Gloster
Aircraft

Since 1917

Three Gladiators of No. 87 Squadron, RAF, flew this 'tied together' formation during a display at Villacoublay in 1938. (*Courtesy Rolls-Royce*)

Gloster
Aircraft
since 1917

Derek N James

PUTNAM

For my sons
William Siward, Benjamin Derek
and Harry Arthur Norman

© Derek N. James 1971 & 1987
ISBN 0 85177 807 0
All rights reserved
Printed in Great Britain for
Putnam, an imprint of
Conway Maritime Press Ltd,
24 Bride Lane, Fleet Street,
London, EC4Y 8DR
by Oxford University Press
Set in Monotype Times
First published in 1971
Second edition 1987

CONTENTS

v

PREFACE

The story of Gloster Aircraft Company is one of great technical achievements paving the way followed by many other companies, and of commercial successes, with rewarding production counted in thousands, interspersed with frustrating years in the aviation wilderness when 'one-offs' were the sole result of enormous expenditure of time, money and effort on private venture designs. It is the story of an engineering company born of war, in a fashionable spa, which, several wars later, was overtaken by the pace of world events to become the first victim of a programme of political and economic stringency which has since decimated British aircraft manufacturing companies. The Gloster story begins with the production of D.H.2s and ends, some 46 years later, amid a mélange of Meteor and Javelin conversions, fire appliances, guided weapon components, vending machines and road tanker vehicles. Although most renowned for its outstanding fighter aircraft built in great numbers for the Royal Air Force, Royal Navy and the air arms of twenty other nations, Glosters were blessed with aeronautical engineers able to run the gamut of design and in consequence the factories at Sunningend, Hucclecote and Bentham saw, for example, the manufacture of seaplane racers, torpedo reconnaissance aircraft, multi-purpose aerial survey aircraft, a tiny ultra-light single-seater, a four-engined bomber-transport and, of course, Great Britain's first turbojet aircraft. At the time of its demise the company was actively studying a number of high sub-sonic and transonic transport projects, some with VTOL capability, several light executive aeroplanes and a remotely-controlled crop-spraying helicopter.

Never a company concerned with living on past achievements Glosters were apparently reluctant to catalogue the details for posterity; moreover, few historical references were retained among the official company documents which wandered to Baginton, Kingston upon Thames and Manchester following the progressive closure of the Hucclecote factory, and much which would have been of interest to students of aviation history has been lost. On the credit side however, a great amount of unpublished information, drawings and photographs has been recovered from a variety of other sources and has made possible a comprehensive narrative of company affairs which includes details not only of those aircraft designed and produced by Gloster Aircraft Company but also others such as the Nighthawk and Nightjar, the AS.31 and the Meteor night fighters in the creation of which some part of the Gloster organization played a major rôle.

This book therefore stems from the work of many people during the past fifty-five years. Outstanding among the thousands, without whose unremitting efforts there would not have been a company with a history to chronicle, there is Hugh Burroughes whose name links every aspect of company activity and whose memory, like his largely unsung contributions to aviation generally, is prodigious. Without the benefit of his help and guidance throughout its elephantine gestation period this Gloster history would have been well-nigh impossible to prepare.

Other ex-colleagues to whom I am greatly indebted for the use of unique records are W. G. Carter and R. W. Walker; John H. Cuss, Percy Braisby, Ron Draper, Chris Jones, Basil Fielding and Douglas Husk whose combined documentary material formed the basis for a number of chapters and appendices; Anthony Laverton who provided a wealth of information about factories, products and people; Russell Adams to whom I turned for many of his fine photographs of Gloster aeroplanes; and Sybil Baker, D'Arcy Hunt, Jack Johnstone, Geoff Mills, Julian Partridge and Hugh Service all of whom gave much to Gloster Aircraft Company during many years. I hope that I have done justice to the works of their hands. I am also exceedingly grateful to Jim Corfield, John Gray and John Gale of Hawker Siddeley Aviation for their ready permission to consult what remained of Gloster historical documents and for their generous help with photographs.

It was invaluable to receive the enthusiastic assistance of such experts as Chris Barnes, William Green, Leslie Hunt, Peter Lewis, Arthur Piercy Jnr, Bruce Robertson, Gordon Swanborough and John W. R. Taylor and of those whose names are recorded against the photographs which they were kind enough to lend to me. Others who put their specialized knowledge and facilities at my disposal were the staff of the Public Record Office and the Air Historical Branch, Ministry of Defence; H. G. Russell and H. Simons (ATP, Ministry of Technology); Ernest Stott, John Bagley and R. C. Wright (RAE Farnborough); Ann Tilbury (*Flight International*); Philip Jarrett (Royal Aeronautical Society); E. Hine (Imperial War Museum); Desmond Clough (Society of British Aerospace Companies); Flt Lieut T. Mason; Flt Lieut A. Thomas and the members of the Sub-Aqua Club (RAF College, Cranwell); E. D. Keen, Douglas Terry and Neville Horne (Dowty Group Ltd); and many other friends in the aircraft industry.

Information and photographs from overseas were of particular value and I am greatly indebted to Reed Kinert, Tom Foxworth, René Francillon and the USAF Photographic Library; Kenneth Meehan, D. P. Woodhall and the RNZAF Photographic Establishment; Mögens Harttung and Hans Kofoed (Denmark); Åke Granhall and Lieut-Col N. Kindberg (Sweden); Pierre Sers and Sud-Aviation (France); Maj D. C. Botha and Cmdt D. B. Prinsloo (South Africa); Koji Hoashi (Japan); Col K. W. Janarmo and Seppo Raivisto (Finland); The Secretary, the Eire Department of Defence; Wg Cdr N. E. Bowen, HM Air Attaché, Oslo; and Col C. A. Humphreys, HM Defence Attaché, Helsinki.

Finally I must record my sincere appreciation of the parts played by

Philip J. R. Moyes who initiated the idea of my authorship of the Gloster book and assisted me in many ways during its preparation; by John Huntington and John Stroud who have given me so much practical help and advice during the last four years; by L. E. Bradford whose masterly drawings grace the following pages; and by Mrs Judy Dobson who so patiently prepared the final typescript.

D.N.J.

Charlton Kings, Glos., 1970

AUTHOR'S NOTE

Gloster types were known either by a name, the specification they were designed to meet, or by project numbers. Occasionally a nickname was also applied.

A series of 'G' numbers with suffix letters purporting to be the system used by Glosters to designate aircraft types and sub-types has been widely published. This system is completely spurious having been evolved in 1948 by the company's publicity department by elaborating on an earlier reference system. By working backwards from the prototype Gladiator, which intially bore the Class B civil registration G.37, and applying numbers and suffix letters indiscriminately to projects, main production and sub-types, it was found possible to allot the type number G.1 to the Mars I.

The inaccurate nature of this scheme is also revealed by the facts that the Goodwood project was allocated G.21, the Grebe was variously G.12, G.18 and G.39, the Gamecock was G.17 and G.27, the Goldfinch was given G.23 and G.30, the Gloster V project and the TC.33 were both allocated G.33 and the D.H.72 became G.35. The ultimate absurdity was the manner in which, when the system was perpetuated and extended outside the company, the plethora of Meteor variants exhausted the alphabet and some of the later sub-types were given new type numbers.

Glosters' main factory site near Gloucester was bisected by the parish boundary line between Hucclecote and Brockworth; thus while the majority of the factory and offices lay in Hucclecote about half of the runway and airfield were in Brockworth. For the purpose of clarity the postal address, which was Hucclecote, is used throughout this book to identify this factory. This address was chosen by the management of the company because, being nearer the City of Gloucester, it had two postal deliveries each day instead of the one in Brockworth.

FOREWORD TO SECOND EDITION

The publication of this second edition coincides with the 70th anniversary of the founding of the original Gloucestershire Aircraft Company. I am most grateful to the many people who have provided me with new information which has enabled me to amend and correct some earlier errors, rectify some omissions and update several sections.

D.N.J.

Barnwood, Gloucester, 1987

Origin and History of the Company

Genesis

The names of the small band of British aviation pioneers of the 1909–10 period who founded their own companies, are well known; among them were Sopwith, Handley Page, the Short brothers, Blackburn, Grahame-White, Sir George White and, less well known perhaps, George Holt Thomas, the founder of the Aircraft Manufacturing Company. With the exception of the last two they were either designers or pilots, or both, and their primary interest lay in building and flying aeroplanes. For George Holt Thomas, however, aviation initially held another attraction.

As the son of the founder of the *Daily Graphic*, young Holt Thomas quickly saw that this new adventure in the air was a splendid source of copy for the newspaper; but soon this qualified interest deepened into something approaching a passion. Whenever possible he visited the various small factories and airfields set up around London where he met these pioneers and saw them and such legendary figures as Gustav Hamel and J. D. North in the air. He was also a frequent visitor to the flying meetings in France where he saw 'the pale Pégoud' flying inverted and looping his

An historic meeting at the Aircraft Manufacturing Co's Hendon factory in 1917. George Holt Thomas, in morning coat and top hat, talking to HM King George V, with Queen Mary and Hugh Burroughes beyond them. At the left of the group are (*left to right*) Capt Geoffrey de Havilland, S. W. Hiscocks, and Guy Peck, who became a director of Gloucestershire Aircraft Company. (*Courtesy Hugh Burroughes*)

1

Blériot monoplane at Buc. All this fired Holt Thomas' imagination and he spent much of his time spreading the aviation gospel in Britain.

During his frequent visits to France Holt Thomas became very friendly with the Farman brothers, particularly with Maurice, and this valuable contact eventually resulted in the Farmans giving Holt Thomas a licence to sell their aircraft in the United Kingdom. At that time France led the world in aviation, particularly in engine development, and Holt Thomas was at once in the fortunate position of being able to offer complete Farman aircraft to the British Government. From 1911 onwards he made the most of his opportunities and his growing success led to the Gnome engine company giving him an exclusive licence for their engines in the United Kingdom. With licences for aircraft and engines in his possession and a growing order book in sight Holt Thomas determined to form his own company and after some searching he acquired a factory at The Hyde, Hendon, another at Walthamstow for making Gnome engines and yet another at Merton to build small airships and kite balloons. In 1912 he realized his ambition, formed the Aircraft Manufacturing Company and enlisted as a working shareholder Clement Cresswell who had been a member of the Grahame-White team.

In 1913 the Aircraft Manufacturing Company was joined by a man who, for the next half century, was to play a major rôle in shaping not only its own progress but also that of British aviation as a whole. He was Hugh Burroughes who, in 1909, had persuaded Mervyn O'Gorman (with whom he had worked as a junior technical assistant at O'Gorman and Cozens-Hardy, Consulting Engineers, of Victoria St, S.W.1) to take him to work at the Balloon Factory, Farnborough, where O'Gorman had just been appointed superintendent. Both Burroughes and his wife were excellent linguists and in consequence became involved with the translation of most of the Farman and Gnome instructional manuals and spare parts lists for the Factory. This brought them into constant contact with Holt Thomas who, in March 1914, offered to Hugh Burroughes the job of manager of the Aircraft Manufacturing Company. Burroughes was Holt Thomas' first 'capture' from Farnborough and 'H.B.', as he was generally known, was instrumental in arranging the second, Geoffrey de Havilland, who was appointed chief designer in June 1914.

With the outbreak of war in August 1914 Hugh Burroughes and Holt Thomas were faced with the twin tasks of building aeroplanes and of administering and expanding the company to cope with a growing order book. When a comparatively large order for 250 D.H.2 single-seat scouts was received by the Aircraft Manufacturing Company, Burroughes realized that the facilities at The Hyde were inadequate to enable them to keep pace with the demand for aircraft, and that additional production facilities were needed. The place to look for them was, clearly, with a reputable woodworking company and Burroughes turned to William Mallinson and Son, Hackney Road, London, the company's principal supplier of spruce and ash, for help and guidance in finding firms with workmen

2

Hugh Burroughes (*left*) and A. W. Martyn. (*Courtesy Mrs I. G. Robinson*)

sufficiently skilled to change to aircraft manufacture. Mallinsons recommended a number, including Vanden Plas, Waring and Gillow and, most important of all, H. H. Martyn and Co Ltd of Sunningend Works, Cheltenham, who were widely known as architectural engineers, particularly for their wood panelling and fittings in ocean liners, and who had an established reputation for first class woodwork.

Hugh Burroughes and Guy Peck, Aircraft Manufacturing Company's production director, visited Sunningend for the first time in April 1915 to

Production of D.H.6 fuselages in H. H. Martyn's aeroplane erecting shop at Sunningend Works, Cheltenham, in 1917. (*Courtesy R. V. Hall*)

3

meet A. W. Martyn, managing director, and Mr Davidson, the works manager, and to see exactly what this company, tucked away on the outskirts of the fashionable spa, could offer to the aircraft industry. Burroughes and Peck were immediately impressed by the range of equipment used by Martyns and by the skill and precision of the craftsmen employed. Shortly after their return to Hendon, Burroughes recommended to the Board of the Aircraft Manufacturing Company that H. H. Martyn should be given the opportunity of proving their worth. The first contract was for spares and components for the Maurice Farman Longhorn and Shorthorn, and this was soon followed by others for the D.H.2 and the B.E.2c, for the innate skill of Martyn's craftsmen had not only carried the company triumphantly through its period of conversion to aircraft manufacture but at the end of it had created a highly efficient production unit capable of building aeroplanes at a great rate. The Sunningend factory was to be a most reliable source of D.H.4 and D.H.6 fuselages, and Bristol and Nieuport fighters during the latter half of the war.

Gloucestershire Aircraft Company Limited

In the spring of 1917 came the first major change in the structure of the company which was to have a far-reaching effect upon its future affairs. This change stemmed from a discussion between Hugh Burroughes and A. W. Martyn during which it was proposed that a new company should be formed in which Martyn and his Board would have a 50 per cent holding with the Aircraft Manufacturing Company holding the other half. It was further proposed that this new company should take over Aircraft Manufacturing's sub-contract work and rent the Sunningend factory from Martyns. It was an ingenious scheme from which both companies obtained benefits and their Boards were enthusiastic about implementing it.

Thus was born The Gloucestershire Aircraft Company Limited, newly registered on 5 June, 1917, with a capital of £10,000 and acquiring the aircraft business previously carried out by H. H. Martyn. Its founding directors were George Holt Thomas (chairman), A. W. Martyn (managing director), Hugh Burroughes, David Longden and Guy Peck. Slowly the labour force grew under the impetus of war and the formation of the new company. The demand for more aircraft and the need for dilution of skilled labour, by the employment of women and boys under 18 years of age, rose considerably during the year. In January 1917 three in every four of the 650 employees were skilled, but by mid-June only two in every three of the 780 men employed were qualified craftsmen.

Orders continued to flow in; for 150 D.H.6 and D.H.9 fuselages, then for 461 complete Bristol F.2Bs and 165 F.E.2bs plus some Nieuport Nighthawks, until Gloucestershire Aircraft Co itself began sub-contracting work to a number of other firms in the Gloucester/Cheltenham district including Savages Ltd and Daniels and Co, of Stroud, and the Gloucester Carriage and Wagon Co Ltd. Where any flying was involved the complete aircraft, minus wings, was towed by a Ford lorry to Hucclecote some seven

4

Gloucestershire Aircraft personalities at Hucclecote; (*left to right*) Larry Carter, H. P. Folland, Capt Gordon W. Charley, who was responsible for overseas sales activities, and Charles Denley, company secretary.

miles away where an Air Board aircraft acceptance park had been built, complete with hangars, during the early part of 1915. By the spring of 1918 Gloucestershire Aircraft Company was capable of building 45 aircraft per week.

Eight months later the Armistice brought with it swingeing changes to Britain's aircraft industry; the forcing house of war followed by the sudden and chilling cessation of military orders left it in a parlous state. At Sunningend the situation by 1919 was particularly depressing for there, although very limited production of the F.2B and Nighthawk continued for a time, there was no design team to strike out on the creation of new types of civil aeroplanes. At The Hyde too, the Aircraft Manufacturing Company was facing its own problems; Hugh Burroughes had decided to leave the company to look after a small engineering firm which he owned, Chelsea Precision Tools, and to represent G.A.C. in London; in addition there was a breakdown of Holt Thomas' health already weakened by a recurring throat ailment. In 1920 Holt Thomas finally sold out to the BSA/Daimler Group who, after a rapid but careful survey of its prospects, decided to close The Hyde factory and those at Walthamstow, Merton, High Wycombe and Camden Town, all of which belonged to the Aircraft Manufacturing Company.

The Government's policy, such as it was, for the industry eventually emerged as a 'stop everything' dictum with no indications of a desire to maintain a nucleus of design or development capacity, only the instructions that all claims should be submitted as quickly as possible. In due course Gloucestershire Aircraft Co made its claim and by the summer of 1919 a settlement of the Nighthawk contract had been made with commendable promptness and a complete reorganization of the Sunningend factory put in hand to enable it to begin on other work. As a part of the settlement G.A.C. bought a very large quantity of Nighthawk components which were surplus to requirements. In the face of Government indifference and the fact that its newly formed Aircraft Disposal Company held substantial stocks of aircraft, aero-engines and spares which were beginning

5

The S.E.4, one of H. P. Folland's remarkably advanced designs.
(*Courtesy H. S. Folland*)

to appear on the market, this part of the settlement showed considerable courage and foresight on the part of the Gloucestershire Aircraft directors, in particular David Longden, who became managing director when A. W. Martyn was named chairman. The remaining claims for the balance of the contracts affected by the cancellations became the subject of a Petition of Right, eventually settled together with a claim for excess profits tax.

During the period 1918–20 the main concern of Martyn and Longden was utilizing the manufacturing resources of the Sunningend factory to

Major Frank Gooden, a Farnborough test pilot, in the cockpit of the first S.E.5, Folland's renowned World War I fighter. (*Courtesy H. S. Folland*)

6

the best effect until such time as its traditional work of fitting out new ships and architectural decoration could begin, and H. H. Martyn could set about rebuilding its pre-war business. Thus a number of contracts were obtained from Rover and Siddeley Deasey for motorcar components, and a motor scooter of very advanced design was built. Named the Unibus, it incorporated a bucket seat, shaft drive, aluminium disc wheels, sprung forks and rear wheel plus a number of other features which have since become standard; but it was ahead of its time and although a handful of scooters were built the whole project was ultimately abandoned.

Behind all their efforts to find engineering work of almost any kind the directors of G.A.C. were also determined to remain as a creative part of the aircraft industry, despite the paucity of orders. One of the major obstacles was the lack of a design team, and David Longden and Hugh

The standard Dragonfly-powered Nieuport Nighthawk of the type built by H. H. Martyn and Co. (*Courtesy C. H. Barnes*)

Burroughes, who had rejoined Gloucestershire Aircraft in 1920 when the firm became disassociated from the Aircraft Manufacturing Co, were adamant that the company could not continue without the services of an experienced designer. But if the general lack of orders for the industry was a daunting prospect for Gloucestershire Aircraft it was also, indirectly, to prove its salvation.

At Cricklewood the Nieuport and General Aircraft Company, a part of the Waring Group, was facing a similarly depressing situation and in November 1920 it was decided that, following a slow run down since the end of the war, the company would be closed, so Gloucestershire Aircraft immediately acquired the design rights of the Nieuport Nighthawk fighter. Fortunately the decision on the closure of the Nieuport factory occurred at the time when G.A.C. were casting around for a design team, and after a preliminary meeting in January 1921, Nieuport's chief designer, H. P. Folland, agreed to act as a consultant designer to oversee the further development of the Nighthawk for production at Sunningend, while he remained at Cricklewood to wind up his affairs with Nieuport. Harry Folland had joined the Balloon Factory at Farnborough in 1912 and established there a great reputation with his designs of remarkably advanced single-seat aircraft. The S.E.4, a fast unarmed scout embodying many unusual aerodynamic practices, and the S.E.4a preceded the renowned S.E.5 and S.E.5a reckoned to be the finest single-seat fighters of the 1914–18 War. In 1917, following the disbandment of the technical staff at Farnborough, Folland joined the Nieuport Company where he produced a workmanlike design for the B.N.1 single-seat fighter. This he followed with the Nighthawk, yet another single-seat fighter, designed to meet the RAF Type 1 specification issued in 1918, and was in the process of developing the London twin-engined bomber when the Cricklewood factory began to close.

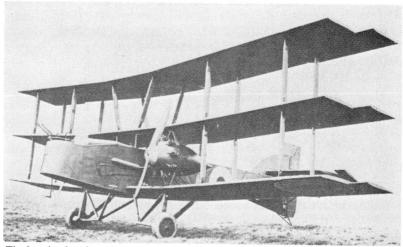

The London bomber, H. P. Folland's last design for the Nieuport and General Aircraft Co, featured a matchboard-covered fuselage and completely interchangeable control surfaces. (*Courtesy C. H. Barnes*)

In 1920 the Japanese Government approached Britain requesting the services of an Air Mission to organize, train and advise the Imperial Japanese Navy's Air Service on its future aircraft requirements. A British Air Mission, led by Col The Master of Sempill, started its work in January 1921 and among its recommendations was the purchase of fifty Nighthawks suitably modified for naval flying. The speed with which these aircraft, renamed Sparrowhawks, were built was the result of the company's very large stock holding of surplus Nighthawk components which had been stored in Cheltenham's Winter Gardens in Imperial Square.

Although this order was a major milestone in Gloucestershire Aircraft's progress it did nothing for the Board's hopes of establishing the company with a reputation for high-speed aircraft, and with this aim in view one of Folland's early tasks was another redesign of the Nighthawk. This was to be the little Mars I/Bamel single-seat biplane racer which was conceived and built in a little under four weeks, surely an all time record for such an effective and successful aeroplane. A short time after its first flight Folland formally joined Gloucestershire Aircraft Company as chief engineer and designer, taking with him from Cricklewood as his assistant, H. E. Preston, who had been with Folland at Farnborough, and the two brothers, G. and T. E. Gibson.

Design and Production

With this vital and dramatic change in the status of the company, a works inspector, approved by the AID, was appointed, the stamp of approval wrung from the Air Board and Gloucestershire Aircraft was in business for the first time not merely as a production organization but as a fully fledged contractor, recognized as such by the Air Board.

It was this august body whose eye the company was aiming to catch when it entered the Mars I/Bamel in the 1921 Aerial Derby and won. It was a hard won victory, for any chance of participation appeared to have vanished only four days before the race when the little racer's tailskid was wrenched off while taxi-ing on the rough, cracked surface of Hucclecote aerodrome causing severe damage to the rear fuselage and rudder. Repairs were completed in time for a check flight on the eve of the race, but there was further trouble when two breather pipes fractured and fell off during the flight to Hendon only a few hours before the start. However, with some rough sketches by Folland as a guide, replacement parts were made at de Havilland's Stag Lane factory, rushed to Hendon in a motor cycle combination belonging to Frank Carter, one of the ground crew, and fitted with only ten minutes to spare before the Bamel was pushed to the starting line.

If this victory failed to draw official attention and approbation then a new British speed record set in December 1921 by the Bamel certainly put Gloucestershire Aircraft in the forefront of the competitive flying scene in the United Kingdom, and for the next three years, with more victories and records to its credit, the company carried forward the whole of British aerial racing.

The name Bamel with which Gloucestershire Aircraft's successful little racer was dubbed, sprang from a chance remark made when Hugh Burroughes first went with Harry Folland to see the aircraft under construction. At that time only the front section of the fuselage was covered and the rear half was bare. Folland commented that in that state, with the large hump of the main fuel tank up front it was 'half bare—half Camel'. This hybrid animal was adopted as an unofficial racing motif and on the side of the Bamel was depicted being ridden by Jimmy James, the company's pilot, with his traditional scarf flying behind him in the wind.

Apart from serving as the basic airframe from which the Bamel and Sparrowhawk were developed, the old Nighthawk was stretched and modified by Folland to produce a whole series of designs for Mars fighter types. Only the Mars VI Nighthawk, re-engined with the Bristol Jupiter III and

9

the Armstrong Siddeley Jaguar II and III under specification 35/22, and the Mars X Nightjar with the B.R.2 rotary engine went into production and then only in small numbers; the remainder of the Mars were to remain as projects or prototypes. Notable among them was the Mars V, a two-seater project with tubular steel construction in the fuselage and other advanced design features.

Although Folland had established his reputation with the design of high-speed military single-seaters he was able to create designs for other types of aircraft with equal skill and facility. Thus the Mars VIII and Mars IX transport projects were a clear break from the military line of development followed by the company with this series. Both aircraft were intended to carry passengers or cargo for approximately 400 miles. The Lion-powered Mars VIII had accommodation for nine passengers or nearly a ton of cargo; the Mars IX with a 360 hp Rolls-Royce Eagle was a smaller version which would have carried seven passengers or three quarters of a ton of cargo.

Jimmy James in the Bamel. Note the 'half-bear, half-camel' motif on the fuselage below the cockpit. (*Musée de l'Air*)

The most unusual feature of both projects was a folding fuselage which hinged at a point midway between the wings and tail unit opening up the whole cross-section of the fuselage to enable bulky loads to be accommodated. This was, almost certainly, the first time a swing fuselage had been envisaged.

In 1923 the first of the *Daily Mail* light aeroplane trials were held at Lympne, and Folland's versatility was again exhibited by his design of the diminutive Gannet which was built for the trials. The Gannet's gross weight was only 460 lb, and with its wings folded it measured only 6 ft 8 in wide, allowing it to be accommodated in the average garage and to be wheeled

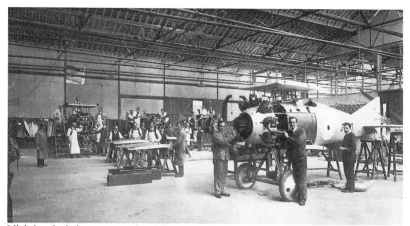

Nighthawks being converted to Mars VI and Mars X in the assembly shop at H. H. Martyn's Sunningend Works.

through a field gateway by one man.

While development of the Nighthawk for production continued, Folland refined the Bamel even further, enabling it to win the Aerial Derby again in 1922 and 1923, and progressed a development programme on wing sections to improve the efficiency of high-speed biplanes. The first fruit of this work was the H.L.B.* combination of different aerofoil sections which produced in a biplane something approaching the wing efficiency of a monoplane; the reduced span and centre of pressure movement endowed aircraft having this wing combination with great manoeuvrability.

*High Lift Biplane.

Flg Off R. L. Atcherley (*left*) and Flt Lieut G. H. Stainforth after winning the 1929 King's Cup race in a Grebe.

The H.L.B. combination was first fitted to a Mars III/Sparrowhawk II fuselage powered by a B.R.2 rotary engine: registered G-EAYN this aircraft became the prototype Grouse I which, like the Nighthawk before it, was the progenitor of a series of successful single-seat biplane fighters which emanated from Sunningend. The Grouse II, presented as a primary trainer, failed to arouse the interest of the Air Ministry and the company sought consolation in the sale of G-EAYN to Sweden; however an earlier demonstration at Hendon had created a favourable impression and resulted in an Air Ministry order in 1923 for three prototypes embodying the H.L.B. wing combination. Thus was born the Grebe, and while the design and experimental departments concentrated on this new replacement for the elderly Snipes in RAF service, the factory built and reconditioned Panthers, D.H.9As and Nightjars until the task of producing Grebes could begin.

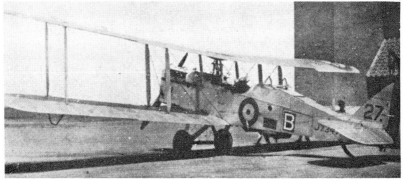

This D.H.9A, J7347, pictured in service with No.27 Sqdn, RAF, was one of the batch built at Sunningend. (*Courtesy Bruce Robertson*)

Like the Meteor which was to follow it into service some twenty years later, the Grebe became a reliable airframe for experimental work. Not only armament and new equipment (the Browning 0.50 in gun and the Hele-Shaw Beacham variable-pitch propeller, for example) were flight tested, but the Grebes were used to develop new techniques such as the flight test of parasite fighters in connection with the Airship Development Programme. These air launching trials, held in October 1926, were from the airship R-33 (G-FAAG), commanded by Flt Lieut Irwin, which was operating from Pulham in Norfolk.

With a great deal of air racing experience, Gloucestershire Aircraft produced the Gloster II seaplane racer for the 1924 Schneider Trophy contest. Two aircraft were built and were powered, like all the company's racers, by Napier Lion engines. Although Folland based his design on the earlier Gloster I, he used every refinement to improve aerodynamic efficiency, but all was in vain. Both aircraft were written off in landing accidents; the prototype, J7504, while alighting on the water at Felixstowe, and the following year when the wheeled landing gear of G-EBJZ collapsed during

The Gloster II on the step at Felixstowe. (*Courtesy H. S. Folland*)

a 200 mph landing at Cranwell. With them went the company's hopes for a Schneider victory that year and also for a new speed record.

While the production of Grebes was being planned Bristol Aeroplane Company had been gaining encouraging results from its Jupiter engine, and during a number of meetings with Folland at Sunningend A. H. Fedden (later Sir Roy), Bristol's chief engineer, pressed the case for fitting this engine in a Gloster airframe. In the event a Grebe, powered by a Jupiter IV, was ordered in August 1924 to meet Air Ministry specification 37/23. This aircraft was the Gamecock prototype.

The development history of the Gamecock is one of dedicated work on the ground and in the air where Capt Howard Saint, the company's test pilot, flew the aircraft to the absolute limits of its performance. Saint was the fourth pilot to join G.A.C. and was responsible for flight testing all the Folland prototypes until he retired in 1936. His work, like that of all

The Gloster II on trestles having just been fitted with its engine cowling panels.
(*Courtesy C. H. Barnes*)

13

The first Kukko, the Finnish-built Gamecock, on the stand of the State Aircraft Factory in the First International Air Exhibition in Helsinki in August–September 1929. (*Courtesy Col K. W. Janarmo*)

the forty pilots who ultimately flew for the company, was of tremendous importance to the industry as well as to G.A.C. and helped to establish the high standard of British test flying which remains unsurpassed anywhere in the world.

Although an immensely popular aircraft, the Gamecock's pilots notes were full of warnings and limitations and it was not an aeroplane for the unwary. In the upper speed range the controls were highly sensitive and effective and spectacular rolls and loops were all part of the accomplished Gamecock pilot's repertoire; even so, coarse aileron applied too quickly at speeds above 135 mph produced wing flutter which could be followed by loss of an interplane strut unless corrective action was taken immediately. The spirited flying of the Gamecock II generated much interest in Finland and in 1928 an order for two pattern aircraft was won. By the early summer of the following year Gamecocks were being licence-built in Finland, where the sole surviving Gamecock components are located.

The Gamecock's major failing was its all wood construction and, although Gloster Aircraft Company ultimately switched to metal and wood structures, it was a contributory factor to the company's long sojourn in the 'aviation wilderness' which began in the later 1920s.

With the quest for greater speed always in mind, Folland was keen to find for the Gamecock a more powerful engine than the 425 hp Jupiter radial and his choice fell on the Napier Lion which was giving such good service in the Schneider Trophy racers. Folland's proposals for a high-

14

performance Lion-powered single-seat fighter in 1924 led to the issue of an Air Ministry contract for three prototypes known as Gorcocks. Although the design was clearly based on the Gamecock all three Gorcocks were different. The first airframe was of wood and metal construction and had a geared Lion engine; the second airframe, also built of wood and metal, featured a direct-drive Lion. Unfortunately the Gorcocks were heir to the Gamecock's wing flutter and no worthwhile trials could be completed to compare the relative merits of the two engine types. The third all-metal airframe was delayed until a metal wing could be embodied and, with a 550 hp direct-drive Lion VIII engine, this Gorcock attained a speed of 174 mph at 5,000 ft.

In an attempt to produce better performance at high altitude, in 1926 Gloucestershire Aircraft turned its attention to the use of supercharged engines and produced the Guan to an Air Ministry order for three experimental single-seat fighters. This time it was the relative inexperience of the engine manufacturers in the techniques of exhaust driven turbo-superchargers which caused the eventual abandonment of the programme after the Guan had achieved high top speeds at altitude and pushed its service ceiling to more than 30,000 ft.

By 1926 Gloucestershire Aircraft Company had become a well known name not only in Great Britain but also in many other countries—where it was almost unpronounceable. Hugh Burroughes and David Longden had become increasingly aware of the problems associated with this unwieldy title and believed that it should be changed to something more simple. For this reason on 11 November, 1926, Gloucestershire Aircraft officially became 'Gloster Aircraft Company Ltd'.

The Gloster board of directors at this time was becoming very concerned about the company's inability to match its earlier successes in obtaining Air Ministry contracts for fighters; they believed that the design team could benefit from an expansion in its numbers to strengthen its technical abilities, and so in 1927 Capt S. J. Waters and F. Duncanson, from the Fairey Aviation company, joined Glosters as assistant designers.

Apart from the technical problems encountered in the development of new manufacturing techniques and the use of new materials and equipment, the British aircraft industry was faced with monumental economic problems of a national character. These had not only caused the Royal Air Force to retain ageing aircraft in squadron service and so reduce the demand for new replacements but had also resurrected the general purpose aircraft which could be 'all things to all men'. Glosters' Goral, built in 1926 to meet specification 26/27, had the accommodating feature of being able to use D.H.9A mainplanes and a number of fuselage components and was designed to enable the metal members of the fuselage joints to be replaced by wooden members if necessary. The result of all this compromise was an ungainly aeroplane which, despite its appearance, performed well in competitive trials at Martlesham Heath, but not sufficiently well to win a production contract for the company.

View of the Goring on floats in the Sunningend factory in May 1928.

More businesslike in appearance but unorthodox in concept and construction was Capt S. J. Waters' Goring day bomber/torpedo aircraft of 1927. It matched, and in some particulars surpassed, its competitors in Martlesham trials; in the event none of them measured up to the requirements of specification 23/25 and, although the sole Goring produced at Sunningend made its own contribution to aeronautical progress through its use as a flying test bed for a variety of aero-engines, it failed to provide much needed work for the Gloster factory.

Hele-Shaw Beacham Propeller

With the object of widening Gloucestershire Aircraft's field of interest, in 1925 Hugh Burroughes made initial contact with Dr Hele-Shaw and T. E. Beacham who were developing an hydraulically-operated variable-pitch propeller in a small mews workshop in Victoria. Many other attempts had been made to produce a propeller of this kind as the need for such a device became fully recognized. All these attempts had failed due either to the bulk or weight of the pitch changing mechanism or because of the amount of attention required by the pilot to maintain the correct pitch.

The following year the company started negotiations to obtain the design rights of the Hele-Shaw Beacham propeller and in August 1926 acquired both the design and manufacturing rights. In addition H. L. 'Pop' Milner joined G.A.C. to continue his work as propeller designer. By December private venture work was well advanced on propellers for the Jupiter VI engine and these units were later test flown on the Grebe demonstrator G-EBHA and on Gamecocks G-EBNT and J8047. Both installations at first showed marginal improvements over the fixed-pitch propellers, in spite of the additional weight, but these early flight trials at least proved the principle and the reliability of the Hele-Shaw Beacham concept.

While further development work and testing proceeded, Burroughes, Beacham and Hele-Shaw tried to interest British engine manufacturers in the propeller but met with failure because those companies believed that they could provide the extra power needed at take-off, admittedly with some weight increase, and that the constant engine speed aspect of the propeller's performance was insufficiently developed. The Ministry's interest was decidedly divided, but by dint of much effort by Glosters some development contracts were promised. In a bid to recover some of the mounting costs of their private venture development programme, in 1928 Glosters granted a licence to the Okura company in Japan who wanted to build variable-pitch propellers themselves.

In January 1929 a contract was finally received for the design and construction of twelve variable-pitch propellers, four for the Jupiter VII in a Bulldog, four for the Rolls-Royce F.XI in a Fox and four for a geared Jaguar in a Siskin. Work began at once and the Jupiter design was completed by May, the F.XI design in September and the Jaguar propeller in February 1930. By October 1930 a Jupiter VII propeller was fitted to a Gamecock. A 50 hr flight test programme with the Gamecock began in November and on its completion at the end of April 1931 some modifications were embodied in the propeller and a further 25 hr were flown starting on 31 October.

One of these propellers was shown on the Gloster stand at the 1929 International Aero Exhibition at Olympia where it served to stimulate the interest of Tom Hamilton of Hamilton Airscrews in the United States, who, having visited Glosters' factory, returned home and quickly patented his two-position propeller! This was later built under licence in the United

Hele-Shaw Beacham variable-pitch propeller on Gamecock demonstrator G-EBNT.

Kingdom by de Havilland. Glosters persisted with the variable-pitch propeller until 1936 at which time Hawker Aircraft, who had earlier acquired Gloster Aircraft, sold the propeller interests to a company formed jointly by the Rolls-Royce and Bristol engine companies which became Rotol Airscrews Limited and subsequently, following acquisition by the Dowty Group in 1961, was renamed Dowty Rotol Limited.

In 1926 too, Folland was already studying the benefits of fabricated metal structures, work which was being paralleled by other designers and by the structures department at the Royal Aircraft Establishment. With his design for an all-metal replacement for the Gamecock, Folland finally grasped the nettle but even though the competitive trials of aircraft to meet the F.9/26 specification extended over a long period enabling the Goldfinch, which was the name given to Glosters' contender, to be virtually rebuilt for a second submission, it fell short of the requirements and was a non-runner quite early in the competition. Nevertheless its maximum speed was only 3 mph less than the Bulldog, the eventual winner, and its service ceiling of 29,600 ft was identical to that of the Bulldog.

Although Gloucestershire Aircraft had made limited use of Hucclecote aerodrome, the company had no hangars there and it was not until 1921 when flight tests on the Bamel began that G.A.C. rented a part of No. 2 hangar from the Air Board for use as a flight shed. As noted earlier it was the practice to take aircraft by road from Sunningend to the aerodrome either on a lorry or towed behind. In the latter case special road wheels were fitted with plain bearings which became overheated if the journey was made nonstop: a regulation halt was therefore instituted conveniently near The Oddfellows Inn, Shurdington, halfway along the route!

This occupancy of one or two rented hangars continued until 1927 when it became clear that, because of the trend toward metal construction and the acquisition of the Steel Wing Company, the factory requirements of Gloucestershire were very different from those of H. H. Martyn who persisted in their traditional woodworking and architectural activities. For this reason further hangar and office space was rented, but this was only a temporary panacea, and in 1928 arrangements were made by Gloster Aircraft Co to buy the entire 200 acre site and all the hangars and office accommodation for £15,000.

The move from Sunningend to Hucclecote was gradually accomplished over a period of about five years beginning in 1925. Although this transfer was of great advantage to the company in that its design, production and flight test facilities were, for the first time, in one place, the move from Cheltenham was not universally popular. In Cheltenham there was some concern about Glosters' move from the town and the view was expressed that 'one can't take a wages bill of £2,500 per week out of a town without making a difference'. However, a news story in the *Gloucester Journal* of 5 October, 1929, read, 'One of the biggest and most important air industries in the British Isles will shortly be established in its entirety at works within 10 minutes drive of Gloucester as the result of the decision by the famous Gloster Aircraft Co Ltd to transfer its activities, now carried on at Cheltenham and Hucclecote, exclusively to the latter place. Up to one thousand men will be employed when the removal is complete and it is anticipated that the greater part of the weekly wages will, in the course of time, be spent in the City and its vicinity, whilst other valuable advantages will accrue to Gloucester in consequence of the firm's important decision.' The Mayor of Gloucester expressed his unqualified delight at the news of the company's move. On the question of transport for employees he recalled that when the Air Park was built during the war a special tramway ran from Gloucester Docks into the aerodrome itself to carry men and materials and he believed that this tramway could be reopened if necessary.

The Gnatsnapper fuselage.

Although Folland was by now convinced that all-metal structures were superior to their wooden counterparts yet his Gambet naval fighter of 1926–27 clung to the traditional material, no doubt because of corrosion problems associated with the operation of aircraft from ships at sea. The licensed production of the Gambet in Japan by the Nakajima company was clearly a feather in Folland's and the company's financial and prestige caps, but it failed to provide work for the shop floor.

Similarly the Gnatsnapper, built to meet specification N.21/26 in 1927–29, ran to no more than two prototype airframes, although the engine manufacturer contributed to their ultimate failure by providing for no fewer than eight different engine installations in the prototype, before it was delivered to Martlesham for the ship fighter competition in May 1929.

19

A feature of the Gnatsnapper was the hinged engine mounting.

Metal Construction

The conversion away from wooden construction to all-metal aircraft was something which was not unanimously favoured by the company's senior executives, most of whom had been concerned with various branches of the old woodworking and architectural engineering business at H. H. Martyn, and they regarded this change to metal construction as premature. However, with the support of David Longden, who had recently succeeded A. W. Martyn as chairman when Martyn severed his connections with G.A.C. in September 1927, Hugh Burroughes put forward such a convincing case for the future of all-metal aircraft that he persuaded his colleagues on the Board to agree that he should buy himself a half interest in the Steel Wing Company. This firm was founded in 1919 by D. J. Mooney to develop the use of steel in aircraft and had been dedicated to its use ever since. In 1928 Burroughes sold his Steel Wing shares to Glosters —at the same price which he paid for them—when G.A.C. finally took over this pioneering concern. D. H. Emby, Steel Wing's chief designer, and a major portion of its expert design staff remained with the company when it moved, at Longden's insistence, first to Sunningend and then to Hucclecote.

This step was to prove of major importance to Glosters who were thus able to secure valuable contracts for the production of the all-metal Armstrong Whitworth Siskin. This was the first occasion on which Gloster Aircraft had built aircraft to another contractor's design. Work began in the autumn of 1927, and 74 Siskin IIIAs were built during the following two years. Glosters were also entrusted with an extensive modification and repair programme on more than 100 Siskins and thus became almost the parent firm for this aeroplane. Another production order which stemmed from Glosters' newly acquired expertise, and which was ultimately worth

20

over £360,000, was one for all-metal wings for the Westland Wapiti. This aircraft, built to the 26/27 specification, had been ordered in quantity after winning the General Purpose Aircraft type competition in which the Goral had also participated. A total of 525 sets of Wapiti wings were built in No. 2 hangar at Hucclecote and delivered to Yeovil during 1929–32. These contracts helped to bridge the great gap of six years from 1928 until 1934 when Gloster Aircraft Company seemed unable to repeat its earlier successes and produce a contract-winning aeroplane.

In November 1928 Glosters took over the responsibility for completing what was to be the first of three de Havilland designed aircraft. In this case de Havilland had spent over a year producing a design study for a twin-engined air survey aeroplane designated D.H.67 but their expanding interests and preoccupation with quantity production of other types led to the delegation of the completion of this machine to Gloster Aircraft. Harry Folland made a number of radical changes in the design, altered the dimensions, specified Gloster constructional techniques, and finally a new aircraft, the AS.31, emerged in 1930. Two were built, G-AADO for the Aircraft Operating Company Ltd, and K2602 which was supplied to the Air Ministry. Both were successful in their widely differing rôles before G-AADO went on to military service with the South African Air Force.

In May 1929 Gloster Aircraft received a most unusual contract to build a unique form of aircraft wing. The project, which was financed by some Italian residents in London, involved the construction of a special variable-camber wing and its fitment to a Breda 15 high-wing monoplane powered by a 100 hp de Havilland Gipsy I engine. Registered G-ABCC, it was the last of a batch of six sold in Great Britain.

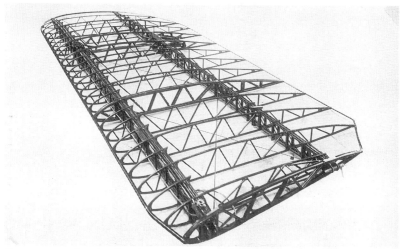

Gnatsnapper wing showing the construction of the Gloster lattice spar and the ribs.
(*Courtesy Royal Aeronautical Society*)

The wing's designer was Signor Ugo Antoni, an Italian aircraft engineer and keen ornithologist who, in seeking to obtain high lift plus the advantages of controlled gliding flight, turned to birds' wings for inspiration. The trailing edge of the Breda's wing was built in three sections; normal ailerons at the tips with a variable-camber section inboard of them and cable-operated from a handwheel in the cockpit. In this section every fourth rib was 'operated' and the three in between were of light construction and flexed to follow the curvature of the main ribs. The third section at the root end was of light metal and multi-ply wooden construction which was free to move up and down through a limited travel similar to the feathers on a bird's wing.

The Breda 15 monoplane showing the variable-camber portion of the starboard wing.

Work was completed by the end of August 1933 and the first flight was on 8 September, 1933. The Italian pilot reported that with the wing at full camber he could hover when the wind speed exceeded the aircraft's minimum speed. Rex Stocken, a Gloster pilot, took over the Breda, which had been fitted with a larger rudder, for a 10 hr flight test programme and flew it for the first time on 14 November. He found the lateral stability was affected by the unusual wing design and control response was different from a conventional aircraft: nevertheless the programme was completed satisfactorily. On 1 December, 1933, the whole project came to an untimely end when, flown by Howard Saint, the Breda encountered heavy turbulence which induced excessive wing flutter and part of the port aileron broke away. The aircraft crashed into trees on Churchdown Hill near the

Designer and pilot. Signor Ugo Antoni with (*left*) Rex Stocken, Glosters' test pilot who flew the Breda 15 with the variable-camber wing built by Glosters.

factory and was a complete write-off. Saint was unhurt and reported that the root end stabilizer sections of the wing prevented a change of attitude which could have stopped the flutter.

While work on this unusual aircraft had been going on, Gloster Aircraft Company had taken over the responsibility for completing the construction of the D.H.72 three-engined night bomber which had been begun at de Havilland's Stag Lane factory in 1928. The Air Ministry had placed an order for a prototype aircraft to meet the B.22/27 specification, and J9184 began to take shape as an enlarged version of the highly successful D.H.66 Hercules transport aircraft but having duralumin mainplanes in place of wood. De Havilland's lack of experience with metal construction, and the need to move the third engine from the fuselage nose to the leading edge of the upper centre section, slowed the progress with J9184 so much that the Air Ministry agreed to move the prototype to Hucclecote for completion. This work was undertaken through an arrangement initiated by C. C. Walker, de Havilland's director and chief engineer, and Hugh Burroughes, which transferred to Gloster Aircraft Company the responsibility for the development of de Havilland's military designs. With the D.H.72 from de Havilland came George Carter who, under Folland's supervision, was to steer this aeroplane (and subsequently the D.H.77) through its final design and development stages.

The D.H.72 was finally completed and first flown in 1931; it was delivered to A and AEE Martlesham in November 1931 where it flew in competition with the Boulton and Paul P.32. It had a giant 95 ft span biplane wing, four main landing wheels, twin fins and rudders, and nose and tail gun positions. It was powered by three 595 hp Bristol Jupiter XFS radial engines and had an all-up weight of 21,460 lb.

The second military aeroplane which came to Hucclecote under the agreement with the de Havilland company was the D.H. 77 single-seat low-wing monoplane fighter designed by W. G. Carter to meet specification F.20/27. Powered by a Napier Rapier I engine, the prototype, J9771, was first flown early in December 1929, completed its Martlesham trials in September 1930 and took part in the RAF Display at Hendon. During the early part of 1931, with its armament removed, it began further flight

23

trials at Hucclecote and completed a 100 hr development programme on the Rapier before moving to the RAE Farnborough in December 1932. This work on these two de Havilland military aeroplanes earned Glosters some £7,000.

Monospars

The monospar system of aircraft construction was evolved in the mid-1920s by H. J. Stieger, a young Swiss engineer, but lack of financial support had prevented the application and commercial exploitation of his novel technique. This system required only one spar in a fully cantilevered wing with torsional strength being supplied by a number of transverse struts in compression and by pyramid-style wire bracing from the apices of these struts to the spar flanges. Drag loads were absorbed through the strengthened leading edge. By 1928 Stieger, with his two associates Sqdn Ldr R. de Haga Haig and Allan Chorlton, had managed to obtain the necessary financial backing and in November 1928 formed the Monospar Wing Company Limited.

Stieger had already designed a small, three-seat cabin monoplane embodying his monospar construction and powered by two Redrup axial-lever engines, a power unit in which the new company was also interested, and early in 1929 he negotiated a £3,350 contract with Gloster Aircraft Company for the manufacture of the aircraft. Work began in August 1929 but when the airframe was nearing completion it was apparent that the Redrup engines were far from airworthy and so the design was modified to accept Salmson engines in their place. These were only half the power of the Redrup engines but, when construction was completed in October 1930, the aircraft's performance was found to be well up to that anticipated with the more powerful engines.

The structure weight of this aircraft, which was sometimes known as the Gloster-Monospar S.S.1, proved to be only 26 per cent of the total weight. In order to test fully the efficacy of the system, the aircraft was flown by Flt Lieut Schofield with unairworthy fabric on the wings and with

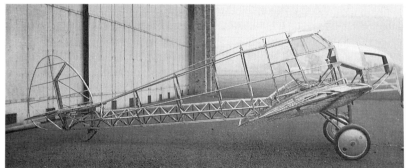

The monospar construction can be seen in the lower half of the fuselage of the Gloster-Monospar S.S.1 built at Hucclecote.

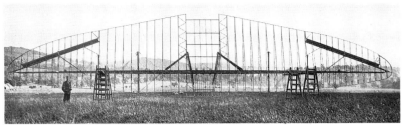

This 63 ft span wing for the Fokker F.VIIb-3m was built by Glosters using the monospar type of construction.

some of the internal bracing wires removed. In this condition it proved completely airworthy and capable of being spun, rolled and looped.

Development of the Monospar and the patent rights were taken over by General Aircraft Limited who later produced a number of successful aeroplanes using this principle. In November 1930 Gloster Aircraft Company received an Air Ministry contract to manufacture a Monospar wing for the three-engined Fokker F.VII. The spar, which was built in one piece, spanned 63 ft and showed that Stieger's design was suitable for large and small aircraft. When completed this wing, which cost £4,100, represented only 10 per cent of the loaded weight of the Fokker F.VII. Although the Steel Wing Company's designs were of a very advanced type, Hugh Burroughes was keen to exploit any new developments in the field of metal construction and on 29 May, 1931, Gloster Aircraft, Armstrong Whitworth, and Boulton and Paul formed the Metal Construction Pool. Under the terms of their agreement, signed by S. W. Hiscocks for Armstrong Whitworth, J. D. North for Boulton and Paul, and by Burroughes, the three companies pooled their patents so that any of them was at liberty to use forms of metal construction covered by patents held by the others. This pool took the name of Aircraft Technical Services Company and opened offices in Clements Inn, London, with Maj Wylie as chief engineer. One of the important developments of ATS was pop riveting, begun at Armstrong Whitworth Aircraft and continued in collaboration with the other two companies, as none had the resources to develop the idea alone. Ultimately this technique was handed to British United Shoe Machinery Co and the three companies drew royalties for the next five years.

In the spring of 1931 the Napier company found that their long and rewarding production of the Lion engine was reaching its end and were seeking new work to replace it. The majority of the Napier Board wanted their company to recommence building motorcars, but H. T. Vane, Napier's chairman, preferred a merger with an aircraft company. Discussions began with Glosters for the purchase of 51 per cent of the G.A.C. shares, but Henry Cooke, Napier's legal adviser, was not keen to follow the Vane plan and, in the depressing economic atmosphere of the time, the takeover bid collapsed.

A change in a quotation by the company's contracts department in

May 1931 directly led to the loss not only of a £2,400 order for internally sprung aircraft wheels but also to that of George Dowty, one of Folland's most brilliant young designers, who conceived the original idea of incorporating landing gear shock absorbers and wheel brakes within the wheel itself. Three experimental wheels had previously been built to his design by Glosters and had passed with flying colours the most arduous tests at RAE Farnborough; such was the company's financial position however that Folland was only able to do what he had done several years earlier, and that was to offer no hope at all that the company would spend money on the wheel's development. But in Japan the Kawasaki aircraft company had read about the wheels in an article written by Dowty to publicize his design and after cabling London for the name of the manufacturer placed a firm order for six wheels.

Because he was still a Gloster Aircraft employee and the company had had experience in making the experimental internally sprung wheels, George Dowty asked Glosters to quote for manufacturing the wheels for Kawasaki. The company quoted him a price of £400 per pair but as soon as he had added his profit and the resulting price of £550 per pair been accepted by the Japanese firm, Glosters told him that they had made a mistake in their estimates and their corrected figure was almost £800 per pair. If there was any doubt in anyone's mind at Glosters about the ultimate success of the wheel, it was not in George Dowty's and he was determined to supply Kawasaki in one way or another, so he resigned from the company in June 1931 and made the six wheels himself with the aid of

Flight deck of the TC.33 viewed from the main cabin during construction.
(*Flight International*)

26

two friends. This modest order was the foundation on which the giant Dowty Group was eventually built.

Another of Harry Folland's digressions from his successful line of fighter development was the TC.33 bomber transport, a four-engined giant which was Glosters' largest aircraft—so large, in fact, that it could not be moved out of its hangar at Hucclecote on completion. However, a little ingenuity, some spades and a winch from Gloucester Docks enabled A. K. Laverton and the works engineer's department to overcome this problem. The TC.33 provided Folland with plenty of elbow room into which he introduced some unexpected features; these included tandem steam-cooled engines, heating and soundproofing for the crew's cabin and for the 30 seated troops or 12 stretcher cases, plus a built-in hoist to load and unload cargo through a large fuselage hatch. But novelty was no substitute for performance expected at bases along the air routes of the Empire where British troops were stationed and where the 'hot and high' requirements would have been far beyond the capabilities of the TC.33. Martlesham was uncompromisingly critical in its report on this particular facet of performance and the TC.33 was scrapped.

A succession of designs built only as prototypes or in very limited quantities had gradually drained Glosters' financial resources, although the company was fortunate in that it still retained its technical strength and potentialities. The benefit of the close and rewarding collaboration between Martyns and the G.A.C., which had been so valuable to both companies right up to 1928, had been impaired by the conversion from wood to metal construction and the two companies fought hard in their own ways to overcome the problem of reduced order books.

By the spring of 1932 Gloster Aircraft Company's fortunes were at their lowest ebb and the company once again embarked on non-aviation work with just sufficient success to absorb their overheads while they strove to develop the SS.18 into an acceptable fighter. Hangars, which had rung to the sound of aircraft manufacture, provided space for indoor tennis and badminton courts, housed silent rows of parked charabancs or gave shelter to squealing pigs and lines of cultivated mushroom beds. Other departments were occupied with the production of car bodies, milk churns, all-metal roll down shop fronts and US-designed Pittman gas-fired fish fryers. At one period the sheet metal department achieved almost as much renown for its work for the motorcar industry as it had for its aircraft components. An interesting development by Gloster Aircraft was the Festing Motorised Barrow designed by Brig-Gen Festing to carry two 500 lb bombs or other stores. Fitted with crawler tracks to enable it to operate over mud and soft ground, the Barrow was powered initially by a Villiers $2\frac{1}{2}$ hp two-stroke engine. Two prototypes were made by A. K. Laverton in the works engineer's department under the direction of H. L. Milner, who was also in charge of the variable-pitch propeller development programme. The two Barrows were extensively tested at Hucclecote and at Catfoss and went to A and AEE Martlesham for Service trials in 1934. About

The Festing Motorised Barrow.

30 Motorised Barrows were subsequently built for the Air Ministry's use.

All this non-aviation work helped in keeping Gloster's factory ticking over during a period when aircraft production contracts were almost non-existent and served to keep together a small but highly skilled nucleus of a labour force against the time when the aviation tempo would quicken.

The Takeover

Gloster Aircraft Company was not alone with these problems: discussions had been in train for a number of months between the Air Ministry and the Industry, through the medium of the SBAC, concerning plans for a reduction in the number of aircraft manufacturers. Visionaries in the Government and Ministry believed that ascendency in the air could best be achieved by accelerating technical progress with an Industry smaller in numbers but with greater individual resources to shoulder the financial burdens rather than expecting Treasury backing. The years of the economic depression were only recently past and support from the Treasury could only be minimal. One proposal envisaged compensation to those companies who could no longer expect to receive offers to tender for Ministry contracts

Glosters' Hucclecote factory, near Gloucester, in 1934.

by a levy on the turnover of those selected to continue. The Government Departments were of the opinion that considerable savings in initial costs and in maintenance costs would ensue if the Services had to cope with reduced numbers of different types of aircraft. In short, the demand was for larger numbers of fewer types. Thirty years later this policy of rationalization was carried to such lengths that there were left only two companies in fixed-wing military aircraft production in Great Britain.

In May 1934 therefore it was Hawker Aircraft Limited who took the first step with a takeover proposal to Gloster Aircraft Company's Board. Hawker's production facilities were inadequate to undertake the large orders which it had and it was clear to David Longden and Hugh Burroughes that these orders could provide a prolonged period of full employment at Hucclecote. For this reason the Gloster Board accepted the Hawker proposal and so ended the life of Gloster Aircraft Company Limited as an independent firm, although in later years it was to regain some of its autonomy. Inevitably there were management changes: David Longden retired after 20 years as managing director, Frank McKenna was initially appointed production manager and later general manager. Hugh

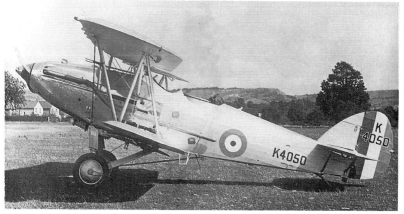

K4050, a Hardy, was the first Hawker aeroplane built by Glosters.

Burroughes continued as a director, and Frank Spriggs (of Hawkers) became chairman of Glosters.

The expected work from Hawkers was soon forthcoming in the form of 47 Hardy general purpose aircraft which were built in three sub-batches during 1934–36. These were followed by 72 Hart Trainers and Hart (Special), 25 Audax (India) Army Co-operation aircraft and two Hartbees ground support aircraft.

While this production programme was in hand between 1934–37 substantial extensions were made to the Hucclecote factory and nearly one million square feet of floor space were available for war production in 1939.

The Schneider Trophy Racing Floatplanes

The demands of Great Britain's Schneider Trophy aspirations exercised Folland's ingenuity to the full for he was so firmly wedded to the biplane configuration that all his skill as a designer and that of Glosters' craftsmen was required to produce aerodynamically clean aircraft. The Curtiss victory and Glosters' second place in the 1925 contest was achieved not so much through the dogged determination and skill of Hubert Broad and Bert Hinkler in the air or the unceasing efforts of the engineers, against all the odds, on the ground, but more by the failure of the Supermarine S.4 monoplane to take part in the event. This opened the door to the biplanes which, let it be said, fought out a tough and thrilling race. The two Gloster III floatplanes built for the contest were never fully tested by Broad or Hinkler before being shipped to Baltimore (Broad had had only a total of five minutes full-throttle flying before the race), and surface radiators, which would have enhanced the performance, were not completed in time to be fitted and tested before shipment. The United States' victory was the result of a more mature development of such components as radiators and propellers and of a five year period of general airframe and engine development which was unmatched anywhere else in the world at that time. Nevertheless, Glosters came nearer to Schneider victory at Baltimore than in any subsequent attempt.

Largely because of the success of the Gloster III, the company used this aeroplane's design as the basis for the next Gloster IVs built for the 1927 contest. However, these new aircraft set a completely new standard of aerodynamic efficiency in biplanes, embodied the latest development in flying control systems for high-speed aeroplanes, and one of them, N223, set an all-time contest record for biplanes with a lap speed of 277·1 mph. On top of these achievements N222, the Gloster IVA, and its Napier Lion engine acquired an enviable serviceability record some two years after the contest during practice and research flying for the 1929 contest.

When Folland finally adopted the monoplane configuration for his racing seaplane designs, it was not wholly of his own volition; rather was he forced to bow to the inevitable because of c.g. problems associated with the installation of the new 1,300 hp Lion VIID engine. In November 1927 design work began on the new Gloster V which was a development of the Gloster IVB and was, therefore, a biplane. It was intended to equip the RAF High Speed Flight with Folland's latest racer for the 1929 contest. In the preliminary wind tunnel tests the models proved highly satisfactory, but problems were encountered at a later stage when it was found that the supercharger on the Lion VIID largely contributed to the weight increase of nearly 300 lb over earlier Lions. When the airframe design was modified to bring the wings further forward to compensate for the shift in centre of gravity, it was then discovered that the front spar of the biplane's upper wing would come over the Lion's centre cylinder block. Thus it was impossible to re-position the upper wing in this manner and at the same

The first Gloster VI waits prudently for another racer, the *Mauretania*, to pass before venturing on to the water at Calshot in August 1929. (*Courtesy Philip Moyes*)

time give the pilot an adequate forward view. For this reason the biplane layout was abandoned, and a monoplane configuration was adopted for the Gloster VI, the last of the Folland line of racing seaplanes.

Despite the paeans of praise which were raised by the technical press when the Gloster VI's graceful shape was first seen, it is performance in the air which wins races and most acclaim, and the Lion engine failed to meet its commitments during the crucial period of pre-race trials. Thus passed for all time Gloster Aircraft Company's chance of a Schneider Trophy victory, although a short-lived world speed record of 336·3 mph in 1929 helped to sweeten the bitter pill of non-participation in the contest that year.

So ended Gloster Aircraft's line of pure racing floatplanes. Was their design and production worth all the problems for such a limited return in terms of contest results? With the benefit of hindsight, there is no doubt at all that apart from the prestige attached to the production of such aeroplanes, the racers formed part of a great storehouse of knowledge on which the company drew when projecting its series of successful military aircraft which for nearly half a century carried the name of Gloster around the world.

The Gauntlet and Gladiator

If Glosters (prior to Hawker's takeover) and other companies in the industry had found it difficult to secure production contracts, they were paralleled by the Air Ministry which was also experiencing difficulties in obtaining from competitive trials at Martlesham a really effective fighter to meet specification F.20/27. This provided a fortuitous breathing space for Folland who was beginning to wonder whether any of his designs would ever find favour with the Ministry. His SS.18, originally designed to the

F.9/26 formula, but progressively developed over several years into the SS.19B, subsequently named Gauntlet, provided the answers to the Air Ministry's, the company's and Folland's problems when it was finally accepted as the Bristol Bulldog replacement. Even then, however, the production specification 24/33 issued in draft to Glosters in September 1933 called for only 24 aircraft, hardly the quantity production order that Glosters so desperately needed. The size of the contract reflected the outward calm of the international situation and at least Glosters could reflect upon the economic manner in which J9125, the original SS.18 airframe, had been progressively modified and re-engined over a period of some six years to bring it up to its contract-winning standard.

The Gauntlet arrived on the aeronautical scene at a time when the first ominous signs of war were appearing in Europe, and these were sufficient to spark off the great military expansion in Great Britain which ultimately was to fit the nation for war some six years later. As the penultimate of Folland's fighters built by Gloster Aircraft Company in quantity, the Gauntlet embodied the results of all his experience in designing high-speed military aircraft. In his determination to avoid the wing flutter problems which had beset some of the earlier Gloster fighters, Folland reverted to a two-bay wing, but, with typical thoroughness, carefully streamlined every strut, bracing wire, joint and excrescence on the aeroplane to produce an exceptionally clean airframe. During its long development, when J9125 carried several different designations, the Air Staff were acutely aware of the

Folland's great attention to detail is apparent in the design of the Gauntlet's early type of spatted undercarriage.

J9125, the Gauntlet prototype, in the 24 ft wind-tunnel at the RAE Farnborough.

inadequacy of the twin-gun armament which was standard in RAF fighters of the period. Glosters were also keen to add weight to the punch of their new fighter and, eschewing the traditional fuselage-mounted Vickers gun, prone to frequent jamming, Folland put in four extra Lewis guns—two under the upper mainplane and two under the lower—firing outside the propeller disc. These four extra guns were discarded, however, for production Gauntlets, which entered service still with only two fuselage-mounted Brownings.

First delivered to the Royal Air Force in May 1934, Gauntlets reached their peak squadron service just three years later when they equipped 14 home-based squadrons. Had Neville Chamberlain failed to win Great Britain a further year of peace at Munich in September 1938, there were still nine home-based Gauntlet squadrons and ten overseas whose pilots were prepared to face the Luftwaffe in open cockpits and with only two guns per aircraft. The Gauntlet's operational activities were confined to co-operating with the Army and the Palestine Police, as part of the Royal Air Force's policing duties to end the attacks of nomadic Arab gangs on small villages in Palestine.

While the Hucclecote factory lay almost empty before the production of Gauntlets, Hardys, Harts and Audaxes got under way, Folland was yet again exhibiting his versatility with a design project for a big 70 ft span monoplane bomber to meet specification B.9/32, powered by two Bristol Perseus VI engines and with a loaded weight of 12,800 lb. A very thick wing contained fuel, bomb load and equipment, and faired smoothly into the fuselage. This specification ultimately produced both the Hampden and Wellington bombers for the RAF. Specification P.27/32, issued in

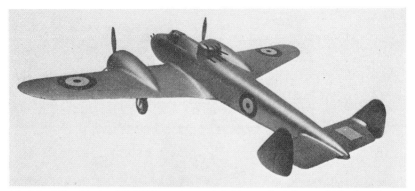

Model of the Gloster F.34/35 turret-armed fighter project from which the Gloster F.9/37 twin-engined fighter was developed. (*Courtesy F. G. Swanborough*)

April 1933, covering an experimental two-seat, single-engined day bomber also produced a proposal from Gloster Aircraft Company during the latter part of the year. Powered by an Armstrong Siddeley Tiger the monoplane design included a retractable landing gear and distinctive inverted V struts from the top of the cockpit to each mainplane. Yet another Gloster project of this period was the two-seat, twin-engined, turret-armed fighter to meet specification F.5/33 which was subsequently developed via F.34/35 into the Gloster F.9/37.

Returning to the early 1930s, while Glosters were working to develop the SS.18/19, the Air Staff were hurriedly drawing up an unrealistic specification for a new fighter. Designated F.7/30 it produced design proposals from almost every major manufacturer, except Gloster Aircraft Company, but failed to produce an aeroplane capable of meeting the specification in all particulars. In this the lack of a suitable engine played a big part, for the preferred power unit, the steam-cooled, inline Rolls-Royce Goshawk, quickly lost favour through installation difficulties and vulnerability to damage in combat. Glosters' apparent disinterest in this specification stemmed largely from Folland's preoccupation with Gauntlet development, but once this burden was eased in 1933 he was able to turn his attention to refining the basic Gauntlet design to effect major performance improvements.

The result of this critical analysis was the SS.37 flown for the first time in September 1934 after very rapid construction of the prototype K5200. Its early trials, during which it was powered by a Mercury VIS engine, were so successful that the company sought permission to enter the aircraft in official F.7/30 trials due to be resumed early in 1935. The winter of 1934–35 was a period of indirect good fortune to Gloster Aircraft Company, for it was then that the steam-cooled Goshawk was finally abandoned as a fighter engine and with it went all the F.7/30 competitors, with the sole exception of the Hawker PV3.

By June 1935 a Bristol Mercury IX powered SS.37 was ready for tender

Some of the 15 Portuguese Gladiator IIs awaiting delivery at Hucclecote in 1939.

to the Air Ministry; it embodied Hawker construction, an enclosed cockpit, a revised tailwheel and a number of other modifications. Within the month specification F.14/35 had been drawn up and issued, Gloster Aircraft Company had received a production order for 23 aircraft and on 1 July the name Gladiator was officially announced. Thus another of Gloster's fighters passed into production, on the first stage of a long and creditable Service career with the Royal Air Force, the Fleet Air Arm and the air forces of eleven other countries including China, Eire, Finland, Norway, Sweden and South Africa.

No. 72 Squadron Royal Air Force was the first to take delivery of its Gladiator Is, on 22 February, 1937, and flew Gladiators until April 1939, longer than any other home-based frontline unit. The introduction of this new fighter was undertaken without any major technical or operational difficulties, but pilots who had had experience of the rather more docile Gauntlet found the Gladiator's higher wing loading and more abrupt stall a little disconcerting initially. However, more experience on the type proved this aeroplane to be an effective weapon not only in the hands of

Gloster and Hawker test pilots with a group of Belgian Air Force pilots at Hucclecote in October 1938 before the delivery flight of a squadron of Gladiators to Belgium.

frontline RAF squadrons, but also in those of the pilots of the Auxiliary Air Force, who began to receive their Gladiators late in September 1938.

The Gladiator II, introduced in February 1938 to meet specification F.36/37, featured the 830 hp Bristol Mercury VIIIA engine plus a number of structural and equipment modifications called for in the light of operating experience and development work by Gloster Aircraft Company. During September 1938, the period of the Munich Crisis, six squadrons of Gladiators were ranged alongside the nine Gauntlet squadrons at home bases as part of RAF Fighter Command!

In the matter of overseas sales Hawker Aircraft's great and recent experience was of much value to Gloster Aircraft Company when promotion of the Gladiator in Europe and elsewhere was proposed. Thus a total of 165 Gladiators was built for direct export and some 120 more were supplied to foreign air forces either from RAF stocks or diverted from Air Ministry production contracts. A number of those supplied to the Norwegian and Finnish Air Forces took part in the defence of their respective capital cities against the might of the Luftwaffe and the Russian Air Force. Swedish volunteers came to the aid of Finland with Gladiators and fought many desperate battles between January and March 1940. In China, Gloster Aircraft Company's fitters found that they and the aircraft they had travelled so far to erect were not accorded the normal protection of a hangar and were constantly harried by Japanese air attacks as they

Hugh Burroughes (*centre*) hands over K8032's logbook to Air Cdre Allan Wheeler, Trustee of the Shuttleworth Trust, in November 1960. Left of the group is E. W. Shambrook, Glosters' managing director.

K8032, attended by Gloster apprentices who helped to restore it to Trust-worthy condition, seconds before its final departure from Hucclecote.

struggled to assemble the Gladiators on a series of outlandish and macabre sites. Latvia and Lithuania, now almost forgotten countries of Eastern Europe, were the first to buy Gladiators, of which several had the unique distinction of being the only known Gloster aeroplanes to carry Soviet markings; this followed the Russian invasion and occupation of the Baltic States and their seizure by the Soviet Union in 1940.

Fortunately one Gladiator—an amalgam of two—remains in an airworthy condition in the hands of the Shuttleworth Trust; though bearing a spurious serial number, this detracts not one bit from the enjoyment of seeing and hearing this example of the RAF's last biplane fighter in its proper element. This aeroplane was restored to its former glories and serviceability through the energetic skill of Gloster apprentices, who undertook the refurbishing of the airframe, the patient enthusiasm of Wg Cdr R. F. Martin, the company's chief test pilot who tracked down the T.R.9 radio, the four guns and much other authentic equipment, and the determination of the Board to see that at least one of Gloster Aircraft's biplanes was kept for posterity—whatever the cost.

Despite Folland's predilection for the biplane configuration he did not fail to grasp the implications of the successive victories of the Supermarine monoplane racers in the last three of the Schneider Trophy contests or of the general trend of airframe development. Thus even while the final design stages and assembly of the prototype Gladiator were in hand he was taking the first steps in the creation of a Gloster monoplane fighter with his SS.34 project of 1933–34. Virtually a monoplane Gladiator, it embodied a retractable landing gear, enclosed cockpit and multi-gun wing-mounted armament. With the issue of specification F.5/34 in 1934, which contributed to the development of the eight-gunned Hawker Hurricane and Vickers Supermarine Spitfire, Folland took more positive action which resulted, in the long term, in his first monoplane fighter, the similarly armed and Mercury-powered Gloster F.5/34. Even then the biplane cast its shadow over its successor at Hucclecote, and because of the company's heavy commitment with production of Gladiators, urgently required to fill RAF squadrons, work on the F.5/34 was retarded and the first flight of the prototype did not take place until December 1937—only a few days

37

prior to initial deliveries of Hurricanes to No. 111 Squadron as replacements for their ageing Gauntlets.

Although the Hawker takeover had been of benefit to Gloster Aircraft Company, it was not welcomed by Folland who felt that the new owners would naturally favour Sydney Camm's designs: it will be remembered too, he became somewhat worried and frustrated at his apparent inability in the early 1930s to design a contract-winning aeroplane. Out of this mental turmoil came a great urge to establish his own company where his particular brand of genius could be applied, unfettered, to the business of designing high-performance aircraft. The change of company status following the takeover was enough to make up his mind, and in 1937 he resigned from Gloster Aircraft Company, and took over the buildings which had belonged to the British Marine Company at Hamble, where he established Folland Aircraft Ltd.

Folland was succeeded by W. G. Carter who was to achieve even greater renown than his predecessor-in-office. George Carter's first design for Glosters was the F.9/37 twin-engined two-seat fighter, which stemmed from development of the earlier F.5/33 and F.34/35 fighter projects, but the Bristol Taurus and Rolls-Royce Peregrine powered prototypes were dogged with engine troubles and landing damage and neither found favour with the Air Staff. Basically, however, this was a good aircraft and was assessed by the A and AEE Boscombe Down as being easy and pleasant to fly with satisfactory stability and light controls for a twin-engined aircraft. Thus when specification F.11/37 was issued in May 1937 to produce

The partly completed mock-up of the Gloster F.18/40 twin-engined fighter.
(*Courtesy William Green*)

Luftwaffe Intelligence photograph of Hucclecote taken in 1939 and showing the partly camouflaged old and new factories.

a two-seat day and night fighter, Carter refined the F.9/37's design to create two sub-types, one to meet the fighter requirement and the other as a high-speed bomber, but neither progressed beyond the project stage. Yet another interesting and unorthodox project, a twin-boom, twelve-gun fighter powered by a pusher engine, was schemed to meet specification F.18/37 (which produced the Typhoon and Tornado) issued in March 1938. Although this, too, did not pass beyond the project stage, it was this design which caught young Frank Whittle's imagination when he first visited Gloster Aircraft Company to meet George Carter early in 1939. Whittle told Carter a little about the work on which he was so secretly engaged and expressed the opinion that the layout of the Gloster F.18/37, which was similar to one he had in mind, seemed very suitable for his jet engine. Thus this project served to create a certain rapport between the two designers which was to prove of benefit during the development of the E.28/39 and the F.9/40.

Like Folland before him, George Carter did not restrict himself solely to fighter projects: two which were produced during 1939 were the B.1/39 four-engined bomber and the N.9/39 two-seat naval turret fighter projects. During 1937–39, while Gloster Aircraft's design and project offices were seeking a successor to the Gauntlet and Gladiator, the factory was busy with production of these and other types. Gladiator production was 279 in 1937, only 158 in 1938 but peaking at 320 in 1939, while production of 200 Hawker Henleys began in October 1938 and continued until September 1940. It was during this period that the wisdom of the factory expansion

39

Hawker Henleys at Hucclecote in 1939 with, in the background, the new No. 2 shadow factory under construction.

programme at Hucclecote was fully realized, for it was apparent that Hawker Aircraft Company would be unable to cope with the large volumes of orders which they were receiving.

As part of this great national expansion programme Gloster Aircraft Company was instructed to take over responsibility for the erection of a shadow factory at Hucclecote to expedite Hawker Hurricane production. Work began on a 43-acre site on 19 August, 1938, and when completed in November 1940 it comprised no less than 24 acres of factory floor area for production work and associated services. Yet another important task was the building of a runway at Hucclecote which hitherto had had only a grass surface and where wet weather flying had been restricted by its condition.

This burden of responsibility for building a new factory was added to those caused by some changes of Air Ministry policy regarding the aircraft to be built by Glosters. In 1939, for example, jig and tool design for the production of the Vickers Wellington was begun and, after a good deal of effort had been expended on this work for about nine months, the company was instructed to deliver to Vickers-Armstrongs or their sub-

One of the 600 Albemarles built in the No. 2 shadow factory. Under the port wing a 1918 tank, used as a Home Guard strong point, can just be seen; behind the starboard wing is the Taurus-powered Gloster F.9/37. (*Imperial War Museum*)

contractors all the drawings and whatever tooling existed. Glosters then undertook all the preparatory work for production of the Armstrong Whitworth Albemarle but this too was taken over by the newly formed A. W. Hawkesley company in the autumn of 1940. This new company was virtually a division of Gloster Aircraft, sharing many of the latter company's facilities and personnel, including test pilots.

When Glosters began their first batch of 500 Hurricanes the company could not have realized the numbers of aircraft which would be built or the rate of production which would be demanded by the Minister of Aircraft Production—the fiery Lord Beaverbrook—or what would be

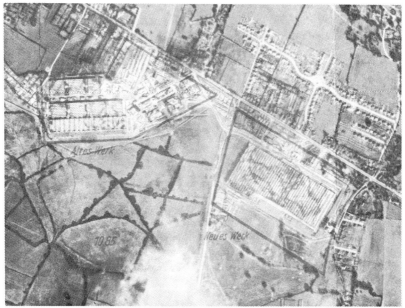

A Luftwaffe aerial photograph, taken some months after the one on page 39, showing the camouflaged Gloster factories. The airfield camouflage is most effective—even though the shadows fall in two different directions!

achieved. The first Gloster-built Hurricane I, L2020, appeared on 27 October, 1939, and by the end of October 1940 the 1,000th aircraft had been completed. During the calendar year 1940, 1,211 Hurricanes were built and this figure was surpassed in 1941 when 1,359 aircraft were completed at Hucclecote. The peak production rate was achieved during the month of October 1940 when 160 new Hurricanes and eight repaired aircraft were delivered to RAF squadrons. Glosters built a total of 2,750 Hurricanes in four production batches which ended with 18 aircraft in March 1942, the last being flown away from Hucclecote during the third week of that month.

Ten months before the last Hurricane left the Hucclecote factory its successor from Sydney Camm's design team at Hawker's, the Typhoon,

41

EK288, a Typhoon 1B, one of the third batch of 700 built by Glosters during 1942–43. Dummy hedges, mounted on wheels and used to camouflage the airfield at Hucclecote, lie on the ground behind the aircraft. (*Courtesy Mrs M. May*)

was appearing on Glosters' production lines. Although Hurricanes had been built in parallel with Hawker Aircraft and Austin Motor Co in the United Kingdom and with Canadian Car and Foundry Corporation in Canada, Gloster Aircraft alone undertook all main production of the Typhoon. The first production aircraft, R7576, was powered by the 2,100 hp Napier Sabre I and was flown by Michael Daunt on 27 May, 1941. A great deal of trouble was experienced with this engine particularly with oil cooling on the climb. Numerous engine failures made test flying a hazardous task and caused at least one Gloster test pilot to crash and others to execute 'dead stick' landings at Hucclecote. Because of these and other problems associated with the airframe and engine, only 28 Typhoons were built during the latter half of 1941, but during the following year 677 were completed in addition to the last 148 Hurricanes. Peak monthly production was in December 1942 when 130 Typhoons were built while 1,165 aircraft were completed in 1944. Glosters' production of Typhoons ended in November 1945 with a single aircraft, SW772, to bring the total to 3,330.

Gloster Jet Aircraft

It was during this pre-war period that the Ministry overseer at Gloster Aircraft Company was Sqn Ldr J. McC. Reynolds, who had been at Cranwell at the same time as Frank Whittle and had maintained contact with him during the years when Whittle was developing his 'Gyrone'. Early in 1938 official interest in this work began to take a practical form when the Air Ministry ordered the first flight engine; in parallel with this the Ministry were also considering which aircraft manufacturer should be encouraged to build an airframe for it. While these deliberations proceeded Sqn Ldr McC. Reynolds arranged the meeting of Whittle and George Carter at Hucclecote where the Design Office was concerned mainly with project aeroplanes. It was, therefore, completely fortuitous that in August 1939 the work load was such that a substantial part of the office was immediately available to tackle the design of Great Britain's—

and the Allies'—first jet-propelled aircraft. But for this the unique task might have been given to another manufacturer. Naturally those at Gloster Aircraft Company liked to believe that they had been specially selected for the job, but the fact was that there happened to be both the facilities and the technical skill available at the right time at Hucclecote. There is no doubt, however, that the Air Ministry were influenced in their choice by the good relations between Carter and Whittle.

Following Whittle's visit, McC. Reynolds made it known at the Air Ministry that Gloster Aircraft were interested in the jet engine and the design of an airframe to suit it; Hawker Siddeley Aircraft Company, of which Gloster Aircraft was a part, included Armstrong Siddeley Motors and they regarded Whittle's engine as a potential product for their factories. Hugh Burroughes was keen that Gloster Aircraft should design and build the airframe and that Armstrong Siddeley should negotiate an agreement to make the Power Jets engine. Unfortunately neither Glosters' Board nor that of Power Jets received this idea with favour, and it proceeded no further.

Shortly afterwards Sir William Farren, at that time Deputy Director of Research and Development (Aircraft) at the Air Ministry, asked George Carter to a meeting with himself and Dr Pye, Director of Scientific Research. There Carter was asked to submit designs for a jet-propelled aircraft; before giving his final acceptance, Carter asked to see a demonstration of the engine and he visited Power Jets' Lutterworth factory for this purpose. Afterwards he said that he had never seen a more unpromising contraption, parts of which glowed a dull red colour; he was of the opinion however that if so much could be accomplished under the rudimentary conditions obtaining at Lutterworth, then it was not difficult to foresee immense possibilities for future development. Later he again visited Lutterworth with T.O.M. Sopwith and Frank Spriggs, both directors of Hawker

W4041/G, the first Gloster E.28/39, at RAE Farnborough.
(*Courtesy L. E. Bradford*)

43

Siddeley Aircraft Company, and Stuart Tressilian, Armstrong Siddeley's chief engineer, and came away more impressed.

In the same way that the good relations between Whittle and Carter had helped the whole project to get under way, so did they persist throughout the job and smoothed the passage of this unique airframe/engine combination from concept to realization. In the incredibly short time of only 15 months from the receipt of contract, the Gloster E.28/39 was in the air on 15 May, 1941, paving the way for the 4,000 Gloster jet aeroplanes which followed it in the ensuing nineteen years. The E.28/39 was, however, very much more than just another 'first' for Gloster Aircraft Company and the British aircraft industry; it proved that jet propulsion really worked. Yet even before the E.28/39 flew, the pressures of war had motivated the development of operational jet aircraft, and Carter was once more called

Michael Daunt fastens his helmet before making the first flight in DG206/G, the H.1-powered F.9/40, at Cranwell. The mechanic holds his ears against the high-pitched whine of the engines. (*Courtesy John Grierson*)

upon to create a fighter for the RAF. Again, speed was the essence of this work and in August 1940 his preliminary design brochures revealed that because he could not rely upon getting engines having very much more thrust than those destined for use in the E.28/39, he had produced a completely new twin-engined design quite unlike anything which had gone before. Three months later the Ministry of Aircraft Production issued specification F.9/40 to cover the Gloster fighter but not before Carter and Burroughes had persuaded the Ministry of Aircraft Production to modify their requirements in respect of the armament and cockpit equipment. On

44

The men and the machine. DG205/G, the fourth prototype F.9/40, with (*left to right*) John Crosby-Warren, Michael Daunt, Frank McKenna, Frank Whittle and George Carter.

the question of the armament the initial demand was for six 20 mm cannon but the Ministry ultimately agreed to accept four cannon instead. Strangely, although this agreement was reached only a few weeks after the brochures were submitted, the F.9/40 front fuselage was built to accept six cannon armament and this basic structure remained virtually unaltered in every mark of Meteor subsequently manufactured. As late as November 1946 the Meteor 4 type record included diagrams of the front fuselage bulkheads

Gloster, Rolls-Royce and USAF personnel with DG210/G, the first Meteor F.1, at Muroc Air Force Base in California. (*Left to right*) four USAF ground crew; Vic Drummond-Henderson, Glosters' assistant experimental department manager; Bill Baldwin, the Gloster inspector concerned with F.9/40s; John Grierson, Glosters' assistant chief test pilot; another USAF crewman and Tim Kendall, one of Rolls-Royce's representatives. (*Courtesy John Grierson*)

with cannon locations marked 1–6, although all the stress calculations were carried out with the two bottom cannon, Nos. 3 and 4, deleted.

An amusing sidelight on the serious business of ordering the new jet fighter was the lengthy difference of opinion between the company and the Ministry of Aircraft Production on the matter of naming the new aeroplane. Only a few weeks after the order for twelve F.9/40 prototypes had been received by Gloster Aircraft Company, the MAP produced an imposing list of possible names; it included Scourge, Terrific, Terrifier, Terrifire, Thunderbolt, Tempest and Cyclone, but an amended list issued two month's later deleted the last two. This was at Glosters' request, for Tempest followed Hawker's natural line of progression from Hurricane, Typhoon and Tornado, and Frank McKenna thought it wrong to usurp this name. Cyclone was rejected because it was the name of a current Wright piston engine. There followed a flood of names: Avenger, Vortex, Wildfire, Skyrocket, Dauntless, Tyrant, Violent and Wrathful, with Gloster Aircraft showing a marked preference for the first one. The issue of a production order for 300 aircraft in August 1941 again stirred up the controversy, for the Ministry wrote to McKenna to say that the name Avenger could not be used because of its similarity to the United States Vengeance; instead the name Thunderbolt had been chosen. McKenna's reply sharply drew the Ministry's attention to Republic Aviation's P-47 fighter which already bore this name—and there the matter rested for a few more months. Finally in February 1942 the MAP settled on Meteor, which did not wholly delight Gloster Aircraft who submitted Annihilator, Ace and Reaper, but the Ministry was adamant, so the F.9/40 became the Meteor.

Late delivery of the Rover W.2B engines almost caused the cancellation of the whole F.9/40 project before it, literally, got off the ground. Although the first engines had been delivered to Gloster Aircraft Company in May 1942, these were 'ground only' units, and as the year slipped by without an airworthy engine becoming available, the Ministry of Aircraft Production considered other means of obtaining an operational jet fighter for the RAF with the minimum delay. The cancellation of Meteor production contracts and the substitution of another Gloster project, the single-engined E.5/42, was one scheme to achieve this. Through the autumn and early winter, proposal and counter-proposal passed between the MAP and Gloster Aircraft, but each one was a variation in the proportion of Meteors to be built either with Rover's W.2B or W.2/500 engines, or Halford's H.1 engine. Then, at the end of November 1942, when the good news of a delivery of H.1 engines was at last given to Frank McKenna at Hucclecote, the MAP ordered production of the Meteor F.1 and all tooling to cease because of the failure by Rovers to keep to their revised programme for production of the W.2B engines. Moreover, the number of F.9/40 prototypes ordered was reduced from twelve to six (although after the first aircraft had flown, wiser counsels prevailed and the order was stepped up to eight aircraft). In addition Gloster Aircraft was instructed to proceed

46

as quickly as possible with plans for the construction of three prototypes to meet specification E.5/42.

This cancellation was the very event that Hugh Burroughes had sought to forestall with his scheme to bring airframe and engine manufacture under Hawker Siddeley control. However, the Meteor was restored to production status soon after the first flight of the H.1 powered fifth prototype on 5 March, 1943, at RAF Cranwell. The pilot was Michael Daunt, Glosters' chief test pilot, who also flew five of the remaining seven F.9/40 prototypes on their first flights. Daunt had undertaken the heavy responsibility of his position when P.E.G. Sayer had been killed in a Typhoon over the North Sea on 21 October, 1942. During the next eleven months every section of Gloster Aircraft Company's technical and administrative facilities was working at full stretch; 955 Typhoons and five F.9/40s were built and flown, development work continued with the E.28/39 and production of the Meteor F.1 began. To these achievements should be added the successful organization and administration of a workforce totalling some 14,000 men and women in 40 factories dispersed over a wide area of Gloucestershire. A great deal of this effort culminated in the first flight of the prototype Meteor F.1 on 12 January, 1944.

For operational service with No. 616 Squadron RAF, the production Meteor 1s differed very little from the F.9/40 prototypes. Powered with Rolls-Royce W.2B/23C Welland engines, these aircraft had a number of airframe refinements which included a fully transparent fairing behind the sideways-opening canopy and four-cannon armament. Based at Manston in Kent the Meteor 1s were used initially in July 1944 against the V 1 flying bombs, but even when Meteor F.3s ventured across the English Channel in January 1945 to join No. 84 Group, 2nd Tactical Air Force, at Nijmegen near to Brussels, their pilots were not allowed to fly over enemy-occupied territory as a precaution against any of the new fighters falling into hostile hands. Later these Meteors took part in fighter sweeps against ground targets but never engaged Luftwaffe jet fighters in combat.

Meteor F.3 centre sections and front fuselages on the five-abreast assembly tracks in the erecting shop during 1946. (*Courtesy Mrs M. May*)

Glosters' private-venture Meteor F.4, G-AIDC, being salvaged after its landing accident at Brussels' Melsbroek Airport in May 1947. (*Hugh Service*)

Post-war Development

With the end of the war, Gloster Aircraft Company began another massive administrative reorganization to dispose of dispersal factories, to centre main production at Hucclecote, experimental design and construction of prototypes at nearby Bentham, and flight test work at Moreton Valence, an ex-RAF airfield some eight miles south of Hucclecote which the company had used since October 1943 for all F.9/40 and Meteor flying. In September 1945, with the agreement of the MAP and the Air Ministry and the co-operation of Rolls-Royce, Gloster Aircraft prepared the Meteor to establish a new World Speed Record and on 7 November achieved this with a speed of 606 mph, at Herne Bay, Kent. A year later two Meteor F.4s, known as Star Meteors, pushed this record up to 616

The private-venture Meteor T.7, G-AKPK, built with some sub-assemblies from G-AIDC, in company with a standard Meteor F.4.

48

mph flying over a course at Littlehampton, Sussex. On both occasions cold weather had dogged the attempts and in warmer flying conditions maximum speeds would undoubtedly have been higher.

For Glosters, the ten years following the war were a period of steady production and full employment coupled with a rewarding export market for Meteors which not only delighted the pilots of 14 air forces, in whose markings they flew, but also caught the public's attention across the world. The company's brilliant carmine-coloured Meteor 4, G-AIDC, and Meteor 7, G-AKPK, demonstrators were a familiar sight on Europe's airports and air bases, and Belgium, Denmark and the Netherlands were major customers during this period. In the Netherlands, where the great Fokker concern was struggling to regain its pre-war eminence, the Meteor was licence-built to equip the Royal Netherlands Air Force and the Belgian

No doubt about the identity of this aeroplane or its engines. In the front cockpit is Bill Waterton, with Gen Lechères, Chief of the Belgian Air Force's General Staff, in the rear cockpit.

Air Force. Apart from absolute speed records, others tumbled to the Meteor's onslaught; the 100 kilometre and 1,000 kilometre closed-circuit records, the time-to-height record and a number of 'capital to capital' records were all claimed by the Meteor.

In Korea on 29 July, 1951, Meteors became the first type of jet aircraft to operate in two wars when Meteor F.8s of No. 77 Squadron Royal Australian Air Force, commanded by Sqn Ldr P. Cresswell, shared a fighter sweep with USAF F-86 Sabres. Although at that time the Meteor F.8 was the RAF's standard interceptor it lagged behind the jet fighter development in other countries; thus, apart from its rate of climb, it lacked the performance of the F-86 and the opposing MiG-15, particularly at high altitude. However the Meteor F.8 continued in the interceptor rôle

49

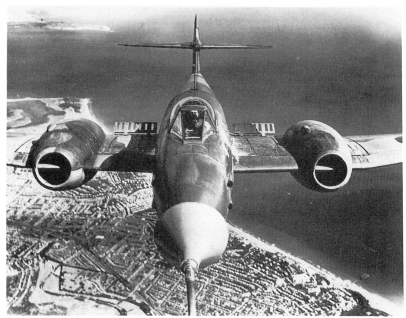

Using the probe and drogue system of flight refuelling, this Meteor F.3, EE397, established a jet aircraft flight endurance record on 7 August, 1949, by remaining airborne for 12 hr 3 min.

The Meteor-packed tarmac at Moreton Valence in the early spring of 1951. Thirty-two aircraft are visible on the hardstandings around the taxiways.

The Sapphire Meteor, piloted by R. B. Prickett, takes off from Moreton Valence early on 31 August, 1951, on its record-setting climb to 12,000 m in 3 min 7 sec.

in Korea with limited success until on 8 January, 1952, it began flying in the ground attack rôle where its rugged construction and excellent power/ weight ratio could be exploited. No. 77 Squadron flew nearly 19,000 sorties in two years' operations in the Korean war, lost 54 Meteors and 32 of their pilots but destroyed three MiG-15s and left countless enemy ground installations in ruins. In addition a number of modifications were embodied in No. 77 Squadron's Meteors and in subsequent production aircraft which increased their effectiveness in service with the RAF and other air forces.

The steady increase in engine power achieved by Rolls-Royce enabled Gloster Aircraft to exploit the potentialities of the Meteor for many operational tasks. Two-seat trainer, single-seat fighter reconnaissance, photo-reconnaissance and ground attack variants were produced for Service use in addition to the vast quantity of single-seat fighter Meteors which poured off the Hucclecote assembly lines. At Baginton, Coventry, Sir W. G. Armstrong Whitworth Aircraft Limited had developed and

Production of Meteor T.7s and F.8s in full swing at Hucclecote in January 1951.

51

WL191, the last Meteor, being assembled in No. 3 factory at Hucclecote in 1954.

built the night fighter Meteors and 551 of this variant were produced, together with 485 other Meteor variants, between 1949 and May 1955 when the last one was delivered. Gloster Aircraft Company's last Meteor, an F.8, WL191, left the factory on 9 April, 1954, flown by Jim Cooksey, to end a line of production stretching back to 1943. Built in 34 sub-types with 21 different types of power unit, the Meteor was a unique aeroplane which materially helped to change the whole course of military aviation in many countries.

During this period there were a number of changes in Gloster Aircraft Company's management, chief among them being the appointments of Percy G. Crabbe as director and general manager to succeed Frank McKenna, who retired in 1947, and George Carter as technical director in

P. G. Crabbe (*left*) was Glosters' director and general manager from 1947 to 1957, and W. G. Carter (*right*), who was successively designer, chief designer, technical director and consultant from 1931 to 1958.

R. V. Atkinson (*left*) was works director at Hucclecote from 1946 to 1959. R. W. Walker (*right*) joined Glosters in 1937 as assistant chief designer, became chief designer in 1948 and a director in 1954.

1948. Carter remained on the Board until 1954, when he too went into semi-retirement as technical consultant to the Company. He in turn was succeeded on the Board by Richard Walker who had been chief designer since 1948 and who had, from July 1943, assumed responsibility for all Meteor development design. Production was the responsibility of R. V. Atkinson, works director, and W. W. W. Downing, production manager.

In 1944 Glosters began building two new airframes, designated G.A.1, to meet the revised specification E.5/42 which had been re-issued as specification E.1/44. Neither airframe was completed as attention turned to an improved variant, the Gloster G.A.2—known unofficially as the Ace —and then to progressively developed versions of the basic airframe to be

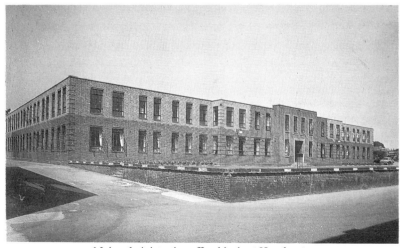

Main administrative office block at Hucclecote.

powered by the Rolls-Royce Nene and de Havilland Ghost engines. This work culminated, in November 1946, in the issue of specification 24/46P to cover proposed manufacture of the G.A.4, but it was not destined to attain production status largely because its performance and development potential were not considered to be sufficiently far in advance of the Meteor; thus work on several airframes was abandoned. The work was not a total loss to Glosters for it had given valuable experience in new production techniques involving machining and forming stainless steel which was used extensively in these airframes.

Aerial view of the Gloster factories. The parish boundary between Hucclecote and Brockworth runs roughly from left to right across the airfield and runway.

British aviation achievements during the immediate post-war era were highly esteemed throughout the world, and in 1946 the Chinese Nationalist Government sent a technical mission to Great Britain to investigate the possibilities of joint basic design of a fighter aircraft, a bomber and a jet engine. Gloster Aircraft Company agreed to collaborate in the design of a single-seat fighter, and a part of the factory, complete with workshop and offices to house a team of 63 Chinese and British designers, was set aside for this work. Designated CXP-102, the initial design was developed into the CXP-1001 which strongly resembled the E.1/44 with the high tailplane and having a nose air intake which also carried four 20 mm cannon in pairs in the upper and lower portions. A part mock-up and a quantity of components were completed when, due to the political situation in China, work was abandoned, and the Chinese party returned home after about a year's work had been accomplished.

The Javelin

Following the end of World War II, the matter of providing a replacement for the Meteor was becoming urgent and the Air Ministry looked chiefly to Gloster Aircraft Company to provide it. It should be remembered that Glosters had a two and a half year lead over de Havilland and their Spider Crab/Vampire, were more than five years ahead of Supermarine with their Attacker, and had designed and built some 400 jet aircraft before Hawker Aircraft flew the first prototype P.1040 in September 1947; moreover neither the Supermarine nor Hawker aeroplanes proved acceptable to the RAF for whom they were intended. An important step in providing this new fighter was taken on 24 January, 1947, with the issue of specification F.43/46 which called for a single-seat fighter for the daylight interception and destruction of single high-speed, high-altitude hostile targets. Because of this rôle very rapid starting was required, a time to height of 45,000 ft in six minutes was to be attained with a service ceiling of 50,000 ft and a maximum speed of 547 kt at 45,000 ft. All the other requirements were aimed at producing a high-performance, highly manoeuvrable interceptor. Concurrently, specification F.44/46 for a two-

The 450-yard long main erecting shop in which more than 9,000 aircraft were built between 1939 and 1959.

55

C

seat night fighter was prepared and issued on the same day. It also called for a rapid take-off, climb to 45,000 ft in a maximum of ten minutes and an endurance of two hours. A comprehensive range of electronic navigation and search equipment was specified together with the heavy armament of four 30 mm guns, full night flying equipment and many aids to crew safety and comfort.

During 1947 the Gloster design office prepared a number of projects to meet these two specifications which, in February 1948, were superseded by specification F.3/48 for a day fighter, and F.4/48 for a night and all-weather fighter. Although originally the intention was to adapt a basic

A Javelin fuselage in the Abbey frame, one of the strength-test rigs in the structural research department.

design for each rôle, Glosters' single-engined project P.275, in which the pilot was housed in the leading edge of the sharply swept fin of a classic delta-winged aircraft, was to meet specification F.3/48 and was quite unlike the massive F.4/48 design. The decision was then taken to concentrate on the all-weather fighter requirement, and with Richard Walker heading the design team, a number of projects were investigated including basic schemes for two, three and four engines; the use of a single Rolls-Royce Avon engine and two 3,000 lb thrust rocket motors; rotating wingtips in place of ailerons and the mounting of fixed armament under the wings. About this time a good deal of information was forthcoming on the work done during the war by Lippisch and other German designers relating to sweptback and delta wings. Little was known in the United Kingdom about the characteristics of either swept or straight wings at high Mach numbers or of the extent of usable lift at low speed on the delta planform. There were widespread misgivings about the apparently poor stall charac-

56

XA568 and XA570, two of the first three Javelin F(AW)1s delivered to the RAF, leave Moreton Valence on 30 December, 1955.

teristics and high angles of attack at low speeds, particularly during landing, but these doubts were to be removed in later years during the early stages of test flying aircraft with this configuration. In many other respects the delta wing appeared to have important advantages over the swept-back 'plank' wing as projected for the Javelin at one stage. The high taper ratio permitted a choice of low aspect ratio for a fighter aircraft combined with a generous wing area for good take-off and landing and at the same time provided an adequate amount of sweepback for the high speed end of the scale. The long root chord allowed a comparatively thin wing to be combined with a large wing volume for stowage of fuel, armament and retracted

One of the engine silencing pens built at Hucclecote and at Moreton Valence.

Javelins WT827, WT830, WT836, XA544 and XA545, en route to the SBAC display at Farnborough on Sunday, 5 September, 1954.

landing gear; it also blended cleanly into the fuselage to form an almost complete delta planform, and it was estimated that through this design the fuselage contributed about 20 per cent of the total wing lift. The structural advantage was clear—the high taper, low aspect ratio and the depth at the wing root led to a low structure weight combined with maximum wing stiffness in bending and torsion. So the design was frozen around this delta wing plan and Gloster Aircraft's G.A.5 emerged in 1951 as a delta-winged aeroplane with a T-shaped tail unit and powered by two Armstrong Siddeley Sapphires.

In direct competition with the G.A.5 was the de Havilland D.H.110 which made its maiden flight in September 1951 exactly two months before the Gloster aeroplane, but in July 1952 the Air Ministry decided in favour of the G.A.5, ordering it into Super Priority production and conferring upon it the name Javelin. This 'Super Priority' category was instigated by Winston Churchill and was a scheme to enable a small number of military aircraft types, specially chosen for their importance to the Services re-equipment programme, to obtain the benefit of priority in acquiring materials, proprietary components and manpower. The development programme was marred by a number of unfortunate accidents to the prototypes, in which three test pilots lost their lives, but by February 1956 production Javelin F(AW)Mk.1 all-weather fighters were reaching the RAF.

In March 1951, Richard Walker had claimed, with some justification, that 'the Gloster F.4/48, as a type, has great potential for future development. Features giving support to this view include the relatively low wing loading—32 lb/sq ft—at the present combat weight of 28,700 lb, the internal capacity available for additional fuel or military equipment and the fact that more powerful engines giving nearly 10,000 lb static thrust can be installed with relatively minor airframe structural modifications.' His claim was amply justified during the ensuing eight years as this aeroplane was evolved through nine variants into Gloster Aircraft Company's last

58

and most potent fighter, the Javelin F(AW)Mk.9. Throughout its development and for much of its operational life—which ended in April 1968—the Javelin was consistently 'sold short' by many who had no appreciation of the important rôle it played so efficiently, or of its many virtues. While the prototype trials were in progress certain sections of the National press were particularly vociferous about the aircraft's inability to exceed Mach 1 until a nocturnal, and 'accidental', sonic boom over London proved otherwise. In RAF service the Javelin was nicknamed the 'Harmonious Dragmaster' due to the organ-like note caused by the airflow over the open cannon ports, but aircrews were generally loud in its praise.

Among the many proposed F.4/48 developments were a day/night photographic-reconnaissance aircraft to meet OR.309 for which Gloster Aircraft Company submitted design brochures in January 1952; single- and two-seat fighters, armed with bombs or rockets in addition to the normal fixed cannon armament, to meet the long-range requirements of the F.5/49 specification; a high altitude escort fighter with a range of more than 3,300 miles; and a two-seat dual control aircraft based on provisions in OR.278 to fulfil a Service rôle of pilot conversion and instrument and gunnery training. This last development formed the basis of the Javelin T.Mk.3 aircraft.

In March 1955 came the first public mention of a new all-weather fighter for the RAF which was being developed from the Javelin by Gloster Aircraft Company. To be powered by two Bristol Olympus engines this aircraft, known as the Javelin T.W.D., or thin wing development, started in 1952 as a logical progressive refinement of the Javelin's basic design to take full advantage of proposed developments of the Sapphire engine giving 14,000 lb thrust. Initially intended to meet a new air staff operational

Neville Horne, a Dowty service engineer, obligingly marks up a Javelin's Canberra 'kills' during Exercise Beware in 1955.

requirement, OR.234, issued in December 1952, it was to be a bomber support aircraft capable of destroying interceptors over enemy bases and its bombers early in their outward flight. Experience in Korea had revealed the difficulties of making interceptions at high speed and altitudes beyond the range of ground control, so search radar and two crew members were to be carried. Armament was to be guns, rocket batteries and guided weapons, but the aircraft's performance was basically high subsonic. These requirements plus the need for increased radius of operation, a high rate of climb and comparatively short take-off and landing capabilities, set Richard Walker and his team a formidable task, but it was anticipated that they would be met by using most of the existing Javelin fuselage structure with a larger, thinner wing, a modified tail unit and 11,000 lb thrust Armstrong Siddeley Sapphire Sa.7 engines.

Model of the thin-wing Javelin for free flight trials. The tailplane has been replaced by a streamlined body of equal drag. Note the large missiles under the wings.

There followed several months of discussion and further investigation and at an advisory design conference on 12 May, 1953, it centred on a thin-wing photo-reconnaissance development to meet specification PR.118D and P but it was emphasized that the fighter version was to be the primary basis for the design, and that performance was in no way to be penalized on account of provisions made for this P.R. rôle. On 20 July, 1953, design studies for the P.R., the day interceptor and night fighter development of the Javelin, having a 7.5 per cent thickness/chord ratio wing and 12,500 lb thrust Sapphire Sa.9 engines, were submitted to the Ministry of Supply. Fitted with up to eight cameras, an array of photo-flash equipment, and rearward-looking radar mounted in the aft end of the fin/tailplane junction fairing, the P.R. variant's estimated top speed was 564 kt at 45,000 ft.

The day interceptor was designed to attain the same speed, armed with two Red Dean and two Firestreak air-to-air missiles plus two 30 mm cannon in the wings; absolute ceiling was to have been 59,200 ft and the endurance $1\frac{1}{4}$ hr. Similarly armed, the night fighter's maximum speed was estimated

Mock-up of the Javelin thin-wing development showing the thickened inboard main-plane and the single pylon-mounted Red Dean air-to-air guided weapon.

to be 561 kt at 40,000 ft with an absolute ceiling of 58,400 ft and an endurance of up to 2 hr. The covering letter to the Ministry noted that as a longer-term project, Gloster Aircraft was preparing design studies around the Bristol Olympus engine, which was coming firmly onto the aviation scene with a 16,000 lb thrust, to meet the newly issued F.153D specification. The company was asked to submit these proposals at an early date and they were submitted in October 1953.

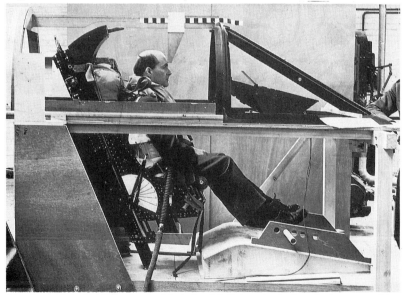
Members of the RAF Institute of Aviation Medicine check the pilot's seat position in a space mock-up of the Javelin T.W.D. cockpit.

In February 1954, the Olympus B.O1.6 was confirmed for the pre-production aircraft and the Sapphire Sa.7 for the prototype, but two months later the Olympus was agreed for all aircraft.

Although more and more thrust was being promised by both Armstrong Siddeley and Bristol, Richard Walker's design team fought an endless battle to limit the increase in all-up weight as the design studies moved from stage to stage. Thus in a letter to the Ministry of Supply on 8 October, 1954, which accompanied the latest details of the Javelin T.W.D. with Olympus B.O1.6, B.O1.7 and B.O1.7SR engines, Walker drew attention to the fact that the all-up combat weight had increased to 43,000 lb.

Treasury approval for a development batch of 18 pre-production all-weather fighter aircraft was given in January 1955, but it was not until May 1955 that the final F.153D specification was received, more than three years after the original O.R. was issued. Meanwhile design work on this new fighter was going ahead to a programme which had been established at the end of 1954 and a quantity of drawings were issued to the factory.

While the design work proceeded, the production planning, in the hands of R. V. Atkinson and W. W. W. Downing, was carefully considered. The policy which was to have been adopted was that all detail manufacture and component assembly could take place in the production shops, leaving the assembly of major components and the installation of controls, systems and equipment to the experimental department. Arrangements were also made to sub-contract to Armstrong Whitworth Aircraft and Air Service Training 20 per cent of the process planning, tooling and manufacture of the aircraft, and an initial forecast made in February 1955 indicated that the flying shell prototype would be completed by the middle of March 1957.

Glosters were not however entirely happy with the situation on several counts. There had been delays in the choice of engine which, when decided, brought delivery promises of late 1957 for the prototype and a year later for pre-production aircraft. There had also been a gross underestimate of the time needed to develop the Red Dean installation which had greatly increased in weight since its inception. Richard Walker felt that the safeguards in armament were being overplayed in providing installations for Red Dean as the primary weapon, Firestreak in case Red Dean failed, and 30 mm Aden guns as a general back up system. Moreover the supersonic fighter was fast becoming the main defensive weapon system, although the 'mother and child' concept of the F.153D system was still a viable proposition particularly for all-weather and night operations. It comprised a high subsonic carrier with long-range acquisition radar and a supersonic collision course weapon. There had been some difference of opinion on this subject of the supersonic fighter, and in May 1956 Glosters re-submitted to the Ministry proposals for a development of the F.153D as a true supersonic fighter, capable of cruising at Mach 1.3. Two stages of development were considered; the first was limited to extending the fuselage fore and aft to improve the area rule distribution and the second was the use of

Close-up view of the underwing external store pylon on the Javelin T.W.D. mock-up and the Red Dean mock-up.

wings and tail surfaces with a 5 per cent mean thickness/chord ratio. In view of the reduction in internal fuel capacity, which would have resulted from the adoption of these thin wings, the second stage was abandoned. Two fully reheated Olympus B.O1.21R engines with about 29,000 lb thrust were specified to power this giant fighter, which was 72 ft long, had a 1,235 sq ft wing which spanned 60 ft 8 in, and an operational weight of 50,500 lb. Preliminary estimates indicated that, with 2,000°K reheat, Mach 1.79 would be attainable in level flight at 45,000 ft.

The development of this Javelin went on despite the signs and portents of a major change in defence policy relating to manned fighter aircraft, but rumour turned to fact in July 1956 when Glosters received notification of the cancellation of the F.153D. The Defence White Paper of 1957 confirmed the Government's shift of policy, and the decision to cease the development of manned fighters for the RAF beyond the Lightning.

Soon afterwards, on 12 April, 1957, a milestone in Glosters' history was passed when the last home-based RAF squadron to operate Meteor day fighters, No 245 based at Stradishall, re-equipped with Hunters.

By the following year it was clear that, as a military aircraft design and production organization, Gloster Aircraft Company's days were numbered. Javelin production continued however, and, in a gallant effort to provide work for its employees, the company accelerated its diversification plans and switched parts of the Hucclecote factory to the manufacture of automatic vending machines and agricultural forage harvesters. Glosters' experience in systems engineering was put to good effect in the formation of the Technical Developments Division which found new industrial

63

A small industrial sweeper made by Alf'd Miles Ltd, a Gloster subsidiary company, in use in one of Glosters' flight sheds.

applications for a range of fluid measuring and controlling equipment and marketed them as well. This Division was taken over by Armstrong Whitworth Aircraft early in 1959 and continued at Hucclecote under the title Whitworth Gloster Equipment.

At the same time, E. W. Shambrook was appointed director and general manager, and H. E. Sidwell succeeded R. V. Atkinson on his retirement as works director of Gloster Aircraft Company, and two Hawker Siddeley

Conversion of Javelin F(AW)7 aircraft to F(AW)9 standard at Moreton Valence.

Aviation directors, J. A. R. Kay and J. T. Lidbury, joined Glosters' Board. The company also acquired Alf'd Miles Limited, an old established firm of coach builders in Cheltenham who were largely concerned with the manufacture of fire appliances and emergency vehicles, and this work, together with the design and production of road tanker bodies, light alloy lighting columns and road sweepers, was transferred to Glosters' No. 3 Flight Shed at Hucclecote.

A new company, Gloster Equipment Limited, was formed in 1959 to take over the vending machine and forage harvester design and production from Gloster Aircraft Company, and to exploit the markets for these specialized products.

On 8 April, 1960, Glosters' last aeroplane built at Hucclecote was

This Javelin F(AW)7, XH965, was the last to be converted to an F(AW)9.

flown by Dicky Martin from Hucclecote to Moreton Valence where modification and servicing of Javelins continued together with conversion of Mk.7 aircraft to Mk.8 standards.

Another company acquired by Glosters in the spring of 1961 to widen the non-aviation interests was Hands (Letchworth) Limited, manufacturers of commercial semi-trailers for road haulage work.

As the full effect of the cancellation of the F.153D and the 1957 White Paper were felt by the company—and the industry—the Hawker Siddeley Group was forced to examine the current and future activities of its aircraft companies with the view to closing those without either a production contract in hand or a new aeroplane to manufacture. Gloster Aircraft appeared to qualify for closure on both counts, although from January 1958 the company had mounted a prodigious programme of market research and project evaluation. As a part of this programme a good deal of thought was given to providing some design and production facilities for the Aviation Traders Accountant twin propeller-turbine transport, and Dicky Martin flew the aircraft on several occasions but was not wholly impressed.

Glosters' design investigations fell into three categories: a short-range jet transport, a small executive jet aircraft and the development and application of V/STOL techniques to civil and military aircraft. Between January 1958 and February 1961 over 50 projects were schemed, including an 80-seat STOL transport with four Bristol Siddeley BE.61 main engines and ten BE.59 lift engines; a 150,000 lb all-up weight military transport; a sweptwing tactical strike reconnaissance STOL aircraft to meet a SHAPE requirement; and a six-seat light aircraft powered by two pusher engines. In addition there were proposals to modify Meteor 7s and 8s to VTOL aircraft using twelve Rolls-Royce RB.108 lift engines; and a remotely controlled crop-spraying helicopter.

In May 1960, J. A. R. Kay and J. T. Lidbury with S. D. Davies, Hawker Siddeley Aviation's technical director, composed the Group's investigating team which visited Glosters to examine and evaluate the viability of these projects. With the exception of the market survey and the technical work on the proposed Accountant programme, none of the projects was considered to have potential value and all were abandoned. Glosters were, nevertheless, instructed to hand over all data on the crop-spraying helicopter to Armstrong Whitworth Aircraft, and on the Accountant to A. V. Roe who later produced their Dart-powered 748 transport bearing a marked similarity to the Accountant.

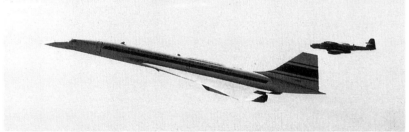

A Meteor NF.11, serialled 6, from Centre d'Essais en Vol at Bretigny, was one of the chase aircraft for the first flight of BAC/Sud Concorde 001 on 2 March, 1969. (*Sud Aviation*)

During the reorganization and run-down of the Gloster aviation activities, other Hawker Siddeley companies provided some sub-contract work and Meteor NF.11s were converted to TT.20s; in addition Argosy, Vulcan, Hunter and Blue Steel components were produced in small quantities.

On 1 October, 1961, Gloster Aircraft Company merged with Sir W. G. Armstrong Whitworth Aircraft Ltd, the combined concern being named Whitworth Gloster Aircraft Limited. It continued under this title until 1 July, 1963, when, following a major reorganization of the Hawker Siddeley Group, the name Gloster finally disappeared when the company became part of the Avro Whitworth Division of Hawker Siddeley Aviation. The name reappeared in a new company, Gloster Saro Limited, which became responsible for production of vending machines, road tankers and

Part of the batch of 18 Meteor NF.11s being converted to TT.20s at Moreton Valence during 1961. The last Javelin F(AW)7 conversion aircraft is seen on the left of the photograph.

refuellers in 1965, and in Gloster Design Services, an independent company established by ex-Gloster Aircraft design office staff at Hucclecote.

Thus the cancellation of the F.153D was fatal not only to the aircraft itself but also to the Gloster company. Once again it had all been a matter of timing which, as noted earlier, so often means the same thing as luck.

Finally on 6 April, 1964, the Hucclecote factory was sold to Gloucester Trading Estates and, almost imperceptibly, the spirit of Gloster Aircraft Company was no more.

Mars I

When Harry Folland first conceived his original design for the Nieuport Nighthawk aircraft he could have had little idea of the ways in which the basic airframe would be modified and adapted to produce two aircraft, one of which was to provide a foreign navy with fighter defences and the other to establish for a thrusting young aircraft company a reputation for high-speed aircraft.

The Mars I racer was the second of these aircraft evolved from the basic Nighthawk by Folland with the sole intention of flying faster than anything else in the sky and thus concentrating the attention of the Air Ministry on the Gloucestershire Aircraft Company. There could have been no one better for this job than Folland, for among his outstanding designs was the Nieuport Goshawk, a single-strut biplane which, although powered by the unfortunate 300 hp ABC Dragonfly radial engine, had earlier established a new British air speed record of 166·4 mph. Clearly bearing the Folland stamp as did so many aeroplanes which followed it, the Mars I achieved its designer's aim and, bearing the nickname 'Bamel', won great fame for itself, its creator and parent company.

Folland was not the first to realize that high speed could be achieved not only by increasing engine power but also by reducing head resistance, but he paid more attention than most others to this second factor. He

The Mars I as first flown with a square radiator, uncowled centre cylinder bank of the Lion engine, and the Nighthawk-type tail unit. In this view a part of the engine cowling is not fitted.

Mars I at Villesauvage for the Coupe Deutsch de la Meurthe contest in September 1921. It carries the hastily painted racing number 1 on the fuselage and the 'Bamel' motif. The pilot is Jimmy James. (*Musée de l'Air*)

replaced the Nighthawk's 230 hp Bentley B.R.2 rotary engine with a large 450 hp Napier Lion twelve-cylinder broad-arrow engine, but careful design concealed its bulk under neat cowlings, and with meticulous attention being paid to streamlining in such details as the propeller spinner, axle, shock absorbing bungee casings and a retractable radiator, the Mars I had a very high top speed.

Conceived and built in less than four weeks, which was in part due to the use of a Nighthawk landing gear, rear fuselage and tail unit, the Mars I had single-bay wings similar to the Goshawk, with single-I interplane struts and with ailerons fitted only on the lower wings. These had squared-off tips which contrasted sharply with the full rounded tips of the upper wings. Built almost entirely of wood, the fuselage had ash longerons with spruce struts and light wooden fairings, to give shape; it was fabric-covered and doped with Emailite X for extra tautness. Spruce landing gear struts were attached to the two lower longerons by metal links which allowed for slight misalignment during assembly, and the single interplane struts were also of spruce attached by a mortice joint to walnut feet spreading out to meet the ash main spars. Ash engine bearers supported by multiply cradles were braced by diagonal steel tubes.

Making its first flight at Hucclecote on 20 June, 1921, it completed its initial tests so successfully that it was entered for the annual Aerial Derby. On 17 July the Mars I, painted silver with red registration letters G-EAXZ and the racing number 21 under the tips of all four wings and on the rudder, was flown by J. H. James, the company's test pilot, to win the race and the Handicap Cup with a speed of 163·3 mph. This was an increase of 10 mph over the speed achieved by the Martinsyde Semi-Quaver, winner of the previous year's race.

This great win by the Mars I inspired the Gloster team who set about refining its design in preparation for the Coupe Deutsch contest held at

Villesauvage, Étampes, France. The wing area was reduced to 180 sq ft from the original 205 sq ft and, because the earlier square radiator was not big enough to allow the full use of the power available from the Lion, when the aircraft arrived in France it was removed and twin Lamblin 'lobster pot' radiators were fitted in its place.

These and other modifications gave an increase of several miles per hour in top speed, but a failure in the stitching of the fabric covering the wings prevented the Mars I from completing the course. After the race G-EAXZ was returned to Sunningend where, once again, it was modified. One radiator and yet another 20 sq ft of wing were removed, streamlined fairings were fitted behind the wheels, the top bank of the Lion's cylinders

G-EAXZ, at Sunningend, prepared for its successful attempt on the British speed record in December 1921. It has wheel fairings, a completely cowled Lion engine, single Lamblin radiator and a high-gloss finish.

was faired-in and many small excrescences were cleaned up; finally it was repainted with a glossy blue fuselage, and ivory-white wings, tail unit, landing gear and registration In this form on 12 December, 1921, it flew to the Aeroplane Experimental Establishment at Martlesham where, one week later, fitted with extra instrumentation which included a radiator temperature gauge and a density meter, it established a new British speed record of 196·4 mph.

Although a fierce protagonist of the biplane configuration, Folland was always seeking means of reducing drag to an absolute minimum; thus for the 1922 Aerial Derby the two wheel fairings were removed, the second Lamblin radiator was refitted, the fin and rudder area was increased and on 7 August, again flown by James, the Mars I romped home the winner

Mars I with wheel fairings removed and with modified fuel tank fairing and windscreen fitted. (*Courtesy C. H. Barnes*)

at 177·85 mph. On 30 September of the same year, Gloucestershire Aircraft once more entered G-EAXZ for the Coupe Deutsch race at Villesauvage and in preparation for this the wing area was reduced still further; unfortunately James' maps blew out of the cockpit during the contest and he lost his way so the efficacy of this measure was not then seen. While in France, however, the Mars I made an attempt on the world's speed record over the official 1 kilometre course and, although it attained 212 mph, this was less than the necessary 4 km/h increase over the existing French record and the attempt failed.

This continued reduction in wing area certainly contributed to the increased top speed, but it also pushed up the stalling speed which reached

Taxi-ing out for the Coupe Deutsch event at Villesauvage in September 1922 for which the Mars I's fin and rudder area were increased. (*Musée de l'Air*)

71

70 mph. However, wings of increased area were fitted when the Mars I later went to Martlesham where, flown by Flt Lieut R. A. de Haga Haig, one of the Establishment's pilots, it was officially timed for rate of climb on 23 November, 1922. A Royal Aero Club Certificate of Performance credited G-EAXZ with a rate of climb of 2,390 ft/min at 5,000 ft and 854 ft/min at 19,500 ft which was reached in 11 min 34 sec.

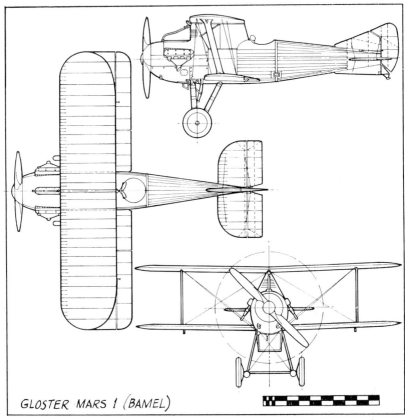

GLOSTER MARS 1 (BAMEL)

Before competing in the Aerial Derby on 6 August, 1923, the Mars I airframe was extensively modified; the wing was completely rebuilt with different ribs to give a new section and a 20 ft span, the fuel tank was moved from its position on top of the fuselage to an internal location, giving the pilot a much improved view forward, the tail unit was reshaped, only one Lamblin radiator was retained, and a more powerful Lion engine, developing 530 hp, was installed. In this form and renamed Gloster I, this aeroplane was flown to victory, despite a severe oil leak, by Larry Carter at 192·4 mph. After the race, G-EAXZ was taken over by Gloucestershire Aircraft's experimental department who used it to flight test various features of the Gloster II racing seaplane. The Air Ministry had

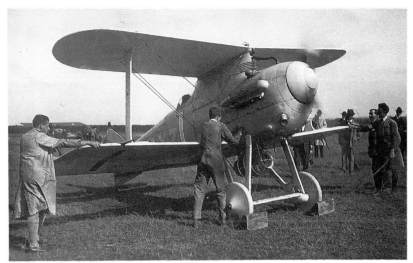

The careful attention to streamlining the wheels, which are encased in linen bags, the bungee casings and cylinder banks, is apparent in this view of G-EAXZ. The cowling bore the amended name 'Gloucestershire Aircraft Mars 1st'. (*Musée de l'Air*)

earlier agreed to buy the aircraft winning the 1923, and last, Aerial Derby, and on 12 December of that year, after some haggling over the £3,000 purchase price, it was transferred to RAF charge and given the serial No. J7234. Mounted on floats it served at Felixstowe from May 1925 as a trainer to enable pilots of the High Speed Flight to gain valuable racing experience in readiness for the 1925 and 1927 Schneider Trophy contests. A number of modifications were embodied which included a header tank on the upper wing and surface radiators on upper and lower wings to give increased performance. It was eventually scrapped in 1927.

G-EAXZ in its Gloster I form in which the fuel tank was housed internally to improve forward view for the pilot.

73

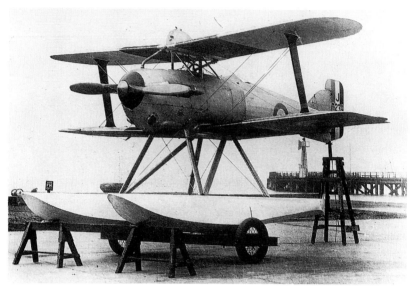

The Gloster I, serialled J7234, on floats at Felixstowe in 1924 and fitted with wing surface radiators, a coolant header tank and revised tail unit. (*Courtesy E. Stott*)

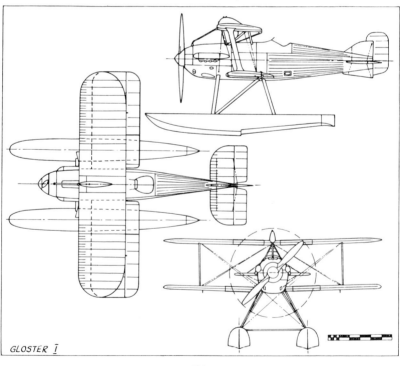

GLOSTER I

74

Description: Single-seat racing biplane. Wood construction with fabric covering.

Accommodation: Pilot in open cockpit.

Powerplant: One 450 hp Napier Lion twelve-cylinder liquid-cooled broad-arrow, driving a Gloster two-blade fixed-pitch propeller (Mars I).

One 530 hp Napier Lion twelve-cylinder liquid-cooled broad-arrow, driving a two-blade fixed-pitch propeller (Gloster I land- and seaplane).

Fuel 50 gal (227 litres); oil 6 gal (27 litres); coolant 8½ gal (38 litres).

Dimensions:	Mars I	Gloster I landplane	Gloster I seaplane
Span	22 ft 0 in	20 ft 0 in	21 ft 0 in
	(6·7 m)	(6·09 m)	(6·4 m)
Length	23 ft 0 in	23 ft 0 in	26 ft 10 in
	(7·01 m)	(7·01 m)	(8·17 m)
Height	9 ft 4 in	9 ft 4 in	11 ft 0 in
	(2·84 m)	(2·84 m)	(3·35 m)
Wing area	205 sq ft	165 sq ft	185 sq ft
	(19·04 sq m)	(15·31 sq m)	(17·18 sq m)

Chord (upper and lower mainplanes) 4 ft 9 in (1·43 m); gap 4 ft 9 in (1·43 m); stagger 1 ft 1½ in (0·341 m); incidence 1½ degrees; dihedral 1¾ degrees.

Weights:			
Empty	1,890 lb	1,970 lb	2,440 lb
	(857 kg)	(893 kg)	(1,106 kg)
Loaded	2,500 lb	2,650 lb	3,120 lb
	(1,134 kg)	(1,202 kg)	(1,415 kg)
Performance:			
Maximum speed	202 mph (325 km/h)	220 mph (354 km/h)	185 mph (297 km/h)
	at sea level	at sea level	at sea level
Stalling speed	55 mph	61 mph	60 mph
	(88 km/h)	(98 km/h)	(96 km/h)
Climb to	10,000 ft (3,048 m)	10,000 ft (3,048 m)	—
in	4·25 min	4·3 min	—

Production: One Mars I/Gloster I built by Gloucestershire Aircraft Co Ltd, Cheltenham, in 1921.

Sparrowhawk

Due to the understandable reluctance of the Air Ministry at the end of the 1914–18 War to encourage the development of new military aircraft for the RAF, Gloucestershire Aircraft turned its attention to overseas where foreign governments were seeking to build up their own air strength having witnessed the effects of air power during hostilities. In January 1921 a British Air Mission, led by Col The Master of Sempill, went to Japan to advise the Imperial Japanese Navy on the equipping of its air arm. In consequence an order was received for 50 modified Nighthawk variants bearing the names Mars II, III and IV, which were subsequently redesignated Sparrowhawk I, II and III respectively following redesign work to fit them for naval service.

Of similar construction to the Nighthawk, the Sparrowhawk's fuselage had a wooden girder type structure, rectangular in section, with light wood fairings. Ash longerons were employed with square spruce struts between them, tapering to fit into circular jointing sockets; the whole fuselage structure was braced internally by round tie-rods. The main spars were also of ash with spruce ribs and struts all internally wire-braced. Metal

JN400, the first Sparrowhawk I modified for service with the Imperial Japanese Navy.

jointing plates in the fuselage and wings were secured by tubular rivets in place of bolts. Powered by the 230 hp Bentley B.R.2 rotary engine, the 30 Sparrowhawk Is were single-seat, land-based fighter-scouts; the 10 Sparrowhawk IIs were basically similar in construction but were two-seat dual control trainers; and the 10 Sparrowhawk IIIs were single-seat, ship-borne fighters, fitted with deck arrester hooks on the landing gear axle, flotation bags in the fuselage and hydrovanes on struts attached to the main landing gear to prevent the aircraft overturning if forced down on water. Twelve of the Sparrowhawk Is and four of the Sparrowhawk IIIs had Leitner-Watts two-blade steel propellers.

In addition to the order for 50 completed aircraft, the contract also covered the provision of spares and sets of components for a further 40 aircraft and these were delivered to a Japanese naval arsenal. The company held sufficient stocks of components, which were bought from the Air Ministry in 1919–20, to enable all the Sparrowhawks to be delivered within six months.

In service all three types of Sparrowhawk proved to be highly reliable, and Japanese naval pilots considered them to be far in advance of the

Sparrowhawks on Kasumigaura naval aerodrome. The aircraft in the foreground is a Sparrowhawk II and the others are Sparrowhawk Is. (*Courtesy Royal Aeronautical Society*)

JN401 was the first Sparrowhawk II two-seat trainer.

French aircraft which they had replaced. For operations at sea, wooden platforms some 30 ft long were mounted on top of the turrets of several Japanese warships. The Sparrowhawks were secured to these platforms which could be traversed into wind and elevated with the guns. For take-off a quick-release hook engaged the landing gear, while the engine was run-

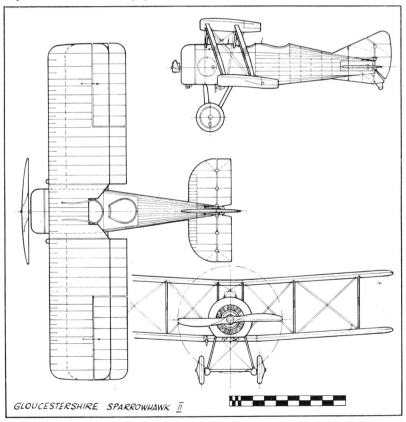

GLOUCESTERSHIRE SPARROWHAWK II

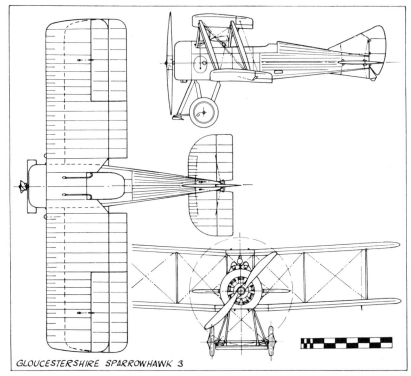

GLOUCESTERSHIRE SPARROWHAWK 3

up to maximum rpm, and was slipped on a signal from the pilot.

Sparrowhawks were in service with Japanese naval air units until 1928.

Gloucestershire Aircraft also built a Mars III/Sparrowhawk II in 1921 for their own use as a demonstrator, and, registered G-EAYN, it was flown in the 1922 Aerial Derby by L. R. Tait-Cox but was forced to retire. This airframe was subsequently rebuilt in 1923 as the Grouse I.

The first Sparrowhawk III, JN442, fitted with the hydrovane attachment in front of the main landing gear.

78

JN442 at Sunningend, showing the longitudinal 'slot' behind the cockpit which was a feature of the earlier Nighthawk fuselage.

TECHNICAL DATA

Description: Landbased naval fighting scout biplane (Sparrowhawk I); two-seat trainer (Sparrowhawk II); shipborne fighter (Sparrowhawk III). Wood construction with fabric covering. Hydrovanes, buoyancy bags and arrester gear on Sparrowhawk III.

Accommodation: Crew of one, or two, in open cockpits.

Powerplant: One 230 hp Bentley B.R.2 nine-cylinder rotary, driving either an 8 ft 9 in (2·65 m) diameter two-blade fixed-pitch wooden propeller or a Leitner-Watts two-blade fixed-pitch steel propeller. Fuel 40 gal (181 litres); oil 8 gal (36 litres).

Armament: Two fixed synchronized Vickers ·303 in machine-guns mounted in top of the engine cowling, with 1,000 rounds of ammunition.

	Sparrowhawk I	Sparrowhawk II	Sparrowhawk III
Dimensions:			
Span	27 ft 11 in	27 ft 11 in	27 ft 11 in
	(8·49 m)	(8·49 m)	(8·49 m)
Length	19 ft 8 in	19 ft 8 in	19 ft 8 in
	(5·99 m)	(5·99 m)	(5·99 m)
Height	10 ft 6 in	10 ft 6 in	10 ft 6 in
	(3·19 m)	(3·19 m)	(3·19 m)
Wing area	270 sq ft	270 sq ft	270 sq ft
	(25·08 sq m)	(25·08 sq m)	(25·08 sq m)
Weights:			
Empty	1,698 lb	1,675 lb	1,850 lb
	(770 kg)	(759 kg)	(839 kg)
Loaded	2,029 lb	2,010 lb	2,165 lb
	(920 kg)	(911 kg)	(981 kg)
Performance:			
Maximum speed	127 mph (204 km/h)	127 mph (204 km/h)	125 mph (201 km/h)
	at sea level	at sea level	at sea level
	105 mph at 15,000 ft	105 mph at 15,000 ft	105 mph at 15,000 ft
	(168 km/h at 4,572 m)	(168 km/h at 4,572 m)	(168 km/h at 4,572 m)
Climb to	15,000 ft (4,572 m)	15,000 ft (4,572 m)	15,000 ft (4,572 m)
in	21 min	21 min	25·5 min
Service ceiling	17,060 ft (5,199 m)	17,060 ft (5,199 m)	16,900 ft (5,150 m)
Duration	3 hr	3 hr	3 hr
Range	300 miles (482 km)	300 miles (482 km)	300 miles (482 km)

Production: A total of 51 Sparrowhawks produced by Gloucestershire Aircraft Co Ltd, Cheltenham, as follows: 30 Sparrowhawk I, 11 Sparrowhawk II, 10 Sparrowhawk III.

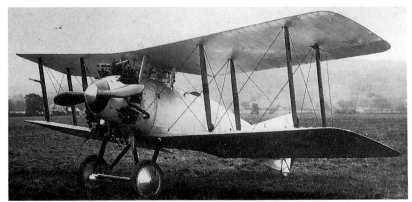

This Mars VI Nighthawk, J6926, seen at Hucclecote with a Jupiter engine, went to No.1 Sqdn, RAF, in Iraq for Service trials in tropical conditions.

Mars VI Nighthawk

The Mars VI single-seat fighter, which emerged during June 1922, was the fifth variant to be developed by Folland from his basic Nieuport Nighthawk, which name it retained after modification and re-engining by Gloucestershire Aircraft. This variant had either a 325 hp Armstrong Siddeley Jaguar II or a 325 hp Bristol Jupiter III engine. In its converted form, the structure of the Mars VI Nighthawk differed very little from the Nieuport-built aeroplane which was a conventional wire-braced, fabric-covered wooden construction in which Folland had paid his usual great attention to detail design and finish. In consequence, for example, in addition to the usual rounded-top wooden fairing to the fuselage there were also full-length fairings, similar in construction, along the fuselage sides which resulted in a neat, well-rounded fuselage shape. Ash longerons were used with square-section spruce struts between them fitting into circular joint sockets. The circular engine mounting plate was of steel-faced multiply wood to which the front struts of the quickly detachable main landing gear were attached. The main spars of the two-bay wings were also of ash, with wire-braced spruce struts and ribs. Ailerons were carried on both the upper and lower mainplanes and were hinged to false spars aft of the main spars. A few aircraft had wings with metal tip bends. The armament was two Vickers ·303 in machine-guns with 500 rounds of ammunition each, mounted under the front fuselage top decking and firing each side of the top cylinder of the engine through the propeller disc. In this way the breech mechanisms were readily accessible to the pilot in the event of a stoppage. The tailplane incidence could be adjusted in flight by a hand lever in the cockpit which was connected by cables to rocking levers on the tailplane.

The first Jaguar-powered Mars VI, H8534, was a Nieuport-built Night-hawk modified by Gloucestershire Aircraft to embody some metal fuselage components and was produced to Air Ministry specification 35/22. This airframe had been in store and was still carrying its wartime overall khaki-green finish. It also carried its two guns externally on top of the front fuselage. It was delivered to the Aeroplane Experimental Establishment at Martlesham on 21 May, 1921, where extensive performance and engine endurance trials were flown between 5 June and 19 August, by which time 50 hr had been logged with the original engine. For eight months it remained in the hangar until a Jaguar IV engine was fitted, and a further 36 hr were flown before this engine was removed to power a Westland Weasel. H8534 was eventually scrapped in July 1922.

Official tests of the Jaguar-powered Mars VI began on 14 July, 1922, when H8544 was flown at RAE Farnborough; the following month it gave an aerobatic display at Croydon piloted by Flg Off P. W. S. Bulman. On 25 September, 1922, J6925 was delivered to Farnborough and in the succeeding two months first J6927 and then J6926, each powered by a Jupiter engine, arrived for comparative trials. They joined J2405 and J2416 which were Nieuport-built and which had been modified to take the Jupiter IV by the RAE under guidance from Gloucestershire Aircraft. J2405 was fitted at one period with an exhaust collector ring and with an oleo-type landing gear in place of the more orthodox pattern with bungee rubber shock absorbers. At Farnborough it was used for acceleration tests and for a series of flight trials during which the wing incidence was checked and the possibility of fitting automatic wingtip slots examined. On

J6926 in the Middle East. The long stack-like carburettor intake pipe is visible between the starboard undercarriage legs. (*Courtesy C. H. Barnes*)

H8544, a Jaguar-powered Mars VI Nighthawk.

7 February, 1923, J6925 was transferred to the Aeroplane Experimental Establishment where it underwent full type trials under the name Experimental Metal Nighthawk. Following 2 hr 45 min flying, J6925 was dismantled and packed for delivery to Iraq for Service trials in high temperature conditions. During the year three, and possibly a fourth, Mars VI went to the Middle East for these trials. The Jaguar-powered H8544 flew with No. 1 Squadron operating Snipes, J6925 went to No. 8 Squadron and a third aircraft, believed to be the Jupiter Mars VI J6926, was flown at the Hinaidi depot. A major problem of operating in this climate was oil cooling and, following a thorough reconditioning (indicated by another change of serial number to JR6925), this aircraft was equipped with a specially designed and most effective cooler made in the squadron workshops. To minimize ingestion of sand and dust, both the Jupiter Mars VIs acquired long carburettor air intake pipes. JR6925 was ultimately

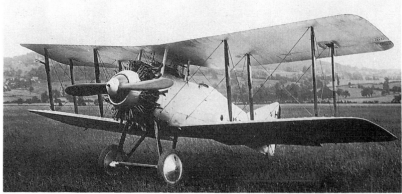
Another view of H8544, showing the propeller spinner with starter dog and the rudimentary cowling of the Jaguar engine.

written off following a crash landing caused by dry rot in the bottom longeron which led to a collapsed landing gear.

Back in the United Kingdom, at the 1923 Aerial Derby in which the Bamel, another Nighthawk derivative, was breaking all records, Flg Off John S. Chick, MC, gave an aerobatic demonstration in which the half loop and roll off the top was judged 'the most impressive' in the Mars VI's repertoire. Of the 230 Nighthawks originally ordered, the total production

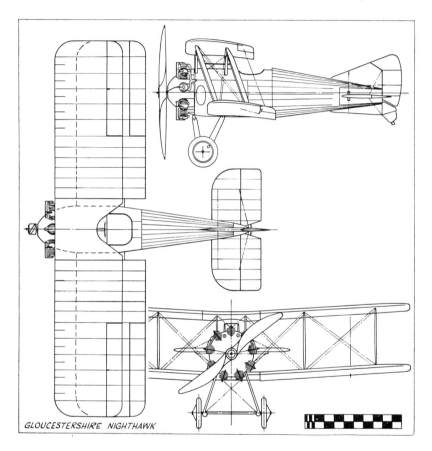

GLOUCESTERSHIRE NIGHTHAWK

of airframes cannot be accurately established as contemporary records differ, and only 128 can be confirmed as being built. It is almost certain that a batch of 17 consecutively serialled Nighthawks, of which J6925 was the first, were older airframes renumbered as they were converted. Their comparatively late delivery, between September 1922 and May 1923, adds weight to this view. Gloucestershire Aircraft Company's list of contracts executed shows that 16 complete aircraft, worth £27,410, were rebuilt as Mars VIs at Sunningend, and that a further 18 Nighthawks built there were converted at a cost of £19,174, either to Mars VI or Mars X Nightjar standards, during the twelve months ending 5 May, 1923. In the following year one more Nightjar and £4,310 worth of Nightjar spares were produced. In addition Gloucestershire Aircraft manufactured quantities of Nightjar spares, beginning in 1919, and also took into store a number of complete airframes built by Nieuport and General Aircraft Co and British Caudron Co. These were later purchased from the Air Board as part of the settlement of contracts in 1919–20.

One of the Mars VI flown by the Greek Army Air Force. (*Courtesy F. G. Swanborough*)

Greek Mars VI Nighthawk

Although the Mars VI Nighthawk was not adopted for Squadron service by the RAF, in 1922 the Greek Government bought 25 Jaguar Mars VIs. These were all Nighthawk conversions and were all delivered within three months of the receipt of the order, reaching Salonika early in 1923 where they were incorporated in the inventory of the Elliniki Stratrotiki Aeroporia (Greek Army Air Force). A new unit, E Mira Dioxeos (E Fighter Squadron), was formed and took on charge 10 Nighthawks and one Breguet 14, but it was short lived, and when the Greco-Turkish Peace Treaty was signed on 24 July, 1923, this squadron was disbanded. The Nighthawks subsequently were transferred to A Mira Aeroplanon (A Aircraft Squadron), which was a mixed unit flying several different types of aircraft and which was eventually expanded to become A Syndagma Aeroplanon (A Aircraft Regiment). The Nighthawks remained in first line Service as fighters until replaced by Polish PZL P.24s in 1938 when they were relegated to training duties.

84

Description: Single-seat fighter biplane. Wood construction with fabric covering.

Accommodation: Pilot in open cockpit.

Powerplant: One 325 hp Armstrong Siddeley Jaguar II fourteen-cylinder air-cooled radial, driving a two-blade fixed-pitch wooden propeller. Later one 325 hp Bristol Jupiter III nine-cylinder air-cooled radial or one 398 hp Bristol Jupiter IV nine-cylinder air-cooled radial, driving a two-blade fixed-pitch wooden propeller.

Armament: Two fixed synchronized Vickers ·303 in machine-guns mounted in the fuselage top decking with 1,000 rounds of ammunition.

Dimensions: Span 28 ft 0 in (8·53 m); length 18 ft 0 in (5·48 m); height 9 ft 0 in (2·74 m); wing area 270 sq ft (25·08 sq m).

Weights:	(Jaguar engine)	(Jupiter IV engine)
Empty	1,816 lb (823 kg)	1,818 lb (824 kg)
Loaded	2,217 lb (1,005 kg)	2,270 lb (1,029 kg)
Performance:		
Maximum speed	150 mph (241 km/h) at sea level 142 mph at 10,000 ft (228 km/h at 3,048 m)	150 mph (241 km/h) at sea level 142 mph at 10,000 ft (228 km/h at 3,048 m)
Stalling speed:	52 mph (83 km/h)	52 mph (83 km/h)
Climb to	20,000 ft (6,096 m)	20,000 ft (6,096 m)
in	24 min	16·5 min
Service ceiling	23,000 ft (7,010 m)	26,000 ft (7,924 m)

Production: 54 Nieuport Nighthawk airframes converted to Mars VI by Gloucestershire Aircraft Co Ltd, Cheltenham, during 1922–23.

Units allocated: Nos. 1 and 8 Squadrons RAF.

Mars X Nightjar

The last of many derivatives of the Nieuport Nighthawk design was the Mars X Nightjar. Developed as a single-seat deck-landing fighter it was fitted with the 230 hp Bentley B.R.2 rotary engine. All the Nightjars were built up from conversions of the Nighthawks' components by Gloucestershire Aircraft Company and so, basically, were identical to the Nighthawk in construction, but embodied a number of modifications to enable them to be used on British aircraft carriers. These modifications included a special wide-track and long-stroke landing gear, the axle casing of which carried 'jaws' to engage the fore and aft deck arrester wires then in use on aircraft carriers. Armament was two Vickers ·303 in machine-guns mounted on the fuselage 'shoulders' outboard of the upper centre section support struts.

The first Nightjar, H8535, went to AEE Martlesham on 8 May, 1922, for trials but was badly damaged on its arrival and so never flew. Almost a year later, on 1 May, 1923, J6941 went to Martlesham and completed 1 hr 22 min flying there before being sent by rail to Leuchars on 7 June where it joined a training flight.

Although intended for naval use, 22 Nightjars were prepared for service with the Royal Air Force, and sufficient Nighthawk airframes and components were retained in Air Ministry stores at Sunningend to provide

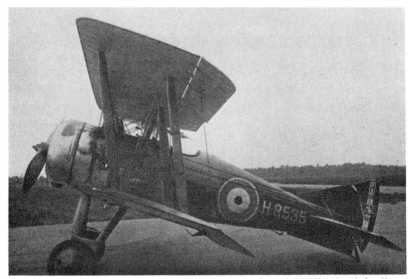

H8535 at Martlesham Heath in June 1922. It was the first of the Nighthawk family to have the B.R.2 rotary engine and was, in effect, the Nightjar prototype. (*Courtesy Royal Aeronautical Society*)

spares for 12 Nightjars over a period of two years' operation. During a brief Service career, which began in July 1922, Nightjars were first flown by No.203 Squadron at Leuchars replacing Sopwith Camels in the Operational Flight. Six Nightjars were taken to the Middle East in September 1922 on board HMS *Argus* and operated during the Chanak crisis period in that theatre. Deck-landing training was the responsibility of Training Flights at Leuchars, but during the eleven months ending in March 1924, when re-equipping with Flycatchers began, there were a number of fatal

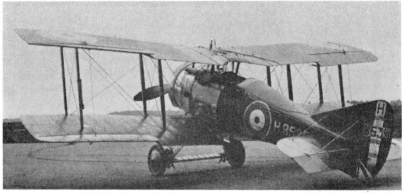

Another view of H8535. Note the thermometer, registering outside air temperature, on the rear port outer interplane strut, and the arrester jaws on the landing gear. (*Courtesy C. H. Barnes*)

H8539, a Mars X Nightjar, at RAE Farnborough in 1922. Note the arrester jaws on the wide-track axle. (*Courtesy C. H. Barnes*)

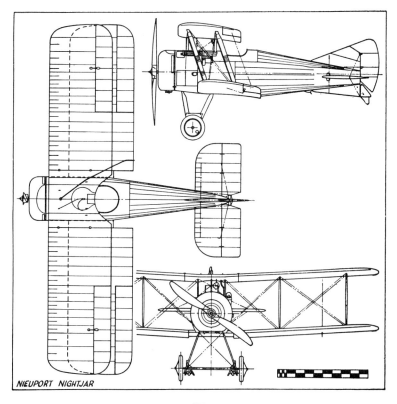

NIEUPORT NIGHTJAR

87

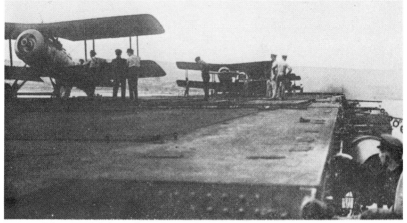

Mars X Nightjars of No.203 Sqdn on HMS *Argus* in September 1922.
(*Courtesy C. H. Barnes*)

accidents in Nightjars mainly through stalling and spinning during the final turn onto the approach to the aerodrome. During this period No. 401 Flight had seven of the Nightjars plus one Nighthawk.

TECHNICAL DATA

Description: Single-seat naval fighter biplane. Wood construction with fabric covering.
Accommodation: Pilot in open cockpit.
Powerplant: One 230 hp Bentley B.R.2 nine-cylinder rotary, driving a two-blade fixed-pitch wooden propeller.
Fuel 34 gal (154 litres) main, 6 gal (27 litres) auxiliary; oil 8 gal (36 litres).
Armament: Two fixed synchronized Vickers ·303 in machine-guns with 1,000 rounds of ammunition.
Dimensions: Span 28 ft 0 in (8·53 m); length 18 ft 4 in (5·58 m); height 9 ft 0 in (2·74m); wing area 270 sq ft (25·08 m).
Weights:

Empty	1,765 lb (800 kg)
Loaded	2,165 lb (981 kg)

Performance:

Maximum speed	120 mph (193 km/h) at sea level
	110 mph (177 km/h) at 10,000 ft (3,048 m)
Climb to	15,000 ft (4,572 m)
in	23 min
Service ceiling	19,000 ft (5,791 m)

Production: A total of 22 Nieuport Nighthawk airframes were converted to Mars X Nightjar by Gloucestershire Aircraft Co Ltd, Cheltenham, during 1922–23.
Units allocated: No. 203 Squadron, No. 401 Flight and a Training Flight RAF.

Grouse

Although the Grouse achieved its place in the public and official eye as a two-seat trainer, it was originally conceived by Folland and built, in 1923, as a private venture research aircraft for use in the investigation of the inflight characteristics of a special combination of upper and lower wing sections, developed by Folland, to combine the merits of biplane and monoplane configurations.

Known as the Gloster H.L.B. section, this single-bay wing combination was fitted to a modified two-seat Sparrowhawk, G-EAYN, which was powered with a 230 hp B.R.2 rotary engine, and comprised a high-lift top wing and a medium-lift bottom wing which gave good lift at take-off speeds. At high speed, however, the lower wing, which was set at a smaller angle of incidence than the top wing, contributed little lift and, because it was of a fairly thin section, created little drag; thus something near to a monoplane efficiency was achieved without recourse to an increased wing span. The centre of pressure travel was also reduced, and with the short fuselage the Grouse was a compact, highly manoeuvrable aircraft.

G-EAYN, the Grouse I, was a modified Sparrowhawk II with a B.R.2 rotary engine and the Gloster H.L.B. wing combination. The front cockpit was faired over during initial flight trials. (*Courtesy C. H. Barnes*)

The two-seat Grouse II powered by a Lynx engine. (*Courtesy C. H. Barnes*)

At that time little was known about cantilever monoplanes, and this wing combination gave almost certainly the best lift/drag ratio ever experienced with biplane fighters. Some indication of the overall efficiency of this arrangement can be obtained from a comparison of the Grouse I, having the Gloster H.L.B.1 section in the top wing and the H.L.B.2 in the bottom wing, and the Mars II with the standard RAF 15 section biplane wings. The wing area of the Grouse I was 65 sq ft less than that of the Mars II, the structure weight at 1,375 lb was 4 per cent down due to the use of thicker wings, and, although the wing loading was higher, the Grouse had a stalling speed of 47 mph compared with the 51 mph of the Mars II.

Despite the almost inevitable lack of initial interest, the Air Ministry ultimately decided to investigate the qualities of Folland's novel wing combination and gave instructions that a special display of Gloucestershire Aircraft's demonstrator Grouse, G-EAYN, was to be arranged at

The Grouse II with constant-chord Grebe-type ailerons and an oleo landing gear.

90

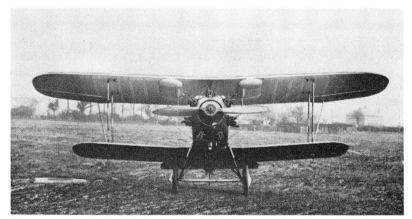

The very neat engine installation and the fuel tanks mounted partially within the upper mainplane are apparent in this view of the Grouse II. (*Courtesy F. G. Swanborough*)

Hendon. This proved the company's claims so convincingly that shortly afterwards the Ministry placed an order for three aircraft to be powered by the 350 hp Armstrong Siddeley Jaguar III radial engine. In this form the aircraft were named Grebe I to distinguish them from the prototype.

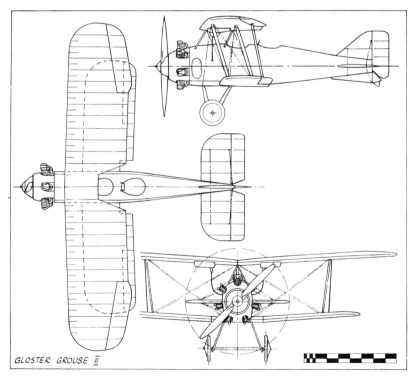

GLOSTER GROUSE II

In 1924 some redesign of G-EAYN was put in hand, and it later emerged as a two-seat trainer powered with a 185 hp Armstrong Siddeley Lynx radial engine. Known as the Grouse II, it was intended as a replacement for the Avro 504, the standard RAF trainer. It was issued with a certificate of airworthiness on 21 April, 1925, and incorporated many of the design features of the Grouse I and the Grebe including, of course, the H.L.B. wing arrangement. It proved to be unusually stable and easy to fly, yet was fully aerobatic. The crisp aileron control was contributed to by the control system; it comprised push rods and bell cranks from the pilot's column out to the lower ailerons, which had differential movement, and this was transmitted to the upper ailerons by external push rods. G-EAYN was later fitted with larger upper ailerons and an oleo landing gear.

The Grouse II in Swedish Army Air Service markings in which the three crowns and the serial number were black. (*Courtesy N. Kindberg*)

Structurally and aerodynamically the Grouse II and the Grebe were very similar and many components were interchangeable; moreover the Lynx and Jaguar engines used the same cylinders, pistons and other components. Unfortunately for Gloucestershire Aircraft, however, the Grouse was not adopted for the RAF, despite its high performance and accommodating similarity to the Grebe; so once again the company looked overseas for a market for its aircraft and found much interest in Sweden. In consequence G-EAYN flew to Sweden where it gave a number of demonstrations at Malmslätt for the Swedish Army Air Service which was quick to realize its value and not only bought the demonstrator, on 9 December, 1925, but gave serious consideration to placing orders for a further eight Grouse IIs. However, this order did not materialize, but the Grouse undoubtedly contributed to the choice and licensed production by Sweden of British air-cooled radial engines in later years.

Description: Single-seat research biplane (I), two-seat trainer (II). Wood construction with fabric covering.
Accommodation: Crew of one, or two, in open cockpits.
Powerplant: One 230 hp Bentley B.R.2 nine-cylinder air-cooled rotary, driving a two-blade fixed-pitch wooden propeller (Grouse I). One 185 hp Armstrong Siddeley Lynx II seven-cylinder air-cooled radial, driving a two-blade fixed-pitch wooden propeller (Grouse II).
Fuel 40 gal (181 litres); oil 3½ gal (16 litres).

	Grouse I	Grouse II
Dimensions:		
Span	27 ft 0 in	27 ft 10 in
	(8·22 m)	(8·47 m)
Length	19 ft 0 in	20 ft 4 in
	(5·79m)	(6·19 m)
Height	10 ft 1 in	9 ft 5 in
	(3·06 m)	(2·86 m)
Wing area	205 sq ft	205 sq ft
	(19·04 sq m)	(19·04 sq m)
Weights:		
Empty	1,375 lb	1,365 lb
	(623 kg)	(619 kg)
Loaded	2,120 lb	2,118 lb
	(961 kg)	(960 kg)
Performance:		
Maximum speed	128 mph (205 km/h)	120 mph (193 km/h)
	at sea level	at sea level
Landing speed	47 mph (75 km/h)	52 mph (83 km/h)
Climb to	10,000 ft (3,048 m)	10,000 ft (3,048 m)
in	11 min	17 min
Service ceiling	19,000 ft (5,790 m)	18,000 ft (5,486 m)
Duration	3·8 hr	3·75 hr
at	10,000 ft (3,048 m)	10,000 ft (3, 048 m)

Production: One Grouse built by Gloucestershire Aircraft Co Ltd, Cheltenham, during 1923.

Gannet

Interest in the light aeroplane may be said to have originated largely in Germany where, hedged around by the restrictions of the Versailles Treaty which prohibited the development of higher powered aircraft, attention turned to this class of aeroplane and to gliders, with some spectacular results. These stimulated a latent interest in Great Britain, and in October 1923 the first Light Aeroplane Trials were organized by the *Daily Mail* at Lympne. It was a matter of lively speculation whether there was any practical value in light aircraft, due mainly to the production costs and the unreliability of the small engines then available, and the trials were intended to promote private ownership by the creation of new, low-cost light aircraft which were reliable and could be overhauled and housed as easily as the family motorcar.

Among the twelve or more designs from British constructors who took up the challenge was the Gannet, which emerged from the Gloucestershire Aircraft factory and which was quite different from anything designed previously by Folland. The diminutive Gannet was remarkably compact and, as one of the tiniest aeroplanes built in Britain, it attracted a good deal of attention at Lympne.

93

The diminutive Gannet as it first appeared with the 750 cc two-cylinder Carden two-stroke engine. (*Courtesy F. G. Swanborough*)

Weighing only 283 lb empty, the Gannet was of all-wood construction, with only a minimum of metal fittings being used. The fuselage, which was built up from four ash longerons, had a small fixed lower centre section, flat plywood sides, a deep top fairing and a shallower bottom fairing of spruce stringers on light plywood formers, all of which was fabric-covered. The thick wings had **I**-section spruce spars and ribs which were built up from cut-out three-ply webs with spruce flanges and struts and internally braced with round-section wires. Four streamlined tubular-steel struts supported the top wing centre section—which housed the 2 gal fuel tank—and similar tubing was used to form the interplane struts. Streamlined flying wires braced the folding wing structure which was arranged to fold at the top and bottom rear spar with quick release pins in the four front spar attachment points. The trailing edges of the top and bottom centre section were hinged to fold clear of the wings in their folded position; the top centre section trailing edge could also be folded up to allow the pilot to enter and leave the cockpit. Spruce landing gear struts and a streamlined axle with rubber shock absorbers were also used. Large semi-span ailerons

With wings folded the Gannet could be handled with ease by one man.
(*Flight International*)

94

G-EBHU at Sunningend in 1924 after being re-engined with a 690 cc inverted-vee twin-cylinder Blackburne Tomtit and fitted with larger wheels.

were fitted on all four wings and the tail unit had an unbalanced rudder and elevators, all fabric-covered.

Particularly remarkable in concept was the 750 cc Carden vertical two-cylinder two-stroke engine which was specially developed for the Gannet.

Only one aircraft was built, G-EBHU, and first flown on 23 October, 1923, and although at the Lympne Trials it carried competition number 7, the Carden engine had not been sufficiently proven before fitting in the Gannet, and persistent overheating and oil failure prevented Glosters'

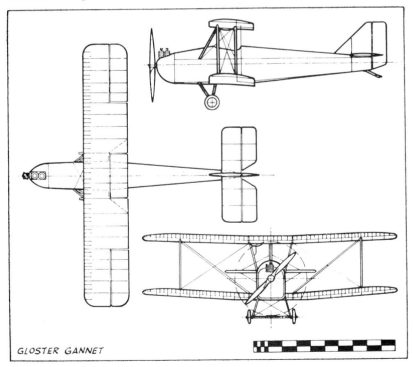

GLOSTER GANNET

95

The Tomtit-engined Gannet with wings folded. Note the folded portions of the upper and lower centre sections.

entry from taking any part in the flying programme. In 1924 the Carden engine was replaced by a 7 hp Blackburne Tomtit inverted-vee twin unit and, thus powered, it achieved a maximum speed of 72 mph.

G-EBHU was never entered for subsequent Light Aeroplane Trials and, although it was maintained in an airworthy condition, it was rarely flown and made its last public appearance, at Olympia in 1929.

TECHNICAL DATA

Description: Single-seat ultra-light biplane. Wood construction with plywood and fabric covering. Folding wings.

Accommodation: Pilot in open cockpit.

Powerplant: One 750 cc Carden vertical two-cylinder air-cooled two-stroke, driving a two-blade fixed-pitch wooden propeller. Later one 7 hp Blackburne Tomtit two-cylinder air-cooled inverted-vee, driving a two-blade fixed-pitch wooden propeller.

Fuel 2 gal (9 litres).

	(Carden engine)	(Blackburne engine)
Dimensions:		
Span	18 ft 0 in (5·4 m)	18 ft. 0 in (5·4 m)
Length	16 ft 6 in	16 ft 6 in
	(5·02 m)	(5·02 m)
Height	6 ft 0 in	6 ft 0 in
	(1·82 m)	(1·82 m)
Wing area	103 sq ft	103 sq ft
	(9·56 sq m)	(9·56 sq m)
Chord	3 ft 1½ in (0·91 m)	3 ft 1½ in (0·91 m)
Width folded	6 ft 8 in (2·02 m)	6 ft 8 in (2·02 m)
Weights:		
Empty	283 lb (128 kg)	330 lb (149 kg)
Loaded	410 lb (190 kg)	460 lb (208 kg)
Performance:		
Maximum speed	65 mph (104 km/h)	72 mph (115 km/h)
	at sea level	at sea level
Landing speed	35 mph (56 km/h)	36 mph (58 km/h)
Climb to	4,000 ft (1,219 m)	4,000 ft (1,219 m)
in	35 min	30 min
Range	140 miles (225 km)	140 miles (225 km)

Production: One Gannet built by Gloucestershire Aircraft Co Ltd, Cheltenham, during 1923.

Grebe

The Grebe was the first Gloster aeroplane to be produced in large quantities for the RAF and shared with the Armstrong Whitworth Siskin the distinction of being the first fighter to be chosen to re-equip post-war squadrons.

Folland's use of the thick high-lift Gloster H.L.B.1 and the thinner medium-lift H.L.B.2 sections in the upper and lower wings respectively of the Grouse trainer had produced excellent results, and this arrangement was therefore retained in the design of a single-seat version of the Grouse, to be powered by a 350 hp Armstrong Siddeley Jaguar III engine, on which work began early in 1923. When properly rigged, this wing combination was claimed to provide near-monoplane efficiency with the strength and advantages in manoeuvrability of a much reduced span.

During the spring of 1923, this single-seat Grouse was flown to Hendon for a demonstration before Air Ministry officials who were so impressed with its performance that Gloucestershire Aircraft Company were soon afterwards instructed to proceed with the construction of three prototypes to contract No. 402023/23 and ordered as Nighthawk (thick winged). The first of these, J6969, became the Grebe prototype: it took part in the RAF's Hendon Air Pageant in June 1923, and during the autumn it went to the A and AEE at Martlesham for trials. There its maximum speed of 152 mph at sea level, compared with the Snipe's 120 mph, and the all-round

The prototype Grebe with its racing number for the 1923 King's Cup race.
(*Imperial War Museum*)

An engine run for G-EBHA, the Gloster demonstrator Grebe at the 1923 RAF Air Pageant when it was demonstrated publicly for the first time. (*Flight International*)

high performance set a new standard for this type of aircraft. All the Martlesham test pilots and other Service pilots who flew it were agreed that the Grebe was far in advance of any fighter previously developed, and their report was largely responsible for the Air Ministry's decision to place production orders with Glosters. J6969 was subsequently returned to Hucclecote for minor modifications to the airframe.

The company's own demonstrator aircraft, G-EBHA, flown by Larry Carter, took part in the 1923 King's Cup race, starting from scratch to win a £100 prize for the fastest circuit, but a broken landing wire at Glasgow on the first day prevented it from completing the course. Later in the same year at the International Aeronautical Exhibition in Gothenburg, piloted by Flt Lieut Bird, it flew the 700 miles between Rotterdam and Gothenburg in record time, outpacing a number of other competitors and winning a special prize awarded by the Swedish Government.

The production aircraft, designated Grebe II, was re-engined with the more powerful 400 hp Armstrong Siddeley Jaguar IV, had an oleo-type landing gear, redesigned fuel tanks, a steerable tailskid and other modifications. The fuselage was built up from ash longerons with spruce struts, which were joined by flat metal fittings, light plywood formers and spruce

G-EBHA after modification to embody a Gamecock-type tail unit and landing gear, and powered by a Jupiter VI engine driving a Hele-Shaw Beacham variable-pitch propeller. (*Courtesy F. G. Swanborough*)

stringers to provide shape, and all fabric-covered. The wings had spruce spars and N-girder ribs braced by metal tie-rods. An unusual feature of the Grebe's elevators was that the spars were held in a cross-tube suspended on bracing wires rather than the more usual practice of being secured to the longerons. The ailerons were hinged on false spars carried at an angle to the main spars and were interconnected by a push rod which transmitted the movement of the lower aileron to the upper unit. There was no upper centre section, the port and starboard wings being joined on the aircraft's centreline and attached to the fuselage by inverted-V struts.

During the years 1923–27 a total of 130 Grebes, worth £313,000, was built including the prototype, costing £2,500, and a small number of two-seat trainers. With the two-seat Grebe, for the first time the Service had a dual-control trainer fast enough to give pilots under instruction some experience of the handling qualities of the single-seat versions which they would ultimately fly. In accordance with Air Ministry instructions Gloucestershire Aircraft divided the production of sub-assemblies between three other aircraft manufacturers. Hawker built the lower wings, A. V. Roe the upper wings and de Havilland produced ailerons and a quantity of other small components. In later years all four companies joined forces as members of Hawker Siddeley Aviation.

An early example of the standard Jaguar-powered Grebe II single-seat fighter produced for the RAF.

The Grebe first entered RAF service in October 1923 when it equipped one flight of No.111 Squadron at Northolt. In the following year No.25 Squadron at Hawkinge became the first to be completely re-equipped with Grebes to replace the long obsolete Snipes. Other squadrons with which the Grebe served were No.19 and No.29 at Duxford, No.32 at Kenley and No.56 at Biggin Hill, but undoubtedly it was with No.25 Squadron, led by Sqn Ldr A. H. Peck, that the Grebe reached the very peak of its Service career with a spectacular public display of synchronized aerobatics and air drill at the 1925 Hendon Air Pageant. The unusual feature of this display was that by the use of radio telephony, which although installed in Service aircraft was still very much in its infancy, HM King George V

99

Grebes of No. 25 Squadron, RAF, on the airfield at Hucclecote. The exhaust collector ring and pipe are evident in this view.

directed some of the Grebes' manoeuvres from the ground. In service the Grebe was fitted with Gamecock-type ailerons and soon established itself as a firm favourite of squadron pilots who, despite its shortcomings in other directions, appreciated its light sensitive controls. There was something particularly appealing about these rather tubby little fighters which seemed to typify the 'bulldog spirit' with which Britons of that era were alleged to be liberally endowed, but, whatever its aesthetic or spiritual qualities in things temporal, the Grebe had a number of shortcomings the most marked of which were the deficiencies of the 14-cylinder Jaguar engine and wing flutter. The Jaguar had a poor power/weight ratio and was ridden with oil system troubles which often led to fires in the air. The wing flutter led to the fitting of outboard V-interplane struts to stiffen the top wing overhang.

The Grebe was used in many advanced flight test programmes, a tribute to its ultimate reliability and handling characteristics. At Martlesham, for example, it was the first fighter to survive a punishing 240 mph terminal

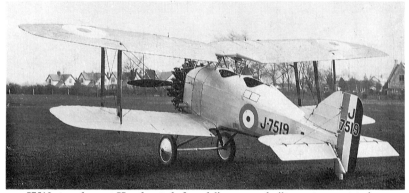

J7519, seen here at Hucclecote before delivery, was built as a two-seat trainer.

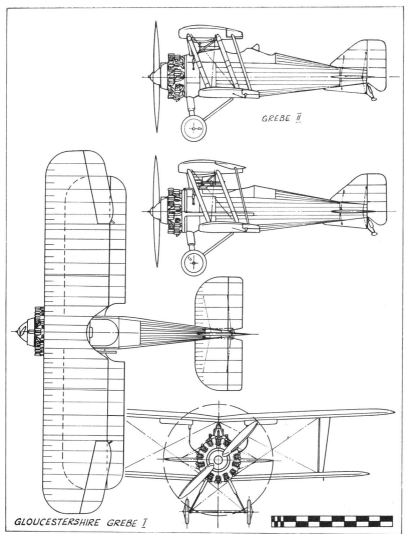

GREBE II

GLOUCESTERSHIRE GREBE I

velocity dive, the only result being a slight stretching of some of the bracing wires, and an interesting feature of this particular test was that, although test pilots were not usually provided with parachutes at that time, on this occasion the Grebe's Martlesham pilot had a US-designed parachute.

During the autumn of 1924 a standard fighter Grebe, J7519, was converted into a two-seat trainer and, following successful acceptance trials, a small batch of these trainers was produced for the RAF in the following year. One of these aircraft, J7520, carrying race number 39 on its rudder, was flown to victory in the 1929 King's Cup race by Flt Lieut R. D. R. Atcherley (who used the name 'R. Llewellyn' for the race) with Flt Lieut

J7520, a Grebe II, being taxied-in after winning the 1929 King's Cup race.
(Courtesy C. H. Barnes)

G. H. Stainforth as navigator. The Grebe was entered in the race by Sir Walter Preston, MP for Cheltenham, and a contemporary report reads, 'It was truly a very fine performance and great praise is due to the navigator for steering such a fine course.' The Grebe's average speed over the 1,160 miles for the two days was 150·3 mph, which was a record for the race. The report also records that although a taxi-ing accident at Blackpool at the end of the first day's flying almost cost Atcherley and Stainforth the race, the necessary spares for the damaged rudder and tailplane were rushed up from Cheltenham during the night and the repairs were completed just in time for the start of the second day's flying.

Grebes served, too, for the testing of new armament, and in April 1925 Gloucestershire Aircraft installed a Vickers ·5 in machine-gun in a Grebe and a similar calibre Colt/Browning gun in a second aircraft for comparative armament trials held at Martlesham during the following September. Although these trials proved the greater fire-power of the ·5 in gun the ·303 in gun was retained as standard.

A Grebe II, at Martlesham, with additional interplane struts and low-pressure tyres.

With the object of improving the pilot's view in Gloster biplanes generally, during 1927–28 three Grebes were modified and used in a series of flying tests. One aircraft had the standard upper wings but with a thinner centre section; a second had the inboard portions of the wings curved downward to fair direct into the fuselage in the style of Canada's McGregor fighter of 1938; the third aircraft dispensed with fabric on the upper centre section leaving an opening 2 ft wide in its place. When the tests were completed in July 1928, it was decided that the thin centre section was superior in terms of pilot's view, rate of climb and maximum speed and this became standard on other aircraft.

A rare photograph showing J7585 in the air. (*Courtesy B. Robertson*)

Two Grebes, J7400 and J7385, were specially modified in 1926 for air-launching experiments in connection with the Airship Development Programme and were carried under the British rigid airship R-33. They were slung from its keel by quick release attachments on the upper wings and were braced by struts from the airship's structure to stabilize them and prevent oscillation. The Jaguar engines were started by means of a Bristol gas starter carried inside the R-33 and connected to the engines by flexible piping. On 21 October, 1926, after an ascent from Pulham in Norfolk, one Grebe, piloted by Flg Off R. L. Ragg, was released at about 2,500 ft and, after diving for about 100 ft, it levelled out and flew for several minutes before landing back at Pulham. The second aircraft, flown by Flg Off C. Mackenzie-Richards, was also successfully released from a slightly higher altitude after some difficulty in starting the engine and made a safe landing at Cardington. Both these pilots came from the Royal Aircraft Establishment at Farnborough.

One of a number of non-standard installations was the Bristol Jupiter VI radial engine fitted in G-EBHA which was used for test flying the Gloster Hele-Shaw Beacham variable-pitch propellers. This demonstrator Grebe had earlier acquired a Gamecock-type tail unit and landing gear and, with

Grebes J7400 and J7385 attached beneath the airship R-33 in 1926.
(*Flight International.*)

its revolutionary propeller, its rate of climb was increased by 200 ft/min. The company announced that its Grebe could 'climb, fly level, loop repeatedly and dive for several thousands of feet without any noticeable variation in engine rpm.' The pilot could also disregard the throttle, leaving both hands free to operate the guns and control the aircraft, knowing that the engine speed would not exceed the desired figure. With a supercharged Jaguar IV engine, a Grebe achieved 165 mph in level flight at 10,000 ft, climbed to 20,000 ft in 16 min and had an absolute ceiling of 27,000 ft.

Grebes remained in frontline RAF service with Nos.19 and 25 Squadrons until the middle of 1928 when they were succeeded by Armstrong Whitworth Siskins. However, at the 1931 Hendon display three Grebes from Martlesham gave their final demonstration of formation aerobatics trailing coloured smoke.

NZ-501 before delivery to the New Zealand Permanent Air Force in 1928.

104

NZ-501 at Wigram Air Base in New Zealand. (*Courtesy D. P. Woodhall*)

New Zealand Grebe

In 1926 Sir Henry Wigram of Christchurch, New Zealand, who had been a great benefactor to aviation in the years immediately following the War, gave the New Zealand Government £2,500 to buy an aeroplane. It was at once proposed that a single-seat fighter should be purchased and that an order should be placed through the British Air Ministry.

Before the end of the year the order was initiated and was received by Gloster Aircraft Company in February 1927. A further twelve months were to pass, however, before the first Grebe arrived in New Zealand. Serialled NZ-501, this aircraft was originally J7381, one of the second production batch of Grebes. Its first test flight in New Zealand was on 2 March, 1928, when Capt J. L. Findlay, NZPAF, flew it at Wigram Air Base watched by Sir Henry Wigram himself. For this and subsequent early flights, the armament and spinner were not fitted; the guns were never, in fact, installed in NZ-501, but G.A.C. supplied a spinner which was reputed to have increased the top speed by 5 mph.

About nine months after NZ-501 was ordered, the New Zealand Government bought two more Grebes, NZ-502 another single-seater and NZ-503 a two-seater. Strangely, throughout their Service lives while on the strength of the New Zealand Permanent Air Force, the three Grebes were always referred to in official statements and reports as 'single-seat fighters'.

The second and third aircraft arrived at Wigram on 23 September, 1928, where they were assembled and test flown and used regularly, despite a number of minor accidents, for training NZPAF pilots. NZ-503, the two-seater, was finally written off in a crash at Hornby on 8 August, 1932, after an elevator control rod end had broken during aerobatics. The pilot, Sqn

One of the NZPAF Grebes, NZ-502, complete with propeller spinner but minus armament, in the air over Wigram Air Base. (*Courtesy D. P. Woodhall*)

Ldr Findlay, and his passenger, Aircraftman J. Simpson, were both seriously but not fatally injured. Following the reorganization of the NZPAF and a change of name to Royal New Zealand Air Force, NZ-501 and NZ-502 were renumbered A-5 and A-6 respectively indicating that they were part of A Flight at Wigram. These markings were applied to the fuselage and the serial number was moved to the fin.

The Grebe's last big moment was a co-ordinated simulated attack on a Vildebeeste photographic aircraft during the RNZAF's first ever display at Rongotai, on 4 June, 1938. By the end of November both A-5 and A-6 had been finally withdrawn from service for use as ground instructional airframes, A-6 going to the Hobsonville engineering school.

TECHNICAL DATA

Description: Single-seat day fighter biplane. Wood construction with fabric covering.

Accommodation: Pilot in open cockpit.

Powerplant: One 350 hp Armstrong Siddeley Jaguar III fourteen-cylinder air-cooled radial, driving a two-blade fixed-pitch wooden propeller (Grebe Mk.I).

One 400 hp Armstrong Siddeley Jaguar IV fourteen-cylinder air-cooled radial, driving a 9 ft 6 in (2·89 m) Watts two-blade fixed-pitch wooden propeller (Grebe Mk.II).

One 455 hp Bristol Jupiter VI nine-cylinder air-cooled radial, driving a 9 ft 10 in (2·99 m) diameter Gloster Hele-Shaw Beacham two-blade variable-pitch metal propeller (G-EBHA).

One 460 hp Armstrong Siddeley Jaguar IV fourteen-cylinder air-cooled supercharged radial, driving a 9 ft 10 in (2·99 m) diameter Watts two-blade fixed-pitch wooden propeller.

Fuel 52 gal (236 litres) in two gravity tanks under the upper wings.

Armament: Two fixed synchronized Vickers ·303 in machine-guns carried in the top of the front fuselage decking, with 1,200 rounds of ammunition. Military load 290 lb (131 kg).

Dimensions:

	Mk.I	Mk.II
Span	29 ft 4 in	29 ft 4 in
	(8·93 m)	(8·93 m)
Length	20 ft 3 in	20 ft 3 in
	(6·16 m)	(6·16 m)
Height	9 ft 3 in	9 ft 3 in
	(2·81 m)	(2·81 m)
Wing area	254 sq ft	254 sq ft
	(23·59 sq m)	(23·59 sq m)

106

Weights: *

Empty	1,720 lb	1,695 lb
	(780·1 kg)	(768·7 kg)
Loaded	2,622 lb	2,538 lb
	(1,189·2 kg)	(1,151·2 kg)

* The Grebe two-seater weighed 1,165 lb (528·4 kg)empty and 2,586 lb (1,173 kg) loaded.

Performance:

Maximum speed	151 mph at 5,000 ft	162 mph at sea level
	(243 km/h at 1,524 m)	(260·6 km/h)
Stalling speed	52 mph	53 mph
	(83·6 km/h)	(85·3 km/h)
Climb to	5,000 ft (1,524 m)	20,000 ft (6,096 m)
in	12·5 min	24 min
Service ceiling	23,000 ft (7,010 m)	23,500 ft (7,162 m)
Duration	2·75 hr	3 hr
at	15,000 ft (4,572 m)	20,000 ft (6,096 m)

Production: A total of 133 Grebes produced by Gloucestershire Aircraft Co Ltd, Cheltenham, as follows:
4 prototypes (1923)
129 Grebe Mk.II production aircraft (1923–27)

Units allocated: Nos. 19, 25, 29. 32, 56 and 111 Squadrons RAF; New Zealand Permanent Air Force.

Gloster II

Although the Aerial Derbies were discontinued after the 1923 race, Gloucestershire Aircraft Company decided to pursue its earlier conceived policy of building high-speed racing aircraft, for it saw in this the best way of enhancing its reputation and keeping the company's name regularly in front of the Air Ministry. The result of this decision was that attention centred on racing seaplanes for the Schneider Trophy contests and the first of these was the Gloster II. Very similar in appearance and construction to its immediate predecessor, the Gloster I, it incorporated every design refinement to improve its speed and aerodynamic efficiency. The 585 hp Napier Lion VA twelve-cylinder broad-arrow engine was the most powerful of its type and drove a Fairey Reed fixed-pitch two-blade metal propeller; the three cylinder blocks were carefully faired-in, in the best Folland style, all external pipework was re-routed and the short centre section struts were enclosed by a fairing which obscured most of the pilot's view directly forward. This lack of forward vision was common to almost all of the Schneider Trophy racers, monoplanes and biplanes alike. Two Lamblin strut radiators were used to reduce the frontal area and were mounted on the forward float struts, and beautifully shaped floats, with small frontal area, were fitted.

Two examples of the Gloster II, costing about £3,000 each, were built to an Air Ministry order during 1924 for the Schneider contest in October of that year. The prototype, J7504, civil registration G-EBJZ went to Felixstowe on 12 September and prepared for test flying by Capt Hubert

J7504, the first of the ill-fated Gloster II racers, on floats at Felixstowe.

Broad. Unfortunately for Glosters, before the pre-race trials could be completed this aircraft sank after one of the float's struts had collapsed while alighting on rough water, and was a complete loss. This accident could have had a serious effect on the whole course of the

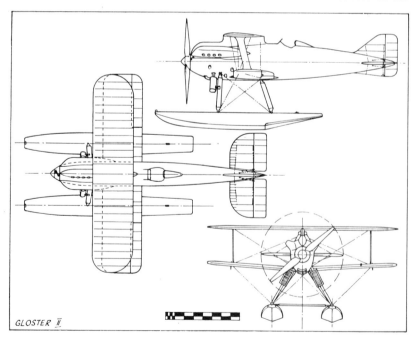

GLOSTER II

108

An unusual view of J7505, the second Gloster II, with wheeled landing gear before its crash landing at Cranwell in June 1925. (*Courtesy C. H. Barnes*)

Schneider Trophy series, because the Italian entries had been withdrawn that year due to recurrent engine trouble, leaving the United States alone in the contest needing only a fly-over to win. However, thanks to a most sporting gesture by the American Aero Club, the race was postponed until the following year.

The floats on the second aircraft, J7505, were removed, a wheeled landing gear was fitted, and the aircraft was prepared for flight-testing a range of metal propellers, radiators and other equipment to be used in a new seaplane racer. Unfortunately this Gloster II was also wrecked, in June 1925, in a landing accident while being flown from Cranwell, one of the few aerodromes in England sufficiently large and with a good enough surface to enable such a fast aircraft to be tested in safety.

During one high-speed run at about 240 mph and at a height of only 40 ft, the aircraft developed elevator flutter and, although Larry Carter

Streamlining of a high order is apparent in this view of J7505.
(*Courtesy C. H. Barnes*)

109

switched off the engine, he touched down at about 200 mph and the tyres and wheels were wrenched off, the landing gear struts collapsed, and it, too, was a complete write-off. Fortunately it did not turn over or catch fire, but Carter sustained a fractured skull, spent a year in hospital but never flew again. He died from meningitis in a Cheltenham nursing home on 27 September, 1926.

TECHNICAL DATA

Description: Single-seat racing biplane with float or wheeled landing gear. Wood construction with fabric covering.
Accommodation: Pilot in open cockpit.
Powerplant: One 585 hp Napier Lion VA twelve-cylinder liquid-cooled broad-arrow, driving a Fairey Reed two-blade fixed-pitch metal propeller.
Dimensions: Span 20 ft 0 in (6 m); length 26 ft 10 in (8·1 m); height 11 ft 0 in (3·3 m); wing area 165 sq ft (15·3 sq m).

	Seaplane	Landplane
Weights:		
Empty	2,500 lb (1,134 kg)	1,920 lb (870 kg)
Loaded	3,100 lb (1,406 kg)	2,400 lb (1,088 kg)
Performance:		
Maximum speed	225 mph (362 km/h) at sea level	245 mph (394·2 km/h) at sea level

Production: Two Gloster IIs built by Gloucestershire Aircraft Co Ltd, Cheltenham, during 1924.

Gamecock

During the five-year period from October 1923, while Grebes were in operational service with RAF squadrons, they were justifiably popular with their pilots who revelled in the unaccustomed combination of great manoeuvrability and a comparatively high top speed. But the Grebe's several shortcomings could not be overlooked, particularly the deficiencies of its power unit, the fourteen-cylinder Armstrong Siddeley Jaguar IV, which was thoroughly unpopular among ground crews who had great difficulty in getting their charges into the air due to engine unserviceability. Folland was only too well aware of the situation and must have been comparing the concurrent success of the Gloster I racing aircraft, powered by a Napier Lion liquid-cooled engine, with the poor performance of the Jaguar.

Fortunately for Glosters, salvation lay only a few miles away at Filton where the Bristol engine company was getting most encouraging results from its development programme on the Jupiter IV which was showing signs of delivering some 400 hp. This was similar to the Jaguar IV, but the Jupiter was a much lighter and far less complex engine and was very much more reliable on test. During the summer of 1924, this Jupiter was undergoing type tests and in July, when they were nearing completion, their results were so promising that the Air Ministry issued specification 37/23 covering development of the Grebe to be powered with the Jupiter IV, and design work began at once. Ordered the following month as the

J7497, the prototype Gamecock I with a Jupiter IV engine and retaining the Grebe-type tail unit.

Grebe II, the design and construction of the prototype, J7497, was completed in less than six months, during which time two more aircraft were ordered: J7756 with a Jupiter IV and J7757 with a Jupiter VI.

The fuselage was constructed almost entirely of wood with ash longerons, and spruce, ash or ply struts and supports with steel tie-rod internal bracings and light wood formers. Nine large bolts attached the engine to the mild-steel front bulkhead, and a second fireproof bulkhead was made of asbestos between aluminium sheet. Two more bulkheads carried the instrument panel, the pilot's seat and the gun mounting brackets while three more bulkheads were used in the rear fuselage. The wings had spruce spars (either laminated or in one piece), struts and ribs, and the ailerons

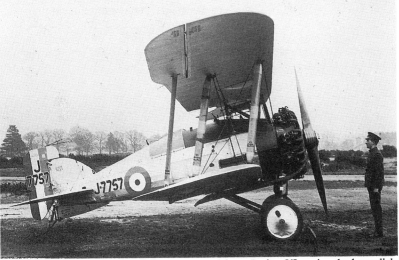

The third prototype Gamecock I was powered by a Jupiter VI engine, had parallel-chord ailerons and was fitted with wireless.

were built up in a similar manner. A wide-track landing gear was used, having rubber in compression shock absorbers with oil dashpots. Fuel was carried in gravity feed type tanks, fitted in the upper wings, with a manual control cock in the cockpit and smaller stop cocks on the feed pipes from the tanks. For the first time the armament, consisting of two Vickers Mk.I ·303 in machine-guns, was carried internally and mounted low on the fuselage side in troughs instead of in the earlier position, which was virtually on top of the front fuselage. Six hundred rounds of ammunition per gun were carried.

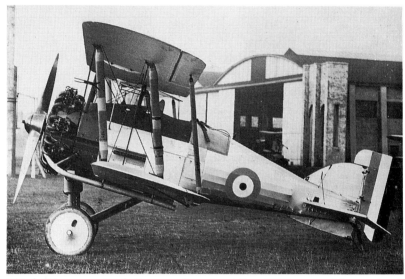

Fitted with narrow-chord ailerons and a centre section, J7910 was used for a series of anti-flutter flight tests at Hucclecote and RAE Farnborough.

The prototype, powered with the Jupiter IV, was delivered to Martlesham on 20 February, 1925. Initially the unbalanced Grebe-type rudder was fitted, but a few weeks after its arrival at Martlesham this was changed to the horn-balanced rudder and larger fin, which was later to typify the Gamecock, with the small ventral fin inherited from Folland's S.E.5. The Gamecock, like its predecessors the Grouse and Grebe, had the same combination of Gloster H.L.B. wing sections, which not only gave high-lift for take-off with minimum lift and drag at high speeds but also reduced the travel of the centre of pressure, thus improving the stability and enabling a short fuselage to be used. These gave the aircraft the same crisp control in pitch that the short-span wings and four large-area ailerons gave in the rolling plane. Yet another factor which contributed to the Gamecock's excellent handling characteristics was the proximity of the engine to the aircraft's centre of gravity. At Martlesham the Gamecock's initial trials were highly successful, and the experienced Service pilots who flew it were enthusiastic about this latest of Folland's fighters. Curiously, however, although the Gamecock was certainly heir to the Grebe's wing and tail flutter troubles and had spinning problems of its own, they appeared to pass unnoticed by these pilots who made no mention of them in reports.

Back at Hucclecote test flying continued, and by July more than 50 hr flying had been accomplished without changing a major component. Then, in September 1925, no doubt encouraged by the successful results of their evaluation, the Air Ministry placed an order with Gloucestershire Aircraft Company for 30 Gamecock I aircraft, worth £79,500, powered by the 425 hp Bristol Jupiter VI nine-cylinder air-cooled radial (as fitted in J7757, the third aircraft) to meet specification 18/25.

The first production aircraft flew in March 1926 and deliveries to No.23 Squadron, based at Henlow, began in May. This squadron flew its Gamecocks longer than any other, retaining these aircraft until after the others had been re-equipped, and it was not until July 1931 that it finally changed to Bristol Bulldogs. In July 1926, shortly after deliveries had begun, Glosters got a further Air Ministry order for 40 Gamecock Is and this was followed up in November by yet another order for 18 aircraft. The value of these two orders was £145,600.

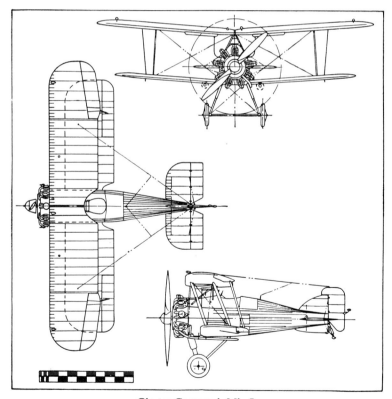

Gloster Gamecock Mk. I.

113

J7891 was the first production Gamecock I with a Jupiter VI engine.
(*Courtesy C. H. Barnes*)

Standard production Gamecock I with exhaust collector ring on the Jupiter VI.
(*Courtesy C. H. Barnes*)

The last of the initial production batch of Gamecock Is, J7920 served with No.43 -
Squadron, RAF, at Tangmere. (*Courtesy C. H. Barnes*)

A Gamecock I with the black and white markings of No. 43 Squadron, RAF.

Meanwhile other RAF squadrons equipped with Gamecocks were Nos.3 and 17 based at Upavon, who, as Night Interceptor Squadrons, received modified Gamecocks suitable for this rôle; No.32 who were joined by No.23 at Kenley; and No.43 at Henlow and Tangmere. Few people who attended RAF Displays at Hendon during 1926–31 will readily forget the splendid aerobatic performances by Gamecocks with their flamboyant squadron and aircraft markings which served to enhance the appeal of their demonstration. In 1931 two of No.23 Squadron's Gamecocks gave a notable display of integrated aerobatics flown by Flt Lieut M. M. Day and Pilot Officer D. R. S. Bader, and Gamecocks were always extremely popular items in air pageants and displays in many parts of Britain.

Although the Gamecock was a delightful aeroplane to fly, was a good gun platform and thus was generally popular among its pilots, the accident rate was high when compared with the number in service, and during their first 19 months in RAF squadrons 22 aircraft crashed, killing eight pilots. The causes varied from total structural failure in the air to spinning and landing accidents.

As mentioned earlier, the Gamecock had inherited the Grebe's flutter and spinning troubles, and one of the modifications embodied late in 1927 to cure the former trouble was additional centre section and outboard V-interplane struts. Glosters and the RAE at Farnborough had also put in hand an exhaustive programme of test flying to sort out these aerodynamic problems. Gamecock J7910 with narrow-chord ailerons was flown on many anti-flutter tests at Hucclecote and Farnborough. The company's pilot, Howard Saint, and a number of Service pilots, including Mutt Summers, made a valuable contribution to Gamecock development by recommending various modifications to improve the handling, and this programme culminated in Saint confidently flying a Gamecock to a speed of 275 mph in a dive and through 22 turns of a spin with complete and accurate recovery. Nevertheless intentional right-hand spins were

J8075, an experimental Gamecock I, was used for flight trials of the Hele-Shaw Beacham variable-pitch propeller which was fitted with a large louvred spinner to assist engine cooling. Note the additional V struts to brace the upper wing overhang, and test equipment on the starboard front strut. (*Courtesy F. G. Swanborough*)

considered dangerous due to almost immediate flattening, and they were banned in the squadrons because the combination of engine torque and lack of rudder control, due to blanketing by the fuselage, made recovery almost impossible.

If the Gamecock had inherited vices from its forbears, it was also heir to some of the earlier Gloster racers' qualities, and in 1927 demonstrated this most forcibly by taking the first three places in the race for the Sassoon

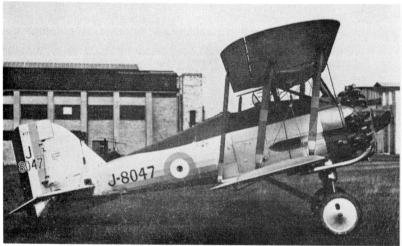

J8047, unofficially known as the Gamecock III, seen during August 1928 with a lengthened fuselage, enlarged fin and rudder and parallel-chord ailerons for an early phase of flight trials. (*Courtesy F. G. Swanborough*)

116

G-EBNT, the Gloster demonstrator Gamecock, with streamlined spinner and cowling assembly. (*Courtesy C. H. Barnes*)

Cup. This was offered annually to fighter squadrons by Sir Philip Sassoon, Under Secretary of State for Air, and entrants were handicapped according to type and carried full Service load less bomb racks and wireless equipment. Flg Off Montgomery in a Gamecock I, bearing No.32 Squadron's diagonal blue and white markings, won the 110 miles event with an average speed of 156 mph, closely followed into second place by Flt Lieut Collier, No.43 Squadron, and Flg Off Macdonald, No.23 Squadron, third.

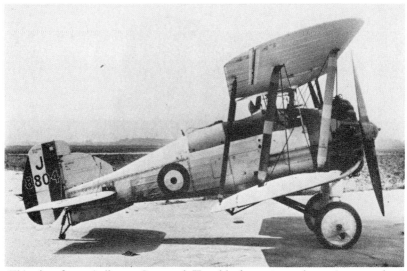

This aircraft was built as a Gamecock II and had a centre section and narrow-chord ailerons, shallower fuel tanks, a larger rudder and other structural modifications. (*Courtesy C. H. Barnes*)

Gamecock I J8047 had a particularly long and exacting life beginning in October 1926, when it was delivered to the RAF Central Flying School at Wittering equipped as a standard day fighter. After completing some 60 hr at CFS, it was transferred to the RAE Farnborough in April 1927 where it was used for spinning trials which resulted in the Gamecocks' wings being re-positioned three inches nearer the tail unit. In the autumn of 1927, J8047 was flown back to Hucclecote for extensive modification and re-building; it included increasing the fuselage length and undercarriage track, fitting a new and enlarged fin and rudder and narrow-chord ailerons. With these alterations, which took almost a year to complete, J8047 was known unofficially as the Gamecock III and was first flown in this form in August 1928. On 28 November it returned to Farnborough, but four months later it went back to Glosters to have a 450 hp Jupiter VII engine in place of its Jupiter VI. Then, like J8075 which was powered by a 450 hp Bristol Mercury IIA, it was fitted with a Hele-Shaw Beacham two-blade variable-pitch metal propeller for the 1929–30 flight trials of this forerunner of the Dowty Rotol propellers. An ex-No.23 Squadron Gamecock was also used for flight testing the variable-pitch propeller.

Gloucestershire Aircraft Company's own demonstrator, G-EBNT, for which a certificate of airworthiness was issued in March 1926, was considerably cleaned up and was, therefore, somewhat faster than standard Gamecocks. In 1928, as a private venture, the company was to have installed the Bristol Orion engine with an exhaust-driven turbo-charger in G-EBOE, a Gamecock I, but this project was abandoned because of the

118

Orion's unreliability and the aircraft's registration was cancelled in March 1928.

In 1932 more spinning trials were undertaken by J8047 fitted with an enlarged area tailplane and powered by a Jupiter VI; then on 10 April, 1934, having logged 202 flying hr, its airframe was sold to a scrap dealer in Hornchurch and purchased in May for £25 by J. W. Tomkins, a farmer of Apethorpe, Peterborough, who rebuilt it as G-ADIN for private flying. It was fitted with a 490 hp Jupiter VIIFP, believed to have been taken from a Bulldog IIA, and a certificate of airworthiness was issued on 24 September, 1935. G-ADIN never flew after its C of A expired 12 months later; but by then time was finally running out for the Gamecock, the last of the RAF's 'wooden walls' in service, and the all-metal Bulldog overtook it to win a production order. Although a company-sponsored design, the Gamecock II gained official approval in January 1928 when J8804 was bought by the Air Ministry. It embodied a number of modifications which resulted from the 1927 series of flight trials and differed from its predecessor principally in the wing design. From the structural point of view, they were little changed except that, instead of the upper mainplanes joining on the aircraft's centreline and being attached to a cabane, a centre section made of steel tube was introduced between them supported on struts from the fuselage. This gave the pilot a much improved field of view, increased the span of the upper mainplanes and, because of their outward displacement, caused the interplane struts to be angled outwards at their tops. Other changes were a larger rudder, narrow-chord ailerons with their linking rods moved outboard to a position midway along their span, aileron false spars replaced by full-span spars to give improved aileron support, wider and shallower petrol tanks which protruded only slightly below the underside of the upper mainplanes, and a redesigned windscreen to give less air disturbance over the tail unit. A second aircraft, J8075, from the second production batch of 40 Gamecock Is, was used for flight testing the Mercury IIA engine but was subsequently brought up to Gamecock II standard.

One of the two pattern aircraft, GA-38, built by Glosters for the Finnish Air Force.

E

Finnish Gamecock

At Martlesham the Gamecock II showed a marked superiority over the Mk.I particularly in handling, where few of its earlier vices remained, but it was not destined for RAF squadron service, and with the end of the Gamecock production Glosters' order book was suddenly and ominously empty. However, an air delegation from Finland had visited Britain during 1927 and had been much impressed with the Gamecock I. On 25 March the

The first pattern aircraft, GA-38, mounted on Finnish-made skis, at Lagus in March 1928. (*Courtesy K. W. Janarmo*)

Finnish Air Pageant was staged on the frozen sea around Helsinki and the final event of the flying programme was an aerobatic display by the Gamecock II flown by Howard Saint. His performance may be judged by a paragraph which appeared two days later in a Helsinki newspaper, the *Hufvudstadsbladet*. 'At the conclusion of the display Capt Saint from England performed English aerobatic flying. First he flew smoothly over the city, then climbing he suddenly seemed but a speck in the sky. Then he tumbled down to within a few metres of the ground. Sometimes his machine turned over, then looped, fell again, rose again and so on. At last he landed elegantly on the ice. His flying really exceeded one's imagination.' Finnish interest in the Gamecock was maintained through the year until in 1928 it won a Government contest and an order. Two pattern aircraft including the Gamecock GA-38 flown by Saint in the Air Pageant, were built at Sunningend, the second aircraft, GA-43, being delivered to Finland during early 1928. By the following year licensed production of the Game-

A Finnish Air Force Kukko mounted on skis. (*Courtesy C. H. Barnes*)

cock, renamed Kukko, had begun in the Finnish National Aircraft Factory at Helsinki and the first of four aircraft, built during 1929 with lengthened fuselage and modified landing gear similar to J8047, and serialled GA-44 to GA-47, was delivered on 5 December, 1929. A further batch of 11 Gamecocks was built during 1930, not without some problems particularly with the steel tube for the centre section which had been ordered from England. Because tube of the wrong specification had been ordered, many of the Gamecocks built in Finland had spruce plugs inserted in the tube for addi-

This Kukko has modified wing-bracing with spacer rods, and a cockpit head fairing. (*Courtesy K. W. Janarmo*)

121

This Finnish Air Force Kukko has enlarged fin and rudder and carries anti-personnel bombs under the lower wings. (*Courtesy William Green*)

tional strength, because the factory wouldn't wait for the correct material to arrive. Initially these Finnish built Gamecocks were powered either with the 420 hp Gnome-Rhône Jupiter IV9Ab or IV9Ak engine, but later aircraft had the more powerful 480 hp Jupiter IV9Ag.

In service with the Finnish Air Force, the Gamecocks equipped Fighter Squadron 24, based at Utti, from 1929 until 1935 when they were relegated to fighter training duties. In this rôle most of them served with the central flying school at Kauhava, but a small number were also attached to Squadrons 29 and 34. At least one Gamecock, GA-46, continued in service with the Finnish Air Force until September 1944 when it was scrapped, having flown 803 hr. GA-38, the first pattern aircraft, had logged 937 hr in the air before it was scrapped on 11 October, 1941.

Gamecock III

This was the unofficial designation of Gamecock J8047 when it was modified and registered G-ADIN.

TECHNICAL DATA

Description: Single-seat day and night interceptor biplane. Wood construction with fabric covering.
Accommodation: Pilot in open cockpit.
Powerplant: Initially one 398 hp Bristol Jupiter IV nine-cylinder air-cooled radial, driving an 8 ft 8 in (2·63 m) diameter Watts two-blade fixed-pitch wooden propeller (J7497 ana J7756).
One 425 hp Bristol Jupiter VII nine-cylinder air-cooled radial, driving a 9 ft 0 in (2·74 m) diameter Watts two-blade fixed-pitch wooden propeller (Gamecock Mk.I and II).
One 450 hp Bristol Mercury IIA nine-cylinder air-cooled radial, driving an 8 ft 10 in (2·68 m) diameter Hele-Shaw Beacham two-blade variable-pitch metal propeller (J8075).
One 450 hp Bristol Jupiter VII nine-cylinder air-cooled radial, driving a Hele-Shaw Beacham two-blade variable-pitch metal propeller (J8047).

One 490 hp Bristol Jupiter VIIFP nine-cylinder air-cooled radial (J8047/G-ADIN).
Fuel 50 gal (227 litres) in two gravity tanks in the upper wings; oil 5½ gal (25 litres).
Armament: Two fixed synchronized Vickers Mk.I ·303 in machine-guns mounted in troughs in the fuselage
sides with 1,200 rounds of ammunition giving 25 seconds duration of fire.

	Mk.I	Mk.II *
Dimensions:		
Span (upper)	29 ft 9½ in	30 ft 1 in
	(9·0 m)	(9·16 m)
(lower)	25 ft 11 in	26 ft 4½ in
	(7·89 m)	(8·02 m)
Length	19 ft 8 in	19 ft 10½ in
	(5·99 m)	(6·04 m)
Height	9 ft 8 in	9 ft 11 in
	(2·94 m)	(3·01 m)
Wing area	264 sq ft	268 sq ft
	(24·52 sq m)	(24·89 sq m)
Track	6 ft 0 in	6 ft 0 in
	(1·52 m)	(1·52 m)
Weights:		
Empty	1,930 lb	2,050 lb
	(875·4 kg)	(929·8 kg)
Loaded	2,742 lb	3,082 lb
	(1,243·7 kg)	(1,397·9 kg)
Performance:		
Maximum speed	145 mph at 10,000 ft	157 mph at 5,000 ft
	(233 km/h at 3,048 m)	(252 km/h at 1,524 m)
Landing speed	49 mph (78 km/h)	52 mph (83 km/h)
Climb to	10,000 ft (3,048 m)	15,000 ft (4,572 m)
in	7·6 min	13·3 min
Service ceiling	22,100 ft (6,735 m)	21,600 ft (6,582 m)
Duration	2·5 hr	2 hr
at	15,000 ft (4,572 m)	15,000 ft (4,572 m)

Production: A total of 96 Gamecocks produced by Gloucestershire/Gloster Aircraft Company Ltd,
Cheltenham and Hucclecote, Glos: as follows:
> 3 prototypes (1924–25)
> 90 Gamecock Mk.I (1925–27)
> 3 Gamecock Mk.II (1927)

A total of 15 Gamecocks/Kukkos built by the Finnish National Aircraft Factory, Helsinki, as follows:
> 15 Gamecock Mk.II/Kukko (1929–30)

Unit allocation: Nos. 3, 17, 23, 32 and 43 Squadrons RAF; Fighter Squadrons 24, 29 and 34 Finnish Air
Force.
> * A and AEE Report No.M/415/C.

N194, the first Gloster III seaplane racer, with the early type tail unit.

Gloster III

In terms of contest results, the Gloster III, of which two were built, was the most successful of all the company's racing seaplanes, because it was flown into second place in the 1925 Schneider Trophy contest at Baltimore.

The United States Navy's victory in the 1923 contest had acted as a great stimulus to both the British and Italian Air Ministries, and Gloucestershire Aircraft Company in particular had made tremendous efforts to develop the Gloster II design into a serious contender for the Baltimore race. So successful were these efforts that a £16,000 order for two aircraft was received in February 1925 and detailed design work began almost immediately. Like its predecessors, the Gloster III was a single-strut biplane with a Napier Lion VII twelve-cylinder engine developing 700 hp, which made it the smallest aircraft for its power ever built in Great Britain at that time. The fuselage was of wooden monocoque construction built up from a light ash framework with three-ply skinning. The 20 ft span wooden wings were fabric covered, but the patent Gloster method of attaching the fabric to the ribs was perfectly adequate even at very high speed. Duralumin floats built by Shorts and weighing an ounce or two over 368 lb were fitted on streamlined, wire-braced struts very carefully faired into the fuselage and float surfaces.

In order to keep the frontal area to an absolute minimum, Folland had designed ingenious wing surface radiators for the Gloster III but unfortunately these were not completed by the time the aircraft was ready to begin

Another view of the Gloster III, N194, showing the large wing radiators.

trials, and so Lamblin radiators were mounted on the leading edges of the lower wing.

Taxi-ing trials began at Felixstowe on 16 August, 1925, and were completed very satisfactorily, despite bad weather and very rough water, in 12 days. On 29 August Hubert Broad made the first flight and reported that all was well apart from some rather unsatisfactory directional stability. It was therefore agreed that dihedral should be introduced in the upper as well as in the lower wings, but as time was short the only major alteration which could be made was an increase in the chord of the dorsal and ventral fins. With these modifications the aircraft were designated Gloster IIIA, and Broad's machine, now serialled N194, made only four flights before being crated for despatch to Baltimore. Bert Hinkler flew the second aircraft, registered G-EBLJ on 3 June, 1925, before being serialled N195 for

The Gloster IIIA at Baltimore with increased chord on the dorsal and ventral fins.
(*US Air Force*)

125

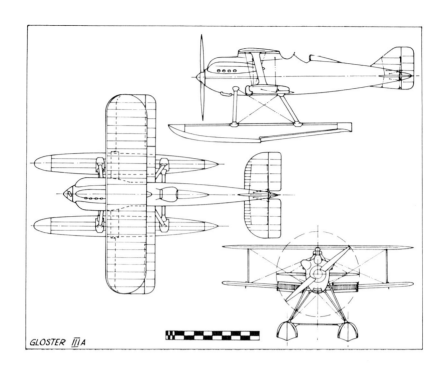

GLOSTER IIIA

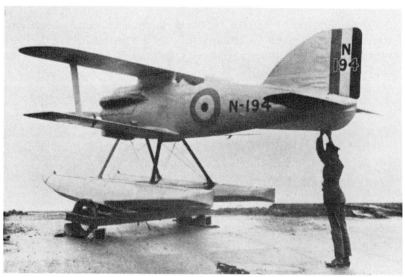

A modified fin was fitted to N194 after the 1925 Schneider Trophy contest.
(*Courtesy C. H. Barnes*)

N194 at Felixstowe after modification to the tail unit. (*Courtesy C. H. Barnes*)

the contest, but he got airborne in it only once from Felixstowe before leaving for the United States.

The Gloster team arrived at Chesapeake Bay in Baltimore on 6 October to find even worse weather conditions, no hangars available for their three aircraft (the Bamel had been taken over for use as a hack machine), or accommodation for the crew. Ultimately a canvas hangar was found for their use, but a hurricane almost wrecked it and the aircraft before navigability trials began on 23 October. To add to Great Britain's misfortunes, the Supermarine S.4 stalled while being flown by Capt H. C. Biard and crashed into the sea, so Hinkler's aircraft, N195, was prepared for the contest as a replacement. Again the weather took a hand, being so bad that Hinkler was unable to begin his navigability tests until the morning of 26 October, the day of the race; then, when he set out on the half-mile taxi-ing test, the waves were so strong that they broke two of the float struts and bracing wires. As a result the nose dropped and the propeller chopped into the floats, putting rapid repair beyond possibility. Thus, with all British hopes pinned on the Gloster IIIA, Hubert Broad, in N194 carrying a blue racing numeral 5 on its fuselage sides, did a magnificent job to take second place in the 217·5 mile race with an average speed of 199·16 mph, some 33 mph slower than Lieut J. H. Doolittle in the winning US Curtiss R3C-2 racer. Broad's fastest lap was in fact only 201·53 mph and he never really looked like winning. Had the surface radiators been fitted and the two aircraft completed earlier to give Broad more than the four hours flying experience he managed to get in before the contest, then the whole pattern of events at Felixstowe and Baltimore would have been

Gloster IIIB, N195, with wing surface radiators and expansion header tank on the upper centre section.

different, and Glosters' name could have been on the Schneider Trophy in 1925. The race was a close run thing nevertheless for the United States team, who flew three identical aircraft, for both Lieut Cuddihy and Lieut Ofstie suffered engine failure, leaving Doolittle alone to complete the course.

After the contest the two Gloster IIIs were returned to Cheltenham where further modifications were embodied in N195. They included the fitting of surface radiators on all four wings, an expansion header tank

Though a biplane, Folland's careful attention to streamlining is apparent in this view of N195. Note the very slim single interplane strut and float struts and the fairing over the Lion's cylinder blocks.

128

on the upper centre section, a revised and enlarged windscreen structure, a fully cantilevered tail unit with all external control levers removed and a curved leading edge to the fin, and the use of streamlined bracing wires for the wings and float struts in place of the round wires used in N194. With these modifications embodied, N195 was redesignated Gloster IIIB. N194 was delivered back to Felixstowe in June 1926, and N195 followed it there in November when both aircraft were used for development flying and as trainers for the pilots of the High Speed Flight preparing for the 1927 Schneider contest.

TECHNICAL DATA

Description: Single-seat racing float biplane. Wood construction with plywood and fabric covering.
Accommodation: Pilot in open cockpit.
Powerplant: One 700 hp Napier Lion VII twelve-cylinder liquid-cooled broad-arrow, driving a Fairey Reed two-blade fixed-pitch metal propeller.
    Fuel 54¾ gal (249 litres); oil 4¼ gal (19 litres).
Dimensions: Span 20 ft 0 in (6·09 m); length 26 ft 10 in (8·1 m); height 9 ft 8 in (2·94 m); wing area 152 sq ft (14·12 sq m).
Weights: (IIIA) Empty 2,028 lb (920 kg); loaded, 2,687 lb (1,218 kg).
    (IIIB) Empty 2,278 lb (1,033 kg); loaded 2,962 lb (1,343 kg).
Performance: (IIIA) Maximum speed 225 mph (362 km/h) at sea level.
    (IIIB) Maximum speed 252 mph (405 km/h) at sea level.
    Alighting speed 80 mph (128 km/h).
Production: A total of two Gloster IIIs built by Gloucestershire Aircraft Co Ltd, Cheltenham and Hucclecote (1925).

Gorcock

The Gorcock was the first military aeroplane with an all-metal structure to be built by Gloucestershire Aircraft, and, although in its design Folland drew largely on his experience with the Lion-engined Bamel and other racers, it helped to pave the way for the company's later general adoption of metal construction.

In May 1924 Gloucestershire Aircraft Co Ltd received a £24,000 contract from the Air Ministry for three experimental single-seat fighters to be powered with the Napier Lion engine. Two aircraft were to have a steel fuselage and wooden wings, and the third was to be all-steel. Design work began in the following month, but a major part of the company's design effort was being concentrated on the Gamecock and, to a lesser extent, on development of the Gloster II racer, and this limited the design progress on the Gorcock. It was therefore more than a year before the first aircraft, J7501, was completed. In appearance it strongly resembled the Gamecock, but the exceptionally neat installation of the 450 hp geared Napier Lion IV, the pointed spinner and the manner in which the three cylinder banks were faired into the fuselage gave an overall impression of sleekness which clearly stemmed from the racers. The two fuel tanks in the upper wings were specially contoured to the wing shape and projected only a small

J7502, the second Gorcock, fitted with the direct-drive Lion VIII engine having stub exhausts and forward carburettor air intakes.

amount below the undersurface, and a Grebe-type tail unit was fitted initially before reverting to the more familiar Gamecock design.

At that time the Air Ministry was considering the relative merits of geared and direct-drive engines, and in order to gain comparative performance figures from the two types of engine the second Gorcock, J7502, was powered by a 525 hp direct-drive Lion VIII. In addition these two wooden-winged aircraft were used initially to flight test different types of radiators. Gloucestershire Aircraft's experimental department had considerable difficulty in getting all three banks of the Lion's cylinders to fire evenly, and engine running was carried out after dark so that the colour of the exhaust flame could be checked; a cure was effected by cutting back the air intake pipes at different angles. As a result of these delays the first two Gorcocks were not delivered until 1927.

Design of the all-metal Gorcock, J7503, with a geared Lion IV, did not

Another view of J7502, showing the Grebe-type tail unit.
(*Courtesy F. G. Swanborough*)

130

J7502 with a Gamecock-type tail unit and re-styled top decking aft of the cockpit, a modified cowling for flush exhaust pipes, and rearward carburettor air intakes.

This D-shaped radiator was one of a number tested on Gorcocks.

J7503, the all-metal Gorcock, with narrow-chord ailerons and Grebe-type tail unit.

131

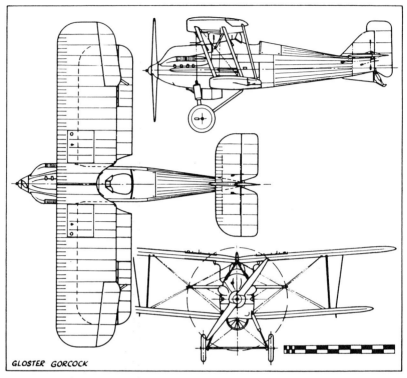

GLOSTER GORCOCK

begin until mid-1925 and construction was not completed until June 1927, delivery being soon afterwards. All three aircraft were heirs to the Gamecock's wing flutter, but additional struts were subsequently added to brace the upper mainplane overhang, and narrow-chord ailerons were fitted.

Although the Gorcock was not ordered into production, these three prototypes were used for research and development flying by the company and the RAE Farnborough for a considerable period. In 1929, for example, a series of tests were put in hand on three types of duralumin propellers on J7502. An unusual feature of the Gorcocks was that despite their research flying rôle each carried two Vickers ·303 in machine-guns in troughs in the fuselage sides.

TECHNICAL DATA

Description: Experimental single-seat fighter biplane. All metal construction, or metal fuselage with wooden wings, with fabric covering.

Accommodation: Pilot in open cockpit.

Powerplant: One 450 hp Napier Lion IV twelve-cylinder liquid-cooled geared broad-arrow, driving a 9 ft 0 in (2·74 m) diameter two-blade fixed-pitch wooden propeller (J7501 and J7503).

One 525 hp Napier Lion VIII twelve-cylinder liquid-cooled direct-drive broad-arrow, driving a 9 ft 2 in (2·79 m) diameter two-blade fixed-pitch wooden or metal propeller (J7502).

Fuel 60 gal (272 litres); oil 5½ gal (25 litres).

Armament: Two fixed synchronized Vickers ·303 in machine-guns mounted in troughs in the fuselage sides. Provision for racks to carry four 20 lb bombs beneath the lower wings.

132

Dimensions: Span (upper) 28 ft 6 in (8·68 m), (lower) 25 ft 0 in (7·63 m); length 26 ft 1 in (7·94 m); height 10 ft 3 in (3·11 m); wing area 250 sq ft (23·22 sq m); track 6 ft 2 in (1·87 m).

Weights: (J7501 and J7502) Empty 2,364 lb (1,072 kg); loaded 3,179 lb (1,442 kg). (J7503) Empty 2,422 lb (1,098 kg): loaded 3,337 lb (1,513 kg).

Performance: (J7501 and J7502) Maximum speed 164 mph at 5,000 ft (263 km/h at 1,524 m); landing speed 57 mph (92 km/h); climb to 15,000 ft (4,572 m) in 11 min; service ceiling 24,000 ft (7,315 m); duration 1·8 hr.

(J7503) Maximum speed 174 mph at 5,000 ft (280 km/h at 1,524 m); landing speed 57 mph (91 km/h); climb to 15,000 ft (4,572 m) in 10·5 min; service ceiling 24,000 ft (7,315 m); duration 1·8 hr.

Production: A total of three Gorcocks built by Gloucestershire Aircraft Co Ltd, Cheltenham and Hucclecote, (1924–27).

The first Guan, J7722, was used to test-fly the turbo-supercharged and geared Lion IV engine. (*Courtesy C. H. Barnes*)

Guan

The Guan was an experimental single-seat high-altitude fighter built to flight test supercharged aero-engines. Similar in construction and appearance to the earlier Gorcock, the Guan had an all-metal fuselage and wooden wings of the Gloster H.L.B. combination, which spanned 3 ft 4 in more than the Gorcock with a 48 sq ft increase in wing area. It was Folland's intention to combine in one aircraft the Gorcock's high top speed, which was nearly 30 mph faster than contemporary Service fighters, with a substantial improvement in service ceiling and this he achieved.

Three Guans, costing £7,500 each, were ordered by the Air Ministry early in 1925 and design work began in February. The first aircraft, J7722, was powered by a 450 hp Napier Lion IV engine fitted with an exhaust-driven turbo-supercharger mounted externally under the propeller shaft. This position for the supercharger resulted in a prominent array of external 'plumbing' which was a feature of the Guan. Completed in June 1926, J7722 was delivered to the RAE Farnborough in August. The second

The second Guan, J7723, with the direct-drive Lion VI having the turbo-supercharger mounted above the propeller shaft. (*Courtesy Imperial War Museum*)

Guan, J7723, was powered by a 525 hp direct-drive Lion VI, also fitted with an exhaust-driven turbo-supercharger which was mounted on top of the cowling above the propeller shaft. This aircraft was completed early in 1927 and was delivered to Farnborough.

Although the supercharging enabled maximum power to be maintained up to 15,000 ft, at which height the Guan had a top speed of 175 mph, and the service ceiling was pushed up to 31,000 ft, the turbo-superchargers were a continual source of trouble. The engine manufacturers made a number of modifications to the units and the system, but very little improvement was achieved and the development was abandoned. This failure led to the cancellation of the third Guan which was to have been powered by the inverted, geared Napier Lioness engine similarly supercharged.

Before the programme was finally terminated, J7722 was fitted with a Hele-Shaw Beacham constant-speed variable-pitch propeller.

TECHNICAL DATA

Description: Experimental single-seat high-altitude fighter biplane. All metal fuselage and wooden wings with fabric covering.

Accommodation: Pilot in open cockpit.

Powerplant: One 450 hp Napier Lion IV twelve-cylinder liquid-cooled geared broad-arrow with an exhaust-driven turbo-supercharger, driving a 9 ft 8 in (2·94 m) diameter two-blade fixed-pitch or variable-pitch metal propeller (J7722).
One 525 hp Napier Lion VI twelve-cylinder liquid-cooled direct-drive broad-arrow with an exhaust-driven turbo-supercharger, driving a two-blade fixed-pitch metal propeller (J7723).
Fuel 124 gal (503 litres); oil 5 gal (22 litres).

Armament: No armament carried but mountings for machine-guns in troughs in the fuselage sides. Projected military load 218 lb (103 kg).

Dimensions: Span 31 ft 10 in (9·69 m); length 22 ft 0 in (6·7 m); height 10 ft 2 in (3·29 m); wing area 298 sq ft (27·68 sq m).

134

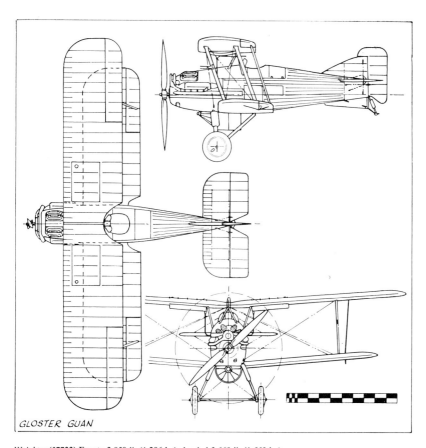

GLOSTER GUAN

Weights: (J7722) Empty 2,859 lb (1,296 kg); loaded 3,660 lb (1,660 kg).
(J7723) Empty 2,972 lb (1,348 kg); loaded 3,803 lb (1,725 kg).
Performance: (J7722) Maximum speed 155 mph at 16,000 ft (249 km/h at 4,876 m); landing speed 55 mph
(88 km/h); climb to 20,000 ft (6,096 m) in 12 min; service ceiling 31,000 ft (9,448 m).
(J7723) Maximum speed 175 mph at 15,000 ft (281 km/h at 4,572 m); landing speed 55 mph (88 km/h);
climb to 20,000 ft (6,096 m) in 12·5 min: service ceiling 31,000 ft (9,448 m).
Production: A total of two Guans built by Gloucestershire Aircraft Co Ltd, Cheltenham and Hucclecote
(1925–27).

135

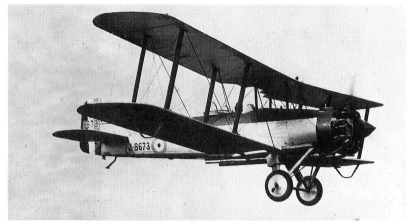

The Goral airborne on surplus D.H.9 wings.

Goral

During the eight or nine years which followed the 1918 Armistice, only a small number of new aircraft were ordered by the Air Ministry to equip the drastically reduced number of RAF squadrons, and by 1927 most of their ageing aircraft were not only long overdue for replacement but, like the Service itself, were being required to perform an ever widening range of duties. Thus the concept of a general purpose aircraft, able to undertake a number of different tasks, was both operationally and economically attractive to the Air Ministry, who were seeking a new type to succeed the ten-year-old D.H.9A which served post war in over 20 RAF and Auxiliary Air Force squadrons at home and overseas: so specification 26/27 was ultimately issued to produce a two-seat aeroplane of this class. Although improved performance and load-carrying capabilities were specified, for reasons of economy it was also stipulated that the new design must incorporate as many D.H.9A components as possible; moreover, an all-metal airframe which would be more durable during operations in the Middle East, for example, and the use of the Napier Lion engine were preferred although not compulsory. This latter proposal was included in the specification as a spur to using up the large stocks of these engines which were in store.

Design of the Goral, which used D.H.9A wings and a number of other components, began in July 1926 and was the responsibility of Capt S. J. Waters under the general direction of Harry Folland. It was one of the very early submissions to be ready, being completed in February 1927 at a cost of £3,000. It was an all-metal aircraft, fabric-covered, and to simplify

J8673, the sole Goral, was produced to specification 26/27 and used surplus D.H.9 wings. (*Courtesy C. H. Barnes*)

transport and erection overseas its slender oval-section fuselage was constructed in three main parts; these consisted of the front fuselage which was complete with the 425 hp Bristol Jupiter VIA air-cooled radial engine but minus the two long exhaust pipes which extended beneath the centre fuselage containing the fuel tank and the fully equipped cockpits, and a rear fuselage which had all the pre-rigged control runs to the tail unit ready to be connected to the pilot's controls in the centre fuselage. Although J8673, the sole Goral to be built, was powered with the direct-drive Jupiter VIA engine, production aircraft were to have been fitted with the 580 hp geared Jupiter VIII.

Apart from their use overseas by RAF squadrons, Gloster Aircraft Company always bore in mind the possible export markets for their designs, and the Goral was conceived with an eye to orders from foreign governments. Thus all the fuselage struts and fittings were rust proofed and all the joints were of a simple non-welded type to enable the struts to be easily detached. These joints were also designed so that any metal member which was damaged could be removed and replaced by one in wood if metalworking facilities were not available. Glosters also offered

The neat engine installation and severe lines of the tail unit are apparent in this side-view of the Goral.

137

The very long exhaust pipes from the Jupiter VIA, the wide-span wings and large fin and rudder typified the Goral.

to supply to customers complete sets of drawings of the wooden members with each aircraft. However ingeniously the Goral had been designed and constructed, it was an unlovely aircraft with its hand-me-down wings and observer's Lewis gun cocked up on a gun-ring mounted high on the rear fuselage decking.

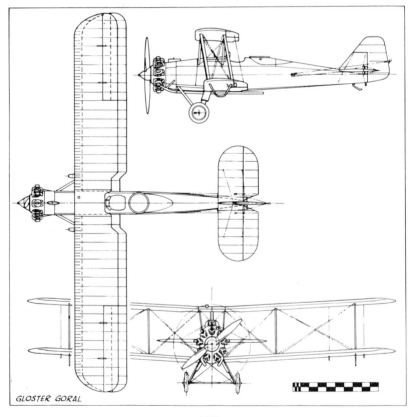

GLOSTER GORAL

Head-on view of the Goral shows the wide-span wings and the well executed propeller and engine installation.

Within a month of its first flight on 8 February, 1927, the Goral was delivered to Martlesham for flight trials where it was in competition with at least seven other 26/27 contenders. In the event the Wapiti was the winner of the type competition, but Westland's success was ultimately shared by Gloster Aircraft who, during the period 1928–31, received orders for some 525 sets of all-metal Wapiti Mk.II wings. The final cost of these wings, which were redesigned to suit their metal construction, proved to be comparable to that of their wooden counterparts.

As late as January 1931 the Goral was proving of interest overseas, and an Argentine purchasing mission in Brussels made extensive enquiries about its capabilities. The mission was, however, unsure of the British factors of safety when compared with those of French aircraft, particularly the Breguet 19 in which they had also expressed an interest. The Air Ministry therefore sent a letter to the Argentinians assuring them that the Goral was stronger than the French aircraft and would stand up to Service use much better than the Breguet design, but it was a fruitless effort and nothing further was heard from the mission.

TECHNICAL DATA

Description: Two-seat general purpose biplane. Metal construction with provision for wooden members to be substituted, and with fabric covering.

Accommodation: Two crew in open cockpits.

Powerplant: One 425 hp Bristol Jupiter VIA nine-cylinder air-cooled radial, driving a 12 ft 0 in (3·65 m) diameter Watts two-blade wooden propeller. Fuel 126 gal (572 litres): oil 14 gal (63 litres).

Armament: One fixed synchronized Vickers ·303 in machine-gun firing forward and one Lewis ·303 in machine-gun on rotatable mounting ring in rear cockpit. Provision for underwing bomb racks to carry two 230 lb (104 kg), four 112 lb (50 kg) or sixteen 20 lb (9 kg) bombs.

Dimensions: Span 46 ft 7 in (14·19 m); length 31 ft 6 in (9·4 m); height 11 ft 4 in (3·3 m); wing area 494 sq ft (45·89 sq m); chord 5 ft 9 in (1·24 m); gap 5 ft 10 in (1·77 m).

Weights: Empty 2,796 lb (1,268 kg); loaded 4,441 lb (2,014 kg).

Performance: Maximum speed 136 mph at 5,000 ft (218 km/h at 1,524 m); landing speed 55 mph (88 km/h); climb to 15,000 ft (4,572 m) in 16·25 min; service ceiling 21,500 ft (6,552 m); duration 6 hr at 10,000 ft (3,048 m); range 750 miles (1,207 km).

Production: One Goral built by Gloucestershire Aircraft Co Ltd, Cheltenham and Hucclecote, (1926).

139

J8674, the only Goring to be built, as it appeared on its first excursion from the factory.

Goring

The Goring two-seat single-engined day bomber/torpedo aircraft designed principally by Capt S. J. Waters, Gloster Aircraft Company's assistant designer, under the supervision of Harry Folland, was a private venture project built at a cost of £7,000 in 1926 to meet specifications 23/25 and 24/25 and was intended as a potential replacement for the Hawker Horsley. The sole prototype, J8674, was flown as a landplane and as a seaplane and, although in appearance it was an orthodox and rather uninspiring single-bay biplane, it had very clean lines and it embodied many features gained from Folland's hard-earned experience with the racing seaplanes.

Constructed mainly in wood with steel fittings, the Goring was nevertheless designed with the ultimate use of an all-metal structure in mind. Ash longerons with spruce struts formed the rectangular fuselage structure

Another view of the Goring showing the inverted-gull lower wings and wide-track landing gear.

140

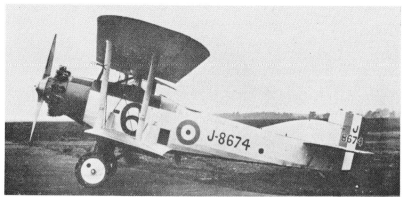

J8674 as it appeared in the New and Experimental Park at Hendon in 1927.
(*Courtesy C. H. Barnes*)

which was wire-braced internally and had a top fairing built of ply formers and spruce stringers. The wing spars and ribs were spruce, and the structure was also wire-braced internally. The lower wings were attached to a small centre section which curved upward to join the fuselage in a manner reminiscent of that used in the Gloster IV seaplane racer, and this feature not only improved the Goring's aerodynamic efficiency but also enabled a short robust main landing gear with a normal cross-axle to be used. To allow a torpedo to be carried to meet specification 24/25, a divided-axle type gear was also designed so that the Goring could operate in this alternative rôle. A major design feature of the wings was their modified Joukowski aerofoil section which gave a very high lift. Two 75 gal gravity feed tanks were carried completely within the thick upper wing. All the control runs between the cockpit and the control surfaces were of swaged rods

The Goring fitted with a supercharged Jupiter VII engine, propeller spinner and modified tail unit.

141

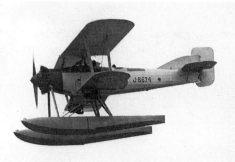

The Goring seaplane during test flying at Calshot with the Jupiter VIII engine and fitted with Gloster-designed floats.

and were routed inside the wings and fuselage with chain and sprocket gear used only for changes in direction. The twin floats were built of anodised duralumin and were of a special Gloster design based on those used in the Gloster IV. An adjustable seat and rudder pedals were provided for the pilot, and the observer's seat could be stowed to enable him to operate his Vickers gun mounted on a Scarff ring, or to gain access to a bomb sight or second gun position fitted in the floor of the rear cockpit.

The Goring was originally designed around the 470 hp Bristol Jupiter VII with a gear-driven supercharger, but on test this engine's unreliability and continual supercharger troubles led to its eventual abandonment for use in the Goring. Thus the design was modified to suit the 425 hp direct-drive Jupiter VI driving a two-blade wooden propeller, and it was with this engine that J8674, having first appeared in March 1927, accomplished a

The Goring undergoing flotation trials at Calshot. (*Courtesy Rolls-Royce*)

142

good deal of flying. A change to the Bristol Orion was also foreshadowed, but because of the failure of this engine and its exhaust-driven super-charger, the Goring appeared in the New and Experimental Aircraft Park at the 1927 RAF Display at Hendon with a 460 hp Jupiter VIII geared radial engine.

The Goring with 570 hp Bristol Pegasus II (*left*) and 670 hp Bristol Perseus IIL (*right*).

In the following year J8674 went to Martlesham where its range and load-carrying abilities were highly praised. However, neither the Goring nor any of its three competitors, the Westland Witch, the Hawker Harrier and the Handley Page Hare, met the 23/25 requirements, a major contri-butory factor being the delay in the development of the supercharged Jupiter VII and X engines. In 1930 the Goring was back at Hucclecote for conversion to the seaplane configuration which included the fitting of an enlarged rudder, and during 1931 was extensively test flown from Calshot by Rex Stocken. At the completion of the trials which included full-load tests with underwing bomb racks, it reverted to a landplane powered by the 575 hp Jupiter XF and was fitted with new vertical tail surfaces of reduced area. Then J8674 was taken over by the Air Ministry and, like the Harrier, it was moved to Filton where, as a Bristol engine test bed, it led a useful life, fitted in turn with the 745 hp Mercury VIIA, the 570 hp Pegasus II and the 670 hp Perseus IIL sleeve-valve engine.

It is rather ironic to recall that although none of the three competitors for the 23/25 contract was successful in winning production orders, two of these aeroplanes ultimately contributed to the development of variants of the Jupiter, the engine which led to their undoing. The third aircraft, the Witch, was used for parachute development work at Henlow.

143

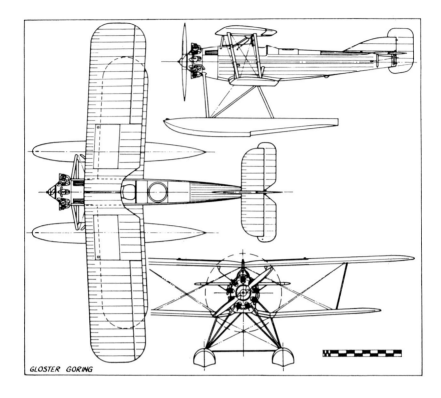

GLOSTER GORING

TECHNICAL DATA

Description: Two-seat day bomber/torpedo biplane with twin floats or wheel undercarriage. Wood construction with metal fittings and fabric covering.

Accommodation: Two crew in open cockpits.

Powerplant: One 425 hp Bristol Jupiter VI nine-cylinder air-cooled direct-drive radial, driving a 12 ft 0 in (3·65 m) diameter Watts two-blade fixed-pitch wooden propeller. Later one 460 hp Bristol Jupiter VIII nine-cylinder air-cooled radial, driving a 12 ft 3 in (3·72 m) diameter Watts two-blade fixed-pitch wooden propeller. Later one 575 hp Bristol Jupiter XF nine-cylinder air-cooled radial.

One 745 hp Bristol Mercury VIIA nine-cylinder air-cooled radial, or one 570 hp Bristol Pegasus II nine-cylinder air-cooled radial, or one 670 hp Bristol Perseus IIL nine-cylinder air-cooled sleeve-valve radial (Bristol test bed duties).

Fuel 150 gal (681 litres) in two gravity tanks; oil 14 gal (63 litres).

Armament: One fixed synchronized Vickers ·303 in machine-gun firing forward and one Lewis ·303 in machine-gun on a Scarff ring type mounting in the rear cockpit. Underwing bomb racks and torpedo crutches under the fuselage to carry 690 lb (313 kg) load.

Dimensions: Span (upper) 42 ft 0 in (12·8 m), (lower) 33 ft 4 in (10·12 m); length (landplane) 30 ft 0 in (9·14 m), (seaplane) 32 ft 3 in (9·82 m); height (landplane) 11 ft. 6 in (3·5 m), (seaplane) 14 ft 2 in (4·3 m); wing area 450 sq ft (41·8 sq. m).

Weights: (Landplane) Empty 2,914 lb (1,321 kg); loaded 5,374 lb (2,437 kg).
(Seaplane) Empty 2,902 lb (1,316 kg); loaded 5,650 lb (2,562 kg).

Performance: (Landplane) Maximum speed 136 mph at 4,000 ft (218 km/h at 1,219 m); landing speed 48 mph (77 km/h); climb to 10,000 ft (3,048 m) in 13 min; service ceiling 16,500 ft (5,028 m).
(Seaplane) Maximum speed 128 mph at 4,000 ft (206 km/h at 1,219 m); landing speed 55 mph (88 km/h); climb to 10,000 ft (3,048 m) in 14·15 min; service ceiling 16,000 ft (4,876 m); duration 6·5 hr at 15,000 ft (4,572 m).

Production: One Goring built by Gloster Aircraft Co Ltd, Cheltenham and Hucclecote, (1926).

144

The Goldfinch being flown at Hucclecote by Howard Saint. (*Flight International*)

Goldfinch

The Goldfinch was the second of Folland's designs to be built and flown with an all-metal structure, and really marked the company's transition to this form of construction.

By the early 1920s the limitations of wooden aircraft structures were becoming increasingly apparent both to Gloucestershire Aircraft Company and the Air Ministry, and G.A.C., who had acquired a half interest in the Steel Wing Company, was undertaking intensive design studies of prototypes with all-metal structures. Folland believed that a bolted-up metal construction with the necessary stiffness could overcome the wing and tail flutter which had plagued wooden aircraft like the Grebe and Gamecock for so many years. Thus in January 1926 the Air Ministry gave Gloucestershire Aircraft a contract worth £10,000 to build an all-metal version of the Gamecock, which was to bear the name Goldfinch, for development as a high-altitude fighter.

The Goldfinch embodied a number of new features apart from its metal structure, and was designed in two distinct forms. The first had all the external appearance of the Gamecock II but had metal wings and tail structure with a mixed metal and wood fuselage; in its revised form the prototype Goldfinch, J7940, had a lengthened fuselage with steel primary structure and a tail unit similar to that on Gamecock J8047 known as the Mk.III. Part of Glosters' work on metal structures had included the design of two types of high tensile steel wing spars and both of these were test flown on the Goldfinch. One was a box-section spar of the type devised by the Steel Wing Company and consisted of high tensile steel rolled to a 'triple barrelled shot gun section' with continuous webs; the second type, known as the Gloster Lattice Girder spar, had booms of heavy gauge drawn high tensile steel strip, the shear being taken through a light steel strip lattice bracing which resulted in an extremely sturdy but

145

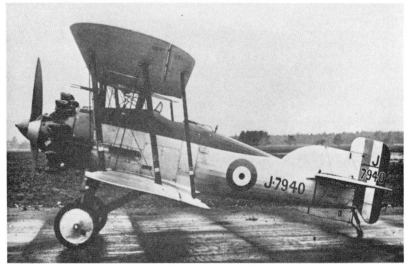

As originally constructed, the Goldfinch had a mixed metal and wood fuselage and Gamecock-type tail unit. (*Courtesy C. H. Barnes*)

lightweight form of structure. These spars were flown in different combinations; in pairs in the upper and lower wings, and with the box-section spar in the thin-section lower wings and the lattice type spar in the deep-section upper wings with Warren-girder type steel ribs. Steel predominated in J7940's fuselage, with some duralumin being used for sub-structures and aluminium for most of the front fairing and the cowling. The forward fuselage was unbraced square-section steel tube all jointed with flat plates bolted through the longerons and struts, while the rear fuselage down to the sternpost was of round tube braced by steel tie-rods and with the joints in the form of pressed steel plates wrapped over the longeron and shaped to grip the strut ends. This metal primary structure was given shape by fairings built up from spruce formers and stringers.

The movable tailplane had a screwjack, cable-operated from the cockpit which was equipped with a pilot's adjustable seat and rudder bar. The wide-track landing gear had rubber in compression suspension with oil dashpot shock absorbers.

The Goldfinch's 450 hp Bristol Jupiter VIIF air-cooled radial was supercharged to enable the aircraft to operate in the high-altitude rôle, and fuel was carried in two gravity feed type tanks in the upper wings with control cocks in the cockpit and feed lines. The standard armament of two fixed Vickers ·303 in machine-guns was carried in troughs in the fuselage side.

Design work on the revised Goldfinch was completed in July 1927 and early in the following December the prototype was ready for its delivery to Martlesham where very satisfactory trials were completed. The excellent all-round performance, with a high top speed of 172 mph at 10,000 ft and 157·5 mph at 20,000 ft plus a 27,000 ft service ceiling and a good rate of

146

The unusual asymmetric arrangement of the centre-section bracing and support struts can be seen in this view of the Goldfinch. (*Courtesy Rolls-Royce*)

J7940, the only example of the Goldfinch, in its initial form before covering.

In its second form the Goldfinch had a longer all-metal fuselage, revised tail unit and the armament was removed. (*Flight International*)

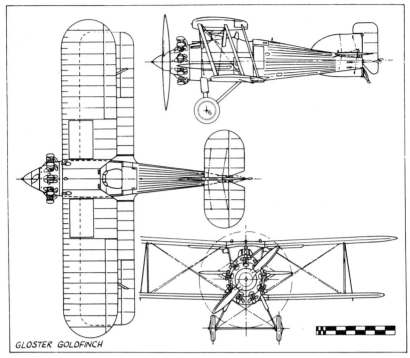

GLOSTER GOLDFINCH

climb, was a glowing testimony to Folland's design. When the Air Ministry issued the official specification F.9/26 for a new all-metal day and night fighter for the RAF, Glosters' hopes ran high and it was believed that the Goldfinch would be chosen for production, but unfortunately it fell short of the requirements in terms of fuel capacity and military load. It was, therefore, eliminated early on in the trials and the Bristol Bulldog was the ultimate winner of the contract.

Although only one Goldfinch was built it was of inestimable value providing further experience in the design and construction of metal aircraft which was to be vital to Glosters in the ensuing years.

TECHNICAL DATA

Description: Single-seat high-altitude day and night fighter biplane. Metal construction with fabric covering.
Accommodation: Pilot in open cockpit.
Powerplant: One 450 hp Bristol Jupiter VIIF nine-cylinder supercharged air-cooled radial, driving a 9 ft (2·74 m) diameter Watts two-blade fixed-pitch wooden propeller.
Fuel 57 gal (259 litres); oil 4½ gal (20 litres).
Armament: Two fixed synchronized Vickers Mk.I ·303 in machine-guns mounted in troughs in the fuselage sides with 1,000 rounds of ammunition.
Dimensions: Span 30 ft 0 in (9·14 m); length 22 ft 3 in (6·7 m); height 10 ft 6 in (3·19 m); wing area 274·3 sq ft (25·56 sq m).
Weights: Empty 2,058 lb (933 kg); loaded 3,236 lb (1,467 kg).
Performance: Maximum speed 172 mph at 10,000 ft (275·7 km/h at 3,048 m); landing speed 56 mph (90 km/h); climb to 20,000 ft (6,096 m) in 16 min; service ceiling 26,960 ft (8,217 m).
Production: One Goldfinch built by Gloster Aircraft Co Ltd, Hucclecote, (1927).

Gloster IV

Early in 1926 the design and production of a new racing seaplane, the Gloster IV, got under way in readiness for the Schneider Trophy contest to be held in Venice the following year. It was, almost inevitably, a biplane, for, although the Italian Macchi M.39, which won the 1926 race against the biplanes of the United States team, and the Supermarine S.4 and S.5 were all monoplanes, Folland was not convinced that in the tough world of Schneider contests the sleeker monoplanes had anything to offer in place of the biplane which, with its short span, greater wing area and rigid method of rigging, made it a more robust design. The Americans, too, appeared to hold similar views and were steadily developing their 1925 winning Curtiss R3C-2 biplanes.

The trend of development in these Gloster IV racing seaplanes was described by H. E. Preston, then assistant chief engineer and designer. 'In the first place we had the Gloster III machines to form a starting point from which to see what could be done to obtain a distinct improvement in performance including flying qualities as well as speed.' He went on to explain that apart from greater engine power the three main factors that influenced further increases in speed were head resistance, airscrew efficiency and landing speed. By careful redesign of the fuselage and floats

The Gloster IV, N224, in its original form at Sunningend. (*Courtesy H. S. Folland*)

149

and by blending the various components where they joined each other, a 40 per cent reduction in head resistance experienced with the Gloster III was achieved. The smooth blending of the wings into the fuselage not only improved the drag characteristics of the wing but also gave a 15 per cent increase in lift. These aerodynamic refinements, plus an increase in engine power, made the Gloster IV around 70 mph faster than its predecessor.

Three Gloster IVs, costing £8,250 each, were ordered and were constructed almost entirely in wood. The monocoque fuselage was built up

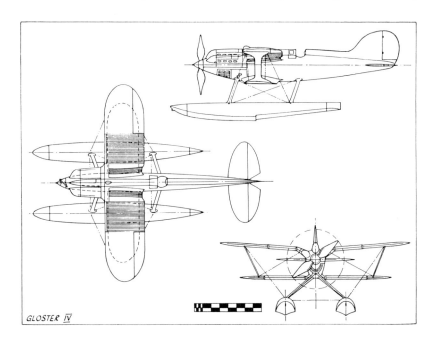

GLOSTER IV

on light formers and ash longerons with two layers of spruce strips about three inches wide laid diagonally in opposite directions to form a stressed skin. A third layer of spruce was used forward of the wings and at all load-carrying points, and the engine mounting was built up from duralumin tube. The broad-chord cantilever fins were built integral with the fuselage. The unstaggered wings were built around a multiple spar and rib structure with two layers of spruce skinning, and the single thin interplane struts were machined from solid duralumin forgings. The roots of the 26 ft 7½ in span upper wings were swept down into a fairing behind the Lion's two lateral cylinder banks, while the roots of the lower wings, which spanned only 18 ft 3½ in, curved upward to meet the fuselage skinning at 90 deg. The main fuel tank was carried in the fuselage with a small gravity fuel tank and the engine cooling system header tank in the fairing aft of the centre cylinder block. Floats received particular attention and, for the first

150

N222, the Gloster IVA with the cruciform tail unit.

The 900 hp Lion VIIA engine, fuel and oil tanks and the pilot were all packed into the Gloster IVA's small cross-sectional area fuselage.

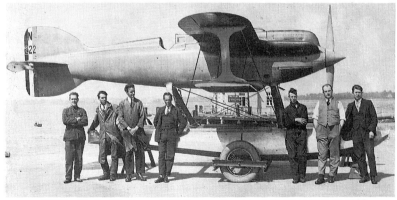

N222 with its Gloster and RAF ground crews at Calshot in July 1927.

time, Glosters designed and built their own with hydrodynamic and aerodynamic tests in tank and wind-tunnel before the final shape of the duralumin floats was accepted. They were carried on tubular steel V-struts with external wooden fairings.

An important feature of the aircraft's flying control system was the Gloster patent variable control gear which provided a 2:3 gear ratio for the small control movements used at high speed and a 3:2 gear ratio for the larger control movements needed in the slow speed condition. This gear was devised when it was found that pilots had difficulty in flying straight and level, the controls becoming over-sensitive at high speed.

Surface radiators of $\frac{3}{16}$ in corrugated copper with brass leading and trailing edges were made on a jig in the form of a sleeve and assembled by sliding onto the wings from the tip end and were secured with stainless steel spokes and brass ferrules. Additional surface radiators on top of the floats gave a total cooling area of 125 sq ft. After some inflight problems with bursting oil tanks, a combined cooler and tank, forming part of the

Flt Lieut S. M. Kinkead afloat in the Gloster IVA at Calshot.

underside of the nose, was fitted and, later, additional corrugated-type coolers were carried along the fuselage sides.

The three aircraft, designated Gloster IV, IVA and IVB and serialled N224, N222 and N223 respectively, were completed in slightly different form. Because of the high efficiency of N224's wing, the area on N222 and N223 was reduced by 25 sq ft down to 139 sq ft and the span was cut to 22 ft $7\frac{1}{2}$ in, without raising the stall and landing speeds dangerously high, which would have prevented the aircraft being put down on limited areas of water. The tail unit on N222 was also redesigned to provide fin and rudder area above and below the fuselage to produce a cruciform shape. In N224 and N222 a direct-drive 900 hp Napier Lion VIIA engine initially drove Gloster-designed and built 6 ft 9 in and 7 ft diameter propellers, respectively, of which the blades were detachable and were machined to the correct pitch and contour from a solid duralumin forging. N223, the Gloster IVB, had a geared Lion VIIB engine delivering about

152

The Gloster IVB, N223, after the upper wing had been raised to improve forward vision, and the addition of support struts and a slightly off-centre header tank.
(*Courtesy Royal Aeronautical Society*)

885 hp and driving a 7 ft 8½ in diameter propeller of similar design and construction.

All three aircraft were delivered to Calshot during July–August 1927 for preliminary flying, which was of surprisingly short duration. N222, for example, which arrived at Calshot on 29 July, was flown for only 40 min before being shipped with N223 to Venice on 16 August. In Venice further practice flying by Flt Lieut S. M. Kinkead added only 72 min to N222's log book, and barely 35 min to that of N223 which was ultimately chosen to fly in the contest. It was during a practice flight on 21 September that, on landing, the propeller spinner came off N223 and damaged one of the blades, but the aircraft was made serviceable again in time for the contest.

Another view of N223 showing the wide-chord section at the head and foot of the interplane struts and the carefully cowled cylinder blocks of the Lion engine.

With bronze wings, cylinder block fairings and tail unit, and a white racing numeral 1 on the sides of its Cambridge blue fuselage, N223 was flown in the race by Kinkead who, after successfully completing all the pre-contest trials, was first away, precisely at 2.30 p.m. on 26 September following a 24-hr postponement due to bad weather. The Gloster IVB lapped steadily at around 275 mph, once going to 277 mph and occasionally faster than Flt Lieut O. E. Worsley in a Supermarine S.5, but never as fast as Flt Lieut S. N. Webster in another S.5. who was the winner with an average speed of 281·54 mph. Then in the fourth lap N223's engine appeared to falter and, after an even slower fifth lap, Kinkead was forced to retire from the contest. When N223 was back in its hangar the propeller was removed and, despite the popular theory that it was a 'thrown spinner' which caused the retirement, it was discovered that the Lion's splined propeller shaft had a crack going three-quarters of the way round it. Thus Kinkead's decision to retire from the contest almost certainly saved the aircraft and his life from an untimely end. This race marked the last appearance of a biplane in the Schneider Trophy series, but Glosters had the satisfaction of knowing that N223's third lap of 277·1 mph had set an all-time record for biplane types.

On 4 October both Gloster IVs were shipped back from Venice to Felixstowe where they remained for flight tests until 21 February, 1928,

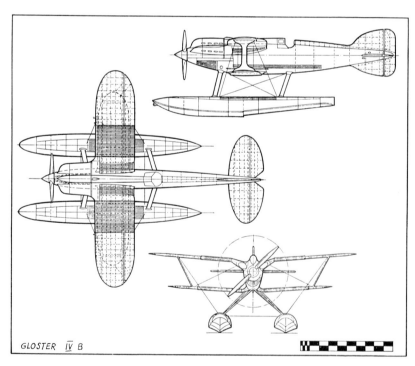

GLOSTER IV B

N224 with special broad-chord Gloster propeller and the tail unit ultimately adopted for the Gloster IVA and IVB in 1929. (*Courtesy L. E. Bradford*)

when they were returned to Glosters' factory for modification and conversion into training aircraft. To improve the pilot's forward view, the top wing was raised to fair directly into the top bank of cylinders, but the clean lines of the aircraft were broken up by adding upper centre section struts and an external header tank. N222 was returned to Felixstowe in July 1928 and with N223 was used for training purposes by the 1929 Schneider team. In March 1929 both aircraft went back to Gloster Aircraft's factory for modifications to the tail unit to cure high-speed yaw, but, although a great deal of ventral fin area was removed and added to the dorsal fin, it made little difference, and a tail unit was fitted of similar pattern to that on the original Gloster IV—which had never experienced this trouble—and all was well.

N224 was eventually sold in 1930 to Amherst Villiers who planned to install an unsupercharged geared Napier Lion engine and fit a wheeled landing gear in place of the floats. A 'well known Schneider Trophy pilot' had undertaken to fly it in an attempt on the 278·5 mph World's Speed Record set by Adjutant Bonnet of France in a Ferbois monoplane but this plan never matured. The two remaining aircraft were used quite regularly at Calshot and Felixstowe for high-speed research and training flying, until on 19 December, 1930, Flt Lieut J. Boothman crashed N223 while alighting in fog and the fuselage broke in two. N222 continued to perform sterling service and in preparation for the 1929 and 1931 Schneider contests made no less than 147 flights. In a letter to Glosters a member of the team wrote, 'You know, of course, how we relied on her, the Gloster IVA N222, for duty when the weather was doubtful and how she kept going, week after week, in spite of heavy weather and constant strains imposed by turning research.' The geared Lion engine, too, performed well and its time-between-overhauls, originally expected to be only two hours, was found to be 15 hours of which about half was actual flying time.

The number of flights made in N222 indicate beyond question that it contributed very largely to the success of the British team in the 1929 and particularly in the 1931 contests. Its handling characteristics were very good, and N222 is known to have been looped and rolled by Kinkead, the first high-speed aircraft of this type to be used for aerobatics.

TECHNICAL DATA

Description: Single-seat racing float biplane. Wood and metal construction with plywood covering.
Accommodation: Pilot in open cockpit.
Powerplant:* 900 hp Napier Lion VIIA twelve-cylinder liquid-cooled direct-drive supercharged broad-arrow (No.63007), driving a 6 ft 9 in (2·04 m) diameter Gloster two-blade fixed-pitch metal propeller (No.6847) (Gloster IV).

900 hp Napier Lion VIIA twelve-cylinder liquid-cooled direct-drive supercharged broad-arrow engine (No.63009), driving a 7 ft 0 in (2·13 m) diameter Gloster two-blade fixed-pitch metal propeller (No.7194) (Gloster IVA).

885 hp Napier Lion VIIB twelve-cylinder liquid-cooled geared supercharged broad-arrow (No.63103), driving a 7 ft 8½ in (2·33 m) diameter Gloster two-blade fixed-pitch metal propeller (No.6927) (Gloster IVB).

Fuel (Gloster IV) 45 gal (204 litres); (Gloster IVA and IVB) 58 gal (263 litres).
Oil (Gloster IV) 6 gal (27 litres); (Gloster IVA and IVB) 7 gal (32 litres).

	Gloster IV	Gloster IVA	Gloster IVB
Dimensions:			
Span	26 ft 7½ in	22 ft 7½ in	22 ft 7½ in
	(8·09 m)	(6·9 m)	(6·9 m)
Length	26 ft 4 in	26 ft 4 in	26 ft 4 in
	(8·02 m)	(8·02 m)	(8·02 m)
Height	9 ft 2 in	9 ft 2 in	9 ft 2 in
	(2·79 m)	(2·79 m)	(2·79 m)
Wing area	164 sq ft	139 sq ft	139 sq ft
	(15·17 sq m)	(12·9 sq m)	(12·9 sq m)
Weights:			
Empty	2,072 lb	2,447 lb	2,613 lb
	(943 kg)	(1,109 kg)	(1,185 kg)
Loaded	2,780 lb	3,130 lb	3,305 lb
	(1,261 kg)	(1,419 kg)	(1,499 kg)
Performance:			
Maximum speed	265 mph	289 mph	295 mph
at sea level	(426·4 km/h)	(465 km/h)	(474·7 km/h)
Stalling speed	76 mph	97 mph	97 mph
	(122 km/h)	(156 km/h)	(156 km/h)
Duration	1·1 hr	1·1 hr	1·1 hr

Production: One Gloster IV, one Gloster IVA and one Gloster IVB built by Gloster Aircraft Co Ltd, Cheltenham and Hucclecote, (1926–27).

* The engine and propeller serial numbers given in these data are those of the units initially fitted to the three Gloster IV aircraft for all flying prior to and during the 1927 Schneider Trophy contest.

The Gambet pattern aircraft, bought by Nakajima Hikoki K.K. in Japan, had arrester jaws and an oleo-type main landing gear.

Gambet

Early in 1926 the Imperial Japanese Navy was seeking a replacement for its Sparrowhawk fighters and in April of that year the Navy's Technical Staff instructed Aichi Tokei Denki K.K., Mitsubishi Jukogyo K.K. and Nakajima Hikoki K.K. to submit designs for a new series of ship-borne fighters. To improve their chance of winning this type competition, the Nakajima company approached Gloster Aircraft Company with the intention of acquiring the manufacturing rights of the Gamecock and one pattern aircraft. However, Folland already had in mind the design of a naval fighter, the Gambet, which he hoped would interest the Air Ministry and serve as a Sparrowhawk successor, and in July 1927 Nakajima acquired one pattern aircraft plus the rights to build the type in Japan.

Powered by a 420 hp Bristol Jupiter VI air-cooled radial, the Gambet was constructed in wood. The fuselage had ash longerons with spruce struts all braced by swaged rods, and the wings, which were of the Gloster H.L.B. type and similar in configuration to those of the Guan, were built entirely of spruce with swaged steel-rod internal bracing. The upper wing extensions outboard of the spruce interplane struts were braced with streamlined wires. The landing gear struts had rubber in compression shock absorbers with oleo-type dampers, and arrester hooks were attached to the axle casing; flotation bags were carried in the fuselage, and pilot's oxygen and night flying equipment were carried. Armament was two Vickers ·303 in machine-guns mounted in troughs in the fuselage sides,

Wire bracing on the upper wing extension and an almost straight leading edge to the fin typified the Gambet. (*Courtesy C. H. Barnes*)

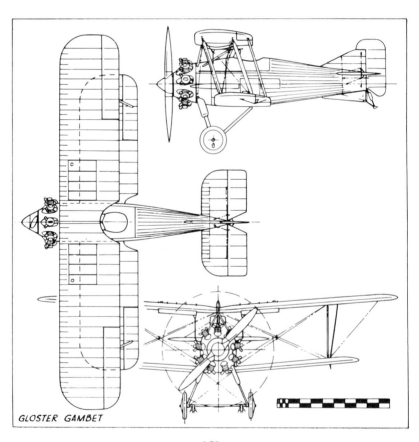

GLOSTER GAMBET

with 1,200 rounds of ammunition, and provision was made to carry four 20 lb bombs on racks beneath the lower wing. The view forward and downward from the cockpit had particular attention during the design stages and resulted in a 51 deg view downward over the leading edge of the wing and 13 deg straight forward over the nose.

Encouraged by the successful flight trials of the prototype, Glosters were keen to submit the Gambet for evaluation at Martlesham, but despite its superiority over contemporary Service ship-board fighters the Air Ministry showed no interest in the aeroplane.

In Japan the design was modified by a team led by Takao Yoshida, Nakajima's chief designer, to meet the requirements of Japanese production techniques. At the same time the pattern aircraft's original Jupiter was

Navy Type 3 Model 2 carrier fighters (Nakajima A1N2s) of the Tateyama Kokutai (Tateyama Naval Air Corps). Note the strut-type main landing gear. (*Courtesy René Francillon*)

replaced by a 520 hp Nakajima-built Jupiter VI and in this form the Gambet was test flown against prototypes of the Aichi and Mitsubishi fighters. The two indigenous aircraft proved to be heavier, less manoeuvrable and no match for the Gambet which was an excellent gun platform and met all the Imperial Japanese Navy's requirements. In April 1929 the Gambet was ordered into production as the Navy Type 3 Carrier Fighter Model 1 or A1N1 (Type 3 indicated the acceptance of the aircraft during the third year of the reign of Emperor Hirohito, A1N1 indicated it was a carrier-borne fighter (A), the first type accepted by the Navy under its new designation system (1), built by Nakajima (N) and the first version (1)).

By the end of 1930 fifty A1N1s had been built, all powered by the Nakajima-built Jupiter VI and armed with two 7·7 mm machine-guns .

While production of the A1N1 proceeded, Nakajima further developed the basic design and replaced the Jupiter VI engine and its two-blade wooden propeller with a 520 hp Nakajima Kotobuki 2 nine-cylinder air-cooled radial driving a two-blade metal propeller. In this form the aircraft's designation was changed to A1N2, and 100 were built during 1930–32.

In service with land-based and carrier-based units, the A1N1 and A1N2 were, without doubt, the best fighter aircraft used by Japan's navy during the early 1930s, and were used extensively during the Shanghai Incident in 1932. The best known action took place on 22 February, 1932, over Sochu, China, when Capt Nogi Ikuda, flying the third A1N2, shot down a Boeing 218 fighter flown by the noted American pilot Robert Short who was serving as an instructor with the Chinese forces. On 26 April A1N2s destroyed a number of enemy aircraft over China to establish a formidable reputation in combat.

Although the A1N1 and A1N2 were taken out of operational units in 1935, many were sold to civilian operators for use as communication aircraft, trainers or weather reconnaissance aircraft. At least one of them, registered J-AAMB, was fitted with a sliding canopy over the cockpit and used as a mail carrier in Japan.

TECHNICAL DATA

Description: Single-seat deck-landing fighter biplane. Wood construction with fabric covering.
Accommodation: Pilot in open cockpit.
Powerplant: One 420 hp Bristol Jupiter VI nine-cylinder air-cooled radial, driving a 9 ft 0 in (2·74 m) diameter Watts two-blade fixed-pitch wooden propeller (Gambet).
One 520 hp Nakajima Jupiter VI nine-cylinder air-cooled radial, driving a 9 ft 2 in (2·79 m) diameter wooden propeller (A1N1).
One 520 hp Nakajima Kotobuki 2 nine-cylinder air-cooled radial (A1N2).
Fuel 72 gal (327 litres); oil 7 gal (31 litres).
Armament: (Gambet). Two fixed synchronized Vickers ·303 in machine-guns mounted in troughs in the fuselage sides with 1,200 rounds of ammunition and four 20 lb (9 kg) bombs under the lower wings. (A1N1 and A1N2). Two fixed synchronized 7·7 mm machine-guns mounted in troughs in the fuselage sides and two 66 lb (30 kg) bombs under the lower wings.

J-AAMB, a civilianized Nakajima A1N1, fitted with an enclosed cockpit, venturi for blind flying instruments and an exhaust collector ring. (*Courtesy René Francillon*)

160

	Gambet	A1N1	A1N2
Dimensions:			
Span	31 ft 10 in	31 ft 10 in	31 ft 10 in
	(9·69 m)	(9·69 m)	(9·69 m)
Length	21 ft 3½ in	21 ft 3½ in	21 ft 3½ in
	(6·47 m)	(6·47 m)	(6·47 m)
Height	10 ft 8 in	10 ft 8 in	10 ft 10 in
	(3·24 m)	(3·24 m)	(3·39 m)
Wing area	284 sq ft	284 sq ft	284 sq ft
	(26·32 sq m)	(26·32 sq m)	(26·32 sq m)
Weights:			
Empty	2,010 lb	2,094 lb	1,944 lb
	(911 kg)	(950 kg)	(881 kg)
Loaded	3,075 lb	3,197 lb	3,031 lb
	(1,394 kg)	(1,450 kg)	(1,374 kg)
Performance:			
Maximum speed	152 mph at 5,000 ft	148 mph at 5,000 ft	150 mph at 5,000 ft
	(244 km/h at 1,524 m)	(238 km/h at 1,524 m)	(241 km/h at 1,524 m
Landing speed	49 mph	48 mph	48 mph
	(78 km/h)	(77 km/h)	(77 km/h)
Climb to	10,000 ft (3,048 m)	10,000 ft (3,048 m)	10,000 ft (3,048 m)
in	7 min	7·05 min	6·3 min
Service ceiling	23,200 ft	24,410 ft	25,520 ft
	(7,070 m)	(7,439 m)	(7,778 m)
Duration	3·75 hr	3·75 hr	3·75 hr
at	15,000 ft (4,572 m)	15,000 ft (4,572 m)	15,000 ft (4,572 m)

Production: One Gambet built by Gloster Aircraft Co Ltd, Hucclecote, (1927).
A total of 50 A1N1s and 100 A1N2s produced by Nakajima Hikoki K.K., Japan (1929–32).

Gnatsnapper

Specification N.21/26 for a single-seat deck-landing fighter resulted from new developments and changes in the operating techniques of naval fighters which demanded greatly increased performance. The specification called for all-metal construction and for the use of the new and untried 450 hp Bristol Mercury IIA nine-cylinder air-cooled radial engine—which almost certainly jeopardized the chance of success of any design which used it.

This class of aircraft had always interested Folland because it was a challenge to the designer and his team, and so, in June 1927, Glosters began design work on an N.21/26 contender. The fuselage aft of the pilot's cockpit was constructed of internally wire-braced round steel-tube frames with oval light-alloy formers; the forward fuselage was a square-section steel-tube structure with integral square-section steel-tube formers to which heavily ribbed metal panels were attached. A feature of the design was the hinged engine bearers which allowed the engine to be swung to either side to facilitate maintenance. For the first time, too, the pilot's comfort was given prime consideration in the design and layout of the cockpit; the seat and rudder bar were made adjustable for height and leg reach for example, and all control levers and switches were carefully sited for easy operation.

Gnatsnapper I, N227, with the Jupiter VII engine, side-mounted armament and plain ailerons.

The single-bay mainplanes incorporated the well proven Gloster lattice-type steel spar construction, which had given highly satisfactory results during structural strength tests, and were of unequal span with N-inter-plane struts. Ailerons were fitted only on the upper wings, which had marked dihedral. The tail unit was wire braced and characterized by large balance areas on the rudder and elevators. A tailskid was retained, but brakes were fitted to the mainwheels.

N227 with the direct-drive Mercury IIA engine and variable-camber wings with inset ailerons. This Mercury had flat valve gear covers on the top three cylinders to keep oil off the windscreen.

N227 as the Gnatsnapper II with the uncowled Jaguar VIII engine, revised tail unit and relocated armament.

Construction work on the £8,300 prototype's airframe was trouble-free and went ahead rapidly, but unfortunately the same cannot be said about the engine development and there were long delays in delivery. When the first Mercury arrived at Cheltenham it weighed 840 lb which was 160 lb more than the original design weight; moreover it failed to deliver its specified power and proved most unreliable. In order to get the prototype, N227, into the air to begin the flight trials, a Jupiter VII engine was fitted as a temporary measure and the first flight was made at Hucclecote in February 1928. As more Mercury IIAs became available at Bristol's Filton factory, they were delivered to Glosters for the prototype, and six

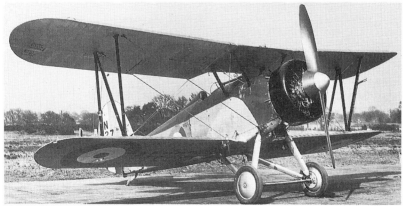

The definitive Gnatsnapper tail unit was fitted in 1930. With this revised tail unit and a cowled Jaguar VIII engine, N227 was used for armament trials at Martlesham.

163

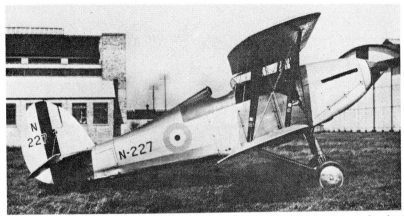

N227 in its final form with the Goshawk steam-cooled engine and condensers fitted to the leading edges of the two-bay wings. (*Courtesy Rolls-Royce*)

engines were installed in succession with very little improvement in performance and reliability. Finally in May 1929, and too late for the Ship Fighter Competition, Glosters delivered their N.21/26 contender, known as the Gnatsnapper, to Martlesham, powered again by the Jupiter VII. During its preliminary handling trials the Gnatsnapper proved itself to be a very satisfactory aircraft particularly in respect to its manoeuvrability and its characteristics in a dive and also in general performance; it was credited with a top speed of 165 mph at 10,000 ft and the ability to climb to 15,000 ft in 12·2 min. Nevertheless, modifications carried out included the fitting of manually operated double-camber wings with steel lattice spars, having inset ailerons; a larger rounded-top rudder and a new landing gear with the ability to withstand higher rates of sink were also fitted. Initially the Mercury IIA was also installed, but it never measured up to the anticipated performance.

While flight development work proceeded, at Glosters' request RAE Farnborough carried out a series of model tests for the Gnatsnapper fitted with slats to prevent autorotation in a spin. Gloster Aircraft provided the models with square, round and duo-curved wingtips and with slats at mid-span and at the tips. RAE Report BA 846 issued in February 1930 showed that the mid-span slats had little effect on autorotation but that the tip-mounted slats were most effective. However, due to weight and complexity, slats were never adopted for the Gnatsnapper.

Meanwhile a second prototype, N254, was being built and, although work had begun in January 1929, it was not until 14 months afterwards that it was completed, fitted with a Mercury IIA engine. This engine was still not a viable proposition, and finally it was discarded as the power unit for this Gnatsnapper, and a Jupiter VII with an exhaust collector system was installed. Similar difficulties with the Mercury IIA were being encountered by other entrants in the Ship Fighter Competition, and

164

this led to the organization of a second contest. For this Gloster Aircraft were instructed to redesign the Gnatsnapper to be powered by a 540 hp Armstrong Siddeley Jaguar VIII, a fourteen-cylinder twin-row geared and supercharged radial; in addition to a number of structural modifications, it was proposed that the armament be removed from the sides of the fuselage to a position immediately in front of the pilot. In April 1930 therefore, having completed its preliminary round of handling trials, the first Gnatsnapper was returned to Glosters' factory for these modifications during which time standard wings with plain ailerons were refitted and a rounded fin and rudder, similar in style to that of the SS.18, was fitted. With the Jaguar VIII engine installed, and designated Gnatsnapper II, this aircraft returned to Martlesham in December 1930.

In the second Ship Fighter Competition the Gnatsnapper's initial tests proved successful, with both the aircraft and the engine performing very satisfactorily, but nearing the end of the competition N227 made a badly judged landing in a high wind and was damaged when it turned over onto its back, fortunately without fatal injury to the pilot. This accident put an end to Glosters' main hopes in the competition, and N227 was returned to the factory for extensive repairs and further modifications. The Jaguar engine, which had been uncowled, was fitted with a Townend ring and in this form the Gnatsnapper was employed on armament trials until mid-1931 when it was again in the factory to have two-bay wings fitted and be re-engined with the Rolls-Royce Kestrel IIS, a steam-cooled vee engine. The condensers were fitted along the leading edges of the upper and lower mainplanes resulting in a neat and effective installation, but their great vulnerability in combat was all too apparent, and the plan to feature this engine and cooling system on other Gloster projects was wisely shelved.

N254, the second Gnatsnapper, at Martlesham. It had a Mercury engine, manually-operated flaps, narrow-chord ailerons on both upper and lower wings, modified undercarriage and enlarged rudder. (*Courtesy G. Leith Smith*)

Nevertheless, N227, redesignated Gnatsnapper III, was returned to Martlesham in June 1931 for further flight trials after which it went to Rolls-Royce at Hucknall for flight testing the 600 hp Goshawk III engine. This Gnatsnapper later served as a company hack aircraft for Rolls-Royce until 1934 when it was scrapped.

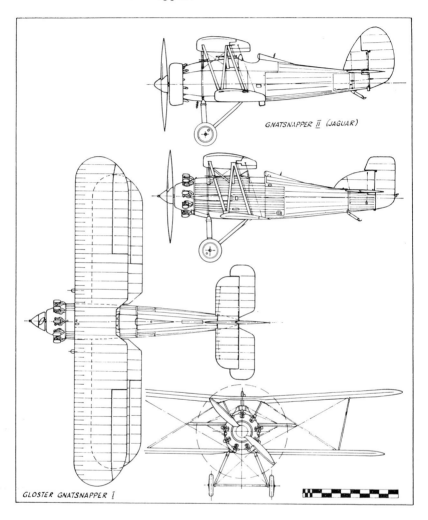

GNATSNAPPER II (JAGUAR)

GLOSTER GNATSNAPPER I

TECHNICAL DATA

Description: Single-seat deck-landing fighter biplane. Metal construction with fabric and metal covering.
Accommodation: Pilot in open cockpit.
Powerplant: One 450 hp Bristol Mercury IIA nine-cylinder air-cooled radial, driving a 9 ft 7 in (2·9 m) diameter Watts two-blade fixed-pitch wooden propeller. Later one 450 hp Bristol Jupiter VII nine-cylinder air-cooled radial, driving a 9 ft 6 in (2·89 m) diameter Watts two-blade fixed-pitch wooden propeller (Gnatsnapper I).

166

One 540 hp Armstrong Siddeley Jaguar VIII fourteen-cylinder twin-row geared and supercharged air cooled radial, driving a Watts two-blade fixed-pitch wooden propeller (Gnatsnapper II).

One 525 hp Rolls-Royce Kestrel II twelve-cylinder geared and supercharged evaporatively-cooled vee, driving a two-blade fixed-pitch wooden propeller (Gnatsnapper III).

Armament: Two fixed synchronized Vickers ·303 in machine-guns mounted in troughs in the fuselage sides with 1,200 rounds of ammunition.

Dimensions; Span 33 ft 6 in (10·20 m); length 24 ft 7 in (7·48 m); height 10 ft 11 in (3·32 m); wing area 360 sq ft (33·44 sq m).

	Mk.I	Mk.II	Mk.III
Weights:			
Empty	2,970 lb	3,095 lb	3,391 lb
	(1,347 kg)	(1,403 kg)	(1,538 kg)
Loaded	3,625 lb	3,804 lb	3,996 lb
	(1,644 kg)	(1,725 kg)	(1,812 kg)
Performance:			
Maximum speed	165 mph at 10,000 ft	177 mph at 15,000 ft	191 mph at 15,000 ft
	(265 km/h at 3,048 m)	(284 km/h at 4,572 m)	(306 km/h at 4,572 m)
Stalling speed	52 mph	53 mph	51 mph
	(83 km/h)	(85 km/h)	(82 km/h)
Climb to	15,000 ft (4,572 m)	20,000 ft (6,096 m)	15,000 ft (4,572 m)
in	12·2 min	19 min	12 min
Service ceiling	20,500 ft (6,248 m)	24,500 ft (7,467 m)	25,000 ft (7,620 m)
Duration	5 hr	5 hr	4·75 hr
at	15,000 ft (4,572 m)	15,000 ft (4,572 m)	15,000 ft (4,572 m)

Production: A good deal of uncertainty shrouds the Gnatsnapper for, despite diligent searching in all the recognized repositories of official reports plus countless discussions with ex-Gloster employees, it has been found impossible to establish without doubt either the total number of Gnatsnappers which were built or their ultimate fate. Most evidence points to the construction of two Gnatsnappers for, although three serial numbers were allocated, it is not considered impossible for one of the airframes to have been renumbered; however, nothing confirming this possibility has come to light. It is only possible therefore to record the broad outlines of the history of those Gnatsnappers which were known to have existed.

Gauntlet

During the seven or eight years following the end of the 1914–18 War the performance of British fighter aircraft was sufficient to enable the nation's air defence system to cope with an attack by the lumbering bombers of the period, but this happy situation was brought to an abrupt end when, in 1925, the Fairey Fox light bomber burst upon the scene. Powered with a US-designed 480 hp Curtiss D.12 (Felix) inline liquid-cooled engine it was built as a private venture, and with its 156 mph top speed it outpaced and outclimbed the RAF's standard fighters causing acute embarrassment to the pilots of the fighter squadrons.

With the knowledge that fighter performance would henceforth need to be stepped up and that the replacement of the Gamecock and Armstrong Whitworth Siskin was an urgent necessity, in April 1926 the Air Ministry issued specification F.9/26 for a day and night fighter with an air-cooled radial engine and armed with two ·303 in Vickers machine-guns. It specified a principally steel or duralumin construction, but having gone this far along the road to modernity it is surprising that it clung tenaciously to the

167

The SS.18 in the air at Hucclecote.

traditional radial engine, despite the use of an inline engine in the Fox, and to the two-gun armament. Nevertheless it was a challenge to the designers and ultimately produced no fewer than nine prototypes.

Glosters' first submission was the Goldfinch which had been considerably altered in appearance and construction since it had been first flown; the modifications included a 2 ft longer fuselage similar to the Gamecock II, a 480 hp Bristol Jupiter VIIF supercharged radial engine and marked dihedral on the upper wings. Two designs of tail unit were also fitted, but the Goldfinch was eliminated quite early on in the quest for this new fighter, and so Glosters decided to prepare a second contestant. However, before this latest of Folland's designs could be brought to the prototype stage most of the requirements of the F.9/26 specification were combined with the experience gained from early trials with other contenders, and a new specification, F.20/27, was formulated and issued in the summer of 1927. Among the numerous prototypes produced and flown during trials which began at Martlesham in July 1927 were the Boulton and Paul

J9125 as originally conceived as the SS.18 powered by a Mercury IIA.
(*Courtesy Rolls-Royce*)

Partridge, Hawker Hawfinch, the Armstrong Whitworth AW.XVI, a modified Bristol Type 105 (Bulldog) and, last of all, Glosters' new fighter the SS.18, J9125, which was powered by the unreliable Bristol Mercury IIA engine developing an alleged 450 hp. The initial cost of J9125 was £8,000.

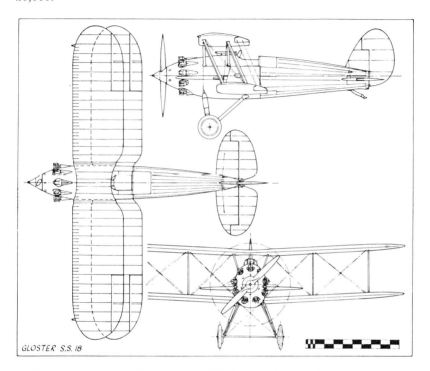

GLOSTER S.S. 18

Construction was all-metal with fabric covering on the wings and rear portion of the fuselage and metal panels on the front fuselage from engine mounting to cockpit. The fuselage was designed in three sections: the front section comprised the engine mounting made of round steel tubes attached to the four longerons by socketed ends, the middle section was of square tube and contained the cockpit and the fuel and oil tanks, and the rear section carrying the tail unit was built of round tube with orthodox internal wire bracing and Gloster plate-type joints. The whole fuselage forward of the cockpit was faired off by metal panels and by fabric-covered light metal formers at the rear. The two-bay biplane wings had high tensile steel main spars and steel ribs, all bracing wire fork-ends and strut ends were sunk below the level of the fabric and the operating levers of the Frise-type ailerons were also carried inside the wing structure. All fabric was attached by the Gloster patented wired-on method. The tailplane was adjustable in flight and a large access door was provided in the rear fuselage to simplify maintenance of the screw-jack and other gear. A conventional

169

wide-track landing gear had rubber blocks in compression to absorb loads, with an oil dashpot to limit bouncing, and the unusual feature of wheel brakes operated by pedals on the rudder bar or from the control column. A split-axle type of landing gear was also designed as an alternative but was never built.

The two-bay wings were an unexpected feature in a fast single-seat fighter, but the very rigid wing structure which resulted prevented aileron stiffness and improved manoeuvrability and greatly simplified the rigging and erection of the aircraft because the wings could be 'boxed-up' on trestles and then attached to the centre section as complete units. The SS.18 was also designed with good accessibility to engine and controls in mind, and it was in consequence an easy aircraft to service and maintain.

Meanwhile the trials of the F.9/26 contenders continued until April 1928 by which time only the Bulldog II and the Hawfinch had survived to be sent for Service trials at five RAF fighter stations, and on the score of easier maintenance the Bristol aeroplane won the competition. The protracted nature of the trials and the apparently small margin by which the SS.18's design performance had been beaten encouraged Harry Folland to press ahead with plans for its further development.

First flown by Howard Saint in January 1929, the SS.18 proved the soundness of Folland's design and of his great attention to streamlining by achieving a top speed of 183 mph at 10,000 ft and climbing to nearly 20,000 ft in 13·5 min.

Difficulties with the Mercury IIA engine, which never delivered the 500 hp which had been promised during its design stages, and the success of the Bulldog, powered with the well-tried Bristol Jupiter VII, persuaded Folland to switch engines. So, with the installation of the 480 hp Jupiter VIIF in mid-1929, J9125 became the SS.18A, the second of seven different designations it was to bear during the subsequent five years. With this new engine in J9125, Glosters began full manufacturer's trials which continued until the following year when, in the light of Saint's flying experience and Service demands, a further increase in power was clearly desirable. These

The first change of designation, to SS.18A, came with the installation of the Jupiter VIIF engine.

170

led to the initial adoption of the 560 hp Armstrong Siddeley Panther III two-row radial, and later of the Panther IIIA, and so to a new designation, SS.18B, for J9125. Fitted with a Townend ring type cowling the Panther was a heavy engine, severely handicapping the design; nevertheless a top speed of 205 mph was attained at over 10,000 ft, but during the climb and descent Saint experienced some handling problems and landing was particularly difficult. Because of this Folland again switched engines, choosing the Jupiter VIIF and giving a new designation to the aeroplane, SS.19, during the summer of 1930.

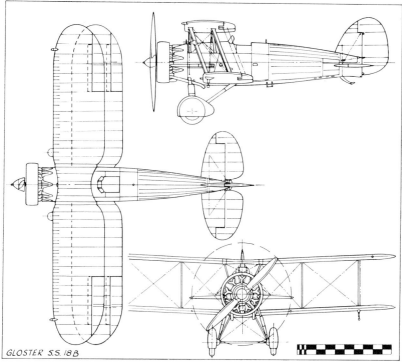

GLOSTER S.S. 18B

As noted earlier, the arrival on the scene of the Fox with its inline engine and very high performance had tipped the air warfare scales in favour of the light bomber and had thus created the need for completely new thinking and a reappraisal of defence requirements by the Air Ministry. Initially the demands were for fighter aircraft with greater speed and heavier armament to offset the anticipated reduction in time during which the fighter would be in attacking range of the bomber and could hold it in the sights.

Specification F.7/30 issued near to the end of 1930 required a top speed of 250 mph and a four-gun armament. Unfortunately this created an installation problem because the Vickers guns specified were prone to persistent jamming and so needed to be mounted within the fuselage where

171

Six guns and a cowled Jupiter VIIF engine distinguish the SS.19 'Multi-gun' here being flown by Howard Saint.

the pilot could reach them in flight and clear the jams. The alternative gun was the drum-fed Lewis which had a distinct disadvantage in that its duration of fire was limited by the small capacity of the drum (97 rounds) and it was not considered possible for the pilot to change drums in combat or in normal flight.

Several earlier specifications had been prepared by the Air Ministry to create fighters capable of beating the bomber threat, and Glosters' proposals to meet specification F.10/27 for a high-altitude single-seat multi-gun interceptor were framed around J9125, powered again by a Jupiter VIIF fitted with a Townend ring cowling, and armed with no less than six guns. Folland had considered that, in order to meet the demand for heavier armament, merely adding two more guns in the fuselage and synchronizing them to fire through the propeller was not a sound solution to the problem. He therefore decided to retain the existing two fuselage-mounted Vickers guns and, despite the limited drum capacity, to use Lewis guns mounted under the wings outboard of the propeller arc where their high rate of uninterrupted fire and comparative reliability could be fully exploited. Thus in 1930, J9125 appeared with the phenomenal armament, for that time, of no less than six ·303 in machine-guns: two Lewis guns under the lower wing and two under the upper wing, all harmonized with the two Vickers guns in the fuselage to converge at a point 150 yards ahead of the aircraft. The guns could also be fired in pairs or all together, which enabled the SS.19 pilot to continue firing for longer than any other fighter pilot in the world. Total ammunition carried was 1,600 rounds, and there was also provision for carrying four 20 lb bombs under the wings. With this heavy armament and the Townend ring the

172

aircraft's weight went up to around 3,520 lb, an increase of some 35 lb, at which the top speed achieved was 188 mph at 10,000 ft. Delivered to Martlesham in September 1930, the SS.19—known colloquially as the 'Multi-gun'—underwent extensive trials and by the end of the year had flown nearly 60 hr without any major defect, and from the handling point of view received the best report on a single-seat fighter up to that time.

Glosters' specification for this aircraft, dated 21 February, 1931, gives a maximum speed of 170 mph at sea level, climb to 20,000 ft in 15 min 14 sec and a maximum speed in a terminal velocity dive of 320 mph. This was with a propeller designed for 1,960 rpm, but an alternative propeller for 2,100 rpm is quoted as giving a top speed of 193·5 mph at 10,000 ft and a 14 min 18 sec climb to 20,000 ft. The specification emphasized the aircraft's low manufacturing and maintenance costs and claimed that it was considerably faster and better on the climb than the best air-cooled fighters in the RAF, in spite of the extra drag of the four wing-mounted guns.

Whatever successes the SS.19 achieved at Martlesham, the Air Staff were unimpressed by its armoury of six guns and went so far as to recommend the removal of the four wing-mounted Lewis guns to enable their weight in night-flying equipment to be carried. Far from being discouraged, Folland decided on other refinements for J9125 and added mainwheel spats and a spatted tailwheel and a redesigned tail unit with increased fin area to improve stability. In this form and redesignated SS.19A, J9125 returned to Martlesham in November 1931 for full Service evaluation trials, during which it achieved a top speed of 204 mph at 10,000 ft, some 30 mph faster than the Bulldog.

Yet another 'anti-bomber' specification was F.20/27 for a single-seat, high-altitude, interceptor fighter armed with two Vickers machine-guns and powered by an air-cooled radial engine. It produced eight prototypes including the almost inevitable Gloster submission based on yet another development of J9125, which, in its SS.19A form, had just about reached the upper limit of its performance with the Jupiter VIIF engine. It was not until October 1932 that Bristols were in a position to offer as a replacement the much improved and highly reliable 536 hp Mercury VIS radial, and in

The SS.19 on the aerodrome at Hucclecote.

173

With wheel fairings and restyled tail unit, a Jupiter VIIF and Townend ring, full night-flying equipment and the removal of the wing guns, J9125 became the SS.19A.

February of the following year, J9125, redesignated SS.19B, went back to Martlesham powered by this engine for preliminary Service evaluation. During these trials, which continued for nearly two months, the SS.19B was flown with a Watts wooden two-blade propeller and a Fairey metal two-blade propeller; it reached a maximum speed of 212 mph at 14,500 ft and climbed to 20,000 ft in 12 min 15 sec. One fault which became apparent almost immediately was the clogging of the wheel spats by turf when operating from Martlesham's soft surfaces, and in June it was agreed that they should be removed. However, K4081, K4082 and K4084, the first, second and fourth aircraft from the first production batch, were subsequently completed with spats, but the others in the batch had Dunlop fairings for the mainwheels.

Bristols continued to put in a lot of development work on the Mercury engine to increase its power, and shortly after J9125 had returned to Hucclecote a 570 hp Mercury VIS, in a Boulton and Paul Townend ring, was fitted. Thus modified, the gallant old prototype was soon back at Martlesham where report M/572/3 issued in August 1933 indicated that 'the SS.19B single-seater day and night fighter aircraft, recently named

The SS.19B had a Mercury VIS engine with a prominent exhaust collector ring, wheel fairings and provision for small bombs under the wings.

174

With the Mercury VIS2 in a narrow-chord cowling with leading-edge exhaust collector ring, and faired tailwheel, the SS.19B was test flown as the Gauntlet prototype. (*Courtesy Rolls-Royce*)

Gauntlet', had an all-up weight of 3,858 lb, attained a maximum speed of 215·5 mph at 16,500 ft and climbed to 20,000 ft in 11 min 43 sec. During diving tests at a weight of 3,550 lb, a maximum speed of 275 mph at 13,000 ft was attained. (These trials were interrupted to allow J9125 to appear at the 1933 SBAC Display at Hendon in June where it was flown by Saint.) This 41 mph margin over the Bulldog's maximum speed prompted the draft issue of a production specification 24/33 to Glosters in September 1933 which called for 24 aircraft, based on the SS.19B, to be produced by March 1935 as replacements for one squadron of Bulldogs. Thus were Folland and the company finally rewarded for their perseverance and resourcefulness in consistently modifying and refining the basic SS.18 design and for their skill in producing originally such a sturdy airframe which so capably withstood the long years of trials which preceded the receipt of this contract.

When the final specification and contract No. 285263/35 were issued to Glosters in February 1934, a number of changes had been called for: they included the more powerful 640 hp Mercury VIS2 engine in a narrow-chord NACA-section cowling with a leading-edge exhaust collector ring, an RAE Mk.IIA compressed-air starter in place of the old Hucks starter claw, two Vickers Mk.V machine-guns mounted in troughs in the sides of the fuselage, and Dowty oleo legs in place of the earlier Vickers struts.

But the receipt of a production contract did not mean that J9125's work was finished, and in April 1935 it was back for acceptance tests at Martlesham where Report M/654 commented on the excellence of the Gauntlet. Delivered under contract No. 279522/33, this aircraft had been fitted with the Mercury VIS2 which was then rated at 643 hp at 12,500 ft and 2,400 rpm. On test with a loaded weight of 3,910 lb, J9125 recorded a maximum speed of 230 mph at 15,800 ft, had a 2,320 ft/min rate of climb at sea level, 2,555 ft/min at 10,000 ft, and a braked landing run of 150 yards in a 5 mph surface wind. With a Watts two-blade wooden propeller, the greatest height reached was 34,400 ft against an estimated absolute ceiling of 35,000

175

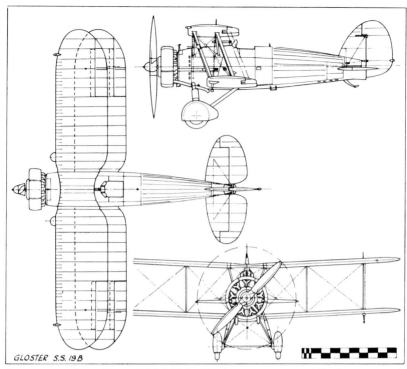

GLOSTER S.S. 19B

ft and a service ceiling of 34,000 ft. During armament trials the guns each fired some 12,000 rounds and operated quite efficiently at heights up to 31,000 ft, with ambient temperatures of −54°C, producing small flash and no dazzle. Damage to the tail unit bracing wires by empty cases was cured by modifying the chutes.

The first production Gauntlet I, K4081, was completed in December 1934 and was first flown by P. E. G. Sayer, Glosters' chief test pilot, on 17 December at Hucclecote and, after several weeks flying, went to Martlesham where Report M/654A of June 1935 recorded that with a Mercury VIS engine giving only 619 hp at 12,500 ft, K4081 was tested at a loaded weight of 3,937 lb and had a service ceiling of 33,200 ft. The second Gauntlet, K4082, was completed to production standard and was flown on test at Martlesham. J9125 continued its outstanding contribution to the Gauntlet's development programme by going into the RAE's 24-ft wind-tunnel for a series of aerodynamic checks on structural design to see whether its high performance could be directly attributed to any specific feature. The estimated maximum speed was 234 mph at 15,000 ft using data obtained in the wind-tunnel drag tests and on the engine test bed, while the actual measured speed was 230 mph. Folland believed that the performance of the Gauntlet, which was, it should be remembered, a two-bay biplane with fixed undercarriage and open cockpit, could be

176

ascribed to the fitting of the structure and equipment into a streamlined fuselage, the use of thin wing sections, submerging all bracing-wire fittings and control levers within the wings, careful design of the wing-to-fuselage and strut-to-wing joints, the use of streamlined bracing wires and landing wheels, plus an overall meticulous attention to the design of all detail fittings.

Twenty of the first production batch of 24 Gauntlet Is were completed by the end of June 1935, and the first two aircraft to be delivered to RAF squadrons flew to No.19 (Fighter) Squadron at Duxford on 25 May. A further 17 aircraft were taken on charge by this squadron during the following five weeks and the rest of the batch was delivered to Waddington and held in reserve. No.19 Squadron had earlier taken on charge one Gauntlet, K4086, for trials on 18 February.

Glosters were fortunate that after such a long development period, full of disappointments, their efforts should culminate not only in a production order but also that the Gauntlet should enter service with this renowned squadron which had earned such a splendid reputation with the Bulldog. Its reputation was quickly enhanced by flying its blue and white chequered Gauntlets with great élan to win the Sir Philip Sassoon Flight Attack Challenge Trophy on 3 June, 1935, at Northolt, performed air drill with great efficiency and precision at the Royal Review, and added even further to its

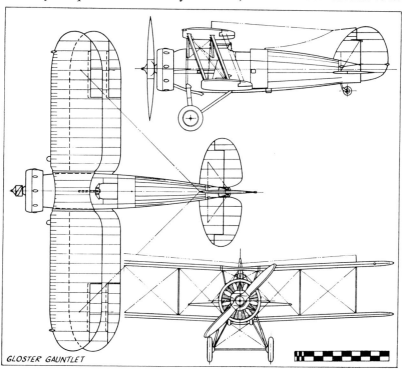

GLOSTER GAUNTLET

177

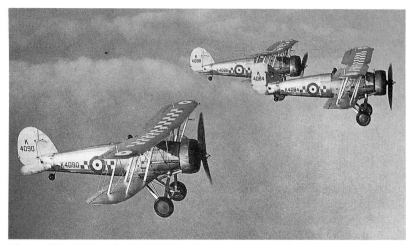

Three of No.19 Squadron's initial batch of twenty Gauntlet Is. Note the blue and white chequered squadron markings and the coloured fin of the Flight Commander's aircraft. (*Courtesy Rolls-Royce*)

laurels when one of its Flight Commanders, Flt Lieut (later Air Chief Marshal Sir Harry) Broadhurst, won the Fighter Air Firing Challenge Trophy at Sutton Bridge in September 1935 and repeated this in 1936. On 27 June, 1936, at the RAF Display three Gauntlets of this squadron, K4097, K4100 and K4094, were flown, 'tied together', by Flg Off J. R. MacLachlan and Plt Off B. G. Morris led by Flt Lieut H. Broadhurst.

Gauntlet II

During 1934 Hawker Aircraft Limited completed its takeover of Gloster Aircraft Company and, although the standardization of design and production methods was agreed upon by the two companies, the Gauntlet I production programme was so well advanced at Hucclecote that it was decided to continue to use Gloster methods throughout. However, design studies indicated that any future aircraft could be built using Hawker structures, and when, in April 1935, a further contract, No. 396880/35, was issued by the Air Ministry for the supply of 104 aircraft designated Gauntlet II, these structures and production methods were adopted.

The Gauntlet II therefore embodied a Hawker-type rear fuselage in which Warren-girder side frames, built up from steel or aluminium tubes joined together by flat steel fishplates, were separated by ball-ended steel-tubes fitting into cup-headed bolts passing through the fishplates. This structure, which was braced by crosswires and turnbuckles, was easier and cheaper to assemble than the welded type and was much easier to repair. The Gauntlet II also had Hawker-type wing spars made up from two comparatively light-gauge steel-strips, cold-rolled to an octagon section and connected by a single plate web.

178

Production of this new Gauntlet was pressed ahead, and by September 1935, when a continuation order, No. 442477/35, for a further 100 aircraft was issued to Glosters, four Gauntlet IIs were already being test flown. Deliveries began in May 1936 when 12 aircraft went to No.56 Squadron and a similar quantity to No.111 Squadron—both based at Northolt—to replace their ageing Bulldogs. On 20 July, No.66 Squadron was formed at Duxford, and as the RAF expansion scheme gathered momentum, the formation of other Gauntlet squadrons quickly followed. No.151 was formed on 4 August from the nucleus provided by a flight from No.56 Squadron at North Weald but did not achieve its full strength of 14 frontline aircraft and five reserves until early in 1938. In the same month the black zig-zag markings of No.17 Squadron appeared on Gauntlets for the first time, and, with their Flight colours painted over the entire top surface of the fuselage and on the wheel discs as well, these aircraft were unique among RAF fighter squadrons. Before the end of 1938 the big red spearhead marking was applied to Gauntlets of No.46 Squadron which had been formed, being closely followed by Nos.32 and 54.

It was in November 1936 that, in conditions of the utmost secrecy, a section of No.32 Squadron's Gauntlets, K7797, K7799 and K7800, was directed by an experimental ground radar unit at Bawdsey Manor to intercept an inbound civil transport aircraft. This was the world's first successful radar-controlled interception and ultimately had a profound effect upon Great Britain's air defence system.

By this time aircraft from the second batch of 100 Gauntlet IIs using the Hawker-type construction were reaching the squadrons. No.80 Squadron, formed in March 1937, and No.54 Squadron flew their Gauntlets only until May when they were re-equipped with Gladiator Is, while No.213 Squadron, re-formed on 8 March, 1937, moved to Church Fenton into the new No.12 Fighter Group where it quickly made a claim to fame by

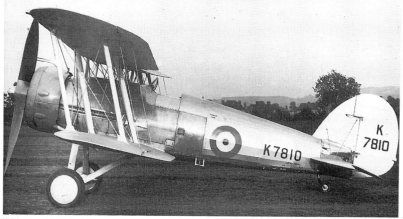

K7810, a Gauntlet II, served with No.111 Sqdn, RAF, and with the RAE where it was a 'target' during early radar trials. (*Imperial War Museum*)

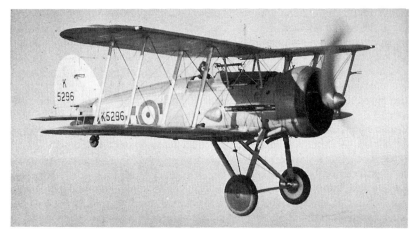

This standard Gauntlet II served with Nos.17 and 56 Sqdns, RAF, and ultimately became ground instruction airframe 2130M. (*Courtesy H. S. Folland*)

winning the Air Firing Challenge Trophy. But there were failures as well as successes; No.79 Squadron, formed at Biggin Hill on 22 March from B Flight, and No.23 Squadron on the same station, suffered many engine failures throughout the year until a remedy for the Mercury's sticking exhaust valves could be found and applied.

No.74 Squadron—the renowned 'Tigers'—was the last to get its Gauntlets, which not only carried its conspicuous black and yellow 'tiger's teeth' fuselage markings with the flamboyance of medieval knights but, by extending these markings the length of the fuselage right to the leading edge of the tailplane and thus occupying the space normally used for the aircraft serial number, the squadron directly contravened Air Staff instructions. Such was the spirit of individuality among the fighter squadrons

One of the 14 ex-RAF Gauntlet IIs sold to Finland during 1940. (*Courtesy William Green*)

180

which were later welded into a formidable defensive team in the air battles over Britain. By May 1937 the Gauntlet had reached its peak in RAF first line strength when 14 squadrons were equipped, and at the RAF Display at Hendon No.66 Squadron's Gauntlet IIs succeeded the Bulldogs for the traditional display of formation aerobatics performed while trailing coloured smoke. But by the end of the year the Gladiator was beginning to replace many of the older Gauntlets in service while No.111 Squadron at Northolt had even received its first Hurricanes. During 1938 most of the remaining Gauntlet Is were withdrawn from home-based frontline squadrons, and were despatched overseas, being replaced by Gauntlet IIs fitted with Fairey three-blade metal propellers and a new type of gun interrupter gear. Some of these went to the Auxiliary Air Force and three squadrons, Nos.601, 602 and 615, were equipped in 1938 and two more, Nos.605 and 616, in the following year. In September 1938 at the time of the Munich Crisis many Gauntlets were quickly and crudely daubed with drab camouflage patterns, some aircraft being painted matt black overall in preparation for night operations. The Night Fighter Flight of No.79 Squadron at Biggin Hill flew Gauntlet IIs with this all-black finish relieved by their flight colour on the fin.

Surprising as it may seem, when war came, Gauntlets were still in service with the RAF in Britain where they equipped Meteorological Flights at Duxford and at Aldergrove in Northern Ireland. From 1936 until 6 December, 1939, when the last Gauntlet meteorological flight took place, four aircraft, K5279, K5280, K5282 and K5283, made twice-daily climbs (known then as 'Thums') to over 20,000 ft to collect weather information of vital importance to the operational squadrons. Gauntlets also flew on many other duties in Station and Communications Flights and as well-loved personal hacks. Overseas No.6 Squadron at Ramleh in Palestine was actively engaged in co-operative operations with the Army and Palestine Police in an effort to stamp out the raiding of remote villages by gangs of nomadic Arab slave traders, while No.33 Squadron at Mersa Matruh and No.112 Squadron at Helwan, although the latter was already equipped with Gladiators, took on charge a number of Gauntlets in February and June 1940 to help with flying training by conserving Gladiator flying hours.

To the Gauntlet had fallen the distinction of being the first of Folland's Gloster fighters of all-metal construction to enter service. The passing of the Gauntlet II from RAF squadron service was also noteworthy as it marked the end of the discomfort—or the delights—of flying in open cockpits for the pilots of Royal Air Force fighters.

The last recorded instance of Gauntlets on RAF strength was as late as 1 May, 1943, when, with a temporary shortage of Gladiators, four Gauntlets went to No.1414 Met. Flight at Eastleigh, Nairobi, for training.

During 1939–40 South Africa acquired four ex-RAF Gauntlet IIs and Rhodesia three Gauntlet IIs.

GT-408, a Finnish Gauntlet II, with main and tail landing gear skis.
(*Courtesy William Green*)

Finnish Gauntlet

Following the Soviet Union's attack on Finland on 30 November, 1939, world opinion was that the Finnish defences would be crushed under the weight of the onslaught in a matter of a few days. In the event, however, Soviet land and air forces met with the most stern and spirited resistance in the bitter winter weather, so much so that Sweden and Great Britain, among other countries, were inspired to offer aid in the form of aircraft. As a result 25 ex-RAF Gauntlet IIs were sent by sea to Finland during January–February 1940 to join 30 ex-RAF Gladiator IIs, also delivered by sea, and were deployed for the defence of southern Finland.

Danish Gauntlet

During the great RAF expansion, the Gauntlet's outstanding perform- ance attracted the attention of several overseas air forces, including that of Denmark. Rather than purchase complete aircraft the Danish Government, in October 1934, obtained a licence to manufacture Gauntlets for which the licence fee charged by Gloster Aircraft Company was £3,750. In addi- tion the Danish Government bought one pattern aircraft, which was supplied uncovered and without engine or armament, for which Gloster charged £2,700. This aircraft was later alloted the Danish serial J-21 and was first flown by Maj H. L. V. Bjarkov in April 1936. The Danish type designation of the Gauntlet was II J.

Seventeen aircraft were built in Denmark by Flyvertroppernes Vaerk- steder (Army Air Service Workshops) in Copenhagen, bearing the serials

J-37 was the penultimate Gauntlet built by Flyvertroppernes Vaerksteder in 1937 for the Danish Army Air Service. (*Courtesy Hans Kofoed*)

J-22 to J-38 and factory serial numbers 86–102. The first two Gauntlets were completed in September, the next 14 aircraft appeared during 1937 and the last one in January 1938. All these Gauntlets served with 1. Eskadrille (No.1 Squadron) at Vaerlose near Copenhagen. Five aircraft were lost in flying accidents and one (J-32) was destroyed during the German air attack on Vaerlose on 9 April, 1940. Following the occupation of Denmark by German Forces the remaining 12 aircraft were placed in storage, but their ultimate fate is unknown. The 17 Gauntlets were originally given an all-silver finish, but this was replaced by camouflage in 1939.

TECHNICAL DATA

Description: Single-seat day and night fighter biplane. Metal construction with fabric covering.

Accommodation: Pilot in open cockpit.

Powerplant: One 450 hp Bristol Mercury IIA nine-cylinder air-cooled radial, driving a Watts two-blade fixed-pitch wooden propeller (SS.18).

One 480 hp Bristol Jupiter VIIF nine-cylinder air-cooled radial, driving an 8 ft 10 in (2·68 m) diameter Watts two-blade fixed-pitch wooden propeller (SS.18A).

One 560 hp Armstrong Siddeley Panther III or IIIA fourteen-cylinder two-row air-cooled radial driving a Watts two-blade fixed-pitch wooden propeller (SS.18B).

One 480 hp Bristol Jupiter VIIF nine-cylinder air-cooled radial, driving a two-blade fixed-pitch wooden propeller (SS.19 and SS.19A).

One 536 hp Bristol Mercury VIS nine-cylinder air-cooled supercharged radial, driving a 9 ft 0 in (2·74 m) diameter Watts two-blade fixed-pitch wooden propeller (SS.19B).

One 640 hp Bristol Mercury VIS2 nine-cylinder air-cooled supercharged radial, driving a 10 ft 9 in (3·26 m) diameter Watts two-blade fixed-pitch wooden propeller or a Fairey three-blade fixed-pitch metal propeller (Gauntlet Mk.I and Mk.II).

Fuel: 62 gal (281 litres); oil 5 gal (22·7 litres) (SS.18, SS.18A and SS. 18B). 58·5 gal (266 litres); oil 6 gal (27 litres) (SS.19, SS.19A and SS.19B). 80·5 gal (365 litres); oil 5·5 gal (25 litres) (Gauntlet Mk.I and Mk.II).

Armament: Two fixed synchronized Vickers Mk.III ·303 in machine-guns mounted in troughs in the fuselage sides with 2,400 rounds of ammunition (SS.18, SS.18A and SS.18B).

Two fixed synchronized Vickers Mk.III ·303 in machine-guns mounted in troughs in the fuselage sides with 1,200 rounds of ammunition, and four fixed Lewis ·303 in machine-guns mounted under the upper and lower wings with 388 rounds of ammunition (SS.19).

Two fixed synchronized Vickers Mk.III ·303 in machine-guns mounted in troughs in the fuselage sides with 1,200 rounds of ammunition (SS.19A and SS.19B).

Two fixed synchronized Vickers Mk.III ·303 in machine-guns mounted in troughs in the fuselage sides with 1,200 rounds of ammunition (Gauntlet Mk.I).

Two fixed synchronized Vickers Mk.V ·303 in machine-guns mounted in troughs in the fuselage sides with 1,200 rounds of ammunition (Gauntlet Mk.II).

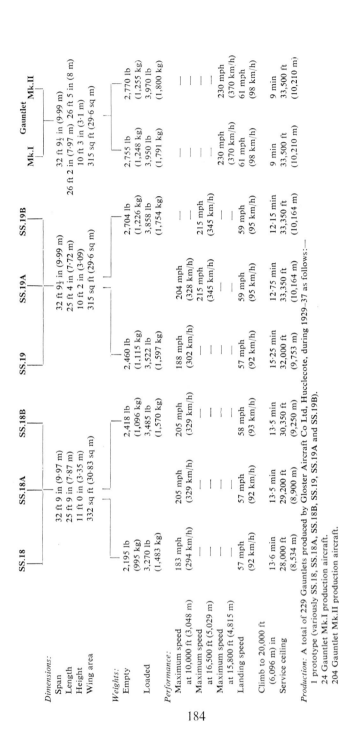

	SS.18	SS.18A	SS.18B	SS.19	SS.19A	SS.19B	Gauntlet Mk.I	Gauntlet Mk.II
Dimensions:								
Span	32 ft 9 in (9·97 m)			32 ft 9½ in (9·99 m)			32 ft 9½ in (9·99 m)	
Length	25 ft 9 in (7·87 m)			25 ft 4 in (7·72 m)			26 ft 2 in (7·97 m)	26 ft 5 in (8 m)
Height	11 ft 0 in (3·35 m)			10 ft 2 in (3·09 m)			10 ft 3 in (3·1 m)	
Wing area	332 sq ft (30·83 sq m)			315 sq ft (29·6 sq m)			315 sq ft (29·6 sq m)	
Weights:								
Empty	2,195 lb (995 kg)		2,418 lb (1,096 kg)	2,460 lb (1,115 kg)		2,704 lb (1,226 kg)	2,755 lb (1,248 kg)	2,770 lb (1,255 kg)
Loaded	3,270 lb (1,483 kg)		3,485 lb (1,570 kg)	3,522 lb (1,597 kg)		3,858 lb (1,754 kg)	3,950 lb (1,791 kg)	3,970 lb (1,800 kg)
Performance:								
Maximum speed at 10,000 ft (3,048 m)	183 mph (294 km/h)	205 mph (329 km/h)	205 mph (329 km/h)	188 mph (302 km/h)	204 mph (328 km/h)	—	—	—
Maximum speed at 16,500 ft (5,029 m)	—	—	—	—	215 mph (345 km/h)	215 mph (345 km/h)	—	—
Maximum speed at 15,800 ft (4,815 m)	—	—	—	—	—	—	230 mph (370 km/h)	230 mph (370 km/h)
Landing speed	57 mph (92 km/h)	57 mph (92 km/h)	58 mph (93 km/h)	57 mph (92 km/h)	59 mph (95 km/h)	59 mph (95 km/h)	61 mph (98 km/h)	61 mph (98 km/h)
Climb to 20,000 ft (6,096 m) in	13·6 min	13·5 min	13·5 min	15·25 min	12·75 min	12·15 min	9 min	9 min
Service ceiling	28,000 ft (8,534 m)	29,200 ft (8,900 m)	30,350 ft (9,250 m)	32,000 ft (9,753 m)	33,350 ft (10,164 m)	33,350 ft (10,164 m)	33,500 ft (10,210 m)	33,500 ft (10,210 m)

Production: A total of 229 Gauntlets produced by Gloster Aircraft Co Ltd, Hucclecote, during 1929–37 as follows:—

1 prototype (variously SS.18, SS.18A, SS.18B, SS.19, SS.19A and SS.19B).
24 Gauntlet Mk.I production aircraft.
204 Gauntlet Mk.II production aircraft.
A total of 17 Gauntlet IIs produced by Flyvertroppernes Vaerksteder in Copenhagen, with the Danish type designation II J, during 1936–38.

Allocation: See Individual Aircraft Notes, pages 352–353.

184

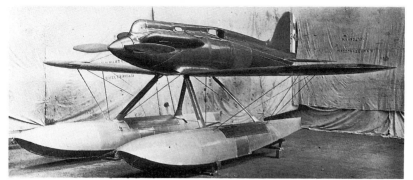

N249, the first Gloster VI, in the factory at Sunningend.

Gloster VI

Glosters' wealth of experience gained in producing many high-speed biplanes was finally put to the test in the design and production of the Gloster VI monoplane racer. Although the adoption of this configuration was virtually inevitable, following the demise of the Gloster V project, Folland and his team tackled the task of designing their first monoplane with characteristic thoroughness, and design and construction began in May 1928; thus when an Air Ministry order for the new racer was received in November 1928 the work was well advanced.

Its structure was a combination of wood and metal; the 24 ft long fuselage was of all-metal semi-monocoque construction having oval former hoops and flush-riveted skinning of duralumin, while the 26 ft span wings with their six main spars were of the multi-spar and multi-rib type of skeleton framework all built of spruce with two- and three-layer spruce laminations laid over this framework to form the skin. All-duralumin flush riveted floats of Gloster design and manufacture contained the equal-capacity main fuel tanks and were carried on steel-tube struts with duralumin fairings. Two engine-driven fuel pumps raised the petrol in equal proportions from each float tank and delivered it to a two-gallon collector tank in the fuselage. Surface radiators, very much thinner in section than any previously used, were fitted to the wings and the oil was cooled by means of a circular oil cooler and tank fitting completely around the fuselage behind the pilot's cockpit and lying flush with the fuselage skin. Additional flat-tube oil-coolers in the upper surface of each float could be used if necessary, the oil passing to and returning from the float coolers via oilways in the leading edge of the struts.

Wing thickness was increased on the outer portions to improve the lateral control at low speeds, because the thinner inboard portion of the wing began to lose lift before the outer part. Maximum chord also occurred at the point of maximum thickness, and the whole design was aimed at combining the advantages of the low-drag thin wing with the thick wing's higher lift.

The Napier Lion VIID twelve-cylinder engine was fitted with a newly developed supercharger which was mounted at the rear to keep the frontal area to a minimum. The three banks of cylinders were carefully cowled to blend in with the general fuselage shape and although the cockpit was, at first, open with only a small completely suppressed windscreen, this was later modified and the cockpit was enclosed under a metal cover with a very large oval cutout on each side of the pilot's head.

Gloster VI with a Lion VIID engine, en route to the water at Calshot.

The construction of the two Gloster VIs, N249 and N250, was completed in July 1929 and cost £25,000. N249 was painted old-gold with blue floats, and thus was born the name *Golden Arrow* which this Gloster VI was given. N250 was no less gorgeously finished, having old-gold wings and tailplane, Cambridge blue fuselage, fin and struts, white floats, and natural copper coloured radiator surfaces. Described by many as being the most beautiful aeroplane of its period, the Gloster VI certainly bore every outward indication of being a winner. One newspaper reported that—'it seems more the conception of an artist who can make and create his own lines by the stroke of a brush, than the work of a designer who is bound by the principles of engineering and the comparative inelasticity of metal and timber. The Gloster Aircraft Company has never produced a finer example of aircraft construction and it is an outstanding testimony to the high standard of their workshop practice just as the design itself is a triumph for Mr H. P. Folland and Mr H. E. Preston.'

Like so many new and experimental engines of that period, the Lion VIID plagued Glosters and the High Speed Flight with a succession of failures. In an effort to provide great power for a small frontal area, in order to offset the increase in weight, the Lion had been over-boosted, being rated at 1,320 hp for limited periods when standard Lions of identical capacity were delivering only 500 hp.

This view shows the exceptionally clean lines of the Gloster VI. Note the thickest section of the wings is well outboard.

N249 was delivered to Calshot on 12 August, 1929, and N250 followed it there on 17 August when they were assembled and successfully completed flotation tests. Although both aircraft were fully prepared, their first flights were delayed by bad weather and it was not until 25 August that Sqdn Ldr A. H. Orlebar was able to get airborne in N249 but experienced engine failure when only 20 ft off the water. After further ground running of both engines, Orlebar got in one flight in N250 just before dark on 31 August, but this brought its problems too and, although the aircraft handled well, the Lion cut out on turns and occasionally in level flight. During the next five days, N249 and N250 were flown by two other High Speed Flight pilots, Flg Off D. D'Arcy Grieg and Flt Lieut G. H. Stainforth, but they were unable to locate the source of the trouble. Even after the Gloster and Napier ground crews worked three days and two nights continuously, neither of the engines could be kept running at full throttle and so it was decided to withdraw the Gloster VI from the Schneider Trophy contest held that year at Cowes.

On 10 September, the day after the race, Stainforth made five runs over the three-kilometre course from Calshot Spit to Agwi Pier in N249 which,

The High Speed Flight handling party launch the Gloster VI at Calshot.

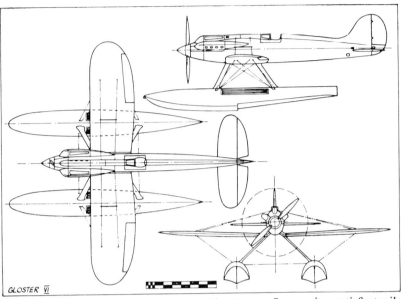

GLOSTER VI

although still giving trouble during the turns, flew quite satisfactorily straight and level. This was amply proved by the last four recorded runs during which N249 attained speeds of 351·3, 328·3, 336·2 and 329·3 mph to give an average speed of 336·3 mph. This was later ratified as an Absolute Speed Record, although even this was well beaten only a few hours later by Orlebar flying a Supermarine S.6. Just a month afterwards, on 9 November, the Gloster VI took part in the Lord Mayor's Show in London.

In 1930 N250 was exhibited in the New and Experimental Types Park at the RAF Display with the Supermarine S.6 and afterwards was returned to Felixstowe where, with a new engine and further modifications to improve the airflow through the carburettor intake, it was used for limited flying, but full power could still not be maintained. N249 was similarly modified with the same results and so, when the High Speed Flight returned to Calshot in May 1931, although this Gloster VI was still on charge as a training aircraft, it was rarely flown.

TECHNICAL DATA

Description: Single-seat twin-float racing monoplane. Metal and wood construction with metal and wood covering.

Accommodation: Pilot in open faired cockpit.

Powerplant: One 1,320 hp Napier Lion VIID twelve-cylinder supercharged broad-arrow, driving a 7 ft 8 in (2·3 m) diameter Gloster two-blade fixed-pitch metal propeller.
Fuel 80 gal (363 litres) in each float with a 2 gal (9 litres) collector tank in the fuselage.

Dimensions: Span 26 ft 0 in (7·9 m); length 27 ft 0 in (8·2 m); height 10 ft 9½ in (3·2 m); float length 22 ft 2 in (6·7 m); wing area 106 sq ft (9·8 sq m); maximum chord 4 ft 8 in (1·4 m).

Weights: Empty 2,284 lb (1,036 kg); loaded 3,680 lb (1,669 kg).

Performance: Maximum recorded speed 351·3 mph (565·3 km/h) at 100 ft (30·4 m); alighting speed 110 mph (177 km/h); stalling speed 92 mph (148 km/h).

Production: Two Gloster VI aircraft built by Gloster Aircraft Co Ltd, Hucclecote, Glos. during 1928–.

188

A fine flying view of the Aircraft Operating Company's Gloster AS.31 G-AADO. The two large doors with small portholes enabled the photographic equipment to be installed in the square-section fuselage. (*Courtesy H. S. Folland*)

AS.31

In the early 1920s air survey was regarded by many people as the key to the further development of the British Dominions and Colonies because, as a logical extension of the wartime art of aerial reconnaissance and mapping, it would enable hitherto unexplored areas of the world to be mapped very quickly. Until 1926 the Aircraft Operating Company Ltd, who were official contractors for aerial survey work to the Ordnance Survey, used converted D.H.9s for the majority of their overseas surveys and with them gained vast experience to enable the company to develop and perfect new and specialized flying and photographic techniques. But by then inevitably these reconditioned and converted war-surplus aircraft were nearing the end of their flying lives, and the company wisely prepared its own specification for an air survey aircraft to meet their specialized needs.

Their experience in Europe, Asia, Africa (where the crew of a single-engined survey aircraft walked 75 miles to the nearest outpost after a forced landing), and South America underlined their need for a twin-engined aircraft of maximum reliability, if the dangers of a forced landing in difficult country encountered with the earlier single-engined types was to

The AS.31 before its delivery to the Aircraft Operating Company at Heston. Note the large glass panel under the nose. (*Courtesy Rolls-Royce*)

be avoided; metal construction was considered essential to enable the aircraft to operate in tropical or arctic regions, and it was desirable that 'in cases of emergency it should be easily transportable in parts.' The Aircraft Operating Company also specified that the aircraft should be able to maintain height with a full load on one engine at 9,000 ft and that the photographer and his camera should be accommodated in a partially enclosed cabin, have a good view, and a means of talking to the pilot and of making instrumental observations.

De Havillands were approached initially and their resultant design study of an all-metal biplane designated D.H.67 was virtually a scaled-down twin-engined version of the D.H.66 Hercules airliner with a single fin and rudder. It featured tandem open cockpits for the pilot and navigator with, beneath them, a position for a prone photographer operating a floor-mounted camera, and a central cabin having three circular portholes for oblique photography. Attachment points for seaplane alighting gear, using two 24-ft Short metal floats in place of the wheeled landing gear, ensured that the aircraft could operate from lakes and rivers if necessary. Its similarity to the D.H.66 was emphasized by the large centre-section

G-AADO carrying the Aircraft Operating Company insignia.

190

fuel tank and the use of ailerons fitted only on the lower wings, which also carried the two 450 hp Bristol Jupiter VI radial engines.

By November 1927 the design had been modified under the designation D.H.67B to embody a biplane tail unit with twin fins and rudders, increased span, and greater gap at the fuselage produced by anhedral on the inboard portions of the lower wing: the open cockpits had been replaced by side-by-side seating for the pilot and navigator in an open cockpit below the leading edge of the centre section and the photographer had been moved right forward into an open cockpit in front of and below them in the nose. Ailerons were also fitted to the upper and lower wings, which were intended to fold, and 480 hp Bristol Jupiter VIII radial engines were introduced to provide improved performance at the same 7,000 lb all-up weight.

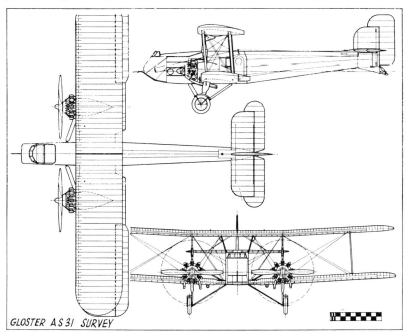

GLOSTER AS 31 SURVEY

But de Havillands were becoming increasingly aware of their involvement with the production of the Moth and Hercules and with other work, and so, in November 1928, responsibility for the construction of the air survey aircraft was handed over to Glosters. Redesign work began in the following month and under Folland's guidance many detail changes were made to the basic design of the aircraft so that it could readily be converted to carry six to eight passengers or cargo, or into a flying ambulance, or a bomber armed with three machine-guns. In this form it bore the Gloster designation AS.31. Fabric-covered all-metal construction was used, and the square-section fuselage was built in three portions: square steel and duralumin tubing was riveted and welded together to reduce the

191

number of loose parts, and duralumin girders and channels supported the plywood flooring.

To simplify repair and replacement in the field, the whole fuselage structure could be dismantled by removing a few bolts and pins and rapidly re-assembled using semi-skilled labour. The wings were of orthodox design with high tensile steel spars using Gloster lattice spar construction, three-section duralumin ribs to simplify replacement, and balanced Frise-type ailerons only on the lower wings. The tail unit, which had a single fin and rudder, had high tensile steel box-spars with built-up duralumin ribs, and the tailplane was fully adjustable in flight. A triangulated V-structure for the landing gear eliminated the usual long axle close to the ground, which could have been unsuitable for use on rough landing strips, and an oleo-type shock absorber was housed in the vertical leg. Dual controls were fitted and push rods used in place of cables throughout the control runs to give long life and positive action. The engines were two 525 hp Bristol Jupiter XI geared air-cooled radials, but performance

In service with the South African Air Force, the AS.31 had large low-pressure tyres without mudguards, and four-blade propellers. (*South African Air Force*)

calculations were made, and mountings were provided in the design, to suit Armstrong Siddeley Jaguar Majors or Jaguar VIs, Pratt & Whitney Hornets, Lorraine-Dietrich 14Acs or Wright Cyclones of similar power.

The Eagle camera, made by Williamson Manufacturing Co of Willesden Green, was carried on a special 'Eyrie' mounting which enabled the camera to be lowered through the bottom of the fuselage to keep it clear of any projections on the aircraft.

Two prototype AS.31s were built at a cost of some £13,000. The first, G-AADO, was inadvertently flown for the first time during its taxi-ing trials in June 1929 at Hucclecote; Howard Saint was the pilot and he had Folland on board with him. Saint completed one taxi run to the bottom of the airfield, then turned round to taxi back up the slope, but having opened the throttles slightly to negotiate some ruts in the airfield surface

K2602, the second AS.31, used for wireless telegraphy trials at the RAE.

he found that he was airborne and heading for the hangars—so gave the engines full throttle, made a steady circuit and landed again.

The second AS.31, K2602, was built for the Air Ministry and was exhibited in skeleton form without its fabric covering at the Olympia International Aero Exhibition in July 1929: it was later completed and, on 19 November, 1931, delivered to the RAE Farnborough for wireless telegraphy experiments. It was last used there on 17 September, 1936.

On 25 January, 1930, G-AADO was flown by Saint from Stag Lane aerodrome to Heston Air Park carrying Lord Thomson of Cardington, then Secretary of State for Air, and F. Montague, Under Secretary, who were accompanied by Alan Butler, H. Hemming and Maj C. K. Cochran-Patrick, all directors of the Aircraft Operating Company. At Heston the AS.31 was impressively demonstrated before a critical gathering which included press men. Less than two months later Alan Butler, accompanied by his wife, a cameraman and Mr Millyard, a ground engineer, delivered G-AADO to Cape Town for service with the Zambesi Basin Survey Expedition. On the 7,000 mile flight which started at Heston on 20 March, 1930, and terminated at Wyabird Aerodrome on 11 April, the AS.31 averaged 128 mph or 3 mph less than its maximum speed. It was subsequently flown on to Bulawayo for the survey operations by Cochran-

An additional rectangular window replaced the camera loading doors in K2602, the glass panel in the nose was omitted and the two-blade propellers were without spinners.

Patrick, and from this base, with Capt Robbins as pilot, it was used during the ensuing year to survey successfully 63,000 square miles of Northern Rhodesia. At the completion, Alan Butler wrote to Glosters to say 'The reliability and good performance of the Air Survey aircraft enabled us to tackle these operations with confidence while the special air survey qualities of the aircraft have proved to be of very great value.' In May 1935, with the completion of these and other surveys in Central Africa, during which it had logged some 500 hr flying without replacement of any components apart from tailskid shoes and tyres, G-AADO was sold to the South African Air Force with which it had the serial number 250. It was based at Zwartkop Air Station, Valhalla, where it was used by the Photographic Section exclusively for aerial photography until it was withdrawn from service in 1942.

The AS.31 also created some interest in Egypt where it was considered for use as a bomber-reconnaissance aircraft, and, following an enquiry, on 4 December, 1930, Gloster Aircraft Company quoted a price of £11,000 per aircraft coupled with a price of £4,500 for the SS.18 single-seat fighter. However, the Egyptian Government did not pursue this enquiry and no contract ensued.

TECHNICAL DATA

Description: Two/three-seat photographic air-survey biplane. Metal construction with fabric covering.

Accommodation: Pilot and navigator in open cockpit, and camera operator in fuselage or nose position.

Powerplant: Two 525 hp Bristol Jupiter XI nine-cylinder geared air-cooled radials, driving two-blade fixed-pitch wooden propellers. Four-blade fixed-pitch propellers subsequently fitted to first aircraft. Fuel: 240 gal (1,091 litres), oil 31 gal (140 litres).

Dimensions: Span 61 ft 0 in (18·9 m); length 48 ft 6 in (14·7 m); height 18 ft 9 in (5·7 m); wing area 1,025 sq ft (95·2 sq m); chord 9 ft 0 in (2·7 m); gap 9 ft 3 in (2·8m); incidence 3 deg; dihedral 3 deg; wing section Clark Y.H.

Weights: Empty 5,614 lb (2,546 kg); loaded (maximum) 8,570 lb (3,886 kg).

Performance: (At normal load of 800 lb (362 kg) of survey equipment, 200 gal (909 litres) of fuel and 27 gal (122 litres) of oil). Maximum speed 131 mph (210 km/h) at 1,000 ft (304 m); cruise 110 mph (177 km/h); stalling speed 47 mph (75 km/h); climb to 10,000 ft (3,048 m) in 7·4 min; service ceiling 21,900 ft (6,674 m); absolute ceiling 23,200 ft (7,071 m); range 495 miles (796 km); endurance at 1,000 ft (304 m) at cruise speed 4·5 hr; endurance at 20,000 ft (6,096 m) at 100 mph (160 km/h) 6·5 hr. (At maximum load of 800 lb (362 kg) of survey equipment, 240 gal (1,091 litres) of fuel and 31 gal (140 litres) of oil.) Maximum speed 130 mph (209 km/h) at 1,000 ft (304 m); cruise 109 mph (174 km/h); stalling speed 48 mph (77 km/h); climb to 10,000 ft (3,048 m) in 11·6 min; service ceiling 21,000 ft (6,400 m); absolute ceiling 22,500 ft (6,857 m); endurance at 10,000 ft (3,048 m) at cruise speed 5·5 hr; endurance at 20,000 ft (6,096 m) at 100 mph (160 km/h) 7·5 hr.

Production: A total of two AS.31s built by Gloster Aircraft Co Ltd, Hucclecote, Glos. during 1929.

The TC.33 bomber transport, Glosters' only four-engined aircraft. The figure beneath the nose is J. B. Johnstone, later to become experimental department superintendent.

TC.33

The TC.33 bomber-transport was Glosters' only four-engined aircraft and was the biggest—but not the heaviest—to emanate from Hucclecote. It was designed in the autumn of 1930 to meet specification C.16/28 which also produced the three-engined Handley Page H.P.43 and which called for an aeroplane capable of carrying 30 fully-armed troops, or their equivalent weight in cargo or bombs, for a distance of 1,200 miles nonstop.

Unusual in that it had a sesquiplane tail unit, and the 95 ft span of its lower wings exceeded that of the upper wings, the TC.33 was another impressive tribute to Folland's versatile skill as a designer. The slender well-proportioned fuselage was an 80 ft long all-metal structure with oval-section formers and metal skinning, and the giant, single-bay unstaggered wings had Gloster lattice spars with metal ribs and fabric covering. From a rectangular centre section the outer wing panels were swept back 7 deg, had parallel-chord ailerons interconnected by cables, and Handley Page automatic slots mounted outboard on the upper wings. The lower wings were carried in the mid-wing position, but the lower centre section had sharp anhedral to lift the inboard ends of the spars clear of the fuselage and provide an unobstructed cabin. Two all-metal fabric-covered end-plate fins and rudders were attached to a pair of strut-braced tailplanes of similar construction. The upper tailplane was mounted above the fuselage on short streamlined struts, and the lower tailplane was positioned on the bottom line of the fuselage. The massive 60 in diameter main landing wheels were carried on triangulated structures, giving a 22 ft 6 in track, with shock absorber units in the vertical members, while a complex strut arrangement under the rear fuselage carried the 30 in diameter castoring tailwheel. Mainwheel brakes were operated by compressed air.

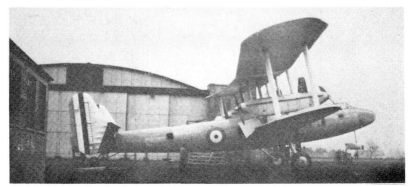

J9832 shortly after being winched out of its assembly hangar at Hucclecote.
(*Courtesy H. S. Folland*)

The single prototype, J9832, had a sound-proofed and heated enclosed cabin for the pilot and co-pilot and for the navigator who was accommodated on a raised platform behind them. Access to the front gunner's open position was by way of a small door below and in front of the co-pilot; a second door in the large rear bulkhead led into the main cabin which was 27 ft 8 in long, 7 ft wide and 7 ft 3 in high. It also was sound-proofed and heated and could accommodate the required 30 fully-armed troops or 12 stretcher cases. A gangway led through the rear fuselage aft of the main cabin to the rear gunner's open position. When operating as a cargo carrier, a very large hatch in the floor of the main cabin could admit loads hauled up by means of a mechanical hoist running on a beam which was integral with the fuselage structure and which was capable of supporting loads of up to half a ton; another smaller hatch in the roof allowed cargo to be lowered by crane into the main cabin.

Power for this graceful giant was provided by four 580 hp Rolls-Royce Kestrel IIS/IIIS steam-cooled engines installed as tandem pairs midway between the upper and lower wings and driving two-blade propellers of which the front pair were larger in diameter than those at the rear. Two

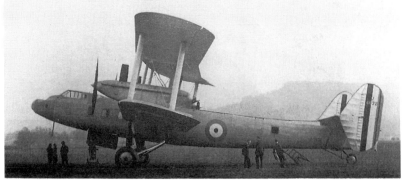

The large freight door can be seen open below the TC.33's nose.

196

The massive proportions of the TC.33 are apparent in this head-on view.

streamlined nacelles were strut-braced to the fuselage and housed the pairs of engines; the Kestrel IIIS units were mounted as tractors and the IIS units as pushers, and a single steam condenser above the Kestrel IIIS provided evaporative cooling for each pair of engines. Only six gallons of water were carried for each engine instead of 14 gallons required for ortho- dox radiator cooling, and this reduction effected a weight-saving of around 250 lb. A system of coloured warning lights on the pilot's instrument panel indicated the direction of water flow through the condensers; green showed the correct direction, while a red indicated a flow reversal for which the only cure was to throttle back to allow the engines to cool.

When the time came for the TC.33's roll-out in January 1932, it was found that the top wings were too high to pass through the doors of Hucclecote's No.2 hangar, and so the works engineer arranged for two trenches to be dug to accommodate the wheels and these enabled J9832 to be winched out of the hangar.

The first flight was on 23 February, 1932, and Howard Saint soon got

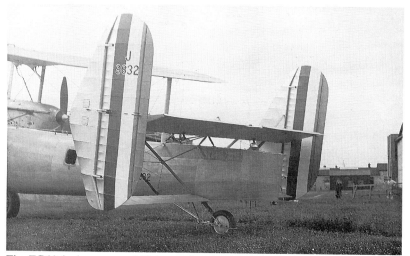

The TC.33 had an unusual biplane tail unit with the main tailplane supported on struts above the fuselage.

197

The TC.33 flying at the 1932 RAF Display at Hendon.

the flight test programme under way, but although the TC.33's performance was good, it ran into tail-flutter problems caused by the servo-tabs
on the elevators and the enormous 9 ft high rudders. Balance weights
ultimately cured the elevator flutter, but the rudder problems persisted.
The Air Ministry test programme called for terminal velocity dives from
high altitude, which was an unusual requirement for such a large aircraft,
and on one 200 mph dive from over 16,000 ft, the rudder pedals began to
vibrate very badly. In an effort to hold the fluttering rudders Saint pushed
so hard with his feet on the pedals that he broke off the back of his seat.
Fortunately Basil Fielding, an inspector who was acting as test observer
on this flight, was equal to the situation and, by sitting back to back with
Saint and bracing himself with his feet against the bulkhead, he provided
the pilot with sufficient support to enable him to fly straight and level
again. When the speed fell, the flutter subsided a little and, although
J9832 was still yawing badly, Fielding with some difficulty went aft to
the rear gunner's position for a visual check on the rudders. He found that
the levers on the servo-tabs had bent over and allowed the operating cables

J9832 before its participation in the 1932 RAF Display at Hendon.
(*Courtesy William Green*)

198

to go slack. After this experience followed by a difficult landing at Hucclecote, design modifications were made in preparation for trials at Martlesham where three more dives were performed without incident.

In 1932, J9832 made a 12 min demonstration flight as part of the RAF Display at Hendon and stayed on there to participate in the SBAC Meeting two days later. Among the visitors was the Italian General Balbo and three of his staff who spent over an hour inspecting the TC.33 and making copious notes and drawings. During its visit to Martlesham in October 1932 for contractor's trials, J9832 recorded a maximum level speed of 141·5 mph at 13,000 ft.

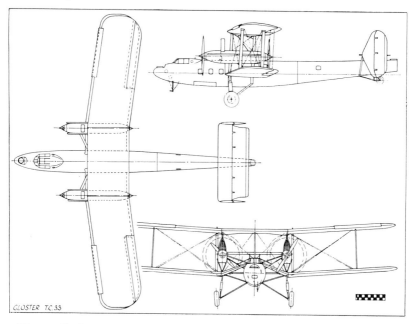

The preliminary report was not very encouraging; the controls were found to be light and effective and well harmonized, landing and taxi-ing were very easy even without the use of brakes, and the cockpit layout and standard of comfort drew warm praise. The take-off performance at full load was very poor, however, and it was found necessary to raise the tail early during the take-off run to enable the aircraft to become airborne in a safe distance. In fact full-load trials at Martlesham were delayed until the wind was blowing in a favourable direction. The landing gear also came in for criticism, as its characteristics varied considerably between take-off and landing loads.

Because of these unsatisfactory features it was considered that the TC.33 was unsuitable for use at RAF aerodromes, particularly those in hot climates overseas: thus Glosters' four-engined 'giant' was not ordered into production.

Description: Four-engine bomber/transport biplane. Metal construction with metal-covered fuselage and wings and fabric-covered tail unit.

Accommodation: Pilot, co-pilot and navigator in enclosed cabin. Front and rear gunners in open positions. Thirty troops or 12 stretchers in main cabin.

Powerplant: Two 580 hp Rolls-Royce Kestrel IIIS twelve-cylinder vee evaporatively-cooled units, driving 12 ft 6 in (3·8 m) diameter two-blade fixed-pitch tractor propellers, serial number A.5436 (port) and A.5435 (starboard), and two 580 hp Rolls-Royce Kestrel IIS twelve-cylinder vee evaporatively-cooled units, driving 11 ft 0 in (3·3 m) diameter two-blade fixed-pitch pusher propellers, serial number A.5437 (port) and A.5438 (starboard). Fuel: 774 gal (3,518 litres); oil 76 gal (345 litres).

Armament: One Lewis ·303 in machine-gun on mounting in both front and rear gunners' positions. 3,600 lb (1,633 kg) bomb load carried externally on racks below the centre fuselage.

Dimensions: Span (upper) 93 ft 11 in (28·5 m), (lower) 95 ft 1 in (28·9 m); length 80 ft 0 in (24·3 m); height 25 ft 8 in (7·8 m); wing area 2,493 sq ft (231 sq m); gap 13 ft 11¾ in (4·2 m); dihedral 2·5 deg; track 22 ft 6 in (6·8 m).

Weights: Empty 18,399 lb (8,346 kg); loaded 28,884 lb (13,101 kg).

Performance: Maximum speed 141·5 mph (227 km/h) at 13,000 ft (3,962 m); landing speed 64 mph (102 km/h); climb to 10,000 ft (3,048 m) in 24·5 min; service ceiling 19,100 ft (5,821 m); absolute ceiling 21,000 ft (6,400 m).

Production: One TC.33 built by Gloster Aircraft Co Ltd, Hucclecote Glos during 1931.

* Ref. A and AEE Report M/618.

S1705, the sole example of the TSR.38.

TSR.38

If specification S.9/30 had produced nothing more than two of the more shapely aircraft to emanate from the Gloster and Fairey factories, it could perhaps have justified itself; in the event, however, the issue of the specification caused Faireys to prepare an alternative design to their own S.9/30 entrant and, although the ugly duckling of the trio, this private venture prototype was ordered into production. Named Swordfish, it secured a place in naval aviation history.

The TSR.38 being flown by Howard Saint at Hucclecote.

Design work on Gloster Aircraft's contender for the order for a three-seat torpedo/spotter/reconnaissance aeroplane, bearing the company designation FS.36, began in November 1930. Powered initially by a 600 hp Rolls-Royce Kestrel IIMS engine, the FS.36 was a fabric-covered non-corrodible all-metal construction with steel wing spars of dumb-bell section, duralumin former ribs and high tensile steel compression ribs. The front fuselage was built up from square-section steel tube and the rear fuselage from round steel tube. In parallel with the other S.9/30 contender, the construction of only one prototype was put in hand, and, as the result of general retarding of aircraft development throughout the industry, work on the FS.36 was kept to a minimum with the effect that it was not until April 1932 that this aeroplane was flown for the first time.

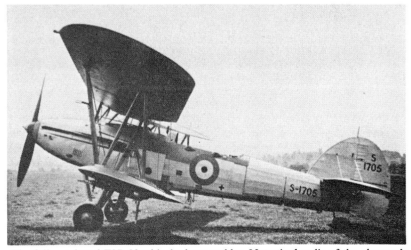

The fully-equipped TSR.38 with the large rudder. Note the handle of the observer's Lewis gun in the stowed position aft of the rear cockpit. (*Courtesy C. H. Barnes*)

Following initial flight trials at Hucclecote, the FS.36, serialled S1705, went to Martlesham for a very brief period during which it was flown in both the reconnaissance and torpedo-carrier configurations. In the former it achieved a top speed of 157 mph and the A and AEE pilot reported that it handled well between 90 and 115 mph; below this speed range the control response was sluggish and manoeuvrability was poor, but these improved at higher speeds. The report also contained good specimens of the observer's handwriting obtained during normal flying in S1705. The pilot's view was considered to be very good, but other faults, such as brake fade at the end of the landing run, were criticized heavily. Back at the factory, a number of modifications were embodied; they included redesigned mainplanes and control circuits and the installation of wing-mounted flotation gear to comply with specification S.15/33, a combination and amendment of the earlier M.1/30 and S.9/30, which was intended to produce a general purpose torpedo/spotter/reconnaissance aircraft.

Other work on S1705 continued in a desultory fashion and finally it reappeared in mid-1933 as the elegant TSR.38 with its exterior appearance very little changed from that of the FS.36. From a short-span centre section the single-bay outer wings, with N interplane struts, could be folded for operation on aircraft carriers. They were sharply sweptback some 10

The TSR.38, with a modified oil cooler under the nose, carrying a torpedo.
(*Courtesy F. G. Swanborough*)

deg and had equal dihedral of 4 deg; a pair of small radiators was mounted one each side below the outer end of the lower centre section which had 6 deg anhedral. The M.6 aerofoil section wings produced fairly thick surfaces and, with automatic slots fitted near the wingtips of the upper wings, gave the TSR.38 much improved lifting and low-speed handling characteristics. The main landing gear was of the divided type to accomodate an 18 in torpedo in crutches between each unit, which was a triangulated structure. A spatted tailwheel was an added refinement and a deck arrester hook was hinged below the rear fuselage. Three separate but closely grouped cockpits were provided for the crew; the pilot sat immediately beneath the large cut-out in the upper centre-section trailing edge, the

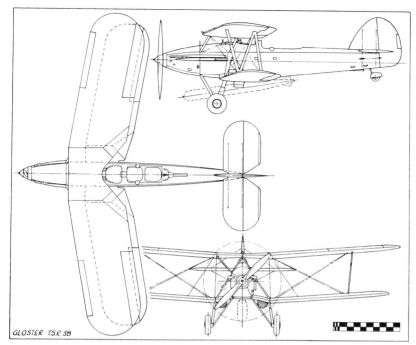

GLOSTER TSR 38

navigator sat behind him protected by a raised coaming which also incorporated the pilot's headrest, while the gunner occupied the rearmost cockpit to operate a Lewis ·303 in machine-gun mounted on a hinged ring and normally carried in the stowed position in the fuselage top decking.

Before returning to Martlesham, further flight trials were undertaken by the company, and as a result the Kestrel engine was replaced by a 690 hp Rolls-Royce Goshawk VIII. S1705 was then transferred to Gosport where it performed a series of dummy deck-landings prior to joining HMS *Courageous* in August 1934 for further test flights and various trials of deck handling equipment and procedures. With these completed, the TSR.38 was again delivered to Martlesham, and Report M.653 of June 1935 credits it with a top speed of 152 mph in the reconnaissance configuration, a climb to 10,000 ft in 9·75 min and an absolute ceiling of 22,000 ft. When carrying a torpedo the figures were 145 mph, 14·25 min and 17,000 ft respectively. By this time, however, Fairey's private venture project, now designated TSR.II, was well advanced on its own flight trials and Glosters' TSR.38 was thus abandoned.

TECHNICAL DATA

Description: Three-seat torpedo/spotter/reconnaissance biplane. Metal construction with metal and fabric covering.

Accommodation: Pilot and two crew in open cockpits.

Powerplant: One 600 hp Rolls-Royce Kestrel IIMS twelve-cylinder liquid-cooled vee, driving an 11 ft 0 in (3·3 m) diameter Watts two-blade fixed-pitch wooden propeller (FS.36).

203

One 690 Rolls-Royce Goshawk VIII twelve-cylinder geared and supercharged evaporatively-cooled vee, driving an 11 ft 5 in (3·4 m) diameter Watts two-blade fixed-pitch propeller (TSR.38).
Fuel 160 gal (727 litres); oil 7 gal (31 litres).

Armament: One fixed synchronized Vickers ·303 in machine-gun and one Lewis ·303 in machine-gun on mounting in rear cockpit. Crutches to carry one 18 in (45 cm) torpedo below the fuselage or 1,700 lb (771 kg) bomb load.

Dimensions: Span (spread) 46 ft 0 in (14 m), (folded) 17 ft 9 in (5·4 m); length 37 ft 4½ in (11·4 m); height 11 ft 6 in (3·5 m); wing area (FS.36) 580 sq ft (53·8 sq m), (TSR.38) 611 sq ft (56·6 sq m); aspect ratio 6·5; incidence 4 deg; dihedral 4 deg; sweepback 10 deg; stagger 3 ft 0 in (0·91 m); gap 6 ft 7 in (2 m); wing section 0·12 thickness/chord ratio M.6 on lower mainplane, and 0·10 thickness/chord ratio on upper mainplane.

Weights: Empty 4,340 lb (1,968 kg); loaded (reconnaissance) 7,100 lb (3,220 kg), (torpedo carrier) 8,038 lb (3,645 kg).

Performance:
(Reconnaissance) Maximum speed at sea level 152 mph (244 km/h); landing speed 52 mph (83 km/h); climb to 10,000 ft (3,048 m) 9·75 min; service ceiling 20,000 ft (6,096 m).
(Torpedo carrier) Maximum speed at sea level 145 mph (233 km/h); landing speed 57 mph (91 km/h); climb to 10,000 ft (3,048 m) 14·25 min; service ceiling 15,600 ft (4,754 m).

Production: One TSR.38 built by Gloster Aircraft Co Ltd, Hucclecote, Glos. during 1931–32.

The SS.37, as originally built, in August 1934.

Gladiator

The Gladiator, built as a private venture to satisfy the requirements of specification F.7/30, was the last and most advanced of the RAF's biplane fighters. Cast in the classic Folland mould, it epitomized this class of aeroplane built between the wars, yet it was almost outdated by the time it entered squadron service. Nevertheless, the Gladiator bridged the gap between the conventional open-cockpit two-gun fighters and the more sophisticated multi-gun monoplanes which so quickly succeeded it.

Clearly a development of the earlier Gauntlet, the Gladiator was born almost by default and was the last of the F.7/30 contenders to be built. This specification issued in the late autumn of 1930 was possibly the most

204

Another view of the SS.37 showing the original engine cowling, and discs on the internally-sprung wheels.

important formulated by the Air Ministry up to that time, calling for a single-seat day interceptor and night fighter with a maximum speed of over 250 mph and an armament of four Vickers guns. It required a great improvement over current fighters in rate of climb, ceiling and manoeuvrability together with a low wing-loading, good vision for the pilot and no exhaust glare, in order to fit the aircraft for its night fighter rôle. The specification also laid great stress on the use of the Rolls-Royce Goshawk, the evaporative-cooled development of the earlier and well proven Kestrel, but its manufacturers were to find that this development work was very much more difficult than they had imagined, and in the end the Goshawk failed because of the impractical nature of its cooling system which was complicated, heavy and vulnerable to enemy fire. Nevertheless, F.7/30 represented an unprecedented leap forward in fighter specifications which could well have daunted many design teams, but it clearly indicated that Britain was aware of the need to re-equip the Royal Air Force with aircraft

Although G.37 was built largely with Gauntlet components, it closely resembled the definitive Gladiator. (*Courtesy H. S. Folland*)

fully capable of coping with any hostile aircraft which might conceivably confront them. As such it was welcomed enthusiastically by the major aircraft manufacturers who, with the promise of big production orders for the successful design, were soon preparing designs to meet the new requirements. Hawker, Fairey, Bristol, Westland and Supermarine had all submitted designs embodying the Goshawk while Vickers and Bristol—with a second F.7/30 aspirant—used a radial engine.

At Hucclecote Glosters were too heavily engaged with Gauntlet development to take very much more than a transient paper interest in the F.7/30 specification. However in 1933 the main effort of Folland and his team was directed toward the improvement of the basic design of the Gauntlet, so that its already good performance could be improved still further. The changes envisaged were the use of single-bay wings with heavier spars and a cantilever landing gear strut to take advantage of Dowty's internally sprung wheel. By discarding two pairs of interplane struts, their bracing wires and fittings, two landing gear struts and an axle spreader-bar, it was anticipated that an extra 15–20 mph would be added to the top speed: in addition the Bristol Mercury ME.30 radial engine was developed sufficiently to provide 700 bhp, and Folland confidently expected his new fighter to have a top speed of 250 mph. Yet even these improvements were insufficient to enable it fully to meet the F.7/30 specification for, like the Gauntlet, the armament was still only two fuselage-mounted guns; however, in February 1934, Bristols indicated that their Mercury ME.35, delivering 800 bhp, would be ready in time to go into production airframes, and this promise of extra power enabled the Gloster project to carry two more guns without detriment to its top speed and so made possible its entry as a contender in the F.7/30 contest.

In order to speed the private venture production of the prototype, designated SS.37, a Gauntlet fuselage was modified to embody the new landing gear, a surface oil cooler on the starboard forward decking and a small streamlined fairing behind the pilot's headrest in the open cockpit. The Gauntlet tail unit and spatted tailwheel were retained, and a 645 bhp Mercury VIS engine was initially selected for this airframe, but ultimately a 530 bhp Mercury IV in a Gauntlet cowling was fitted when it was flown for the first time on 12 September, 1934. The pilot was Glosters' P. E. G. Sayer, who had transferred from Hawkers following their purchase of the G.A.C. Initially the top speed attained was only 236 mph, but on 28 October, by which time the Mercury VIS had been fitted, the SS.37 reached 242 mph at 11,500 ft carrying two fuselage-mounted Vickers guns and two drum-fed Lewis guns beneath the lower wings.

Trials continued at Hucclecote and Martlesham with only minor modifications being made to the airframe, and on 3 April, 1935, this prototype SS.37 was transferred to the Air Ministry bearing the serial K5200. In June an improved version was proposed by Glosters having the more powerful 830 bhp Mercury IX engine, a fully enclosed cockpit with sliding canopy, redesigned tail unit and landing gear, Vickers Mk.V guns

Still in its original form, but serialled K5200 for Martlesham trials, the SS.37 bears the Hendon Experimental Aircraft Park numeral 1 on the fuselage nose.

and embodying the Hawker-type construction. The top speed was calculated to be in excess of 252 mph at 14,000 ft and the landing speed was 48 mph. Spurred on by the urgent requirements of the RAF's Expansion Programme, the Air Ministry's formalities were completed very rapidly and within a fortnight of the receipt of Glosters' tender, a production specification F.14/35 was prepared and issued, 23 production aircraft were ordered, and on 1 July, 1935, the aircraft was named Gladiator. The following day K5200 returned to Hucclecote from Martlesham, where it had completed its initial evaluation programme, and on 4 July it flew to Hendon, bearing the Experimental Aircraft Park No.1, to take part in the RAF Display. Following its return to the factory, K5200 was modified to bring it up to near Gladiator I standard and an 830 bhp Mercury IX engine with a slightly heavier Watts wooden propeller of coarser pitch was fitted.

Because of the unreliability of the Vickers machine-gun, the Air Ministry had evaluated a number of British and foreign guns with the result that licensed production of the US-built Colt ·300 in gun, under the name Browning and with a ·303 in calibre, was planned for BSA; thus Glosters decided to make provision for its use in later versions of the Gladiator and to replace the under-wing mounted Lewis guns with the greatly improved Vickers Mk.V guns until BSA's new Browning gun was available.

Flight testing of the modified K5200 began again at Hucclecote in September 1935—by which time a further 180 Gladiators had been ordered, with instructions to Glosters that all deliveries to the squadrons should be completed before the end of 1937. For these renewed trials, a Fairey Reed three-blade fixed-pitch metal propeller was fitted as an alternative to the Watts unit, and on 23 October, 1935, K5200, powered by a Mercury IX engine having a standard ·5:1 ratio reduction gear, flew back to Martlesham for comparative trials. On landing there the port cantilever leg collapsed when the fulcrum pin on the longeron sheared off. The subsequently lengthy and exhaustive trials, which followed the rapid repair work on K5200's damaged lower wing, revealed that the metal propeller had little to offer over the two-blade wooden type. Martlesham Heath Interim Report M/666B/Int.2, dated 10 September, 1937, described comparative tests carried out with Gladiator I, K7964, with a 10 ft 6 in diameter Fairey Reed propeller driven by a Mercury IX delivering 840 bhp

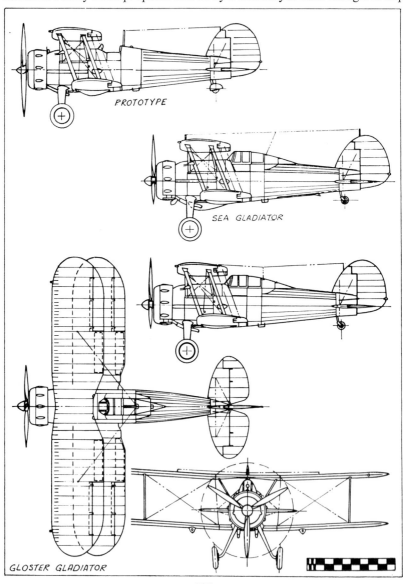

PROTOTYPE

SEA GLADIATOR

GLOSTER GLADIATOR

208

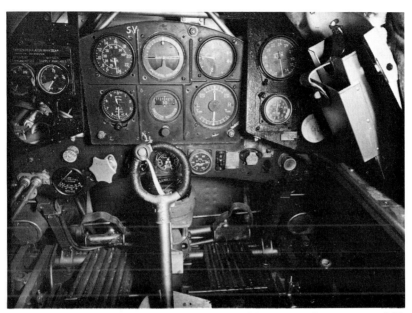

Gladiator cockpit. Compare this layout with that of the Meteor shown on page 266.

at 14,000 ft and with a ·572:1 ratio reduction gear, against K5200 flying with a standard Mercury IX having its normal ·5:1 ratio reduction gear. This was one of many tests performed with the main object of achieving smoother running of the Mercury engine, during which K5200 was flown with both the three-blade metal propeller and the two-blade wooden type. With the Fairey Reed unit, it had a maximum speed of 253 mph at 14,500 ft and the engine performed satisfactorily up to 32,000 ft, but with the Watts propeller its top speed was 248 mph at 14,600 ft. K7964 reached 245 mph at 14,200 ft and had a service ceiling of 32,000 ft. As a result of these trials and others on K8049, during which it was concluded that the increased gear ratio and two-blade wooden propeller reduced the take-off ground run by some 55 yards but also cut the maximum speed, it was decided in future to use the three-blade metal propeller and the ·572:1 gear ratio to meet specification F.36/37 as Gladiator Mk.II.

Gladiator I

While these trials and their resultant modifications were in hand, production of the first batch of aircraft was being undertaken, with the manufacture of all major components being completed before final assembly began. Initial check flights on the first three production aircraft K6129–K6131 were undertaken in January 1937; the first of the batch was taken on RAF charge on 16 February and the remainder in little over the two following weeks.

No.72 Squadron, formed at Tangmere on 22 February, was the first of nine squadrons to get their Gladiators during the year. Most of the remaining aircraft in the first batch went to No.3 Squadron at Kenley in April 1937 to replace their Bulldogs. On 27 April, No.54 Squadron at Hornchurch was the first to re-equip with Browning-armed Gladiators, with No.74 following suit soon afterwards. In the following month No.80

K6131, the third production Gladiator I, with the enclosed cockpit.

Squadron forsook the Gauntlets, re-equipped with Gladiators and then spent nearly a year at Henlow in preparation for service in the Middle and Near East where it earned a great reputation in combat. Other squadrons re-equipped during 1937 were No.65 at Hornchurch, who began on 1 June, Nos.73 and 87 at Debden on 8 June and No.56 at North Weald beginning during July. In addition a number of aircraft were flying in a variety of trials at Hucclecote, Martlesham and other establishments. Through the rest of the year these squadrons took part in air exercises and the RAF Display at Hendon; No.87 was placed second in the Sassoon Trophy competition in October, and in September, with the Air Ministry playing the part of gracious host, a party of senior Luftwaffe officers including Maj-Gen Ernst Udet, Lieut-Gen Stumpff and Gen E. Milch inspected Nos.54 and 65 Squadrons as part of a tour of RAF units in Britain.

During the winter months of 1937–38 a number of crashes marred the records of some squadrons; the Gladiator was also criticized as a gun

Gladiator Is of No.72 Sqdn, RAF, at Farnborough during an exercise in 1937. These aircraft were part of the first production batch. (*Courtesy William Green*)

platform because in a dive overspeeding of the Watts two-blade propeller caused vibration, and pilots found that they were unable to hold their sight firmly on a target. By March 1938 most production Gladiator Is were being fitted with the three-blade propeller—but by this time Hurricanes were appearing in more squadrons. No.3 converted to the new monoplane fighter in March and April, and its Gladiators were crated ready for despatch by sea to Egypt. Gladiators replaced by Hurricanes were occasionally used to re-equip Gauntlet squadrons, although on 10 July at the Villacoublay Air Display three Gladiators of No.87 Squadron flew tied-together formation aerobatic sequences with cord connecting their interplane struts.

As the autumn approached, the five remaining fully operational Gladiator squadrons prepared to meet enemy air attacks on the United Kingdom; No.25, flying camouflaged aircraft carrying the large white squadron letters ZK on the fuselage sides, moved to Northolt as part of London's defences, with Nos.54 and 65 Squadrons performing a similar

A Gladiator I in 1939 fighter camouflage. Red and blue roundels were carried, and the undersurface of the port and starboard mainplanes was black and white respectively. (*Courtesy William Green*)

211

rôle at Hornchurch. No.607 was the first Auxiliary Air Force squadron to get Gladiators, its first aircraft, K6137, being acquired at the end of September, with others arriving in October on transfer from No.25 Squadron.

From about the middle of 1938 in the Middle East, Gladiator Is, flying from their base at Ramleh in Palestine, were regularly used on operations against Arab marauders, and when war began in September 1939 four squadrons of Gladiators and one of Gauntlets formed the main air defences of this region.

Operating in the defence of Aden, No.94 Squadron's Gladiators were used for a variety of tasks including interception, ground attack and even anti-shipping patrols during which, on 18 June, 1940, they were instrumental in effecting the surrender and capture of an Italian submarine, the *Galileo Galilei*. Later, in May 1941, this squadron moved north into the Suez Canal Zone and while there, awaiting its re-equipment with Hurricanes, was ordered to the defence of RAF Habbaniyah in Iraq.

Three other Gladiator squadrons plus a few ageing Gauntlets were available for the defence of Egypt when Italy entered the war in June 1940, and these were soon in combat with the Regia Aeronautica, scoring many victories. Within six weeks, No.33 Squadron's Gladiators had destroyed 58 enemy aircraft in the air and on the ground and the squadron had lost only four pilots and eight aircraft.

In Greece and Crete however, Nos.33, 80 and 112 Squadrons lost many more aircraft in winning a number of air battles with Italian and German formations and ultimately withdrew to Egypt.

Most renowned of all the Gladiators' operations in the Mediterranean theatre was the dogged defence of Malta by Sea Gladiators, about which much has already been written, with a good deal of literary licence being taken over the part played by *Faith*, *Hope* and *Charity*. Nevertheless the Sea Gladiators based on the island acquitted themselves magnificently in operations against the Regia Aeronautica until reinforced by Hurricanes,

The most notable Gladiator pilot was unquestionably Flt Lieut M. T. St. J. Pattle, DFC, a South African, who was credited with more than 30 enemy aircraft destroyed, a large proportion of them while flying Gladiators, including five shot down in one sortie against Italian formations over the Albanian frontier on 28 February, 1941.

Nearer home, Nos.607 and 615 Squadrons began their operations from Merville in France during November 1939 as part of the British Expeditionary Force but lost almost all their aircraft in the air or on the ground during the desperate days of May 1940. The achievements of No.263 Squadron, when operating off the frozen Lake Lesjaskog and from Aandalsnes in Norway in support of British and Norwegian ground forces, are among the most outstanding of the war. After all its 18 Gladiators were lost in the period 22–26 April, 1940, the squadron returned to the United Kingdom to re-equip and on 14 May, with a further 18 Gladiators, it sailed back to Norway in the aircraft carrier *Glorious*. Eight

One of the first batch of four Sea Gladiators taken on charge by the RAF in Malta in April 1940, N5519 retains part of its naval colour scheme and the arrester hook cradle and has a Fairey three-blade metal propeller. (*Imperial War Museum*)

days later it was operational again, flying no less than 54 sorties during the first day. One classic engagement occurred on 2 June when Plt Off L. R. Jacobsen, DFC, attacked by eight German aircraft, forced one Ju 88 to fly into a mountain, destroyed three He 111s and almost certainly destroyed a fourth. The squadron was ultimately evacuated from Narvik on 7 June on board *Glorious* but on the next day the carrier was intercepted and sunk by the German warships *Scharnhorst* and *Gneisenau*, and the entire squadron, all the aircraft and most of the pilots were lost. Only N5641 remains as a reminder of this gallant campaign, and at the time of writing it stands in a dismantled state inside a specially built hut at Dovre in Norway.

Gladiator II

Because of the increased demand for Gladiators in the Middle East following the Palestine troubles in 1938, 24 of the last batch of 28 Gladiator Is were specially modified for service in this theatre during January–February 1939. The work was undertaken at RAF Shawbury by No.27 Maintenance Unit after their initial delivery had been delayed by Glosters to allow certain structural modifications to be embodied. As recorded earlier, these changes detailed by the Air Staff in specification F.36/37 included the use of the 830 bhp Mercury VIIIA which was among the engines built under the Ministry of Aircraft Production's shadow factory scheme. It was designated Mercury VIIIAS and had Hobson mixture control boxes and a partly automatic boost control carburettor. Improved cockpit instrumentation was flight tested in a Gladiator I, K7919, and included a blind-flying panel carrying a Smith's airspeed indicator, Kollsman altimeter, Sperry artificial horizon and directional gyro, Hughes rate of climb indicator and a Reid and Sigrist turn and slip indicator. A vacuum

213

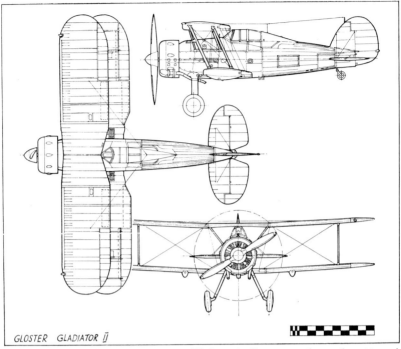

GLOSTER GLADIATOR II

pump, desert equipment storage, a Vokes air filter over the carburettor air intake and electric starting equipment were also fitted.

In this form with the Mercury VIIIAS driving a 10 ft 6 in diameter Fairey three-blade metal fixed-pitch propeller, the aircraft was designated Gladiator II. Despite the increase in loaded weight the maximum speed, climb and airfield performance all showed a noticeable improvement over those of the earlier mark; in addition both the range and endurance of the Gladiator II were increased. During 1938 Glosters received an initial production order for 50 Gladiator IIs, 38 of which were modified as Sea Gladiators (Interim) as noted below. It was soon apparent, however, that this quantity was insufficient to meet the requirements of both the Air Ministry and the Admiralty and, later in 1938, a major order for 300 aircraft, both Gladiator IIs and Sea Gladiators, was placed with Glosters.

Sea Gladiator

During the 1930s naval aviation was sadly neglected by the Admiralty and little or no attention was paid to the development of fleet fighters. Thus, in 1937, finding its fighter units equipped with the out-of-date Nimrods, the Admiralty approached the Air Ministry with a request for them to suggest which aircraft, already in service with the RAF or under development, would be most suitable for conversion for use by the Royal Navy. As a stop-gap the Fairey P.4/34 project was acquired, and the production aircraft, named Fulmar, was ordered. Because of the Gladiator's well-established production programme, it was nominated by the Air Ministry as being suitable for conversion for sea-going service, and in March 1938 Glosters received an Admiralty order for Sea Gladiators. These aircraft, N2265–N2302, were the first 38 Gladiator IIs off the production line and were retained at Hucclecote for airframe modifications which included a tubular cross-member between the two lower longerons and pivot points for the V arrester hook. The Royal Navy's TR.9 radio and an airspeed indicator reading in knots were also fitted.

All 38 aircraft, designated Sea Gladiator (Interim), were taken on charge during December 1938 and 13 were delivered to the naval air station at Worthy Down for initial training of squadron pilots and instructors, while the remaining 25 aircraft went to Donibristle, Hatston (Orkney) and Eastleigh.

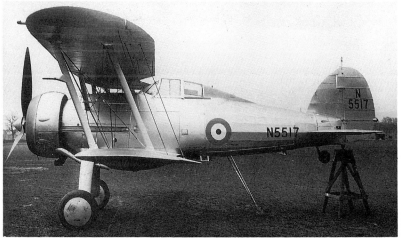

A standard Sea Gladiator, N5517, demonstrating the operation of the deck arrester hook. In 1939 this aircraft went to No.801 Sqdn for trials in HMS *Courageous*.
(*Imperial War Museum*)

The main Sea Gladiator order was placed with Glosters in June 1938 after further modifications had been agreed. These included emergency dinghy stowage, deletion of the internal collector boxes for spent ammunition cases and links, extension of the case chutes to jettison the cases and links clear of the dinghy, and the installation of catapult strong-points. The order was for 60 aircraft out of the main production batch of 300 Gladiators IIs, all built by Glosters and delivered before the middle of February 1939. During January–February the first production Gladiator I, K6129, was flown at Martlesham and Worthy Down on development trials for the navalized Gladiator, and on 19 April it was cleared for gun firing with the new installation. The three-blade metal propeller proven in trials with earlier Gladiators was adopted as standard on all Royal Navy Sea Gladiators.

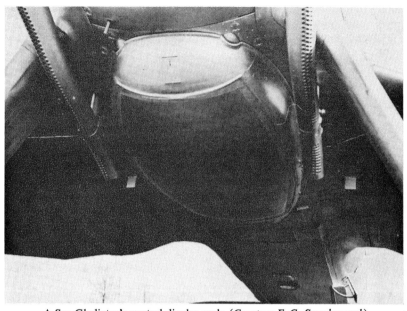

A Sea Gladiator's ventral dinghy pack. (*Courtesy F. G. Swanborough*)

Four Sea Gladiators began sea trials in *Courageous* in March 1939 and the first squadrons embarked soon afterwards were Nos.801 and, in *Glorious*, 802. On 3 September a total of 12 Sea Gladiators (Interim) and 42 Sea Gladiator IIs were on Admiralty charge and remained there until May 1941, when Sea Gladiators were finally withdrawn from front-line operations. The type saw service in Norway, the Mediterranean and the North Sea with No.804, No.813 in *Eagle*, and No.885 Squadrons fighting the Luftwaffe and Regia Aeronautica in many stirring and valiant engagements. Thereafter numerous Airfield Defence and Station Flights continued to use Sea Gladiators, including RNBS Yeovilton which operated them until 1943 and possibly even later.

Meteorological Gladiators

Operational flying ended for the Gladiator with the interception and destruction of an Italian bomber over Libya by No.6 Squadron's aircraft on 26 September, 1941, but Gladiators continued to perform many other duties in RAF service until 1945. An important task undertaken was weather observation flights from a number of airfields in the United Kingdom and overseas, and no fewer than 12 Meteorological Flights— Nos.1401, 1402, 1403, 1411, 1412, 1413, 1414, 1415, 1560, 1561, 1562, 1563—and No.521 Met. Calibration Squadron flew Gladiators. The last of these vitally important weather flights was made by a No.1402 Flight aircraft on 7 January, 1945, from RAF Ballyhalbert in Northern Ireland.

216

K6143, a Gladiator I, with armament removed and meteorological equipment mounted between the interplane struts. (*Imperial War Museum*)

Gladiators also flew on airfield defence, communications and radar calibration duties and served on several flying training schools and No.1 School of Army Co-operation until the middle of 1941.

In February 1948, L8032, the last of the final production batch of 28 Gladiator Is built during 1937, was bought by Glosters, together with N5903, a Gladiator II, after both aircraft had gathered dust in various parts of the factory for nearly four years after the cancellation of an order to convert them for meteorological flying. One aircraft, L8032, subsequently was delivered to Air Service Training at Hamble in November 1950, while N5903 went to their Ansty establishment; they were intended for use as ground instructional airframes. In 1951 when Ansty closed they were acquired at a 'peppercorn' price by V. H. Bellamy of Flightways who retained the two-blade wooden propeller and the reduction gear of the Gladiator I's Mercury IX engine and fitted them to the Mercury VIIIAS taken from the Gladiator II. The new engine/propeller combination was

The last airworthy Gladiator, with civil registration, before refurbishing by Gloster apprentices.

217

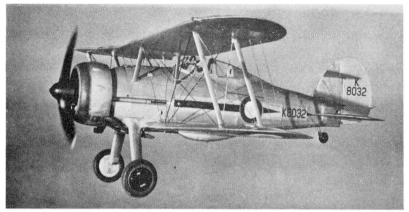

On delivery to the Shuttleworth Trust, the last airworthy Gladiator complete with armament and radio, and bearing No.72 Sqdn, RAF, markings with a spurious serial number.

installed in L8032's airframe, the aircraft was registered G-AMRK and Bellamy flew it in several displays. In August 1953 it was again bought by Glosters and was flown with civil markings until 1956 when it was decided to restore L8032 to operational trim. It was rewired, fitted with a TR.9 wireless, an original pattern gun-sight and four guns and finally, with Air Ministry permission, it was repainted in the markings of No.72 Squadron (one of the first two squadrons which flew Gladiators) and given the serial K8032 previously carried by an earlier production Gladiator. It was flown by Gloster pilots at a number of displays and was finally handed over to the Shuttleworth Trust on 7 November, 1960.

Latvian Gladiator I

During March 1937 a Latvian air mission visited the United Kingdom with the aim of buying British aircraft for the Latvian Air Force. The mission saw the Gladiator at Hucclecote and on 27 May placed an order for 26 Gladiator Is fitted with four Vickers Mk.VM 7·7 mm guns. These aircraft were shipped to Latvia during August–November. The cost of these Gladiators, plus three Hawker Hinds ordered in January 1938, was £120,000 and the money was raised by a State lottery.

Lithuanian Gladiator I

The second overseas customer for Gladiators was Lithuania which ordered 14 aircraft only a few days after the receipt of the Latvian order by Glosters. After being test flown at Hucclecote they were dismantled, crated and shipped during October and November 1937 and were re-assembled at air bases at Vilna and Kaunas. Gladiators from Latvia and Lithuania are known to have flown bearing Russian markings following the seizure of these two countries by the USSR in 1940.

218

This Latvian Gladiator I was among the first batch to be delivered.
(*Courtesy C. H. Barnes*)

One of Lithuania's fourteen Gladiator Is. (*Courtesy C. H. Barnes*)

Norwegian Gladiators 421 and 423 taxi-ing before take-off from Steinsfjorden on 9 April, 1940. (*Courtesy William Green*)

Norwegian Gladiator I and II

Norwegian interest in the Gladiator began to be evinced in April 1937 and initial discussions were centred round the supply of six complete aircraft to be followed by licensed production in Norway. These plans were modified to provide for the initial supply of 12 aircraft and when six Mark Is had been delivered to Fornebu Airport, near Oslo, on 15 July, 1938, the contract was revised and six Gladiator IIs, the last to be built, were switched from the Air Ministry to Norway to meet the contract. These aircraft, armed with four Colt ·300 in guns, took part in the defence of Oslo against the Luftwaffe air attacks and, although all 12 were subsequently lost either in the air or on the ground (at least two broke through the ice of the frozen lake from which they were operating and were abandoned), they destroyed at least four enemy aircraft.

A J8A Gladiator II of Flygflottilj 8, Royal Swedish Air Force, in the winter colour scheme of 1939. (*Courtesy William Green*)

Swedish Gladiator I and II

In 1937 Royal Swedish Air Force expansion plans included the purchase of 55 Gladiators of which the first 37 were Gladiator Is (redesignated J8s) powered by 640 bhp Mercury engines driving Watts two-blade wooden propellers. Deliveries began in June 1937 and about nine months later Glosters received a further order for 18 Gladiator IIs (redesignated J8As) powered by 740 bhp Mercury VII engines licence-built in Sweden and driving three-blade metal propellers. Forty-five aircraft were allocated to the three squadrons forming Kungl Svea Flygflottilj–No.8 Fighter Wing, and ten were held in reserve. The Wing was formed on 1 July, 1938, under the command of Överste E. G. Gärdin and was based at Barkarby near Stockholm. These Gladiators first went into action in January 1940 as part of a Swedish volunteer force which aided Finland in the war with

220

GL270 was one of the Gladiator IIs sold to Finland in December 1939 which retained its wheeled undercarriage. (*Courtesy William Green*)

Russia. Many of the aircraft were fitted with ski-undercarriages designed in Sweden and underwing bomb-racks to carry eight lightweight bombs, and for more than two months, during which three Gladiators were lost, they operated very successfully against Russian air attacks despite the severe winter weather.

Gladiators remained in frontline service with the Swedish Air Force until the spring of 1941.

Finnish Gladiator II

Thirty Gladiator IIs, all of them ex-RAF aircraft, were supplied for use by the Finnish Air Force during December 1939–February 1940. It was recorded that these aircraft formed part of the fighter defences of southern Finland during the Russo-Finnish war.

A Finnish Gladiator, with ski landing gear, taxi-ing on snow. (*Courtesy William Green*)

221

Belgian Gladiator I

The scramble by overseas customers seeking to buy Gladiators was continued by an order from Belgium for 22 Gladiator Is with deliveries beginning on 12 September, 1937, and continuing through until May 1938. During this period there were protracted discussions between the Belgian Government and Glosters for the licensed production of the Gladiator by Avions Fairey in Belgium but this plan never materialized. The Belgian Air Force operated them until at least the middle of May 1940.

Belgian Gladiators on a delivery flight from Hucclecote. Note the Belgian markings and the Class B serial numbers. (*Courtesy Rolls-Royce*)

Chinese Gladiator I

In October 1937 when China and Japan were at war, the Chinese Government ordered 36 Gladiator Is. These aircraft were to be delivered by sea to Hongkong where they would be erected at Kai Tak aerodrome by a team of Gloster engineers. In the event, due to diplomatic considerations, the crated aircraft were taken by rail and then by junk up the Pearl River to Canton and delivered to Tien Ho aerodrome where three or four were assembled in the open despite regular attacks by Japanese aircraft. The remainder of the first 20 Gladiators were assembled in December 1937 and January 1938 on a variety of open-air sites, including a roadway, White Cloud aerodrome and a graveyard, and on completion were immediately flown about 300 miles away to be out of reach of further Japanese bombing and where training could continue without interruption. Tien Ho was used again on several occasions for the assembly of the remaining 16 Gladiators which took part in the defence of Siuchow later in 1938.

222

Four Gladiator Is were supplied to Eire. They are seen at Baldonnel in the initial colour scheme which underwent two subsequent changes. (*Eire Department of Defence*)

Irish Gladiator I

In 1938 the Irish Army Air Corps received four new Gladiator Is, ordered during the previous year, which were delivered by air from Hucclecote to Baldonnel where they served until 1941. These Gladiators were the first of a number of British aircraft acquired by the Government of Eire as part of a re-equipment programme for its Army Air Corps.

Greek Gladiator I and II

Two Gladiator Is were bought from Glosters in January 1938 by Zarparkis Homogenos, a Greek business man, who presented them to the nation for use by the Royal Hellenic Air Force. The two aircraft complete with a quantity of spares and ground equipment cost £9,400. Towards the end of 1940 arrangements were concluded between the British and Greek Governments for the transfer of a number of RAF aircraft to the Royal Hellenic Air Force and, beginning in December 1940, a total of 13 Gladiators were given up by Nos.33 and 80 Squadrons and a further four were transferred from RAF Middle East stocks.

Portuguese Gladiator II

In February 1939 the Portuguese Government placed an order with Glosters for Gladiator IIs and to meet its request for early delivery 15 standard RAF aircraft were switched from an Air Ministry contract. The Portuguese also expressed an interest in purchasing a further 30 Gladiator IIs but this order never matured. G5 was test flown at A and AEE Martlesham in July 1939.

223

One of the Portuguese Gladiator IIs, with a Mercury VIIIA engine and Fairey three-blade metal propeller, showing the radio installation.

Three Portuguese Gladiator IIs at Hucclecote in 1939. This is an enlargement of part of the picture on page 35.

This Portuguese Gladiator II was test flown at Martlesham in 1939. An outside thermometer was carried on the port rear interplane strut. (*Courtesy William Green*)

224

An Egyptian Air Force Gladiator I fitted with a filter on the carburettor air intake. (*Courtesy F. G. Swanborough*)

Egyptian Gladiator I and II

Eighteen Gladiator Is modified up to Mk.II standard were handed over to the Royal Egyptian Air Force by the RAF during March–April 1939. A number of these aircraft were later taken back on charge by RAF Middle East and were subsequently modified again for use by Meteorological Flights. In 1941, 27 Gladiator IIs were similarly transferred to the Egyptian Air Force and several of these were also taken back on RAF charge.

Iraqi Gladiator I and II

The Royal Iraqi Air Force took over nine Gladiator Is during 1940–42, all transferred from RAF Middle East, some of which were returned. In March 1944 five Gladiator IIs from the same source were handed over to the Iraqi Air Force as replacements and at least two of these were flying from Mosul as late as 1949.

South African Gladiator II

In January 1939 one Gladiator I, K7922, was transferred from No.72 Squadron RAF to the South African Air Force for evaluation, and 11 Gladiator IIs were subsequently handed over by the RAF beginning in April 1941. These aircraft were used by Nos.1, 2 and 3 Squadrons, SAAF, for training and operational flying in the Middle East and East Africa.

225

TECHNICAL DATA

Description: Single-seat day fighter biplane. Metal construction with metal and fabric covering.

Accommodation: Pilot in enclosed cockpit.

Powerplant: One 530 hp Bristol Mercury IV nine-cylinder air-cooled radial, driving a two-blade fixed-pitch wooden propeller (SS.37).

One 645 hp Bristol Mercury VIS nine-cylinder air-cooled radial, driving a two-blade fixed-pitch propeller (SS.37).

One 830 hp Bristol Mercury IX nine-cylinder air-cooled radial, driving a 10 ft 9 in (3·22 m) diameter Watts two-blade fixed-pitch wooden propeller (Mk.I).

One 830 hp Bristol Mercury VIIIA or VIIIAS nine-cylinder air-cooled radial (delivering 840 hp with manual boost override), driving 10 ft 6 in (3·19 m) diameter Fairey three-blade fixed-pitch metal propeller (Mk.II and Sea Gladiator).

Fuel (Mk.I and II) 70 gal (318 litres), (Sea Gladiator) 83 gal (377 litres); oil 5 gal (22·7 litres).

Armament: Two fixed synchronized Browning ·303 in machine-guns mounted in troughs in the fuselage sides and two machine-guns mounted under the lower mainplanes firing outside the propeller disc. (First 60 Gladiator Is had Lewis ·303 in machine-guns under the lower mainplanes with 97-round drums of ammunition. The next ten aircraft had Vickers K gas-operated ·303 in machine-guns under the lower mainplanes with 100-round drums of ammunition.) 600-round box of ammunition for each fuselage gun and provision for a 400-round box for each lower mainplane gun. Latvian and Lithuanian Gladiator Is were fitted with four Vickers Mk.VM 7·7 mm machine-guns. Belgian and Chinese Gladiator Is were fitted with Vickers Mk.V machine-guns. Norwegian Gladiator IIs were fitted with Colt· 303 in machine-guns.

Dimensions: Span 32 ft 3 in (9·8 m); length 27 ft 5 in (8·2 m); height (Mk.I) 11 ft 9 in (3·57 m), (Mk.II and Sea Gladiator) 11 ft 7 in (3·52 m); wing area 323 sq ft (29·9 sq m); track 7 ft 2½ in (2·1 m).

	SS.37	Mk.I	Mk.II	Sea Gladiator
Weights:				
Empty	3,062 lb	3,217 lb	3,444 lb	3,554 lb
	(1,398 kg)	(1,458 kg)	(1,562 kg)	(1,612 kg)
Loaded	4,339 lb	4,594 lb	4,864 lb	5,020 lb
	(1,967 kg)	(2,082 kg)	(2,206 kg)	(2,272 kg)
Performance:				
Maximum speed	236 mph at	253 mph at	257 mph at	253 mph at
	10,000 ft	14,500 ft	14,600 ft	14,600 ft
	(380 km/h at	(407 km/h at	(414 km/h at	(407 km/h at
	3,048 m)	4,419 m)	4,449 m)	4,449 m)
Stalling speed	51 mph	53 mph	54 mph	55 mph
	(82 km/h)	(85 km/h)	(87 km/h)	(88 km/h)
Climb to	10,000 ft	10,000 ft	10,000 ft	10,000 ft
	(3,048 m)	(3,048 m)	(3,048 m)	(3,048 m)
in	5·25 min	4·75 min	4·5 min	4·75 min
Service ceiling	27,000 ft	32,800 ft	33,500 ft	32,300 ft
	(8,229 m)	(9,996 m)	(11,570 m)	(9,844 m)

Production: A total of 747 Gladiators produced by Gloster Aircraft Co Ltd, Hucclecote, Glos. during 1934–39 as follows:

One prototype (1934).

378 Gladiator Mk.I production aircraft (1935–38).

38 Sea Gladiator (Interim) production aircraft (1937–38).

60 Sea Gladiator production aircraft (1938–39).

270 Gladiator Mk.II production aircraft (1938–39).

Allocation: See Individual Aircraft Notes, pages 354–357.

K5604, one of two F.5/34s built, was Glosters' first monoplane fighter to fly.
(Imperial War Museum)

F.5/34

Known unofficially as the Gloster 'Unnamed Fighter', the F.5/34 was the
last of H.P. Folland's designs for the company on which he began work
early in 1935 in close collaboration with H. E. Preston.

The F.5/34 specification, which ultimately produced the Hurricane and
Spitfire, was a most ambitious step forward in fighter design requirements,
calling as it did for a single-seat aircraft with the heavy armament of six
or eight Browning machine-guns each with 300 rounds of ammunition to
give a 15 sec duration of fire, retractable landing gear, enclosed cockpit
and pilot's oxygen supply, maximum speeds of 275 mph at 15,000 ft and
265 mph at 20,000 ft, a service ceiling of 33,000 ft and a 90 min endurance.
Thus in this one specification were combined all the far reaching and
advanced design features which were calculated to step up the performance
and operational efficiency of what were to be the RAF's first generation
monoplane fighters.

The Gloster F.5/34's fuselage was a monocoque structure built up from
light, fabricated oval-section rings with duralumin skinning. Heavier-gauge
rings provided strong-point attachments for the mainplane and tailplane
and for the engine bearers. The mainplane was built in one piece with the
light-alloy spars running through from tip to tip and ribs made from
channelling with steel and light-alloy tube struts. Duralumin stressed-skin
was used on the mainplane and tail unit with fabric-covered Frise ailerons,
rudder and elevators. The split trailing-edge flaps were all-metal and
hydraulically operated. A large braced tubular-steel crash arch was

227

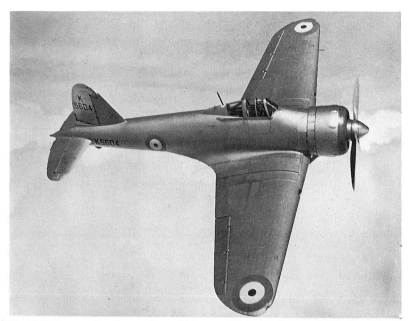

The F.5/34's geared and supercharged Mercury IX engine drove a de Havilland three-blade controllable-pitch propeller. (*Courtesy Rolls-Royce*)

housed inside the fixed portion of the cockpit canopy behind the pilot's head. All three units of the Dowty landing gear retracted, the mainwheel units swinging rearwards and upwards into the wing leaving a large segment of each wheel protruding below its lower surface. In this position they could take the full weight of the aircraft in the event of a wheels-up landing. The tailwheel retracted in a similar manner, also leaving a portion of the wheel exposed. The armament, consisting of eight Browning ·303 in guns, was mounted in the mainplanes outboard of the propeller disc; in this position the guns had an unimpeded rate of fire, eliminated the weight

This view of the Gloster F.5/34 shows the marked similarity to both the Gladiator and the E.28/39, particularly in the shape of the cockpit and tail unit. (*Flight International*)

228

The prototype F.5/34 climbs away from Hucclecote. (*Flight International*)

and complexity of synchronizing gear and took full advantage of the remotely-operated Browning's growing reliability. Large hinged panels in the upper surface of the wing provided good access to the guns for quick turn around between sorties.

The engine was an 840 hp Bristol Mercury IX nine-cylinder geared and supercharged air-cooled radial neatly enclosed in a long-chord cowling with a leading-edge exhaust collector ring and controllable cooling gills, and driving a 10 ft 6 in diameter de Havilland three-blade controllable-pitch propeller.

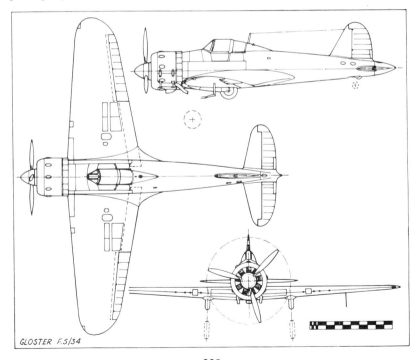

GLOSTER F.5/34

K8089, the second F.5/34, which carried eight wing-mounted machine-guns.

Mainly because of the company's involvement with the development and production of the Gauntlet and Gladiator, which was absorbing all of its design office manpower, only slow progress was made with the task of building K5604, the prototype F.5/34, and the first flight by Gerry Sayer was not made until December 1937. A second aircraft, K8089, which was similar in concept, flew for the first time in March 1938.

By that time of course, the Hurricane was in RAF squadron service and the Spitfire was in production, and, although Glosters' F.5/34 had a top speed of 316 mph at 16,000 ft, could climb to 15,000 ft in 7·8 min and had a 32,500 ft service ceiling plus pleasant handling characteristics, it failed to win a production order. Both K5604 and K8089 were transferred to Air Ministry charge and were used for experimental flying at RAE Farnborough and other Establishments until about May 1941 when they became ground instructional airframes serialled 2232M and 2231M respectively.

TECHNICAL DATA

Description: Single-seat day fighter monoplane. Metal stressed-skin construction with fabric-covered control surfaces.

Accommodation: Pilot in enclosed cockpit.

Powerplant: One 840 hp Bristol Mercury IX nine-cylinder geared and supercharged air-cooled radial, driving a 10 ft 6 in (3·19 m) diameter de Havilland three-blade controllable-pitch metal propeller. Fuel 68 gal (309 litres); oil 6 gal (27 litres).

Armament: Eight fixed Browning ·303 in machine-guns mounted in the wings with 2,600 rounds of ammunition.

Dimensions: Span 38 ft 2 in (11·5 m); length 32 ft 0 in (9·7 m); height 10 ft 2 in (3·09 m); wing area 230 sq ft (21·3 sq m); incidence 1 deg; mean chord 7 ft 1 in (2·1 m); track 10 ft 3 in (3.11 m).

Weights: Empty 4,190 lb (1,900 kg); loaded 5,400 lb (2,449 kg).

Performance: Maximum speed 316 mph at 16,000 ft (508·5 km/h at 4,876 m); stalling speed 68 mph (109 km/h); climb to 20,000 ft (6,096 m) in 11 min; service ceiling 32,500 ft (9,905 m).

Production: A total of two F.5/34s built by Gloster Aircraft Co Ltd, Hucclecote, Glos. during 1936–38.

230

The pilot of the F.9/37 had an excellent field of vision. (*Courtesy William Green*)

F.9/37

A twin-engined, single-seat day and night fighter, the F.9/37 was the last of Glosters' pre-war piston-engined designs, being evolved through a series of projects over a four-year period beginning in 1933.

Although specification F.5/33 for a two-seat fighter with turret armament was issued with the intention of providing a replacement for the Hawker Demon, it failed to produce a prototype, but three companies undertook design studies; they were Armstrong Whitworth with their AW.34, Bristol whose project was the Type 140, and Glosters. The Gloster project to specification F.5/33 was a twin-engined design with a four-gun power-operated turret and was to have been powered by the 625 hp Bristol Aquila sleeve-valve air-cooled radial engine. The work done on the F.5/33 at Hucclecote was put to use in 1935 when design studies began on an aircraft to meet specification F.34/35. They resulted in a proposal for a twin-engined two-seat fighter, mounting a four-gun power-operated dorsal turret and with fixed armament in the nose. An RAF serial number, K8625, was allocated for the prototype, but it was abandoned when the Boulton Paul Defiant, built to specification F.9/35, was ordered to cover the requirements of both specifications.

When specification F.9/37 was issued some 18 months later calling for a twin-engined single-seat fighter with fixed armament, Glosters' new chief designer, W. G. Carter, rapidly revised the earlier design, and, with the turret removed, it formed the basis of his submission to meet the new requirement.

231

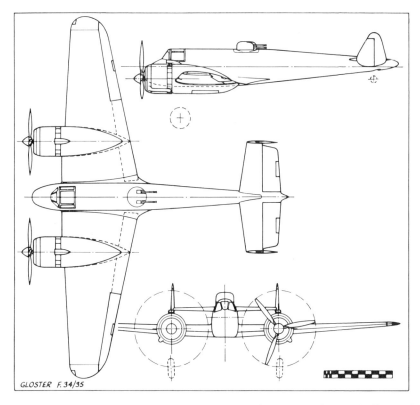

GLOSTER F.34/35

This was George Carter's first design for Glosters and he used all-metal stressed-skin construction throughout with the exception of the control surfaces which were fabric covered. The fuselage was built in two main sections, with detachable nose and tail cones, using light-alloy fabricated ring-type bulkheads with solid plate-type web bulkheads at the main and tailplane attachment points. The front main section of the fuselage contained the cockpit and the two-cannon armament: the rear main section was made up of two sub-assemblies one of which carried the four grouped 20 mm cannon and the mainplane attachments, and the other the tailplane attachment points and the retractable tailwheel mounting structure. Carter's original design made provision for a gunner's position in the rear section of the fuselage, but during the early development it was decided to adhere to the requirements of specification F.9/37 and to omit the second crew position. The detachable nose gave access to the camera-gun, heater, instrument panel and rudder pedals; the tail cone carried the rear navigation light and provided access to the tailwheel.

The mainplanes were also built up in two portions each side; the centre plane and the outer wing. The centre plane housed the two main fuel tanks and carried the engine bearers and landing gear attachment points. Two

232

L7999, the first Gloster F.9/37, with the Taurus engines and Rotol propellers and spinners.

parallel **I**-section spars of duralumin channel were used with lattice-type ribs made up from duralumin channel and round steel or duralumin tube with squared ends. The two root-end ribs were made with a panel web so that the cannon bay in the fuselage could be made gas tight. A duralumin false-spar carried the inboard segment of the flaps. The outer wing was of similar construction and carried the fabric-covered ailerons and the outboard segment of the metal-covered flaps. All control runs were of the push rod type except for the rudder which was cable operated.

The F.9/37 was intended for dispersed production by semi-skilled operators and so the entire structure was broken down into comparatively small sub-assemblies which could be made in simple jigs and pre-assembled on the bench before final erection of the complete aircraft. A retractable single-leg overhung wheel-type landing gear of Dowty design was used and the whole unit, complete with hydraulic jack and up-lock, could be assembled in a stand jig ready for bolting direct to the centre-plane attachment points.

Component construction for the two prototypes began in February 1938 and L7999 was the first to be completed. Powered by two 1,050 hp Bristol Taurus T-S(a) fourteen-cylinder twin-row radial engines driving 10 ft

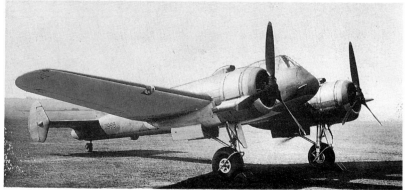

The first F.9/37 with the derated Taurus T-S(a) III engines and minus spinners.

233

View of L7999, showing the tail layout.

diameter three-blade variable-pitch Rotol propellers, it made its first flight from Hucclecote on 3 April, 1939, piloted by P. E. G. Sayer. It was soon seen to be an aircraft with great potentialities and the initial trials were pressed ahead to such good effect that on 23 May, less than seven weeks after its initial flight, it made a cross-country flight to RAF Northolt where it made a brief but spectacular high-speed appearance before a group of astonished MPs before returning to the factory. After further flying at Hucclecote, L7999 was delivered to A and AEE on 8 July, 1939, for preliminary handling, and the Establishment subsequently reported very favourably on the cockpit layout and view, its comfort and ease of access and egress. In the air it was reported to be light on the controls, stable about all axes and in all examined conditions of flight except in the climb when, with the Taurus' cooling gills open, the stability deteriorated; it was found however to be quite satisfactory in this respect when the gills were closed or partially open. The maximum speed attained was 360 mph at 15,000 ft, and L7999 had a 2,460 ft/min rate of climb at 12,000 ft and a service ceiling of 30,000 ft.

Unfortunately for Glosters all development of this most promising and important fighter came to an abrupt halt after only a few preliminary flights, when L7999 was badly damaged in a landing accident at Boscombe

L8002, the F.9/37 powered with Peregrine engines. Note the nose-mounted armament.

Another view of L8002. (*Imperial War Museum*)

Down. It was sent back to the factory for repair and reconstruction, but it was not until April 1940 that this work was completed and the aircraft returned to Boscombe Down. When it did so its original 1,050 hp Taurus T-S(a) engines had been replaced by 900 hp Taurus T-S(a) IIIs which reduced the maximum speed to 332 mph at 15,200 ft and the rest of the performance suffered equally. Continuing unserviceability of the engines and airframe delayed completion of the trials until July 1940, but L7999 earned good reports for its pleasant handling characteristics and stability.

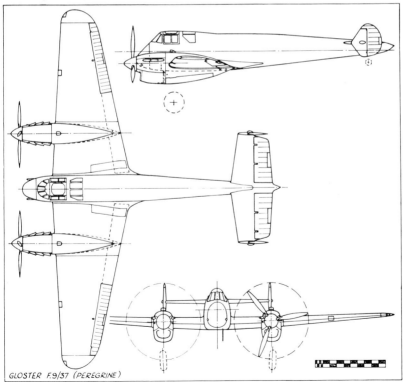
GLOSTER F.9/37 (PEREGRINE)

235

While L7999 was being rebuilt and re-engined, the second prototype, L8002, was steadily nearing completion at Hucclecote and it made its first flight from there piloted by Sayer, on 22 February, 1940. Powered by two 885 hp Rolls-Royce Peregrine twelve-cylinder liquid-cooled vee engines, it reached a maximum speed of 330 mph at 15,000 ft during flight trials.

Although the heavily armed F.9/37 prototypes proved to be probably the most tractable, vice-less twin-engined aircraft which had then been built, capable of being looped and rolled with ease and possessing the docile landing characteristics of a biplane, neither version was chosen for production. The issue of specification F.18/40 for a two-seat day and night interceptor raised Glosters' hopes again, and during 1940–41 L8002 was experimentally loaded for use in a series of tests on its suitability for this rôle, but the project was abandoned before either the tests or the construction of a mock-up were completed.

TECHNICAL DATA

Description: Single-seat day and night fighter monoplane. Metal stressed-skin construction with fabric-covered control surfaces.

Accommodation: Pilot in enclosed cockpit.

Powerplant: Two 1,050 hp Bristol Taurus T-S(a) fourteen-cylinder twin-row air-cooled radials, driving 10 ft 0 in (3·04 m) diameter Rotol three-blade variable-pitch metal propellers (L7999).
Two 885 hp Rolls-Royce Peregrine twelve-cylinder liquid-cooled vees, driving 10 ft 0 in (3·04 m) diameter Rotol three-blade variable-pitch metal propellers (L8002).
Fuel 170 gal (772 litres); oil 15 gal (68 litres).

Armament: Two fixed British Hispano 20 mm cannon mounted in the fuselage nose and four fixed British Hispano 20 mm cannon mounted in the fuselage. Provision under the centre section for two 20 lb (9 kg) bomb carriers.

Dimensions: Span 50 ft 0½ in (15·24 m); length 37 ft 0½ in (11·27 m); height 11 ft 7 in (3·3 m); wing area 386 sq ft (35·85 sq m); track 15 ft 9 in (4·6 m).

Weights:
(L7999) Empty 8,828 lb (4,004 kg); loaded 11,615 lb (5,269 kg).
(L8002) Empty 9,222 lb (4,183 kg); loaded 12,108 lb (5,492 kg).

Performance:
(L7999) Maximum speed 360 mph at 15,000 ft (579 km/h at 4,572 m); landing speed 68 mph (109 km/h); climb to 28,000 ft (8,534 m) in 19·6 min; service ceiling 30,000 ft (9,144 m).
(L8002) Maximum speed 330 mph at 15,000 ft (531 km/h at 4,572 m); landing speed 69 mph (111 km/h); climb to 25,000 ft (7,620 m) in 19 min; service ceiling 28,700 ft (8,747 m).

Production: A total of two F.9/37s built by Gloster Aircraft Co Ltd, Cheltenham, Glos. during 1938–40.

Ref. A and AEE Report No.756.

W4041, the first E.28/39, with heat-sensitive paint strips on the rear fuselage sides.

E.28/39

Timing—a word which often means the same thing as luck—played a great part in Glosters' history but probably at no point did it contribute so much to the company's story as in August 1939. Then, while Great Britain stood on the brink of war for the second time in a quarter of a century, a decision was taken by the Air Ministry to build a jet-propelled aeroplane using an engine designed by Flt Lieut F. Whittle.

Through personal contact George Carter and Frank Whittle were aware of each other's current projects, Carter with his F.18/37 twin-boom fighter project and Whittle, of course, with the development of his W.1. gas-turbine, for which in March 1938 the Air Ministry had given Power Jets Ltd a contract to build a flight engine.

By chance the design programme at Glosters was such that a large part of the drawing office was then available to undertake the work of designing an aeroplane capable of accepting Whittle's engine, and so, after being allowed to see the engine running at Lutterworth and hearing from Whittle what thrust he hoped to obtain from it, Carter agreed to begin design work at once.

The official contract, SB/3229, for the design and construction of the aeroplane to the E.28/39 specification was issued to Glosters on 3 February, 1940, and paragraph two read—'The primary object of this aeroplane will be to flight test the engine installation but the design will be based on the requirements for a fixed-gun interceptor fighter as far as the limitations of size and weight imposed by the power unit permit. The armament equipment called for in this specification will not be required for the initial trials but the contractor will be required to make provision in the design for the weight and space occupied by these items.'

237

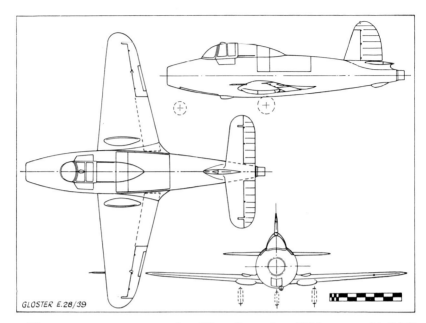

GLOSTER E.28/39

The armament was to consist of four Browning ·303 in guns with 2,000 rounds of ammunition and the maximum speed stipulated in this contract was 380 mph with an engine thrust of 1,200 lb.

Glosters had 'to pay to Power Jets Ltd a sum of £500 (five hundred pounds) in respect of the contribution made by that firm to the design of the Gloster-Whittle aircraft.'

The design of the E.28/39 was conceived by George Carter with the very close collaboration of Frank Whittle, and there is little doubt that the ultimate success of the project was, in no small way, due to the mutual understanding and respect of these two giants in their field.

The general layout of the aeroplane envisaged a small and compact low-

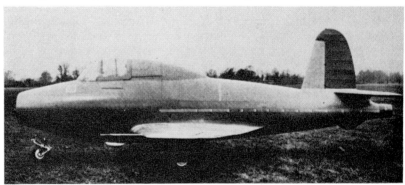

Another view of W4041. Note the fabric-covered rudder and small-diameter jet pipe.

wing monoplane with a single fin and rudder and having a tricycle landing gear. This landing gear configuration was necessary because of the position of the engine, which was to be mounted inside the fuselage and aft of the cockpit, and the 81 gal fuel tank. With a conventional tailwheel landing gear, Carter believed that there would have been some difficulty in raising the tail for take-off. Air for the engine was to be led from a pitot-type intake in the nose of the aeroplane through flat-sided ducts passing on each side of the pilot's cockpit to the engine mounted in a plenum chamber.

Among the early decisions which had to be taken was the method of dealing with the installation of the jet-pipe, and two possible means were considered. One was to take the jet-pipe straight from the engine through the length of the fuselage to exhaust through an orifice aft of the tail unit; the other method was to delete the rear portion of the fuselage, carry the tail unit on two booms and allow the engine to exhaust straight out from a very short jet-pipe. It was considered that the short jet-pipe and fuselage would give increased jet efficiency and result in an increase of some 14 mph in maximum speed, but as the jet efflux could have given rise to unknown airflow conditions over the boom-mounted tailplane, the first configuration was adopted despite the loss of about 1 per cent thrust due to the 6 ft longer jet-pipe.

All the initial construction of the two E.28/39 prototypes, W4041 and W4046, was undertaken in the experimental department at Hucclecote, but the threat of enemy action against aircraft factories was too great to be ignored, and so W4041, which was planned to be ready first, was dispersed to the premises occupied by Regent Motors in Cheltenham. There, under the guiding hand of Jack Johnstone, Glosters' experimental department superintendent, work was continued in great secrecy.

Of all-metal monocoque construction, the E.28/39's fuselage was circular in section and had a light-alloy stressed skin. The mainplanes were two-spar construction with a stressed skin, tapering in chord and thickness and joining at the centreline of the fuselage into which they were recessed. Fabric-covered ailerons with automatic balance tabs were fitted, and hydraulically-operated split trailing-edge flaps were powered by a hand pump in the cockpit. Large-area fabric-covered elevators and rudder were used to compensate for the lack of propeller slipstream at low airspeeds. Two sets of wings were built for the first aeroplane, one set had the 'high speed' EC 1240 section, and the other had a NACA 23012 section. The 81 gal fuel tank was mounted between the cockpit and the engine in the space separating the two air intake ducts.

Dowty's tricycle landing gear had a steerable telescopic-strut nosewheel unit which retracted backwards and knee-action mainwheel units which retracted inwards into the wing. Retraction was by hydraulic pressure supplied by an accumulator which was manually charged on the ground before each flight. In an emergency a compressed-air system, working off a bottle, could blow down all three units. Brakes and oleo-pneumatic shock absorbers were also fitted on the three units.

The only known photograph of the first flight of the E.28/39 from Cranwell, on 15 May, 1941. (*Courtesy N. Daunt*)

Whittle's W.1 engine, which produced 860 lb thrust at its maximum permitted 16,500 rpm, needed radiators capable of dissipating some 70 hp, under ground level conditions, in order to cool the rear bearing, and these were mounted internally, one being fitted in each of the intake ducts in front of the engine. Initially, $3\frac{1}{2}$ gal of coolant were required, but following early flight tests one radiator was blanked off and finally both were removed and the bearing was cooled quite adequately by air bled from the compressor.

While construction of the airframe went ahead in Cheltenham, Power Jets built a 'ground taxi-ing only' engine, designated the W.1X, using components which were considered below standard for the W.1 flight engine, plus a quantity of spare parts. Although this test engine's performance fell short of what was anticipated, nevertheless it was a great improvement on earlier engines, and it conserved the W.1 for the all important flying programme.

On 7 April, 1941, W4041, fitted with the NACA 23012 section wing, was taken by road from Regent Motors to Hucclecote for initial taxi-ing trials. At 8 p.m. P. E. G. Sayer, Glosters' chief test pilot, began a series of runs. Of these he reported that, possibly due to the spongy grass surface of the aerodrome, the wheels did not commence to rotate until 10,000 rpm had been reached and that at the maximum permitted 13,000 rpm the acceleration was very poor. Controllability was very good indeed and the load on the rudder bar to steer the nosewheel was satisfactory. Darkness curtailed further tests that day.

The following day the throttle stop was moved to allow 16,000 rpm to be reached, and during the third taxi-ing test Sayer accomplished three short 'hops' about 6 ft off the ground and varying in distance between 100–200 yards.

Elevator control difficulties due to the lack of propeller slipstream were less serious than expected and only the throttle control came in for criticism during this test. Whittle taxied W4041 for a short time before the second test and then again after Sayer had made the hops.

240

Following these initial brief taxi-ing tests, the E.28/39 was taken to Crabtree's Garage in Cheltenham, which was another site taken over by Glosters for use as a dispersal factory. A new nose landing-gear unit with longer travel was fitted and retraction tests were begun on the complete landing gear which had been locked down for the taxi-ing trials.

With the successful completion of the first stage of the E.28/39's tests, it was dismantled and taken by road to Cranwell for flight trials. Cranwell had long runways and there was the advantage that trials could be conducted in greater secrecy out in the wilds of Lincolnshire than in the more densely populated Gloucester/Cheltenham area.

By 14 May the W.1 engine was fitted and Sayer taxied the aircraft once more. The following day, 15 May, 1941, the weather was completely unfavourable for the scheduled first flight; it was not until 7 p.m. that the clouds cleared and there seemed a possibility of getting airborne, so with only 50 gal of fuel, Sayer taxied out to the runway. At 7.45 p.m. he opened the throttle and took-off. His flight report reads: 'The pilot's cockpit hood was in the full open position for take-off and the elevator trimmer was set to give a slight forward load on the control column as during the unsticks at Hucclecote it was felt that the nose tended to rise rather rapidly as soon as the aeroplane was in the air. The flaps were full up for the first take-off.

'The engine was run up to the maximum take-off revolutions of 16,500 with the brakes held full-on. The brakes were then released and the acceleration appeared quite rapid. The steerable nosewheel enabled the aeroplane to be held straight along the runway although there did not appear to be any tendency to swing, feet off the rudder bar.

'The aeroplane was taken-off purely on the feel of the elevators and not on the airspeed. After a run of approximately five hundred to six hundred yards it left the ground, and although the fore and aft control was very sensitive for very small movement the flight was continued.

'The rate of climb after leaving the ground and with the undercarriage

A rare photograph of W4041 in the air.

241

still down is slow and the aeroplane appeared to take some time to gain speed. The undercarriage was raised at 1,000 ft after which the climb and increase in climbing speed improved. The fore and aft change of trim when raising the undercarriage did not appear to be appreciable.

'The thrust available for take-off is 860 lb at 16,500 rpm and as the aircraft weight is approximately 400 lb up on estimate the take-off run of five hundred to six hundred yards is considered to be quite reasonable. As soon as the aeroplane was on a steady climb the engine revolutions were reduced to 16,000 which is the continuous climbing condition. The engine appeared quite smooth and noise in the cockpit resembled a high-pitched turbine whine.

'The ailerons feel responsive and quite light at 240 ASI at small angles. The elevators are very sensitive indeed and on first impressions will require some adjustment. The rudder feels reasonably light at small angles and possibly slightly overbalanced. Further investigations to be carried out during later flights.

'The aeroplane feels unstable fore and aft but this may be due to the over-sensitive elevators. It is very left wing low flying level at 240 ASI and carries quite a lot of right rudder. The jet-pipe is slightly out of alignment, and looking up the pipe it is off-set to the left which may possibly be the cause of the turning tendency to the left.

'Gentle turns were carried out to the left and to the right and the aeroplane behaved normally. The engine ran well and the temperatures appeared satisfactory up to the revolutions reached during this short flight. The aeroplane was trimmed to glide at 90 ASI with the flaps fully down and the throttle slightly open for landing. The approach was carried out in very gentle gliding turns and the controllability was very good.

'The aeroplane was landed on the runway slightly on the main wheels first, after which it went gently forward onto the nosewheel. The landing was straightforward and the landing run with the use of brakes was quite short.'

Sayer's very detailed report on this historic first flight of the E.28/39, which lasted 17 min, ended a day of triumph not only for George Carter, Whittle and Sayer but also for the small band of Gloster and Power Jets designers and fitters who had toiled so long to create this pioneering British aeroplane which, by this flight, had confounded its many critics.

The following day a notice was posted up in Glosters' design office at Bishop's Cleeve. It read, 'Last night a short flight was successfully completed.'

During the next 13 days, 10 hr of flying were accumulated in 15 test flights without the need to remove the engine cover. W4041 was flown on several climbs to 20,000 ft, and on one it reached 25,000 ft. Full fuel load of 81 gal was carried on these flights to bring the all-up weight to 3,690 lb and provide an endurance of up to 56 min.

This indeed was success and few new inventions can have proved themselves so successfully at their first attempt.

The first E.28/39 takes off from Farnborough with ventral camera and additional fins on the tailplane. (*Courtesy William Green*)

At the end of these trials the E.28/39 was returned to the factory pending the completion and delivery of the new and more powerful W.1A engine from Power Jets, but seven months were to pass before the aeroplane was again prepared for flight.

During this period it was decided to transfer the flight testing from Cranwell to Edgehill, in Warwickshire, which was chosen because it was conveniently placed both for Gloster personnel at Hucclecote and Power Jets' people at Lutterworth. On 4 February, 1942, initial taxi-ing trials began on W4041 which was now fitted with the 'high speed' wing and the W.1A engine incorporating a barostat to reduce automatically the fuel flow with the decrease in atmospheric pressure during the climb and at altitude.

But these tests did not go so well with the engine, and after 2 hr 20 min flying, it was removed because the exhaust cone had wrinkled with the heat and the clearance between the turbine blade tips and the shroud ring had shrunk to below safe limits. The trouble was cleared in 10 days and tests re-started, but a failed turbine-blade on the eighth flight during a climb to 30,000 ft again put a temporary stop to the programme. After repairs Sayer again attempted an altitude test, but a fault in the barostat caused a power reduction and curtailed the test.

Sayer's first experience of engine failure and a forced landing came on 6 June when, after a climb to 30,000 ft and a two-minute level speed run, he had an impression that a bearing had broken because of a harsh grinding noise in the engine before it flamed-out. When he landed back at Edgehill, fortunately without damage to the aircraft, his diagnosis was proved correct as oil in the feed pipe had congealed and cut off the flow to the front and rear bearings.

Another W.1A engine, with a modified oil system to prevent freezing at high altitude, was prepared and after a delay of three and a half months Sayer again took W4041 into the air at Edgehill watched by some distinguished United States visitors. But 'immediately after take-off the high oil pressure began to fall' reported Sayer 'although the low pressure still

243

indicated 8 lb'. He flew straight and level to gain speed in case of another engine failure but noted that 'the high oil pressure had dropped to 5 lb from 34 lb per square inch'. He managed to land safely but unfortunately the port wing tip touched the ground and damaged the bottom skin. This was Sayer's last flight in the E.28/39. He was killed on 21 October when he crashed into the sea in a Typhoon which he was flying during a visit to RAF Acklington in Northumberland with R. Fitzgibbon Carse, Glosters' service manager.

Fortunately Sayer had kept his assistant, Michael Daunt, very well informed so that he was able to continue with the test programme with little delay once repairs on the aircraft had been completed.

Gloster Aircraft were now asked to transfer W4041 to Farnborough so that it could be flown by Service pilots, and it was delivered there by road where, after reassembly, it was flown by Daunt to complete the 10 hr test of the new oil system which he had begun at Edgehill.

Meanwhile the airframe of the second E.28/39, W4046, which had been completed was eventually fitted with the long-awaited new Rover W.2B engine with 1,200 lb thrust, and the aircraft flew for the first time on 1 March, 1943, piloted by John Grierson, Glosters' development test pilot. During the next 14 days, he made 12 flights in W4046 and on 17 April made the first cross-country jet flight in Britain to take the aircraft from Edgehill to Hatfield for a demonstration before Winston Churchill.

A few weeks later, on 3 May, this aircraft was flown to Farnborough by John Crosby-Warren, another Gloster pilot, where it was fitted with a new Rover W.2B engine giving 1,526 lb thrust. During May 1943 it was used for a number of tests including a series of five flights by RAE pilots to check the effect of flap and landing-gear position on the take-off run. On 30 July the aircraft was carrying out a ceiling climb and had reached 37,000 ft when the pilot, Sqn Ldr Douglas Davie, found that the ailerons had jammed, and after experiencing an inverted spin he baled out at 33,000 ft, the first pilot to do so from a jet aircraft.

Meanwhile the first E.28/39 had returned to the factory and reappeared in May fitted with Power Jets' W.2/500 engine, which produced 1,700 lb thrust, and, equipped with an auto-observer, Michael Daunt made the initial flight from Hucclecote and then handed over the aircraft to John Grierson to complete the programme of engine development at Barford St John, a new dispersal airfield. Between 12 and 29 June, 1943, 23 flights were made of which several were above 41,000 ft, and a number of repairs and modifications were completed. John Grierson, wearing a pressure waistcoat, attained a height of 42,170 ft on 24 June after inhaling pure oxygen for 30 min before the flight.

On 30 June the high-speed E-type wing was delivered to Barford St John and by the end of the week was fitted to W4041, but it was found that the new wing resulted in a 4 mph increase in stalling speed.

Towards the end of the year the Ministry of Aircraft Production asked for the aircraft to be handed over to RAE Farnborough, and, because there was a delay in the delivery of a new W.2/500 engine due to bearing troubles, W4041 was despatched engineless by road. After arrival and pending the installation of the new engine, which was to produce 1,760 lb thrust, end-plate fins were fitted to the tailplane to cure some instability, and a jettison hood was incorporated. Flying began again in April 1944, and the aircraft was used on a 10 hr programme to obtain various aerodynamic data.

This prototype was finally put on permanent display in the Science Museum in Kensington on Saturday 28 April, 1946, a fitting resting place for such an outstanding aviation pioneer.

TECHNICAL DATA

Description: Single-seat experimental monoplane. Metal stressed-skin construction with fabric-covered control surfaces.

Accommodation: Pilot in enclosed cockpit.

Powerplant: Initially one 750 lb (340 kg) thrust Power Jets (ground only) turbojet. Later one 860 lb (390 kg) thrust Power Jets W.1 and later still one 1,160 lb (526 kg) thrust W.1A turbojets were fitted. Ultimately one 1,700 lb (771 kg) thrust Power Jets W.2/500 turbojet was installed, the power being subsequently increased to 1,760 lb (798 kg) (W4041).

One 1,200 lb (544 kg) thrust Rover W.2B turbojet. Later one 1,526 lb (692 kg) thrust Rover W.2B turbojet was fitted (W4046).

Fuel 81 gal (368 litres); oil 1 gal (4·5 litres).

Dimensions: Span 29 ft 0 in (8·8 m); length 25 ft 3¾ in (7·6 m); height 9 ft 3 in (2·7 m); wing area 146·5 sq ft (13·5 sq m); wing thickness/chord ratio (root) 0·012, (tip) 0·009; dihedral 4 deg; incidence 1·75 deg; aspect ratio 5·75; fin area 4·25 sq ft (0·39 sq m); rudder area 8·55 sq ft (0·79 sq m); tailplane span 12 ft (3·6 m); track 7 ft 10 in (2·1 m).

Weights: Empty 2,886 lb (1,309 kg); loaded 3,748 lb (1,699 kg).

Performance: Maximum speed 466 mph at 10,000 ft (749 km/h at 3,048 m); landing speed 86 mph (138 km/h); climb to 30,000 ft (9,144 m) in 22 min; service ceiling 32,000 ft (9,756 m).

Production: A total of two E.28/39s built by Gloster Aircraft Co Ltd, Hucclecote, Glos. during 1940–42.

Meteor

Long before the first E.28/39 began to take material form in Glosters' factory, plans were in hand to develop operational jet aircraft. Even though the feasibility of a jet-propelled aeroplane had not then been proven by actual flight experience, it was apparent to George Carter that the most practical and attractive application of jet propulsion would be first to a fighter and only when engine powers had increased, to a bomber. He also realized that the task of developing an engine capable of delivering more than 2,000 lb thrust would take very much longer than the time required to design and build a fighter airframe. This effectively killed any plans which he or the Air Ministry had for future military development of the single-engined E.28/39; thus Carter had no alternative to selecting a twin-engined layout for the first British jet fighter.

George Carter's preliminary brochure submitted in August 1940 showed that he had combined the unorthodox with the well proven, by choosing a tricycle landing gear and high tailplane with the engines

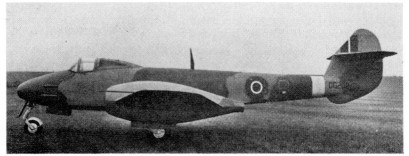

DG202/G, the first F.9/40, with the fluted canopy fairing and without the torpedo fairing at the fin/tailplane junction. (*Courtesy William Green*)

housed in separate mid-mounted nacelles on the low-set wings. In November 1940 the Ministry issued specification F.9/40 written around Glosters' proposals for a twin-engined jet fighter and design arrangements were finalized in December.

The decision to use two engines, to mount them in the wing and to fit a tricycle landing gear, however enforced they may have been, undoubtedly contributed to the aircraft's ability to accept a number of different power units and to its long and successful operational life. This layout provided for a neat landing gear stowage, a continuous landing flap under the fuselage and an effective pair of air brakes close to the fuselage; the mid-wing nacelles allowed the spars to run across the entire centre section without assembly joints, thus saving weight, and resulted in a clean aero-dynamic and compact engine installation.

Three of the Air Staff's requirements for a fighter of this kind were (i) a six-cannon armament with 120 rounds of ammunition per cannon; (ii) a seat to provide a 'deck chair attitude' for the pilot; and (iii) provision for the use of a pressure suit. However, George Carter was concerned about the aircraft weight and the uncertainty of the thrust which would be available from the engines. This lack of power clearly coloured all his fundamental

DG202/G undergoing deck handling trials on HMS *Pretoria Castle*. Note the sideways-opening canopy, the torpedo fairing, and housing for the anti-spin parachute aft of the tailplane.

design thinking on the F.9/40 and influenced official acceptance of the aircraft with a reduced load of four cannon and the promise that requirements relating to the pilot's seat and pressure suit would be kept in mind for future investigations. By the end of January 1941 a mock-up of the fuselage, cockpit and one mainplane was complete, and the final conference took place at Glosters' Bentham Experimental Factory on 11 February when the F.9/40 was approved for prototype production with only a few minor modifications.

On 7 February, 1941, Glosters received an order from the Ministry of Aircraft Production for 12 'Gloster Whittle aeroplanes' to the F.9/40 specification. The contract, SB21179/C.23(a), also required the manufacture of jigs and tools to reach a production rate of 80 aircraft per month. The serial batch DG202–DG213 was allocated to the first twelve F.9/40s. This contract was followed on 21 June, 1941, by an MAP letter of intent to order 300 F.9/40 (Whittle) aeroplanes, and the contract A.C1490/41 was received on 8 August. The first F.9/40 was allocated to Glosters for flight trials; the second was for engine development work; the third for pressure cabin and gun-firing trials; the fourth for trial installations of equipment; and the fifth for A and AEE trials. The sixth F.9/40 was reserved for an exchange arrangement with the US-built Airacomet; the seventh and eighth were allocated to RAE; the ninth and tenth were not allocated; and the last two were for air experience flying by Fighter Command and the Air Fighting Development Unit. The number of prototypes was reduced to six in November 1942, but was increased to eight after the first F.9/40 had flown.

Delays in the delivery of the W.2B engines being built by Rover Motors of Coventry and failure to meet delivery dates by Glosters' sub-contractors, lengthened the development of the prototypes, but ground running of two 'ground only' engines in DG202/G took place on 29 June, 1942. Three days later the aircraft went by road to Newmarket Heath, an RAF emergency airfield in Cambridgeshire, for taxi-ing trials which began on 22 July. By this time the F.9/40 had been named Meteor, and the name Welland chosen for Rover's production W.2B Series 3 engine, although continuing delays in delivery prompted the MAP to encourage the development of two other types of engine by de Havilland Engines and Metropolitan Vickers for test flying in the F.9/40s. This policy was proved correct, as month after month passed without the production of an airworthy W.2B, and it was de Havilland's H.1 engines which powered DG206/G, the fifth prototype, on the first flight of an F.9/40 on 5 March, 1943. Flown by Michael Daunt, this took place at RAF Cranwell, Lincolnshire. Redesignated F.9/40H, the centre section of DG206/G was 15 in wider than the other prototypes, giving a 44 ft 3 in wing span, an anti-spin parachute was carried in a fairing behind the fin/tailplane intersection and a fully transparent canopy was fitted. The Metropolitan Vickers F.2 axial-flow engines were installed in the third prototype, redesignated F.9/40M, in underwing nacelles, but, due to delays caused by their high idling thrust,

I   247

The third prototype F.9/40, DG204/G, powered by Metropolitan Vickers F.2 axial-flow turbojets in underwing nacelles, prepared for engine running at Bentham. (*Courtesy William Green*)

A rear view of DG204/G showing the underslung engine nacelles and the anti-spin parachute housing.

DG206/G, powered by Halford H.1 turbojets, was the first F.9/40 to fly and had a clear-view canopy fairing and rear-view mirror. (*Courtesy William Green*)

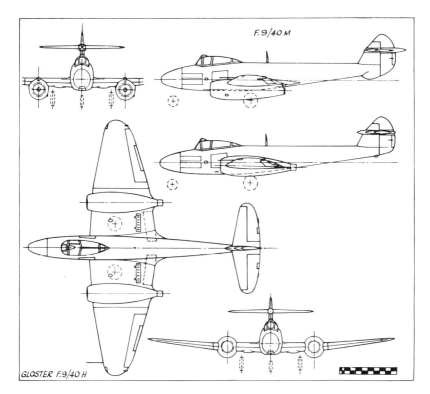

F.9/40 M

GLOSTER F.9/40 H

the engines were returned to their manufacturers. Before Glosters could fly DG204/G with the re-installed F.2s, the MAP ordered the aircraft to be handed over to RAE Farnborough, and it was from there that the first flight took place on 13 November, 1943.

Directional instability was a major problem encountered during development flying with the F.9/40s, and modifications to cure it included an enlarged fin and rudder, test flown on DG208/G, which also had air brakes, the use of flat-sided rudders and a torpedo-shaped fairing at the fin/tailplane intersection.

The first prototype, DG202/G, had W.2B/23 engines, and, after flight trials by Glosters and Rolls-Royce, it was flown to Abbotsinch by Eric Greenwood on 11 August, 1945, for deck handling on HMS *Pretoria Castle* lying in the Firth of Clyde. DG207/G, the sixth F.9/40, was used as the prototype Meteor F.2 fitted with H.1 Goblin engines, and DG209/G, the eighth and last prototype, had Rolls-Royce W.2B/37 engines.

Meteor F.1

The prototype, EE210/G, was first flown by Michael Daunt on 12 January, 1944. It was basically a military version of the F.9/40 with

249

The prototype Meteor F.1, EE210/G, carried United States markings when it went to Muroc Air Base in 1944 in exchange for a Bell Airacomet. (*Courtesy William Green*)

W.2B/23C Welland engines, four 20 mm cannon armament and a clear-view canopy. This aircraft went to Muroc Air Force Base in the USA in February 1944 in exchange for a Bell XP-59 Airacomet which had been assembled and flown at Moreton Valence during September 1943. Like all the F.9/40 prototypes and the many marks of Meteor which followed it, the Meteor F.1 was of all-metal stressed-skin construction. The fuselage, which was built up around four light-alloy and steel longerons with pressed light-alloy frames and rolled stringers, was in three main sections: front fuselage containing the nose landing gear, cockpit, armament and ammunition bay; centre section carrying the main fuel tank and provision for a ventral tank, main landing gear, engines, flaps and air brakes; rear fuselage and lower fin. The wing was built up around two light-alloy and steel spars with main ribs at the root, inboard and outboard of the engines; the outer wings carried the ailerons. The tail unit comprised the one-piece tailplane, elevators, top fin, and top and bottom rudder. Control runs were push rods and cables to the tail unit and push rods to the ailerons.

Twenty Meteor F.1s were ordered, and all but five were delivered to the RAF to meet their immediate need for an operational jet fighter. Twelve aircraft went to No.616 Squadron, the first, EE219, reaching Culmhead

This Meteor F.1, EE223/G, was the first to be powered by Derwent I engines installed in short-chord nacelles. (*Imperial War Museum*)

250

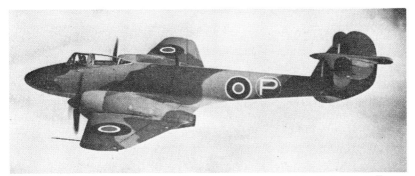

EE227, the world's first propeller-turbine aircraft, was powered by Rolls-Royce Trents driving Rotol five-blade propellers and had additional fins on the tailplane. (*Courtesy William Green*)

on 12 July, 1944. About two weeks later the squadron moved to Manston with their Spitfire VIIs, but having a detached flight of seven Meteors, EE215–221, and by the end of August had completely converted to Meteors. The squadron's first 'kill' was on 4 August when Flg Off Dean 'knocked down' a V 1 flying bomb with the wingtip of EE216 after his guns jammed while making an attack. Under the command of Sqdn Ldr Andrew McDowell, No.616 also took part in trials with the USAAF to give the crews of US day bombers and escorting fighters some experience of jet fighter tactics. EE227, 18th production Meteor F.1, went to RAE Farnborough after completing 80 hr operational flying and was used for directional stability trials, during which it flew with the top fin and rudder removed. In February 1945 it reverted to Meteor F.1 standard and went

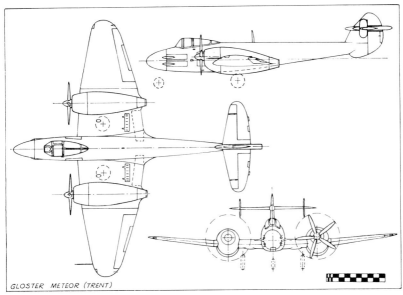

GLOSTER METEOR (TRENT)

EE212/G, the third Meteor F.1, with reduced rudder area and minus the ventral fin. (*Courtesy William Green*)

to Rolls-Royce, Hucknall, for installation of the RB.50 Trent propeller-turbines fitted with 7 ft 11 in diameter Rotol five-bladed propellers. Its first flight, by Eric Greenwood, took place at Church Broughton on 20 September, 1945. This was the world's first flight by a propeller-turbine aircraft.

EE211/G had long-chord nacelles, and EE215 went to Power Jets Ltd for experiments with reheat installations. EE219 was fitted with two auxiliary fins on the tailplane and the ventral bumper was removed for further directional stability trials. EE224 was converted at A and AEE to accommodate a second seat in place of the ammunition bay.

Meteor F.2

The long delay in the delivery of the Rover W.2B engines for the proto-type F.9/40 prompted the MAP in October 1942 to instruct Glosters to give priority to an operational H.1 engined F.9/40, designated Meteor 2, and the airframe allocated for this was DG207/G, the sixth prototype. During the following six weeks several schemes to produce 50 Meteor 2s were investigated, but largely because the MAP wanted de Havilland to proceed as quickly as possible with development of the Vampire with the Goblin engine, production of the Meteor 2 did not go beyond this one prototype.

Before going to No.616 Sqdn, EE214/G was used for ventral fuel-tank trials. (*Courtesy William Green*)

252

The steel protective shoe on the bottom of the ventral fin was removed from EE219 for trials to improve the Meteor's handling.

Meteor F.3

The Meteor F.3 was designed to take full advantage of the more powerful W.2B/37—or Derwent I—engine and embodied a sliding canopy, increased internal fuel capacity, slotted air brakes and a strengthened airframe. Because Derwents were not available, the first Meteor F.3, EE230, made its maiden flight early in September 1944, powered by W2B/23C Wellands. The first 15 aircraft were similarly powered; EE245 was fitted with the first pair of Derwents, and the remaining 195 production F.3s also had the 2,000 lb thrust Derwents. Following experience of long-chord nacelles on EE211/G, the last fifteen F.3s were fitted with this type of nacelle.

Deliveries of Welland-powered Meteor F.3s to the RAF began on 18 December, 1944, when EE231 went to No.616 Squadron at Manston. In January 1945 one flight went to the 2nd Tactical Air Force in Belgium and was later joined by Meteors of No.504 Squadron. Derwent-powered F.3s equipped Fighter Command's first jet fighter wing comprised of

A Meteor F.3 of No.616 Sqdn in overall white finish adopted for operations in Western Europe in 1945.

253

The 71st Meteor F.3, powered by Derwent Is, was used for engine flight development work by Rolls-Royce at Hucknall, logging some 250 hr before re-issue to the Central Gunnery School. (*Courtesy Rolls-Royce*)

The four cannon were removed and nose-mounted cameras installed in Meteor F.3 EE338. (*Courtesy William Green*)

EE311 at Rockliffe, Ontario, for winterization trials by the Royal Canadian Air Force in 1945–46.

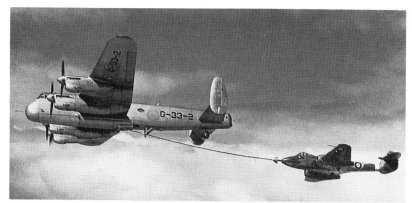

Early flight-refuelling trials were conducted with EE389 and a Lancaster tanker. (*Courtesy Rolls-Royce*)

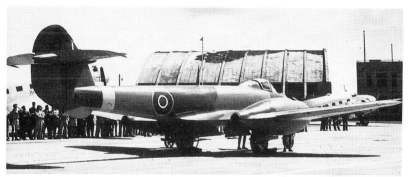

Meteor F.3, EE395, was reserialled NZ6001 for a tour of New Zealand in 1945. (*Courtesy Royal New Zealand Air Force*)

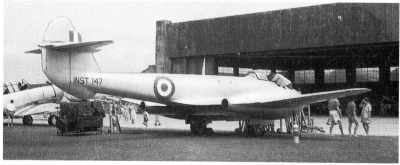

NZ6001 was reserialled INST 147 when it became an RNZAF instructional airframe at Hobsonville. (*Courtesy D. P. Woodhall*)

255

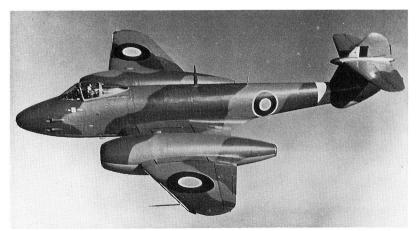

EE457, being flown by Eric Greenwood, was a long-span Meteor F.3 modified to have long-chord nacelles.

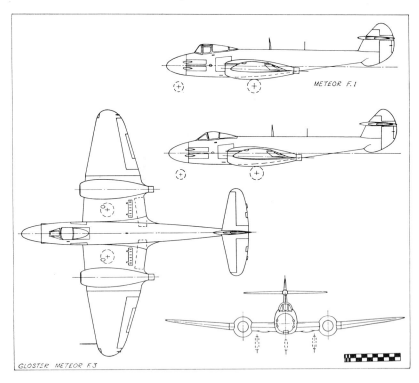

Nos.56, 74 and 245 Squadrons at RAF Bentwaters. A second wing at Boxted was similarly equipped. On 14 August, 1948, No.500 (County of Kent) Auxiliary Squadron was the first auxiliary unit to get them.

Of the 210 Meteor F.3s produced, more than 30 were used for various development trials, and notable among them were EE246, EE338 and EE416 used by Martin Baker for ejector seat trials; EE311 used for winterization trials at Rockliffe, Canada; and EE445 with a Griffiths wing for boundary layer control tests. Unique among Meteor trials was the deck-landing assessment of EE337 and EE387. Boscombe Down report No.817/f of 28 April, 1950, covered 32 landings on HMS *Implacable* during which pilots found the Meteor to have better deck-landing qualities than any other jet aircraft tested at A and AEE. Both aircraft had Derwent 5 engines in short nacelles, a strengthened landing gear for 11·5 ft/sec rate of sink and a Sea Hornet V-frame arrester hook under the rear fuselage.

Meteor F.4

Following successful flight tests with long-chord nacelles on a Meteor F.1, EE211, during which its sea-level maximum speed had been increased by 60 mph, Glosters undertook an intensive programme to develop the high-speed, high-altitude characteristics of the Meteor. Concurrently Rolls-Royce were producing a scaled-down version of their 4,000 lb thrust Nene engine, which had been too big to fit into the Meteor's engine bay. Named Derwent 5, it successfully passed a 100 hr test at a 3,000 lb thrust rating and was first flown in a Meteor F.3, EE360, by Eric Greenwood on 17 May, 1945.

EE454 prepared for the 1945 attempt on the World Speed Record at Herne Bay, Kent.

The Service version of this aeroplane, designated Meteor F.4, was extensively modified to meet the requirements of the increased performance. Changes from the F.3 included a strengthened airframe, which gave an ultimate strength pull-out factor of 10 at 500 mph, and a pressurized cockpit. Gross weight with 325 gal of internal fuel and 1,000 lb of lead ballast was 14,460 lb. Meteor F.4s were cleared for a maximum level speed of 600 mph at sea level and Mach 0·85 at 30,000 ft, which altitude was reached in a 6 min climb.

In the autumn of 1945 two Meteor F.3s, EE454 and EE455, were taken from the production line, brought up to F.4 standard, less VHF mast and armament, and given a special high-speed finish for an attack on the

257

RA382 was the first Meteor F.4 to have the 30-inch insert in the fuselage between the main fuel-tank bay and the ammunition bay.

world's speed record by the re-formed RAF High Speed Flight. On 7 November Grp Capt H. J. Wilson in EE454, named *Britannia*, set a new record of 606 mph at Herne Bay, and on the same day Eric Greenwood achieved 603 mph in EE455, which had an all-over yellow finish to make it easily discernible by the recording cameras.

In squadron service the F.4's rate of roll was being penalized by the 43 ft long-span wings which were not sufficiently stiff. Rather than delay delivery to the RAF by redesigning the wing to meet specification F. 11/46, the span was reduced to 37 ft 2 in, producing a 6 per cent cut in wing area, which improved the rate of roll to more than 80 degrees per sec but increased take-off and landing speeds. Three Meteor F.4s with this new wing, EE549, EE550 and EE548, were supplied to the High Speed Flight for a further attempt on the speed record made on 7 September, 1946, at Tangmere when Grp Capt E. M. Donaldson in EE549 raised the world

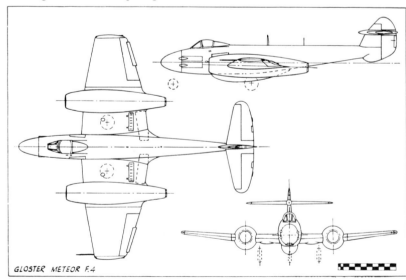

GLOSTER METEOR F.4

258

This Meteor F.4 of No.245 Sqdn was fitted with a ventral fuel tank and nose-mounted probe for trials by Flight Refuelling.

speed record to 616 mph. On 6 February, 1948, VT103, flown by Bill Waterton, set a new world record of 542 mph over a 100 km closed-circuit, starting and finishing at Glosters' Moreton Valence aerodrome.

A total of 489 Meteor F.4s for the RAF were built by Glosters, and 46 by Armstrong Whitworth who began producing components in 1946 and delivered their last F.4, VZ436, on 27 April, 1950. VZ438 was the last Gloster-built F.4, delivered on 16 February, 1950. Thirty-one RAF and Auxiliary squadrons and other units were equipped with the F.4 and they remained in service with the training units long after they had been supplanted in frontline squadrons by the Meteor F.8. The first jet fighters to be based in Scotland were No.222 Squadron's F.4s which arrived at Leuchars in May 1950.

Directional instability had never been completely cured on the Meteor until the T.7 two-seat trainer, having a 30 inch longer front fuselage, made its first flight in March 1948. The improvement in stability was most marked and in consequence an F.4, RA382, was modified by the addition of a similar length section inserted in the front fuselage between the ammunition bay and the main fuel tank and containing a 95 gal fuel tank.

Many Meteor F.4s were used for experimental flying, among them were EE520 which was used for landing-gear drop tests by Glosters but never flew; RA418 had a photographic-reconnaissance nose; Derwent 5 engines with reheat were fitted in RA435; RA476 flew from Turnhouse, near Edinburgh, to Bovingdon, Herts, a distance of 313 miles at an average speed of 627 mph piloted by Sqdn Ldr J. Lomas; RA490 was initially

A Meteor F.4 and two F.8s of No.245 Sqdn, fitted with flight-refuelling probes, take-off from RAF Horsham St Faith.

259

This Meteor F.4, VT196, on loan from the MoS, was used in Canada by the National Research Council for flight trials of a reheat system. Both Derwent 8 engines had reheat tailpipes but only the port engine had a reheat fuel system. (*Courtesy National Research Council*)

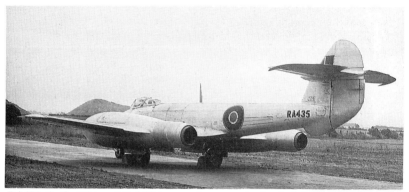

RA435, the first RA-serialled Meteor used as an engine test bed, had modified nacelles to accommodate a reheat system on its Derwent engines. (*Courtesy Rolls-Royce*)

Meteor F.4 RA490 fitted with Metropolitan Vickers Beryl axial-flow engines. Its further development is illustrated opposite.

260

RA490, a heavily modified Meteor F.4, was fitted with specially adapted Nene engines for trials with a jet deflection system. (*Courtesy William Green*)

fitted with Metropolitan Vickers Beryl axial-flow engines, then later used for jet deflection trials powered by two special Rolls-Royce Nene engines; RA491 had Rolls-Royce Avon and later SNECMA Atar engines; VT196 went to Canada for trials of a Canadian-designed reheat system; VW790 was fitted with long-span wings for Ministry of Supply trials of Vickers rocket missiles; VZ389 was used by Flight Refuelling Ltd for probe and drogue trials. Glosters' demonstrator Meteor F.4, G-AIDC, was painted carmine with cream registration letters; it was used for a tour of Europe

RA491 in its original F.4 form as it was used for flight trials of the Rolls-Royce Avon axial-flow turbojet. (*Courtesy Rolls-Royce*)

RA491, with a Meteor F.8 front fuselage, was powered by SNECMA Atar engines when Avon flight trials were completed. (*Courtesy F. G. Swanborough*)

beginning in April 1947, but a landing accident at Brussels, when it was being flown by a Belgian Air Force pilot, curtailed the tour. The serviceable major components of G-AIDC were subsequently embodied in G-AKPK, a Meteor T.7 demonstrator.

Argentine Meteor F.4

The first export order for Meteors came from the Argentine Republic in May 1947 and was for 100 F.4s. The contract provided for the training of 12 pilots of the Fuerza Aerea Argentina and six of the aircraft were retained at Moreton Valence for this purpose. Glosters also made available EE367, EE460 and EE470. In order to provide a rapid delivery, the first 50 F.4s were ex-RAF aircraft re-serialled 1-001 to 1-050, but the remainder were new aircraft produced for Argentina and serialled 1-051 to 1-100. The first few aircraft were uncrated at the dockside in Buenos Aires, partly assembled in a nearby park and towed on their own landing wheels some 12 miles to El Palomar airbase. The great majority were taken direct to El Palomar, where Gloster personnel assisted FAA ground crews to assemble and prepare the aircraft for flight testing by Bill Waterton, the company's chief test pilot. He was later relieved by Digby Cotes-Preedy, another Gloster pilot.

Meteors were used both by the Government and the rebel forces during the anti-Peronist revolution in September 1955 and, despite the fact that many of these aircraft rarely received the servicing they required, in July 1970 about 20 were still airworthy and in service with a further 22 being repaired and overhauled.

Dutch Meteor F.4

The Netherlands Government bought 38 Meteor F.4s ordered in small batches beginning in June 1947. The first, I-21, was delivered exactly a year later, and all were delivered to the Fighter School at Twenthe,

262

A Meteor F.4 and a T.7, with wing and ventral fuel tanks, before delivery to Egypt.

except I-50 which crashed at Thorney Island during its delivery flight. From Twenthe, the F.4s went to 327 and 322 Squadrons at Soesterberg and to 323 and 326 Squadrons at Leeuwarden. Dutch Meteor F.4s were identical to RAF aircraft. Twenty-seven ex-RAF F.4s were subsequently purchased by the Netherlands.

Egyptian Meteor F.4

A British Government embargo placed on sales of all war material to the Middle East, in April 1948, caused a 17-months delay in the delivery of two F.4s ordered by the Egyptian Government in August 1948. A second order for three F.4s was received in January 1949 and a year elapsed before they were delivered. This was followed in October 1949 by a third order for a further seven aircraft which were delivered by 22 May, 1950. All these aircraft were similar to RAF Meteor F.4s except that provision was made for desert equipment to be carried in the rear fuselage.

Belgian Meteor F.4

In March 1949 Belgium ordered 48 Meteor F.4s and all were delivered by the end of September 1949. Built to RAF standard, these aircraft carried the serials EF-1 to EF-48 and were operated by Nos.349 and 350 Squadrons of No.1 Wing, Belgian Air Force, at Beauvechain.

A Meteor F.4 of the Belgian Air Force.

263

Danish Meteor F.4s

Some 17 months before the Danish Army and Naval Air Arms amalgamated on 1 October, 1950, to form the Royal Danish Air Force, Denmark ordered 20 Meteor F.4s. The first F.4 was delivered on 6 October, 1949, to equip the 3rd Air Flotilla of the Naval Air Arm formed at Karup two weeks later. Danish F.4s were similar to RAF aircraft except that they had a glossy green and grey camouflage finish. Their serial numbers were 461 to 480.

Meteor F.R.5

This was an experimental one-off fighter-reconnaissance version of the F.4. Earlier tests with camera installations in F.3 and F.4 aircraft had not been wholly successful due to icing up of the camera windows and other installation problems. The prototype airframe, VT347, was adapted to take vertical cameras in the rear fuselage and others for oblique photography in the nose. The first flight on 15 June, 1949, ended in disaster when the aircraft crashed at Moreton Valence killing Rodney Dryland, a Gloster test pilot. The cause was traced to the failure of the centre-section tank bay side-skins, and complete disintegration of the aircraft following a high-g pull-up over the airfield. A number of redesign and strengthening modifications were subsequently embodied in Meteors as a result of this accident.

Meteor T.7

In 1947, with a 600 mph fighter becoming operational in rapidly mounting numbers in RAF squadrons and overseas, training was beginning to be a vast problem. The need was for a two-seat trainer Meteor and,

A Meteor T.7, flown by Brian Smith, gets smartly airborne on a test flight from Moreton Valence.

264

Glosters' PV Meteor T.7 demonstrator was built from major sub-assemblies from the F.4 demonstrator, G-AIDC, and was painted carmine with ivory markings.

under the leadership of R. W. Walker, Glosters' design team quickly produced schemes as a private venture for adapting the F.4 airframe to accommodate a pupil and instructor seated in tandem unpressurized cockpits under a long heavy-framed canopy.

Speed of development was imperative and the experimental department overhauled the centre section, outer wings and rear fuselage of the F.4 demonstrator, G-AIDC, and built a new front fuselage 30 in longer than standard to house the additional seat. Unarmed and with all essential controls duplicated, this Meteor variant had Derwent 5 engines. Designated Meteor T.7, the first flight took place at Moreton Valence on 19 March, 1948, piloted by Bill Waterton. This prototype was painted carmine with the ivory registration letters G-AKPK.

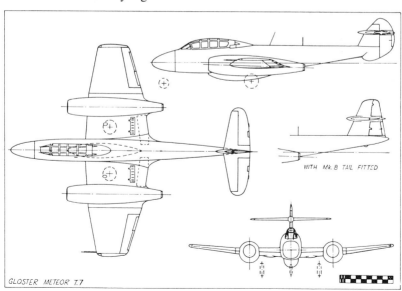

GLOSTER METEOR T.7

WITH Mk.8 TAIL FITTED

A Meteor T.7 on a production test flight from Moreton Valence, before final painting.

Front cockpit of a Meteor T.7 two-seat trainer.

Slotted air-brakes, shown extended on this Meteor T.7 flown by Mike Kilburn, were standard on all Meteors.

The RAF Central Flying School's aerobatic team of 1953 was one of many which flew Meteors—inverted. This formation is traditional with the CFS teams.

Although at that time there was no official requirement for a jet trainer, the T.7's performance was sufficiently impressive to cause the Air Ministry to issue specification T.1/47 to cover an RAF version. G-AKPK was subsequently used as a demonstrator in a number of countries, including France, Italy and Turkey, before being sold to the Royal Netherlands Air Force in November 1948 re-serialled I-1.

Production T.7s were basically similar to the F.4s with the exception of the front fuselage; provision was made for a 175 gal ventral drop fuel tank and two 100 gal underwing drop tanks, the 1,000 lb of lead ballast in the F.4s was reduced initially to 462 lb and then to 300 lb as various modifications were embodied, and the IFF equipment was initially removed. With the total weight reduced by nearly 350 lb, the T.7's rate of climb and take-off performance were somewhat better than the fighter variants and the longer nose enhanced directional stability. Early production T.7s had Derwent 5 engines, but later aircraft were powered by

Meteor T.7, WA634, fitted with an F.8 tail unit and modified cockpit canopy, was used by Martin Baker Aircraft for the first live runway-level ejection-seat trials.

267

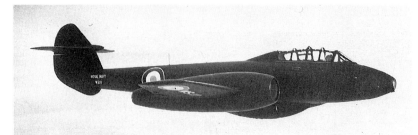

This Royal Navy Meteor T.7 had a black gloss finish, a flat glass camera port in the nose and was used by Sperry Gyroscope Company for special trials of equipment.

Derwent 8s and in consequence had larger diameter air intakes.

The first production Meteor T.7 was first flown on 26 October, 1948, and the type entered RAF service early in 1949 with No.203 Advanced Flying School at Driffield. Forty-three T.7s were supplied to the Royal Navy as their standard shore-based jet trainer.

In total 640 Meteor T.7s were produced during 1949–1954 and supplied to 96 RAF and RN squadrons (most of which had one or more T.7s) and training units. The last MoS T.7 was XF279, but the last aircraft delivered was XF278 on 27 July, 1954. Export orders for T.7s totalled 72.

A considerable number of Meteor T.7s, some fitted with an F.8 tail unit, were used for experimental and development flying and among them were VW411 and VW412 which were fitted with an automatic air brake system; VW412 also took part in trials of asymmetric loads simulating the carriage of one Red Dean missile; VW413 was used at RAE Farnborough for trials in connection with the development of the U.Mk.15 target drone and was later converted by Armstrong Whitworth into the aerodynamic prototype NF.11; WA634 was used by Martin Baker for development of the zero-feet rocket ejector seat; WE867 was fitted with a tail parachute; WL375 had a camera nose and an F.8-type tail unit. Some

Meteor T.7, WA619, was used for a series of touch-and-go trials on HMS *Ark Royal* during 1955. (*Courtesy Hawker Siddeley Aviation*)

A Meteor T.7 of No.77 Sqdn, Royal Australian Air Force. The radio compass antenna fairing can be seen above the fuselage.

WL364 was used for several years by Glosters as the photographer's aircraft for aerobatic sequences.

Meteor T.7s continued in service at RAF and Ministry of Technology establishments as late as 1969 and were used as high-speed communications aircraft and personal hacks. WH166 was still in use by the CFS Examining Wing at RAF Little Rissington in July 1969.

Dutch Meteor T.7

Ordered in November 1948, 43 T.7s were delivered to the Royal Netherlands Air Force in seven batches between 1949 and 1956. The first T.7 delivered was Glosters' private venture demonstrator, G-AKPK, re-serialled I-1 and brought up to full RAF standard. Early RNAF T.7s had Derwent 5 engines, but later deliveries had Derwent 8s and large diameter air intakes.

Belgian Meteor T.7

Between 1948 and 1952, Belgium acquired 42 T.7s by direct purchase of three new aircraft from Glosters, 19 ex-RAF aircraft and 20 which were ex-Belgian Air Force F.4s rebuilt as T.7s by Avions Fairey at Gosselies, using front fuselages provided by Glosters. T.7s were used as advanced trainers and served with Nos.1, 7 and 13 Fighter Wings at Beauvechain, Chièvres and Brustem respectively. Avions Fairey also modified a small number of T.7s to take the F.8 tail unit, and some of these aircraft were subsequently sold to Israel.

Egyptian Meteor T.7

One T.7 was ordered by Egypt in August 1948, but due to the British Government's ban on export of arms to the Middle East, it was not delivered until October 1949. Two more T.7s were delivered early in 1950 and three ex-RAF aircraft in September 1955.

Syrian Meteor T.7

The Syrian Government ordered two Meteor T.7s in January 1950 and, serialled 91 and 92, they were accepted by the customers' representative at Moreton Valence on 10 June, 1950. Although these aircraft were used by

Meteor T.7s for the Syrian Air Force at Moreton Valence during 1952.

Glosters to train four Syrian pilots, the arms embargo prevented their delivery to Syria, and both aircraft were refurbished for export to France. Two ex-RAF T.7s, WL471 and WL472, were subsequently delivered to Syria in November 1952 following the lifting of the ban. These aircraft were similar in all respects to standard T.7s with Derwent 8 engines.

Danish Meteor T.7

Nine T.7s were ordered in 1950 for use by an Operational Conversion Unit of the Royal Danish Air Force at Karup.

Meteor T.7s of the Brazilian Air Force formate over Burnham-on-Sea during pre-delivery test flying.

Brazilian Meteor T.7

Ten T.7s and 60 F.8s were ordered by the Brazilian Government in October 1952, but, because Brazil had little convertible currency, the British Government agreed to accept 15,000 tons of raw cotton as payment. Two of the first four T.7s delivered in April 1953 were ex-MoS aircraft, WL485 and WL486. All T.7s were powered by Derwent 8 engines, had whip aerials replacing the earlier rigid type and at least two had radio compasses. Serial numbers were 4300 to 4309. Several T.7s were among the 50 Meteors still reported as being airworthy in November 1969.

French Meteor T.7

Apart from two T.7s, originally allocated for delivery to Syria, a total of 12 more aircraft, all ex-RAF, were delivered to France during 1953–55. They were primarily used for training aircrews from No.30 Squadron, Armée de l'Air, which was equipped with Meteor NF.11 night fighters.

Wet weather work at Moreton Valence as a Meteor T.7 is prepared for delivery to France.

A number of T.7s were also used at the CEV Bretigny for trial installations of equipment including ejector seats, radio and navigation equipment. Similar to RAF T.7s these aircraft were mainly supplied without the Type 1934 and 1935 VHF radio.

Israeli Meteor T.7

Four T.7s were delivered to Israel in June 1953, serialled 2162 to 2165. Similar to RAF T.7s they were fitted with special target-towing lugs attached to the ventral tank rear support structure, the frangible fairing being omitted.

Swedish Meteor T.7

On 29 July, 1955, the first of three Meteor T.7s ordered by the Royal Swedish Air Force Board for operation by a Swedish company, Svensk Flygtjänst AB (Swedair Ltd), was delivered. Painted yellow, it was an ex-RAF aircraft, WF833, bearing the civil registration letters SE-CAS in black, and was for target-towing duties. These duties were performed by

Engine runs for G-ANSO fitted with standard Meteor T.7 rear fuselage and outer mainplanes prior to painting and delivery, as SE-DCC, to Sweden.

272

Two of Svensk Flygtjänst's target-towing Meteor T.7s at Bromma, Stockholm.
(*Courtesy Svensk Flygtjänst*)

Svensk Flygtjänst for all branches of the Swedish and Danish defence forces under contract to the two Governments. A second aircraft, ex-WH128, was refurbished and converted by Flight Refuelling and, registered SE-CAT, it was delivered in September 1955. It crashed on the approach to Visby airfield on 21 January, 1959. The third and last T.7, SE-DCC, was originally Glosters' private venture ground-attack fighter G-AMCJ, of 1950, which became G-7-1 in 1951 and G-ANSO in 1954. Basically an F.8, the single-seat front fuselage was replaced by a two-seat T.7 front fuselage in 1954, and for four years was used by Glosters as a photographic aircraft. In November 1958 Svensk Flygtjänst agreed to buy G-ANSO on condition that a standard T.7 rear fuselage and outer wings were fitted. SE-DCC was painted yellow like its two predecessors but had white registration letters and was delivered by John Towle, a Gloster pilot, on 11 August, 1959.

Meteor F.8

From 1950 until the end of 1954 when the Hunter began to appear in considerable numbers in RAF squadrons, the Meteor F.8 was the main single-seat day interceptor in Fighter Command.

Development of the F.8, which began in 1947, was primarily intended to improve the Meteor's performance, which was being surpassed by that of newer jet fighters. Early trials in 1949 with the 'long nosed' Meteor F.4 RA382, and experience with the T.7, showed that the increased fuselage length greatly enhanced longitudinal stability, but the expendable 95 gals of fuel carried in the 30-in insert in RA382's front fuselage, and the

273

VT150, the prototype Meteor F.8, was a modified F.4 airframe with restyled tail unit and cockpit canopy.

forward shift of the ammunition bay, caused the aircraft's centre of gravity to move beyond acceptable limits when fuel and ammunition had been used, leading to instability in pitch. The situation was partly attributable to the removal of 275 lb of lead ballast from the 15 in webs adjacent to the cannon.

Control with the F.4 tail was very difficult, but a solution to the problem was found, almost by chance, at the RAE Farnborough, where the third prototype E.1/44 was undergoing wind-tunnel tests with a new tail unit. In slightly modified form it was fitted to RA382, and the aircraft's handling trials at A and AEE Boscombe Down in February 1949 were so successful that it was decided to fit this tail to all F.8s even though 100 aircraft with the F.4 tail unit had been ordered.

The first prototype F.8, VT150, was a modified F.4; it flew on 12 October, 1948, at Moreton Valence piloted by Jan Zurakowski. In January–February 1949, VT150 was refitted with an F.4 tail unit and in this form was flown at Boscombe Down before the decision was taken to use the E.1/44 tail on all production F.8s. A and AEE Report 817/e (part 2)

During the latter part of its life, VT150 was used to air-test anti-spin parachutes for the Javelin.

The eleventh production Meteor F.8, with small-diameter engine air intakes, metal canopy fairing and rigid VHF aerial.

indicated that it was unacceptable as a fighter aircraft due to the heavy elevator forces. Under a comparable war load VT150's stick force per g was 4 lb greater than on the F.4. With the E.1/44 tail again fitted, VT150 was at Boscombe Down during August–December 1949 for handling and cockpit assessment and A and AEE pilots reported that the limiting Mach number was 0.02 better than the F.4, rudder forces were lighter, and there was a 15 kt IAS reduction in minimum speed for safe control with one engine out. Spinning trials were performed in November 1950 and A and AEE Report 817/e (part 10) records that up to 40,000 ft spinning and recovery characteristics were satisfactory to cover incipient spin. However, when rotation ceased, the snaking, yawing, nose-down pitch and associated negative g which occasionally occurred were decidedly 'unpleasant'. VT150 was used at a later stage to flight test the Javelin's

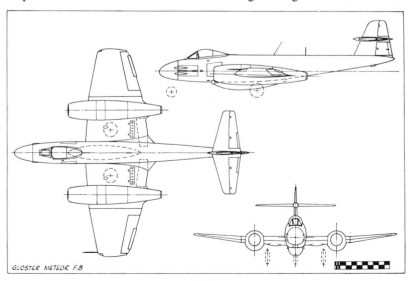

GLOSTER METEOR F.8

275

This Meteor F.8 of No.1 Sqdn, RAF, was one of a number with a target-towing lug on the ventral tank rear attachment bracket. (*Courtesy William Green*)

anti-spin parachute and Meteor fuselage noses with different construction to check the effects of gun blast. The engines were Derwent 8s. The first production F.8, VZ438, flew in September 1949 and was delivered to No.1 Squadron RAF at Tangmere on 10 December, 1949. A large one-piece powered sliding canopy with a metal rear fairing was fitted to early production F.8s, and a Martin Baker ejector seat was standard on all aircraft. Spar webs and parts of the centre section and rear fuselage structure were strengthened by the use of high tensile steel components to meet the increased stress demands resulting from the higher performance of the F.8. The soundness of the design may be gauged from the results of a check made on 1 May, 1954, when it was found that Meteor F.8s in service in the United Kingdom had averaged 660 flying hours each.

A total of 1,183 Meteor F.8s were built for export and for use by 32 RAF squadrons and units and 11 RAuxAF squadrons: of this total 89 served in Korea with No.77 Squadron Royal Australian Air Force, and 50 were subsequently refurbished for export.

Numbers of F.8s were converted to Meteor U.16 and U.21 target drones by Flight Refuelling and used extensively for guided-weapon trials

VZ460 was used for bomb and rocket trials.

Nose-mounted flight-refuelling probe on WA829, a Meteor F.8, of No.245 Sqdn, RAF.

in the United Kingdom and Australia. The total of F.8s so converted by January 1970 was about 108.

The Meteor F.8 was built in larger numbers by Glosters and Armstrong Whitworth than any other mark, and about 60 were used for experimental flying. Among the more important and interesting were: VZ439 with a metal cockpit canopy for pressure-cabin tests; VZ460 for bomb-pylon trials; VZ496 set a 1,000 km closed-circuit record on 12 May, 1950; VZ517 was fitted with an Armstrong Siddeley Screamer rocket engine under the centre fuselage; WA775 was used for nose radar trials for the Hunter with Firestreak missiles; WA820 with Armstrong Siddeley Sapphire 2 engines established four time-to-height records flown by R. B. Prickett from Moreton Valence on 31 August, 1951: time to 12,000 m was 3 min 9·5 sec; WA857 for trials with US HVAR rocket projectiles; WE855 for tests of runway barriers; WH483 used on trials of spring-tab

WA829 refuelling in flight.

Meteor F.8 used to flight test the two wingtip-mounted Rolls-Royce Soar lightweight jet engines. This was one of the two Meteor airframes known to have had four engines.

VZ517 had an Armstrong Siddeley Screamer rocket motor attached below the centre section. The undersurface of the rear fuselage was skinned with stainless steel, and an extended tail bumper was fitted. (*Courtesy F. G. Swanborough*)

The Sapphire-powered Meteor F.8, showing the very large nacelles and the bumper mounted under the rear fuselage.

ailerons; WK660 modified for installation of two 30 mm guns. In October 1950 VZ473 went to Boscombe Down for brief handling trials with 25 lb and 60 lb warhead rocket-projectiles in single and double tier underwing mounting. A and AEE Report 871/e (part 8) indicated that it was not a good rocket-projectile platform due to heavy aileron forces. The type was cleared for Service use of RPs however in December 1952 with the introduction of spring-tab ailerons.

In 1952 Armstrong Whitworth received an MoS contract to convert a Meteor F.8 to accommodate a prone pilot. WK935 was selected and a new cockpit was built onto the front of the nosewheel bulkhead containing a specially designed foam rubber couch, with arm and chin rests for the pilot. A short control column was offset to starboard and hanging pedals operated by ankle movements controlled the rudder. Engine and other ancillary controls were similar to those in the main cockpit, to which they

WL191, the last Meteor to be built, climbs away from Hucclecote en route to Moreton Valence for testing.

Meteor F.8 modified for trials of a prone pilot position at RAE Farnborough. Note the increased fin area to compensate for the extra keel surface forward.

were connected. A Meteor NF.12 tail unit with additional fin area was fitted to compensate for the long nose, and all control surfaces were power boosted. The first flight of WK935 in this form was on 10 February, 1954, at Baginton, Coventry, piloted by Eric Franklin, Armstrong Whitworth's chief test pilot. A total of 99 flights were completed by Institute of Aviation Medicine and RAE Farnborough pilots. Unfortunately Bristol Aircraft's rocket-powered interceptor project, for which this research flying was undertaken, was cancelled, and the need for WK935 passed.

Egyptian Meteor F.8

In October 1949 the Egyptian Government ordered 19 F.8s and followed this with another order for five F.8s in December 1949, but the British Government's ban on sale of arms to Middle East countries prevented completion of these orders. Ten of these aircraft were diverted to Denmark, and the remaining 14 were converted to standard for MoS delivery.

In December 1952, 12 ex-RAF F.8s were refurbished and serialled 1415 to 1426. Only four had been delivered to Egypt when the order was cancelled, but it was finally re-instated and completed in 1955 with the delivery of eight ex-RAF aircraft re-serialled 1415, 1419 to 1421, 1423 to 1426.

Belgian Meteor F.8

In 1949, with their Meteor F.4s rapidly becoming out of date, the Belgian Government sought to modernize their fighter equipment by ordering 23 F.8s and completing negotiations for licensed production of the type in Belgium by Avions Fairey. The order was met by refurbishing 23 ex-RAF aircraft which were re-serialled EG-201 to EG-223. A second order for 150 F.8s (EG-1 to EG-150) was met by N.V. Koninklijke Nederlandse Vliegtuigenfabriek Fokker in Holland. In 1950 Fokker supplied 30 sets of F.8 components to Avions Fairey who assembled and delivered them to the Belgian Air Force serialled EG-151 to EG-180; in 1951 Glosters supplied 37 sets to Avions Fairey to construct EG-224 to EG-260.

One of the Meteor F.8s built in Belgium by Avions Fairey for the Belgian Air Force.
(*Courtesy William Green*)

Danish Meteor F.8

The first overseas order for new F.8s which was fulfilled came from Denmark and was received in April 1950. Twenty aircraft were ordered to RAF standard and were delivered between January and June 1951, serialled 481 to 500.

Syrian Meteor F.8

The 1951 embargo halted the production of 12 F.8s for Syria and the aircraft reverted to the RAF programme, but the order was re-instated and delivery began in December 1952. A further seven ex-RAF F.8s were delivered to Syria in 1956.

Dutch Meteor F.8

N.V. Koninklijke Nederlandse Vliegtuigenfabriek Fokker built 155 F.8s, serialled I-101 to I-255, between January 1951 and February 1954. Five ex-RAF aircraft were delivered on 26 July, 1951, serialled I-90 to I-94. Meteor F.8s served with Nos.322, 323, 324, 325, 326, 327 and 328 Squadrons of the Royal Netherlands Air Force from 1951 to 1956, when they were replaced by Hunters.

Meteor F.8s at Moreton Valence awaiting delivery to the Royal Danish Air Force.

Production of Meteor F.8s by KNV Fokker for the Belgian Air Force.

Australian Meteor F.8

Meteor F.8s equipped No.77 Squadron, Royal Australian Air Force, in Korea from February 1951 until the cease-fire on 27 July, 1953. During that time 48 aircraft were lost and the squadron had destroyed three enemy MiG-15s, heavily damaged ground installations and a number of other enemy aircraft. The Meteors were all ex-MoS aircraft, initially built and delivered to RAF standard, but under the impetus of operational flying a number of modifications were embodied: these included a completely

A Meteor F.8 of No.77 Sqdn, Royal Australian Air Force.

282

clear-view cockpit canopy, the installation of a radio compass and, on later batches, underwing rocket rails.

The F.8s operated in a number of rôles including high altitude interceptor, bomber escort, ground attack and target defence. At the end of the war 41 F.8s returned to Australia where they were relegated to training duties or issued to the Citizen Air Force. A small number were converted for target-towing, or as target drones by Fairey Aviation Co.

Brazilian Meteor F.8

The order from the Brazilian Government in October 1952 for 70 Meteors, in exchange for 15,000 tons of raw cotton, included 60 F.8s. Deliveries began in April 1953 and were completed by the year's end. These F.8s were similar in most respects to RAF F.8s except that radio compasses were fitted in all the aircraft. They were serialled F.8 4400 to F.8 4459. More than 40 Meteor F.8s were reported to be airworthy in August 1970.

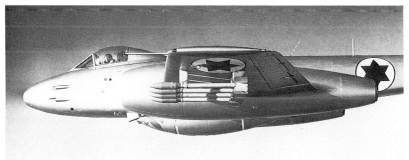

An Israeli Meteor F.8 en route to Lyme Bay for live-firing trials with HVAR projectiles.

Israeli Meteor F.8

Eleven F.8s were ordered by Israel in February 1953 and produced to a special standard, being equipped to tow targets, carry HVAR projectiles on underwing rails and fitted with the Martin Baker M2E ejector seat. Firing tests with the HVAR projectiles were conducted over the Lyme Bay range with aircraft 2166, and Israel supplied all the cannon for their aircraft, which were serialled 2166 to 2169 and 2172 to 2178. Deliveries began in August 1953 and were completed by January 1954.

Ground Attack Fighter

Sometimes referred to as the GAF or the Reaper, this variant of the Meteor F.8 was built in 1950 as a private venture. The intention was to widen the range of the Meteor's operational capabilities and so extend its production life. Basically an F.8 airframe with strengthened outer wings of increased span, the ground attack fighter was first flown on 4 September, 1950, at Moreton Valence by Jim Cooksey and a few days later appeared

Meteor ground attack fighter with 24 rocket projectiles and 100 gal wingtip tanks.

G-7-1, the Meteor GAF, armed with four 1,000 lb bombs.

Asymmetric load trials with G-7-1 carrying one full 100 gal fuel tank on the starboard wingtip.

Port wingtip fuel tank on the Meteor GAF.

in the static aircraft park in the SBAC Exhibition at Farnborough. In common with earlier PV Meteors, it was painted carmine with ivory registration letters, G-AMCJ. It carried a representative war load of 12 RPs and two 1,000 lb bombs under the fuselage and wings, two 100 gal tip tanks, and six dummy 1,500 lb/6 sec RATOG bottles around the rear fuselage. Alternative loads included 24 RPs, four 1,000 lb bombs, two 20 mm cannon in an under-fuselage pod, or 580 gal of fuel.

During 1951 G-AMCJ was flown extensively with various combinations of external load until the end of July when it was painted silver and re-registered G-7-1 in accordance with a new Air Ministry Class B civil markings scheme. These markings were in red, and with similarly coloured RPs and tip tanks it was flown again on 9 August, 1951, by Zurakowski in preparation for his memorable display at Farnborough the following month where he daily performed one and a half vertical 'cartwheels' at the

For the 1950 SBAC Exhibition the Meteor GAF, registered G-AMCJ, carried a dummy RATOG installation around the rear fuselage.

The Meteor GAF, with a T.7 two-seat front fuselage, was painted larkspur blue with ivory registration letters G-ANSO, cheat line and tip tanks.

top of a steep climb. Zurakowski initiated this manoeuvre by throttling back one engine while maintaining full power on the other.

Firing trials with double-tier mounted 3-in RPs on the ventral and wing stations were undertaken at A and AEE Boscombe Down between August and October 1952, and Report 817e/P.V. records that when the aircraft's cannon were fired there was some marked but acceptable damage to the ventral RPs. Unfortunately Glosters were unable to obtain orders for the ground attack fighter, and in 1954 the single-seat front fuselage was replaced by a T.7 two-seat front fuselage. Painted larkspur blue with ivory letters and tip tanks, it was re-registered G-ANSO and appeared in the static park at the SBAC Exhibition. This aircraft's subsequent history is described under Swedish Meteor T.7.

In its final form the Meteor GAF acquired a T.7 tail unit and outer wings, was painted all-over yellow and bore the Swedish registration SE-DCC.

Meteor FR.9

The fighter-reconnaissance version of the Meteor was introduced to replace the RAF's ageing Spitfire XVIIIs and the design was based on the Meteor F.8 airframe with the camera nose intended for the FR.5 and subsequently flown on a number of T.7s and F.8s. A type F.24 camera was carried on type 25 mountings attached to the nosewheel bulkhead; the camera was remotely operated by the pilot with a type 48 controller, and three glass panels in the nose allowed oblique photography to either side

Prototype Meteor FR.9 photo-reconnaissance fighter. Note the camera windows in the nose and the extensions on the ammunition empty case and link ejection chutes.

or ahead. Camera heating was provided by means of hot air piped from the compressor casing of the starboard Derwent 8. The normal F.8 armament of four 20 mm cannon was retained.

Jan Zurakowski first flew the prototype FR.9, VW360, on 23 March, 1950, and in July 1950 this aircraft went to A and AEE Boscombe Down for brief handling trials and functioning checks of the F.24 camera installation.

All the 126 Meteor FR.9s were built by Glosters and the first squadron to get them was No.208 with the delivery of VW363 on 28 July, 1950. Most of the squadrons operating the FR.9 were based overseas, either with 2nd Tactical Air Force in Germany or in the Middle East.

A small number of Meteor FR.9s were used for development flying and included VW360 which was converted to F.8 standard and used for HVAR projectile trials; VW362 used on gun and camera-heating trials before going to Ferranti Ltd where large spotlights were mounted in wingtip

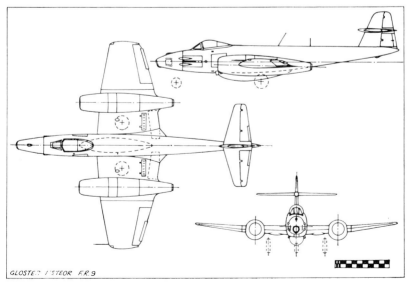

GLOSTER METEOR F.R.9

287

VZ608, a Meteor FR.9, with a fuselage-mounted Rolls-Royce RB.108 jet-lift engine replacing the main fuel tank. The dorsal intake was styled on that for the Short S.C.1 VTOL aircraft. (*Rolls-Royce*)

VZ608 taxi-ing with both Derwents and the RB.108 operating. (*Rolls-Royce*)

fairings; and VW364 engaged on ejector seat trials. VZ608 was delivered to Rolls-Royce, Hucknall, in March 1951 for various engine tests including the Short S.C.1's RB.108 jet-lift engine which, in June 1955, was fitted in the centre section in place of the main fuel tank and exhausted through a hole in the bottom of the fuselage. Fuel for the RB.108 and the main engines was carried in the underwing tanks, which limited flight duration to 30 min. VZ608 was later modified by Miles Aircraft Ltd to flight test the RB.108 in a vertical position in the fuselage, and for this series of tests a replica of the S.C.1.'s dorsal air intake was fitted into the top surface of the centre fuselage. This aircraft is now in Newark Air Museum, Nottinghamshire.

Ecuadorian Meteor FR.9

Undoubtedly influenced by the presence of Meteor fighters in the Argentine, in May 1954 the Government of Ecuador ordered 12 FR.9s to equip one squadron. This order was met by refurbishing ex-RAF aircraft which were re-serialled 701 to 712 before shipment to Ecuador in 1954–55.

288

A Meteor FR.9 of the Ecuadorian Air Force. The pilot's step has failed to retract when the canopy was closed.

These aircraft were to RAF standard and were refurbished by Flight Refuelling Ltd. In November 1969 eight Meteor FR.9s were reported to be still in service.

Israeli Meteor FR.9

Seven ex-RAF FR.9s were refurbished by Flight Refuelling for delivery to Israel in 1954–56.

Syrian Meteor FR.9

Two ex-RAF FR.9s were delivered to Syria in 1956.

Meteor PR.10

Designed and developed in parallel with the FR.9, the Meteor PR.10 was intended as an unarmed, high-altitude photo-reconnaissance aircraft. It utilized the single-seat FR camera-equipped front fuselage, less armament, and the long-span wings and tail unit of the early Meteor F.4s. In addition to the camera installation in the nose, which was identical to the FR.9, there was a ventral camera installation in the rear fuselage consisting of two type F.52 cameras on type 39 mountings, all remotely-operated by the pilot through a type 35 No.8 controller in the position normally

VS968, the first Meteor PR.10, at Moreton Valence. Note the long-span wings, metal canopy fairing and absence of armament.

A Meteor PR.10 on production flight test before final painting. Yet another aircraft with the pilot's step in the down position.

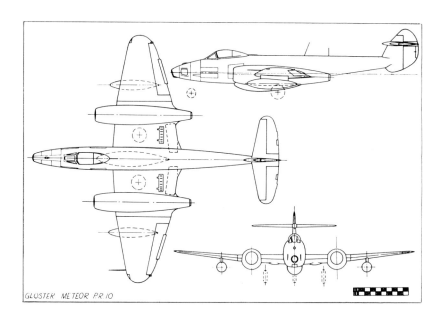

GLOSTER METEOR PR.10

VS968 in service with No.541 Sqdn, RAF, at Laarbruch, West Germany, in 1954. The aircraft has a camouflage finish, and ventral and underwing fuel tanks are carried.

290

occupied by the gyro gunsight. Camera heating was by means of hot air piped from the starboard engine compressor casing to the nose installation and from the port engine to the ventral cameras, heat being confined to the camera-bay in the rear fuselage by a canvas curtain. To protect the camera windows from mud or stones thrown up during taxi-ing or take-off, jettisonable metal covers were fitted. The PR.10 had a service ceiling of 47,000 ft and a maximum endurance of 3 hr 40 min.

The prototype PR.10, VS968, was first flown by Zurakowski on 29 March, 1950, and in August was delivered to Boscombe Down for brief handling trials with wing and ventral tanks.

Fifty-nine Meteor PR.10s were built, and the first delivery was on 2 February, 1951, when VS968, arrived at Gütersloh, Germany, for No.541 Squadron.

VW413, the fourth production Meteor T.7, after conversion to the NF.11 aerodynamic prototype.

Meteor NF.11

The issue in January 1947 of specification F.44/46 for a two-seat, twin-engined night fighter produced a number of proposals, but none of the designs met the RAF requirements, largely through a lack of knowledge of high-speed flight and associated problems, with the result that Glosters were asked to develop the Meteor for this rôle as an interim measure. The company had been concerned with extensive tests of airborne radar in Meteor F.3s and F.4s in 1946 and, following the failure of their F.44/46 proposal, undertook several design studies including one in October 1949 embodying reheated Derwent engines and broad-chord wings with marked sweepback on the outer panels.* However the design office was heavily overloaded with work on the Meteor F.8 and the Javelin, and in 1949 it was decided that development and production responsibility for the night fighter should be transferred to Armstrong Whitworth.

The aerodynamic configuration of this Meteor fighter, designated NF.11, was flight tested on the fourth production T.7, VW413, which first flew in

*P.300. See page 391.

This Meteor NF.11, WD597, was used by Rolls-Royce for flight trials of the Derwent 8.

October 1949. The first true prototype NF.11, WA546, was first flown on 31 May, 1950, by Eric Franklin. In appearance the Meteor NF.11 featured the T.7's cockpit, the F.8's tail unit and the long-span wings similar to the PR.10; to this was added a lengthened di-electric nose containing the scanner for the Mk.10 AI radar. A major modification was the re-positioning of the four 20 mm cannon in the wings, outboard of the Derwent engines, together with 160 rounds of ammunition for each cannon. The need for quick and easy access to the cannon made large 30 in square access doors essential; because of their size and location they were part of the stressed structure and were of patented construction to withstand shear loads, thus maintaining the outer wing stiffness and strength. Yet another important modification was the introduction of a pressure cabin in what was virtually a T.7 front fuselage, and, to achieve this, all the structure between the nosewheel bulkhead and front spar bulkhead was sealed. The

Meteor NF.11s of No.85 Sqdn, RAF, in formation for the Royal Review of the RAF at Odiham in 1953.

292

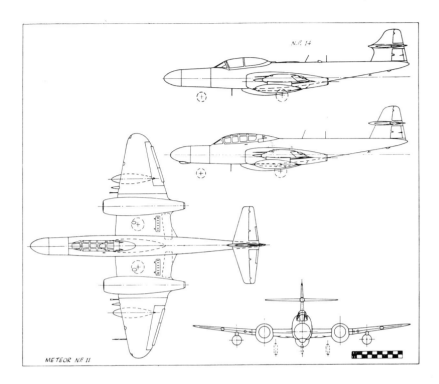

N.F. 14

METEOR N.F 11

pressurization was supplied by tapping the Derwent 8 compressor casing giving a working differential pressure of 8 psi to provide an equivalent cabin altitude of 24,000 ft at a true height of 40,000 ft. This differential pressure was identical to that on Meteor F.8s, FR.9s, and PR.10s.

The AI radar scanner installation presented quite a formidable aerodynamic problem, for it was discovered that, with the fuselage lines decided, the bottom bearing, on which the scanner swung, protruded below the lower surface of the nose. A great deal of flight-test work was required before the best fairing shape was achieved. The power demand on the aircraft's electrical system was considerably more than on earlier Meteors and power was supplied by two 28 volt 6 kilowatt engine-driven generators charging two 12 volt accumulators. The electrical equipment included the AI, VHF, IFF and Gee navigational aids and an AYF radio altimeter.

The first production Meteor NF.11, WD585, was delivered to No.29 Squadron early in 1951 and the last aircraft, WM403, left Baginton in May 1954. A total of 341 NF.11s, including three prototypes, were produced and served with 15 RAF squadrons and No.228 OCU; in addition Belgium, Denmark and France bought a number of NF.11s.

Because of its high performance, wing strength, two seats, and ability to carry a considerable load of electronic equipment in its long nose, the

293

Meteor NF.11, WM372, was one of a number employed by Fairey Aviation for trials of the wingtip-mounted Fireflash guided weapon. The modified nose housed electronic gear and had two large camera ports. (*Courtesy William Green*)

NF.11 was adapted for many experimental programmes in connection with the development of guided weapons and guidance systems. Among the aircraft used for this purpose were WD585 and WD587 which were fitted with di-electric noses of different shapes by the Telecommunications Research Establishment; WD643, WD743, WD745, WD746, WD782, WM372 and WM374 were used by Fairey Aviation during trials with the Fireflash (Blue Sky) air-to-air guided missile; WM232 was used for Firestreak (Blue Jay) air-to-air guided missile trials by de Havilland Propellers Ltd; WM262 and WM295 were each fitted with a Sperry auto-stabilizer and Decca Navigator for trials of the EMI-Vickers (Blue Boar) weapons system; WM295 was also used for tests of a Vickers missile.

Other Meteor NF.11s used for experimental and development flying included WD604 which undertook extensive testing of a jettisonable wingtip tank installation; WD767 was adapted for flight testing Radop radar dart targets at A and AEE Boscombe Down; and WM252 was used as a chase aircraft during trials of the Short S.C.1 VTOL research aircraft. WD687 went to Boscombe Down in February 1953 for brief handling

Meteor NF.11, WM374, carrying trials equipment and Fireflash guided weapons. The aircraft had an overall glossy white finish. (*Courtesy William Green*)

trials fitted with a modified fin in which the area was increased by one square foot. During earlier trials rudder overbalance was experienced in low-altitude sideslips and severe fin stalling was encountered at high altitude. A and AEE Report No. 817/i (part 2) revealed that the increased fin area and restricted rudder movement had cured these faults. WD687 was back at Boscombe Down in April 1953 for spinning trials fitted with an extended nose representative of the later Meteor NF.12, and Report No.817/i (part 3) showed that the spin characteristics were satisfactory for Service use. A number of NF.11s were also converted to TT.20 standard and were used to tow high-speed non-radar or radar-responsive targets stowed internally.

Danish Meteor NF.11

Twenty Meteor NF.11s were ordered in the spring of 1952 for the Royal Danish Air Force and the first four, serialled 501 to 504, were delivered on 28 November, 1952; the remainder, 505 to 520, were all in Denmark by the following March. These aircraft were operated by No.723 Squadron until 1958 when four of them, 508, 512, 517 and 519, were converted to TT.20 standard by Armstrong Whitworth Aircraft and registered SE-DCH, SE-DCF, SE-DCG, and SE-DCI respectively. The last two were scrapped during the spring of 1966 and SE-DCF and SE-DCH were sold to Kjeld Mortensen in Denmark in March 1969 after all four aircraft had been operated by Swedair Ltd for target-towing duties in Denmark. SE-DCF and SE-DCH were later sold to West Germany.

French Meteor NF.11

A total of 32 Meteor NF.11s, all ex-RAF aircraft, serialled 10–41, were delivered to the French Air Force between January 1953 and April 1955 and were operated by the 30th Fighter Squadron, the first all-weather fighter unit in the French Air Force to re-equip with jet aircraft. One NF.11 was fitted with two SFECMAS S-600 ramjets, installed one under each wing, in addition to its two Derwent 8 engines. A number of other

This Meteor NF.11 carried two SFECMAS S-600 ramjets below the outer mainplanes for high-speed and high-altitude flight trials in France. (*Courtesy F. G. Swanborough*)

One of the NF.11s used by CEV, Bretigny, in France for research flying. (*Courtesy F. G. Swanborough*)

NF.11s were subsequently operated by the Centre d'Essais en Vol, Bretigny, for various flying duties; one was used as chase aircraft during the first flight of Concorde 001 at Toulouse.

Belgian Meteor NF.11

In 1957, 24 Meteor NF.11s were the subject of a Government to Government deal with Belgium, all the aircraft being ex-RAF re-serialled EN-1 to EN-24. These aircraft were issued to No.10 and No.11 Squadrons of No.1 Fighter Interceptor Wing at Beauvechain and served with this wing until 1959.

Meteor NF.12

Although Glosters played little part in redesign or production of the later marks of the Meteor night fighter, these aircraft used major airframe

A Meteor NF.11 from CEV, Bretigny, was one of the chase aircraft during the early flights of Concorde 001 from Toulouse. This photograph was taken during the first flight on 2 March, 1969. (*Sud Aviation*)

One of two Meteor NF.11s converted to NF.12 standard, WD790 was flown by Ferranti Ltd on radar trials with this modified nose. (*Ferranti Ltd*)

components originally designed and manufactured in great quantity by Glosters.

First flown on 21 April, 1953, the NF.12 production prototype, WS950, was a progressive development of the NF.11 having a 17 in longer nose of improved aerodynamic shape to accommodate the US-built APS.21 AI radar. The extra keel surface forward was balanced by a larger fin, produced by adding small fairings to the upper and lower fin at the tailplane junction. Derwent 9 engines, producing 3,800 lb thrust each, replaced the earlier Derwent 8s and the limiting Mach number increased to 0.81. Some local strengthening of the wing structure was again necessary to enable the NF.12 to operate safely at the higher speeds.

One hundred Meteor NF.12s were manufactured by Armstrong Whitworth Aircraft and deliveries began late in 1953 when WS590 arrived at No.238 OCU; WS721 was the last to be taken on charge, by No.25 Squadron. NF.12s were operated by nine RAF squadrons and two OCUs.

Meteor NF.13

This night-fighter variant antedated the Meteor NF.12, the prototype WM308 having first been flown by J. O. Lancaster on 21 December, 1952. The Meteor NF.13 was basically a tropicalized NF.11 with a number of small modifications to fit the aircraft for service overseas. These included

The fairing over the radar scanner's lower mounting bracket was omitted in the Meteor NF.12 and an increased area fin was embodied as shown on this aircraft of No.25 Sqdn, RAF.

aerials on the outer wings for distance measuring equipment (DME), a radio compass loop on the rear of the canopy fairing and two cold-air intakes on the fuselage just forward of the ventral tank position. Some of the later aircraft in the batch of 40 which were produced, had additional flap area outboard of the engine nacelles to compensate for the extra 450 lb weight of the NF.13 over the NF.11.

Only two RAF squadrons, both attached to the Middle East Air Force, were equipped with the Meteor NF.13: they were No.39 and No.219.

Egyptian Meteor NF.13

Six ex-RAF Meteor NF.13s, WM325-6, WM328, WM338, WM340 and WM362, were sold to the Egyptian Air Force in June 1955 and re-serialled 1427 to 1432.

French Meteor NF.13

Two ex-RAF Meteor NF.13s, WM364-5, were sold to France and re-serialled NF-F364 and NF-F365.

Israeli Meteor NF.13

Six ex-RAF Meteor NF.13s, WM366, WM334, WM312, WM309, WM320 and WM335, were sold to Israel and re-serialled 4X-FNA to 4X-FNF respectively.

Syrian Meteor NF.13

Six ex-RAF Meteor NF.13s, WM332, WM336, WM330, WM337, WM341 and WM333, were sold to Syria and re-serialled 471 to 476 respectively.

Meteor NF.14

The first prototype of the NF.14, the last production version of the Meteor, was WM261, a converted NF.11. It was first flown on 23 October, 1953, by W. H. Else. The major external difference between the NF.14 and

A standard Meteor NF.14 of No. 85 Sqdn, RAF. with clear-view canopy and extended nose radome.

G-ASLW resplendent in an overall pale blue finish with dark blue and light blue cheat line and white registration letters. This NF.14 was powered by Derwent 8s.

earlier Meteor night fighters was the two-piece blown cockpit canopy which replaced the old-type heavy-framed hood. Other less apparent differences were a revised windscreen to match the new canopy and an even longer nose to give a 51 ft 4 in overall fuselage length. Spring-tab ailerons, developed by Glosters, and an auto-stabilizer were fitted to improve directional stability. The Derwent 9s had large-diameter air intakes.

A total of 100 Meteor NF.14s were produced and issued to 13 RAF squadrons and three other units between March 1954 and 26 May, 1955, when the final production aircraft, WS848, was delivered.

Rolls-Royce's demonstrator Meteor NF.14, G-ASLW, ex-WS829, in the camouflage finish it carried when flown by No.238 OCU. Some operational equipment, cannon fairings and unpainted radome are still retained. (*Rolls-Royce*)

NF14-747 was the sole Meteor NF.14 sold to France. (*Courtesy F. G. Swanborough*)

299

Wingtip camera pods and various command aerials were carried by RA421, the prototype U.15 target drone which was converted from a Meteor F.4. (*Courtesy William Green*)

Meteor U.Mk.15 and U.Mk.16

In the early 1950s it was apparent that the rifled barrel gun, either as an offensive or defensive weapon on the ground or airborne, was obsolete, and the emphasis in armament development was on air-to-air and surface-to-air guided missiles. A prime requirement in the development programme was a high-speed target against which defence missiles such as Red Duster (Bloodhound), Red Shoes (Thunderbird), and Seaslug, or offensive weapons like Blue Sky (Fireflash), Blue Jay (Firestreak), or Red Dean could be used.

The need was for a high-speed target of similar size and capable of reproducing the performance and tactics of a hostile aircraft while carrying the necessary equipment to evaluate the weapon system and provide pilotless remote control throughout the flight. The Meteor, which was available in large quantities, was chosen as the most suitable aircraft for conversion to the target-drone rôle. On 2 September, 1954, VW413, a Meteor T.7, was flown on preliminary trials by the RAE Farnborough to test a throttle control unit made by Ultra Ltd. The first pilotless take-off under automatic control was accomplished on 17 January, 1955.

Because Glosters were heavily committed to Javelin production, the conversion of Meteor fighters to target drones became the responsibility of Flight Refuelling at Tarrant Rushton, and on 11 March, 1955, RA421,

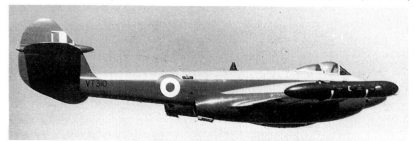

An unmanned flight by VT310, a U.15, from RAE Llanbedr. Note the acquisition flares below the jet-pipe fairings. (*Courtesy William Green*)

The first U.16 delivered to RAE Llanbedr was WH284 which retained the small engine air intakes. (*Courtesy Arthur Piercy, Jr*)

the first Meteor to be so converted, made the first fully automatic take-off controlled from the ground. A month later it completed the cycle with the first fully automatic landing. Flight Refuelling converted 92 Meteor F.Mk.4s to target drones designated U.Mk.15, of which the majority were shipped to the Weapons Research Establishment at Woomera, Australia, and about 20 were allocated to the RAE Llanbedr. The major modifications included the installation of radio link equipment, infra-red homing flares, special instrumentation gear and an automatic pilot, plus command aerials and wingtip pods containing a camera system to record the final stage of the missile's flight path in intercepting the target. The camera pods were jettisonable and recoverable, having a parachute, buoyancy bag and homing beacon contained in a section of the outer mainplane to which the pod was attached and which could be separated from the rest of the mainplane on command.

Because the U.Mk.15 had its technical limitations and was beginning to be in short supply, it was decided to develop a drone conversion of the Meteor F.Mk.8. Conversion of the F.8s to U.Mk.16 target drones involved structural modification which included a redesigned nose section, some 30 in longer than before, to house radio control gear, autopilot, batteries and other equipment. A total of 108 U.Mk.16 drones were pro-

This Meteor F.8, A77-884, was the first to be converted to a U.21 target drone by Fairey Aviation of Australasia using modification kits supplied by Flight Refuelling in the United Kingdom. (*Courtesy William Green*)

301

duced to January 1970 by Flight Refuelling, the majority being allocated to the RAE Llanbedr. A variant, the U.Mk.21, was also produced to meet an Australian specification and supplied as a complete aircraft and also as a do-it-yourself kit.

Meteor TT.Mk.20

Sir W. G. Armstrong Whitworth Aircraft Ltd developed the Meteor TT.Mk.20 from the NF.11 night fighter, principally to satisfy the Navy's requirements for a high-speed target-towing aircraft for worldwide shore-based operation of ground-to-air gunnery and guided missile practice.

The TT.20 could carry four high-speed radar, or non-radar, responsive targets, either 15 ft long and 3 ft diameter or 20 ft long and 4 ft diameter, which were stowed in the specially modified rear fuselage and launched

WM242 was one of a number of Meteor NF.11s converted to TT.20 standard for target towing and used by the Royal Navy. (*Courtesy William Green*)

while the aircraft was airborne. An M.L. Aviation type G fully-feathering windmill-driven winch was mounted on a streamlined pylon on the starboard centre section and was used to pay out or haul in the 6,100 ft long towing cable. Near-miss recording gear, together with conductive cable and target microphone, was carried on the targets and with this equipment projectile shock waves were used to detect near misses which were signalled via the towing cable to an indicator on the winch operator's control panel in the rear cockpit.

The towing cable was routed from the rear of the winch to a pulley at the trailing edge of the wing through a tubular strut to a pulley below the fuselage and thence through a cable-cutter to the target exchange and release unit. The cable-cutter's blade-trip mechanism was remotely control-lable from the rear and front cockpits. Apart from the installation of the target winch, stowage canisters and the associated control and indicating equipment, the rudder and elevator control cables were re-routed through the rear fuselage in the region of the target canisters, the four wing-mounted guns were removed together with the magazines and magazine feed necks and other non-essential items of equipment. This enabled the TT.20 to operate at weights comparable to those of the standard NF.11 Meteors and have similar airfield performance.

In addition to modifying ex-RAF NF.11s for the Royal Navy's use, Armstrong Whitworth also modified four Danish Air Force NF.11s,

302

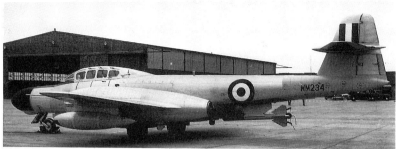

This Meteor TT.20 carries a Rushton towed target equipped with miss-distance and hit recorders plus a flare pack. (*Courtesy Arthur Piercy, Jr*)

serialled 508, 512, 517 and 519, which were returned to Baginton for this purpose. These aircraft were subsequently registered SE-DCH, SE-DCF, SE-DCG and SE-DCI respectively and, although they were owned by the Danish Air Board, were operated by Svensk Flygtjänst AB in target-towing for the Danish Defence Forces. SE-DCF was taken out of service in November 1964 and the three remaining aircraft in March 1965. SE-DCG and SE-DCI were scrapped during the spring of 1966, while SE-DCF and SE-DCH were refurbished by Swedish Airworks Ltd at Malmö during 1968 and were returned to Denmark on 14 March, 1969, on being sold to Kjeld Mortensen. A few weeks later they flew to Cologne on delivery to the German Federal Republic for target-towing duties, but in February 1970 both aircraft were being advertized for sale again by Mortensen and were located in Brussels.

During service as target-tugs all four aircraft were painted silver overall with fluorescent red bands around the rear fuselage, nose and wingtips.

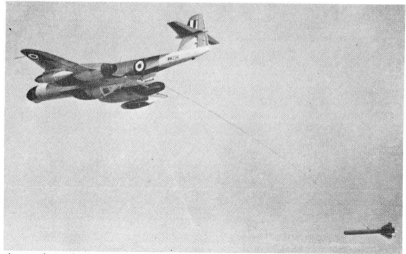

A rare air-to-air view of Meteor TT.20, WM234, trailing a Rushton towed target. The normal length of the tow was 6,000 ft. (*Courtesy Arthur Piercy, Jr*)

SE-DCF, one of the Meteor TT.20s operated by Svensk Flygtjänst in Sweden and Denmark. (*Svensk Flygtjänst*)

F.9/40

Description: Single-seat day fighter. Metal stressed-skin construction.

Accommodation: Pilot in enclosed cockpit.

Powerplant: Two 1,400 lb (635 kg) thrust Rover W.2B turbojets, or two 1,650 lb (748 kg) thrust Power Jets W.2/500 turbojets, or two 1,600 lb (725 kg) thrust Rolls-Royce W.2B/23 turbojets (DG202/G, DG203/G, DG205/G, DG208/G and DG209/G).
Two 1,900 lb (861 kg) thrust Metropolitan Vickers F.2 axial-flow turbojets (F.9/40M).
Two 2,300 lb (1,043 kg) thrust de Havilland Halford H.1 turbojets (F.9/40H).
Fuel 300 gal (1,363 litres) in all F.9/40s except DG204/G which contained 330 gal (1,500 litres); oil 3 gal (13 litres).

Armament: Four fixed British Hispano 20 mm cannon in the front fuselage sides with 600 rounds of ammunition.

Dimensions: Span 43 ft 0 in (13·1 m), (DG206/G and DG207/G) 44 ft 3 in (13·4 m); length 41 ft 3 in (12·5 m), (DG206/G and DG207/G) 41 ft 5 in (12·6 m); height 13 ft 0 in (3·9 m), (DG204/G) 13 ft 8 in (4·1 m); wing area 374 sq ft (34·74 sq m); track 10 ft 5 in (3·2 m).

Weights: Empty 9,654 lb (4,378 kg) (DG202/G, DG203/G, DG205/G, DG208/G and DG209/G), 9,996 lb (4,533 kg) (DG204/G), 9,885 lb (4,483 kg) (DG206/G and DG207/G).
Loaded 11,775 lb (5,351 kg) (DG202/G, DG203/G, DG205/G, DG208/G and DG209/G), 13,081 lb (5,933 kg) (DG204/G), 13,300 lb (6,033 kg) (DG206/G and DG207/G).

Performance:

	DG202/G, DG203/G, DG205/G, DG208/G, DG209/G	DG204/G	DG206/G and DG207/G
Maximum speed at 30,000 ft (9,144 m)	420 mph (676 km/h)	440 mph (708 km/h)	480 mph (772 km/h
Maximum speed at sea level	385 mph (619 km/h)	390 mph (627 km/h)	460 mph (740 km/h)
Climb to 30,000 ft (9,144 m)	17 min	16·5 min	11 min
Service ceiling	37,000 ft (11,277 m)	41,000 ft (12,496 m)	45,000 ft (13,716 m)
Absolute ceiling	42,000 ft (12,801 m)	45,000 ft (13,716 m)	48,000 ft (14,630 m)

Production: A total of eight F.9/40s built by Gloster Aircraft Co Ltd, Hucclecote, Glos. during 1941–44.

Allocation: See Individual Aircraft Notes on pages 357–358.

Meteor

Description: Single-seat day fighter (Mks.1, 3, 4 and 8).
Two-seat trainer (Mk.7).
Single-seat photographic-reconnaissance fighter (Mk.9).
Single-seat photographic-reconnaissance aircraft (Mk.10).
Two-seat night fighter (Mks.11, 12, 13 and 14).

Unmanned target drone (Mks.15, 16 and 21).
Two-seat target tug (Mk.20).
Metal stressed-skin construction.
Accommodation: Pilot and crew in enclosed cockpits.
Powerplant: Two 1,700 lb (771 kg) thrust Rolls-Royce W.2B/23C Welland Series I turbojets (Mk.1).
Two 2,000 lb (907 kg) thrust Rolls Royce W.2B/23C Welland or Derwent Series I turbojets (Mk.3).
Two 3,500 lb (1,587 kg) thrust Rolls-Royce Derwent 5 turbojets (Mk.4).
Two 3,500 lb (1,587 kg) thrust Rolls-Royce Derwent 8 turbojets.
Two 3,800 lb (1,723 kg) thrust Rolls-Royce Derwent 9 turbojets.
Fuel 300 gal (1,363 litres) (Mk.1), 325 gal (1,567 litres) (Mks.3, 4 and 7), 420 gal (1,904 litres) (Mks.8, 9 and 10), 325 gal (1,567 litres) (Mks.11, 12, 13, and 14). Ventral tank 175 gal (795 litres), wing tanks 100 gal (454 litres).
Armament: Four fixed British Hispano 20 mm cannon mounted in the front fuselage sides with 780 rounds of ammunition (Mks.1, 3, 4, 8 and 9).
Four fixed British Hispano Mk.V 20 mm cannon mounted in the outer mainplanes with 640 rounds of ammunition (Mks.11, 12, 13 and 14).
Single or double tier underwing racks for RPs were available for Mks.8 and 9.

	Mk.1	Mk.3	Mk.4 (Short span)	Mk.4 (Long span)	Mk.7	Mk.8
Dimensions:						
Span	43 ft 0 in	43 ft 0 in	37 ft 2 in	43 ft 0 in	37 ft 2 in	37 ft 2 in
	(13·1 m)	(13·1 m)	(11·3 m)	(13·1 m)	(11·3 m)	(11·3 m)
Length	41 ft 3 in	41 ft 3 in	41 ft 0 in	41 ft 0 in	43 ft 6 in	44 ft 7 in
	(12·5 m)	(12·5 m)	(12·49 m)	(12·49 m)	(13·2 m)	(13·5 m)
Height	13 ft 0 in	13 ft 0 in	13 ft 0 in	13 ft 0 in	13 ft 0 in	13 ft 0 in
	(3·9 m)	(3·9 m)	(3·9 m)	(3·9 m)	(3·9 m)	(3·9 m)
Wing area	374 sq ft	374 sq ft	350 sq ft	374 sq ft	350 sq ft	350 sq ft
	(34·7 sq m)	(34·7 sq m)	(32·5 sq m)	(34·7 sq m)	(32·5 sq m)	(32·5 sq m)
Weights:						
Empty	8,140 lb	10,519 lb	11,217 lb	10,529 lb	10,645 lb	10,684 lb
	(3,737 kg)	(4,771 kg)	(5,088 kg)	(4,777 kg)	(4,829 kg)	(4,846 kg)
Loaded (clean aircraft)	13,795 lb	13,920 lb	14,545 lb	14,460 lb	14,230 lb	15,700 lb
	(6,258 kg)	(6,314 kg)	(6,597 kg)	(6,558 kg)	(6,454 kg)	(7,121 kg)
Performance:						
Maximum speed (clean aircraft) at 10,000 ft (3,048 m)	415 mph	415 mph	580 mph	575 mph	590 mph	598 mph
	(675 km/h)	(675 km/h)	(933 km/h)	(925 km/h)	(949 km/h)	(962 km/h)
Climb to 30,000 ft (9,144 m) (clean aircraft) in	15 min	15 min	6 min	6 min	5·6 min	6·5 min
Serving ceiling (clean aircraft)	40,000 ft	40,000 ft	44,500 ft	52,000 ft	45,000 ft	43,000 ft
	(12,192 m)	(12,192 m)	(13,563 m)	(15,849 m)	(13,716 m)	(13,106 m)

	Mk.9	Mk.10	Mk.11	Mk.12	Mk.13	Mk.14
Dimensions:						
Span	37 ft 2 in	43 ft 0 in	43 ft 0 in	43 ft 0 in	43 ft 0 in	43 ft 0 in
	(11·3 m)	(13·1 m)	(13·1 m)	(13·1 m)	(13·1 m)	(13·1 m)
Length	44 ft 7 in	44 ft 3 in	48 ft 6 in	49 ft 11 in	48 ft 6 in	51 ft 4 in
	(13·5 m)	(13·1 m)	(14·7 m)	(15·2m)	(14·7 m)	(15·5 m)
Height	13 ft 0 in	13 ft 0 in	13 ft 11 in	13 ft 11 in	13 ft 11 in	13 ft 11 in
	(3·9 m)	(3·9 m)	(4·2 m)	(4·2 m)	(4·2 m)	(4·2 m)
Wing area	350 sq ft	374 sq ft	374 sq ft	374 sq ft	374 sq ft	374 sq ft
	(32·5 sq m)	(34·7 sq m)	(34·7 sq m)	(34·7 sq m)	(34·7 sq m)	(34·7 sq m)
Weights:						
Empty	10,790 lb	10,993 lb	12,019 lb	12,292 lb	12,347 lb	12,620 lb
	(4,894 kg)	(4,986 kg)	(5,451 kg)	(5,575 kg)	(5,600 kg)	(5,724 kg)
Loaded (clean aircraft)	15,770 lb	15,400 lb	16,542 lb	17,223 lb	17,333 lb	17,287 lb
	(7,153 kg)	(6,985 kg)	(7,502 kg)	(7,812 kg)	(7,862 kg)	(7,841 kg)
Loaded (ventral and wing tanks)	19,135 lb	18,765 lb	20,035 lb	20,380 lb	20,485 lb	21,200 lb
	(8,679 kg)	(8,541 kg)	(9,088 kg)	(9,244 kg)	(9,291 kg)	(9,626 kg)

	Mk.9	Mk.10	Mk.11	Mk.12	Mk.13	Mk.14
Maximum speed (ventral and wing tanks) at 10,000 ft (3,048 m)	396 mph (638 km/h)	576 mph (927 km/h)	554 mph (891 km/h)	554 mph (891 km/h)	576 mph (926 km/h)	578 mph (930 km/h)
Climb to 30,000 ft (9,144 m) (clean aircraft) in	6·5 min	6·2 min	—	—	—	—
Climb to 30,000 ft (9,144 m) (ventral and wing tanks) in	—	—	11·2 min	12 min	14 min	13·2 min
Service ceiling (clean aircraft)	44,000 ft (13,411 m)	47,000 ft (14,325 m)	—	—	—	—
Service ceiling (ventral and wing tanks)	41,000 ft (12,433 m)	44,000 ft (13,411 m)	40,000 ft (12,192 m)	40,000 ft (12,192 m)	36,000 ft (10,972 m)	40,000 ft (12,192 m)
Performance:						
Maximum speed at 10,000 ft (3,048 m)	598 mph (962 km/h)	575 mph (925 km/h)	580 mph (933 km/h)	580 mph (933 km/h)	585 mph (940 km/h)	585 mph (940 km/h)

Production: A total of 3,545 Meteors produced by Gloster Aircraft Co Ltd, Hucclecote, Glos, 1942–54 and Sir W. G. Armstrong Whitworth Aircraft Ltd, Baginton, Coventry, during 1949–55 as follows:
    20 Meteor Mk.1 production aircraft (1942–45).
    210 Meteor Mk.3 production aircraft (1944–47).
    658 Meteor Mk.4 production aircraft (1947–49).
    712 Meteor Mk.7 production aircraft (1948–55).
    1,183 Meteor Mk.8 production aircraft (1949–54).
    126 Meteor Mk.9 production aircraft (1949–52).
    58 Meteor Mk.10 production aircraft (1949–52).
    8 Meteor Mk.11 prototype aircraft (1949–50).
    335 Meteor Mk.11 production aircraft (1950–52).
    100 Meteor Mk.12 production aircraft (1953–54).
    40 Meteor Mk.13 production aircraft (1953–54).
    100 Meteor Mk.14 production aircraft (1954–55).
A total of 330 Meteors produced by N.V. Koninklijke Nederlandse Vliegtuigenfabriek Fokker Schiphol, Netherlands, during 1951–54 as follows:
    300 Meteor Mk.8 production aircraft.
    30 sets of Meteor Mk.8 components supplied to Avions Fairey, Belgium, for assembly.
Allocation: See Individual Aircraft Notes pages 358–369.

E.1/44

During September 1942 the non-delivery of Rover and Halford engines for the Gloster F.9/40 prototypes had caused the Ministry of Aircraft Production to consider cancelling this twin-jet fighter in favour of another single-engined project to meet specification E.5/42, but fortunately the MAP plan was ultimately abandoned following the successful first flights of the F.9/40. However, Glosters continued to refine the early design which had envisaged the use of the 2,300 lb thrust H.1 or H.2 engine, and during April–August 1943 preliminary tests were run in the RAE low-speed wind-tunnel with a 1:4·5 scale model E.5/42 designed to accommodate one or other of these engines.

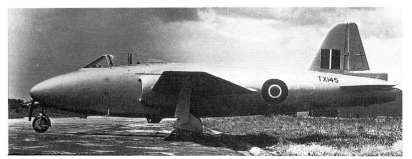

The pre-production E.1/44 prototype, TX145, at Moreton Valence. Note the low-set tailplane, and housing for the anti-spin parachute above it.

In November 1943 construction of two GA.1 airframes to a modified E.5/42 specification was begun at Bentham. The first, SM801, was to have been purely a flying shell while the second, SM805, would have been the operational prototype, and both were intended to have been powered by 5,000 lb thrust Rolls-Royce Nene engines. With the revision of the E.5/42 and its re-issue as E.1/44 in the following year, all work on these two airframes was abandoned, and construction of the third airframe, the GA.2 SM809, began late in 1944.

The E.1/44's structure was extremely robust and followed the established Gloster pattern, being all-metal with stressed skin and divided into major sub-assemblies to simplify sub-contract production. The fuselage was divided into five such sub-assemblies; the nose, front, centre, rear and tail sections. Two fore and aft webs, the cockpit floor and walls which carried the top longerons, two outer webs carrying the four cannon, and the bottom longerons, all formed the front fuselage section on which all contour-forming members were based. The front fuselage was attached by the four longeron pick-up points to the centre fuselage, which housed the engine, and which was built up from reinforced Z-section frames with heavy double-channel-section frames for the main spar and engine attachments. A semi-monocoque structure was used for the rear fuselage which

TX145 with flaps and air-brakes extended. The light-coloured sections of the nose are unpainted panels. (*Courtesy William Green*)

307

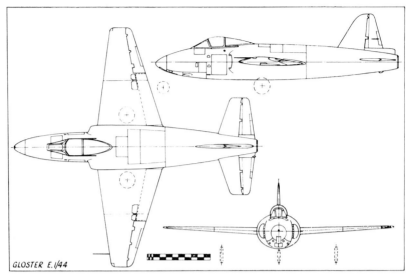

GLOSTER E.1/44

was riveted to the centre fuselage. The wings were built in four parts, two centre plane and two outer plane sections, and had a single high tensile steel spar with an auxiliary light-alloy rear spar with a stressed-skin covering. Apart from the upper fin which was of wood, the entire tail unit was an all-metal stressed-skin structure. All the control runs were of the push rod type, spring-tabs were fitted to the elevators and ailerons, and a balance tab was used on the rudder. The very wide-track tricycle landing gear had hydraulically-operated inward-retracting mainwheel and rearward retracting nosewheel units. Fuel was carried in five internal tanks contoured to fit the fuselage.

While construction of SM809 proceeded, a programme of model and full-scale tests was in progress at RAE Farnborough. In February 1945 measurements were made of the E.1/44's longitudinal and directional

The clean lines of the E.1/44 are apparent in this view of TX145 in the air.

Two views of TX148, the second E.1/44, with the tail unit of the type subsequently adopted for the Meteor F.8. Note the slightly enlarged air intakes and the open plenum chamber doors. (*Courtesy William Green*)

stability with five different arrangements of thrust spoilers in the jet-pipe nozzle; the resulting changes in trim and stability were reported to be small. These experiments were followed by others in the wind tunnel on a 1:4·5 scale model to prove the suitability of two types of underwing fuel tanks, while in May and June there were investigations of a 1:2·5 scale model intake duct to measure the duct losses when fitted to a Rolls-Royce B.41 engine. In the autumn model ditching tests showed that the E.1/44's ditching characteristics were superior to those of many single-engined propeller-driven fighters. Construction of SM809 was completed in July 1947, and it was prepared for delivery by road to A and AEE Boscombe Down. Unfortunately, *en route* the Queen Mary type vehicle jack-knifed while descending a hill and the airframe sustained almost irreparable damage. Immediately, building of the second airframe, TX145, was accelerated and this aircraft was first flown at Boscombe Down on 9 March, 1948, by Bill Waterton. Following initial handling trials and checks on the hood jettison system in the Boscombe 'blower' rig, TX145 returned to the factory for a number of small modifications.

Performance of the E.1/44 was up to the initial expectations, a top speed of 620 mph being achieved with a satisfactory rate of climb, but it fell short of requirements with regard to handling, and design of a new restyled tail unit was begun. Model tests of this new unit, which featured a high tailplane position similar to the Meteor, were undertaken in the high-speed wind-tunnel at Farnborough, and this design proved so effective that it was also incorporated in TX148, the third prototype E.1/44, which first flew at Boscombe Down in 1949. However, although the aircraft performed quite satisfactorily, it was its limited development potential compared with that of the Meteor which was a primary reason for the abandonment of the E.1/44, with TX150, the fourth prototype, nearing completion. The prototypes earned their keep for several years at RAE Farnborough where they were used for various trials including runway braking-parachute development and flight trials of flying control systems. The date of their final withdrawal from this service cannot be accurately established, but it is known that TX148 was flying during 1951.

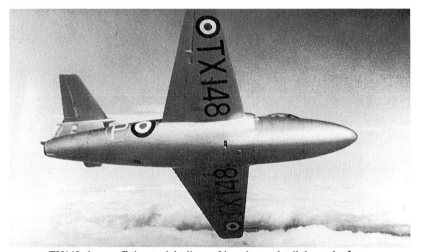

TX148 shows off the straight lines of its wing and tailplane planform.

TECHNICAL DATA

Description: Single-seat day fighter. Metal stressed-skin construction with wood upper fin.

Accommodation: Pilot in enclosed cockpit.

Powerplant: One 5,000 lb (2,268 kg) thrust Rolls-Royce Nene II turbojet.
   Fuel 428 gal (2,030 litres); oil 1·25 gal (5·6 litres). Provision for two 100 gal (454 litres) underwing fuel tanks.

Armament: Four fixed British Hispano 20 mm cannon mounted in the fuselage nose with 720 rounds of ammunition.

Dimensions: Span 36 ft 0 in (10·7 m); length 38 ft 0 in (11·5 m); height 11 ft 8 in (3·5m); wing area 254 sq ft (23·6 sq m); track 17 ft 6 in (5·3 m).

Weights: Empty 8,260 lb (3,746 kg); loaded 11,470 lb (5,203 kg).

Performance: (*Clean aircraft*) Maximum speed 620 mph (997 km/h) at sea level; landing speed 105 mph (169 km/h); climb to 40,000 ft (12,192 m) in 12·5 min; service ceiling 44,000 ft (13,411 m); absolute ceiling 48,000 ft (14,691 m); duration 1 hr at 30,000 ft (9,144 m).

Production: A total of six prototypes built by Gloster Aircraft Co Ltd, Hucclecote, Glos. during 1943–49 as follows:
   2 E.5/42 (1943–44) partially built.
   4 E.1/44 (1944–49) of which the last was uncompleted.

The first flight of the GA.5 on 26 November, 1951.

Javelin

Because aircraft development is a continuous process, it is difficult to pinpoint the exact moment in time for the conception of the Javelin as far as its basic configuration is concerned. Although the Javelin's delta planform was very different from that of its straight-winged predecessors, the Meteor and E.1/44, in the late 1940s Glosters produced and submitted to the Ministry of Supply a number of design proposals for single- and two-seat day and night fighters as Meteor replacements, and it was these which bridged the apparent gap between the two distinct types of configuration. Among these were proposals to specifications F.43/46 and F.44/46.*

In December 1946 the Air Staff issued two operational requirements, OR227 for a two-seat night fighter and OR228 for a single-seat day interceptor. By the early months of 1948 these had crystallized into the F.4/48 and F.3/48 specifications. Meanwhile, in February 1947, Glosters' proposals to specification F.44/46 for a two-seat night fighter strongly resembled the Meteor, and provision was made to install either the 6,500 lb thrust Rolls-Royce AJ.65 (later to become the Avon) or the 7,000 lb thrust Metropolitan Vickers F.9 (which became the Armstrong Siddeley Sapphire) using the same nacelle structure. Design of the structure was based on the Meteor practice and embodied a moderately swept wing

*See Appendix A.

The first GA.5, WD804, carried a nose-mounted pitot boom.

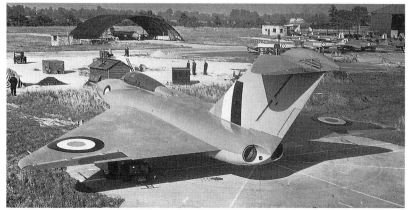

WD804 showing the original delta wing shape and jet-pipe fairing with the engine oil vent pipes conspicuous. The fences beside the anti-spin parachute housing prevented the shrouds jamming the elevator and movable tailplane.

with a 9 per cent thickness/chord ratio. The armament was either four 30 mm guns or a single $4\frac{1}{2}$ in recoilless gun mounted in the front fuselage. Developed at Fort Halstead this recoilless gun was a cross between a shell-firing cannon and a rocket projector and was basically a tube firing an anti-aircraft shell forward while simultaneously ejecting backwards a counterweight of equal mass so that no recoil reaction was felt on the airframe. There were two versions: one with a hopper feed for seven rounds and a second with a 2 ft 6 in diameter magazine, like a giant revolver, which was partly housed in a blister on the underside of the fuselage.

By October 1947, and while discussions proceeded with the Air Staff on their two operational requirements, Glosters had given consideration to some fairly major changes in specification requirements relating to their

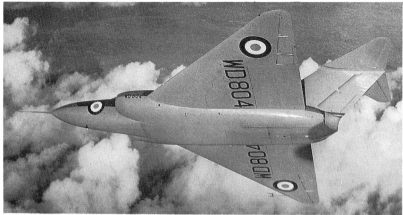

The first modification to WD804 was the introduction of this interim jet-pipe fairing. Note the shadow of the photographic Meteor's nose and engine nacelle on this fairing and starboard wing.

A fine view of the massive GA.5 showing the large-area delta wing and tailplane. Also discernible are the small oil vent pipe extensions on the jet-pipe fairing.

F.43/46 proposal which had been instigated by the MoS. These omitted the 30 mm guns and substituted either the Red Hawk missile or six rocket projectiles as a possible alternative to the $4\frac{1}{2}$ in recoilless gun which had a high installed weight of 1,810 lb. Other equipment included a 42 in nose-mounted scanner for the AI radar operated by a second crew member. The result was an aeroplane very similar in appearance to the Javelin, having a loaded weight of 21,000 lb, a large-area delta wing and a slab tailplane mounted on top of a massive swept fin to cope with the trim changes anticipated through the wide speed range of this aircraft.

In parallel with this proposal Glosters were also preparing design studies for another single-seat day fighter as well as for a two-seat night fighter. The day fighter design emerged as a single-engined classic delta without a tailplane but with the pilot seated in the leading edge of an enormous sharply-swept fin. Power was provided by an unspecified 12,000 lb thrust engine with reheat to give a maximum speed of Mach 0·94 or 620 mph at 45,000 ft. The F.4/48 design, with AJ.65 engines and a loaded weight of 25,500 lb, followed closely the earlier two-seat delta configuration with provision for rotating wingtip controls instead of ailerons 'because of the

Second prototype GA.5, WD808, taking-off from Moreton Valence on its first flight.

313

scanty information on lateral control associated with the delta planform'. An alternative design, with increased sweepback on the wing and without a tailplane, was also proposed but was not proceeded with.

Thus the basic shape of the Javelin was evolved through design proposals based on the results of work by Lippisch and other German scientists on swept and delta wings which were analysed by the RAE Farnborough after World War II. The RAE had undertaken a far-reaching delta-wing research programme for which Boulton Paul Aircraft designed and built their P.111 to specification E.27/46. A high-speed research aircraft, the P.111 had a very thin wing and was powered by a single Rolls-Royce Nene engine, but unfortunately the P.111 was slow in reaching flight

WT827, the third prototype GA.5, was the first to carry a radome and armament. In this view it is seen with an experimental bull-nose radome.

status and it was not until 6 October, 1950, that it made its first flight. By the time useful data were becoming available from the RAE, they were too late to influence the design of the F.4/48 and merely served to confirm certain of its established design features. Boulton Paul also built a second aircraft for this research programme to specification E.27/49. This was the P.120 which was similarly Nene-powered, but incorporated a tailplane, and which made its first flight on 6 August, 1952. Unfortunately this aeroplane crashed before it was able to make any significant contribution to the programme. A. V. Roe were also heavily involved in probing into this new sphere of aerodynamics with the creation of a whole fleet of 707 delta-wing research aircraft to specification E.15/48 with which to overcome the paucity of flight experience of this planform. One of these Avro 707s flew for the first time on 4 September, 1949, but crashed on 30 September killing its pilot, and it was not until a year later, on 6 September, 1950, that the second aircraft, a 707B, made its first flight. This also was too late to

314

The GA.5's and Javelin's orthodox landing attitude, unlike that of other contemporary delta-winged aircraft, is seen in this view of WT827 with flaps down, landing at Moreton Valence.

provide other than corroboration of the F.4/48's design features; it did, however, provide the opportunity for Bill Waterton to fly a delta-wing aircraft and to experience some of the low-speed characteristics in preparation for the flight test programme of the F.4/48.

In March 1948 the Ministry of Supply decided that four Gloster F.4/48 prototypes would be required. Four months later the design was stabilized around the 9,000 lb thrust Armstrong Siddeley Sapphire 2 engine but a further proposal increased the loaded weight to 29,200 lb and the wing area from 900 sq ft to 1,100 sq ft. This was followed in August 1948 by yet another proposal reverting to a 900 sq ft wing, with orthodox power-boosted ailerons in place of the moving wingtip controls, using an all-moving tailplane with elevators and substituting 7,500 lb thrust Sapphires. On 13 April, 1949, Glosters received from the Ministry an instruction to proceed with the manufacture of the four prototypes bearing the Gloster designation GA.5, plus one airframe for structural test work in the company's Abbey frame. As an economy measure two of these prototypes were subsequently cancelled in November 1949, and it was not until March 1951 that the manifest impossibility of doing all the development flying of such a complex aeroplane with only two prototypes was fully appreciated

On early prototypes the entire cockpit canopy slid back. The pilot of WT827 is Bill Waterton.

315

by the Ministry, and the order was increased to one trainer and five fighter prototypes. This shortsighted action by the Ministry completely disrupted the development plan by throwing extra work onto Glosters' design office and dislocated work already under way in the factory. This was forecast repeatedly by the company and, when the additional prototypes were reinstated, they were too late to avoid the break in continuity in design, manufacture and flight testing. In consequence, the first production aircraft appeared before the prototype order was complete.

The prototype specification issued on 10 June, 1948, called for an aircraft with an essentially subsonic performance, the maximum speed at 40,000 ft being required to be not less than 525 kt, for the interception of 480 kt targets. The maximum diving speed for stressing purposes was specified as Mach 0·95 (but with no requirement for it to exceed 565 kt EAS), the service ceiling was to be 45,000 ft, the endurance not less than two hours including the climb to 40,000 ft and 15 min combat at that height. Very rapid starting was of primary importance, with an ideal start-up time of only five seconds between the pilot receiving the order and the engines running at idling speed ready to open up for take-off. The rate of climb was required to be such that from the time the pilot pressed the starter switch to the aircraft reaching 45,000 ft not more than 10 min should elapse.

Although of unorthodox appearance with its delta wing and a tailplane of similar planform mounted on top of a large fin, structurally the Javelin was quite conventional, using aluminium alloys almost exclusively, the exceptions being a few edging members in steel. The fuselage was built up from four sub-assemblies, the two largest of these being the front and centre fuselage which were permanently joined during manufacture. The Hycar radome was the fuselage nose; on Javelins F(AW)Mk.1, 4, 5 and 7 with the British AI radar, it was removed from the aircraft to gain access to this equipment. On Javelins F(AW)Mk.2, 6 and 8 with the US-built radar, the radome was larger and could be pulled forward on special hinges and swung to one side. In the front fuselage, which carried the Dowty nose landing gear, the pressurized cockpits were made by a thick inner shell sealed at the front and rear by solid bulkheads and were enclosed by the armoured windscreen and the electrically-operated sliding canopy. The hood on the first prototype, WD804, was in one piece, the forward portion over the pilot being Perspex but the rear section over the radar operator was metal with two small round portholes on each side and an access hatch in the top. Because of the immediate adverse comments by radar operators, the area of window was increased, and finally a new hood embodying twin canopies was flown on the fifth prototype, WT836, and, with small modifications, on all production Javelins. The engine air intakes were built separately and attached to the fuselage sides and contained the ducts leading to the engine compressor casings. The servicing bay was located below and behind the rear cockpit and between the air ducts; it housed the starter equipment (initially the cartridge type but on

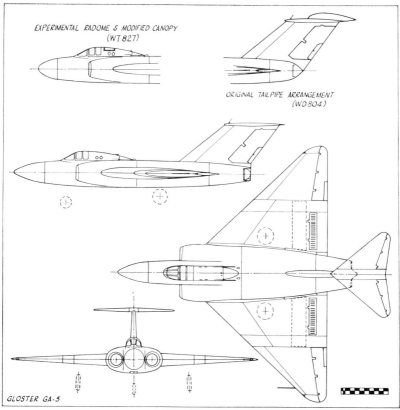

EXPERIMENTAL RADOME & MODIFIED CANOPY
(WT 827)

ORIGINAL TAILPIPE ARRANGEMENT
(WD 804)

GLOSTER GA-5

later aircraft iso-propyl-nitrate starting was used), auxiliary gearbox, hydraulic panel, generator control, electrical distribution panel and some radio equipment. Access to this bay was through a large panel in the fuselage bottom skin. The centre fuselage was made up from a longitudinal box-beam structure of diabolo section with large frames forming the two engine bays on each side. Rails were fitted inside the bays so that the engines could be rolled into place in the airframe through the open rear end of the fuselage. The front and centre fuselage sub-assemblies were joined at frame 12, a massive fabricated light-alloy structure which carried the wing main-spar attachment points. The rear fuselage was a semi-monocoque fairing over the two jet-pipes.

In the wings the main spar, together with the leading-edge ribs and the light-alloy skin, formed a torsion box running out to the tip. The inboard section of the wing was built as a unit and contained fuel tanks, the Dowty main landing gear, flaps, airbrakes and the gun and ammunition bays. It was joined during manufacture to the outboard section which carried the Lockheed Servodyne aileron-control units and the mass-balanced ailerons. The entire wing was attached to the fuselage by standard

317

WT827 with another experimental radome and a modified canopy, having a square window above the rear cockpit. The white rear section of the canopy is a Durestos fairing for the Gee aerial.

pin joints at the front and rear spars. The fin was built up around two fin posts and light-alloy ribs, and the small 'centre section' for the tailplane, which was built integrally with the fin, housed the bearings for the tubular spar joining the two halves of the movable tailplane.

With the development of the GA.5 the flying control system underwent a number of changes. Initially, operation of the ailerons, elevators and rudder was power-assisted by hydraulic control units having a boost ratio of 5:1, 5:1 and 7·4:1 respectively. In this system a proportion of the aerodynamic loads on these surfaces was transmitted back to the control column to give 'feel' for the pilot. On the fourth prototype, WT830, fully powered ailerons with an hydraulic Q-feel simulator were tested and were subsequently adopted for later aircraft. On all the prototypes, most of the Javelin 1s and some Javelin 2s, an electrically-operated variable-incidence tailplane was fitted, but on all other aircraft an hydraulically-operated 'all-flying tail' was used in which the electric motor was replaced by a screwjack driven by two hydraulic motors. In this system the elevators acted as anti-balance tabs, and twin simulators introduced into the control circuit a resistance or load proportional to the indicated airspeed.

Prototype Production and Flying

Work on the prototype airframe, WD804, began in April 1949 at Hucclecote, where components for all of the prototypes were built, with assembly of the first two aircraft being completed in Glosters' experimental department at Bentham. The major sub-assemblies of WD804, which had an all-metal nose in place of the radome and was without armament, were moved to Moreton Valence in July 1951 where a further three months of re-assembly and installation work and a month's ground testing and taxi-ing culminated in the first flight on 26 November, 1951. The pilot was Sqdn Ldr W. A. Waterton, and his 34 min in the air resulted in the discovery of rudder buffeting and the first of many minor changes to the aircraft's external appearance. Waterton reported severe rudder vibration in the air, and back on the ground an inspection quickly showed it to be caused by interference between the jet efflux and airflow around the rear fuselage. The path of the offending airflow could be seen clearly,

318

because oil escaping from the Sapphire's centre and rear bearings (which were lubricated on the total loss system) via two vents below the rudder, was streaked across its lower surfaces. To prevent recurrence of this, the fairing around the jet-pipes was lengthened after further flight tests with a wool-tufted rear fuselage.

Test flying with WD804 continued with the usual test instrumentation and an anti-spin parachute housed in a streamlined fairing on top of the

The revised wing shape with a kinked leading edge on the fourth prototype GA.5. Note the slots in the leading edges of the flaps.

tailplane. Then, on 29 June, 1952, while flying at high speed on its 99th flight, both elevators were lost following violent flutter. Waterton was able to retain some control in pitch by means of the electrically-operated variable-incidence tailplane and, although the response rate was slow due to the comparative difficulty of moving the large trimming wheel, he made several 'approaches' and 'landings' at altitude to get the feel of his elevator-less aircraft before finally touching down on the long main runway at Boscombe Down. As the result of the necessarily very high landing speed, the impact caused the landing gear to collapse and, despite some difficulty in opening the canopy, Waterton stepped out unscathed. For his skill in saving the auto-observer records and 'courage beyond the call of duty' he was subsequently awarded the George Medal.

In spite of this setback, the Ministry of Supply decided to order the GA.5 in quantity, announcing this on 7 July, 1952, with a 'super priority' production classification and naming the aircraft Javelin.

Fortunately the second prototype, WD808, was nearing completion and flew for the first time from Moreton Valence on 21 August, 1952, with Waterton as pilot. It was not armed and had an all-metal nose displaying the Hawker Siddeley winged laurel-chaplet badge in preparation for its

The fifth prototype GA.5, WT836, had the interim shaped radome and twin canopies for the pilot and navigator.

public debut which it made a few days later at the SBAC Display at Farnborough. Although there were severe limitations on the aircraft until the cause of WD804's crash had been fully investigated, Waterton gave an impressive display of low altitude, low speed flying. On its return to Moreton Valence installation of a flight resonance system in WD808 began, and flight trials, the first with a British aeroplane carrying such equipment, got under way in January 1953. Several Gloster pilots were now joining with Waterton in the Javelin's development flying and Jan Zurakowski, Brian Smith, Geoff Worrall and Peter Lawrence plus Sqdn Ldr Peter Scott, the RAF project liaison pilot, got airborne in WD808.

The third prototype, WT827, first flown by Waterton on 7 March, 1953, was the first to carry the four wing-mounted 30 mm Aden guns, AI radar and a nose radome. It was used for a series of highly successful trials which included gun heating and firing, generator cooling, general engineering, radome development and flight refuelling. For these last-named trials WT827 was fitted with a probe on the starboard wing, but its location aft of the pilot made the flight refuelling operation hazardous and difficult. During the radome development programme it was found that rain or hail quickly eroded the neoprene protective skin on the Hycar radome, and, after many attempts to improve the adhesion had failed, it was decided to modify the shape. A number of alternative shapes was tried, and the most effective, both aerodynamically and electronically, was found to be the pointed one used on all production Javelins.

In March 1953, as part of an evaluation of various European aircraft by United States Air Force test pilots under the Mutual Defense Aid Program, Cols R. Johnson and P. Everest visited Glosters to fly the Javelin. One feature of the design which received a good deal of criticism was the capacity of the internal fuel tanks which held 765 gal, and on 4 June, 1953, WT827 flew for the first time with two 250 gal ventral tanks, which, because of their location and appearance, became known as bosom tanks.

Earlier wind-tunnel tests and a good deal of high altitude flying experience with the first two prototypes, showed a requirement for a modified wing shape to improve manoeuvrability at altitude. This was achieved by reducing the sweepback on the outer wing panels from outboard of the

320

cannon bay, which increased the tip chord and reduced the thickness/chord ratio. The decreased taper ratio reduced the spanwise airflow and improved both the tip stalling and the lift coefficient at high subsonic speeds. The modified wing was fitted to WD808 and first flew on 28 May, 1953. Two weeks later on 11 June this prototype was completely destroyed in a crash at Flax Bourton, near Bristol, after experiencing super stall conditions during tests with the c.g. further aft than had previously been tried. Peter Lawrence, the pilot, delayed ejecting to avoid crashing on school children in a playing field and finally left the aircraft too low to allow his parachute to open fully. Lawrence gave almost no comment on his radio during the very rapid descent in an apparently completely stable nose-up attitude from which he was unable to regain control, and only the information from the auto-observer, which was recovered from the wreckage, enabled a complete record of this tragic accident to be compiled. This was the first recorded occasion of the super stall condition, and an interesting facet was that during the 60 sec descent from about 11,000 ft there was no airspeed recorded on the auto-observer trace. This accident was in no way attributable to the new wing shape, but was primarily due to the use of the very large flaps at too low an airspeed and with the wing at high angles of attack, which resulted in complete loss of elevator control due to blanketing. Instructions were therefore issued concerning the use of flaps at certain speeds and conditions of flight to alleviate the problem.

Spinning in the Javelin was, for those unprepared for it, an alarming experience for, although the rotation was comparatively slow, the nose of the aircraft pitched through about 70 deg during each turn. A series of model dropping-tests from a captive balloon some 5,000 ft over Cardington helped to develop a technique for recovery from a spin. R. F. 'Dicky' Martin proved this technique in nearly 200 spins in Javelins which involved the application of into-spin aileron, pushing the control column forward and adjusting the tailplane setting to give a nose-down attitude.

The fourth prototype, WT830, was the first to be fitted with full power ailerons and 7·5:1 boost ratio on the elevators; it was also the first to fly out of Hucclecote, Waterton making this flight on 14 January, 1954. This aircraft was used by Glosters for aerodynamic and stress research flying.

WT836, the last of the Javelin fighter prototypes, made its first flight on 20 July, 1954, piloted by Dicky Martin who, in March of that year, had replaced Bill Waterton as Glosters' chief test pilot. A feature of this aircraft was the double transparent canopies, with a more markedly curved top line to accommodate the new bone dome helmets of the pilot and radar operator, which became standard on all subsequent Javelin fighters. This new 'high line' canopy was fitted when it was found that under conditions of negative g the new nylon seat harness eased sufficiently to allow the crew to move upwards and leave insufficient room above their helmets for their hands to grasp the ejector-seat blind-handle. WT836 was used for a number of trial installations of equipment and also for hood jettisoning trials in the Boscombe Down 'blower' rig.

Javelin F(AW)Mk.1

The first production aircraft, XA544, was flown for the first time on 22 July, 1954, by Dicky Martin and was used for operational checks on armament, instrumentation and other trial installations. It was the forerunner of 40 Javelin Mk.1 aircraft from the Hucclecote production lines, powered by 8,000 lb thrust Armstrong Siddeley Sapphire Sa.6 engines, of which 29 were delivered to the RAF to equip No.46 Squadron at Odiham and subsequently No.87 Squadron at Wildenrath in Germany. The remaining 11 Javelins were retained as CA aircraft for use by Glosters and various Ministry Establishments during 1954–56. Among these aircraft were XA545 with the first all-flying tail unit; XA546 fitted with a Gee installation; XA547 which was equipped with four underwing weapon pylons for initial trials of the de Havilland Firestreak missiles; XA548 with an anti-spin parachute, tail bumper, drooped wing leading edge and slats for the very lengthy spinning trials; XA549 which was equipped with various types of radar installations; XA552 which was transferred to de Havilland to have 10,000 lb thrust Gyron Junior engines with reheat; XA560, the first Javelin to have reheated Sapphire Sa.7 engines which flew for the first time on 30 September, 1955; XA561, another aircraft used for spinning at Boscombe Down fitted with an anti-spin parachute and tail bumper bar; and XA562 which went to Rolls-Royce for installation of two RA.24R

Dicky Martin goes aboard XA544, the first production Javelin F(AW)1, for its first flight from Hucclecote. This aircraft still had the 'low-line' cockpit canopies.

XA548 was flown with slats and vortex generators. In this view the slats are just visible locked in the closed position. The pitot head was moved to the nose for these trials.

engines. XA544 and XA546 took part in the SBAC Display at Farnborough in September 1954, but this second aircraft was lost on 21 October when Flt Lieut R. J. Ross, an RAE pilot, crashed into the Bristol Channel off Weston super Mare. He was apparently attempting to recover from an intentional spin at too low an altitude, and the Javelin's very high rate of descent, reckoned to be about 240 ft/sec in an established spin, gave him no time to regain level flight before he hit the water. There were the usual crop of rumours, including a detailed letter and sketch from someone in Chepstow showing the jet-pipes 'melted away', and a reported sighting of the pilot on Steep Holm, a small island, but Ross's body was not recovered and the aircraft's location in the turgid waters was never established.

By this time the Javelin was attracting the interest of European air forces and, only a short time before XA546 was lost, it had been flown by Lieut-Cols C. Roman and G. de Beuger accompanied by Major H. Cabolet, a radar observer, all members of a Belgian Air Force evaluation team. During 1955, development and display flying went ahead rapidly. In June XA556 took part in the flying display at the Paris Air Show flown by Geoff Worrall, but only after much overnight work by the Gloster ground crew at Le Bourget who repaired the jet-pipe fairing damaged by flames

A rare high-altitude photograph of XA548 showing the slats locked in the open position.

323

XA552, a Javelin F(AW)1, fitted with two ventral tanks. The white lines on the tanks indicate lifting and support positions.

from a very wet start following a flame-out in the air. The following month XA544 appeared at the RAE Golden Jubilee Celebrations at Farnborough, and XA564 and XA565 were there for the SBAC Display in September. During Operation Beware, the annual air defence exercise, XA554 and XA559, fitted with two 250 gal bosom fuel tanks, were flown from RAF Coltishall by Sqdn Ldr P. Scott with Flt Lieut P. Jeffries as his radar operator/navigator, Wg Cdr E. O. Crew with Sqdn Ldr J. Walton, and Dicky Martin with Flt Lieut R. Williamson. The Javelins delighted everyone, not least the Air Staff, by fulfilling their specified operational rôle in intercepting and claiming the destruction of Canberras some 100 miles out from the coast and 'jumping' some stray USAF F-100 Super Sabres *en route*.

The Javelin F(AW)Mk.1 received its official CA release on 30 November,

Rudder buffeting was overcome by this 'pen-nib' fairing above the jet-pipes and was embodied on all production Javelins with Sapphire Sa.6 engines.

An unusual view of a Javelin, XA550, showing the massive fuselage and tail unit and the close-coupled jet-pipes.

This Javelin F(AW)1 had hot-air spray pipes to de-mist the inside surface of the cockpit canopies. The pipes appear as dark lines on the canopies.

Three prototype and two production Javelin F(AW)1s fly in formation to Farnborough for the 1954 SBAC Display.

Despite trouble with wet starts and a burnt jet-pipe fairing, XA556, photographed at Le Bourget, flew in both displays at the 1955 Paris Air Show.

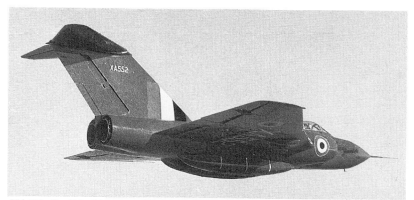

XA552 after it had been modified to flight test the de Havilland Gyron Junior engines. It carried a metal nose with a pitot boom and was finished overall blue with white markings. (*Courtesy Rolls-Royce*)

XA562, a Javelin F(AW)1, powered by two RA.24R Avons with reheat, was used by Rolls-Royce. Note the bulges below the inner mainplane and the metal nose fairing replacing the radome.

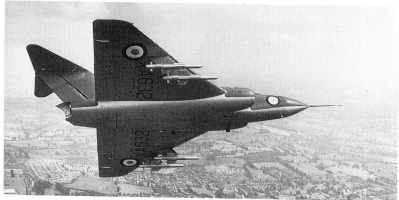

XA632, a Gloster trials aircraft, with a nose-mounted pitot boom and carrying four de Havilland Firestreak guided missiles.

1955, and the first three Javelins to be delivered to the RAF were XA568, XA570 and XA572 which flew from Moreton Valence to No.23 MU at Aldergrove, Northern Ireland, on 30 December, 1955, for routine checks and installation of the AI.17 radar before issue, on 29 February, 1956, to No.46 Squadron at Odiham for intensive flying. Under the command of Wg Cdr H. E. White, DFC, AFC, the intensive flying programme was soon in full swing with the aim of achieving 1,000 flying hours as quickly as possible. To this end pairs of Javelins took-off at 30 min intervals from 08·30 hr to 02·30 hr each day, practising every operational procedure until, within eight weeks, the required total was reached. No.87 Squadron, based at Wildenrath in Germany, was the second to get Javelin F(AW)Mk.1s, their first aircraft, XA623, arriving on 2 August, 1957, from Odiham where it had previously been flown by No.46 Squadron, who ultimately handed over 14 Javelins to No.87 Squadron.

The first Javelin F(AW)2, XD158, piloted by Sqdn Ldr P. Scott, taxi-ing at Moreton Valence.

Javelin F(AW)Mk.2

The prototype Javelin 2, XD158, flew for the first time on 31 October, 1955, piloted by Dicky Martin, and the first production aeroplane, XA768, on 25 April, 1956. The main difference between this Javelin variant and the Mk.1 aircraft was the use of the US-designed AI.22 (APQ43) radar equipment in the place of the British AI.17. The most noticeable difference was the asymmetric shape of the radome which was hinged to allow it to be opened, rather than removed, for radar servicing as in the AI.17-equipped aircraft. XD158 was fitted with an all-metal nose which was camouflaged in the standard aircraft pattern. CA release for the Javelin F(AW)Mk.2 was received on 31 May, 1957, and delivery to the RAF began on 27 June, 1957.

A total of 30 production aircraft were built by Glosters at Hucclecote of which 26 were issued to the RAF to replace the Javelin 1s in No.46 Squadron and also to equip Nos.85 and 89 Squadrons. The remaining four aircraft and the prototype were retained for test flying by Gloster and Ministry Establishments. XA769 was used for radar, electrical system and generator trials; XA770 had special armament controls fitted; XA771

Painted orange dayglo this Javelin F(AW)2, XA778, was a calibrated test vehicle with an F(AW)7 engine installation with F(AW)8 flying control system. It was used as a pacer aircraft at A and AEE to determine ASI pressure error correction on other aircraft.

was flown on missile-carrying trials and XA778 ultimately became a 'pacer' aircraft at A and AEE Boscombe Down, painted a brilliant fluorescent orange, while XD158 also went to A and AEE for radar installation trials.

Javelin T.Mk.3

In spite of the complexity of the Javelin and the fact that not only was it the largest fighter ever adopted by the RAF but also the world's first delta-winged aircraft to enter service, initially squadrons converted to this new aeroplane without the aid of a dual-control trainer. To prepare for the conversion from the Meteor NF.12s and 14s with which No.46 Squadron had been equipped, the commanding officer and a flight commander went to Boscombe Down for initial Javelin experience, then returned to Odiham to convert the remaining pilots. In this way all conversion training was completed on the squadron in under four weeks.

Glosters had begun design work on a trainer variant of the GA.5 early in 1950 to meet OR278 for a pilot conversion, instrument, and gunnery training aircraft. Design studies for tandem and side-by-side seating were

The prototype Javelin T.3 two-seat trainer. Note the tailplane Q-feel pitot heads on top of the fuselage and the enlarged cockpit canopies.

considered, but in the dual interests of making minimum modifications to the existing airframe structure and providing the pupil pilot with a cockpit layout and instrument presentation identical to that which he would find in the operational aircraft, the tandem seating scheme was chosen and specification T.118D was issued to cover this aircraft. Based on the Javelin F(AW)Mk.6 with Sapphire Sa.6 engines, the prototype T.3, WT841, was assembled by Air Service Training at Hamble using Gloster-built components, and first flew on 26 August, 1956, piloted by Zurakowski. The Javelin trainer embodied a 44 in long insert in the front fuselage to counteract the aft movement of the c.g. caused by the removal of the nose-mounted AI radar equipment. A greatly enlarged cockpit

The large canopy and housing for the instructor's periscope sight on the Javelin T.3.

canopy was used to accommodate the rear ejector seat which was raised $9\frac{1}{2}$ in above the level of the front seat to provide the instructor with a clear view forward over the top of the pupil pilot's head. The fixed wing-mounted armament of four 30 mm Aden guns was retained for gunnery instruction, and a twin horizontal periscope sight protruding from each side of the fuselage was provided for the instructor in the rear cockpit. Two 50 gal fuel tanks were fitted in the fuselage insert.

The first production Javelin T.3 first flew from Hucclecote on 6 January, 1958, and a total of 23 aircraft was built. The first batch was delivered to RAF Fighter Command's Javelin conversion unit, No.228 OCU, which was based at Leeming from October 1957 until 15 September, 1961, when it was disbanded. At that time it was believed that an adequate number of aircrews had been trained to meet the demands of the remaining Javelin squadrons until they were phased out of service. This view was substantially revised in the light of the subsequent operations by Javelins of Nos.60 and 64 Squadrons in safeguarding Malaysian airspace in the confrontation

The second production Javelin T.3 before delivery to No. 228 OCU.

with Indonesia which clearly indicated that there was a continuing need for two-seat fighters with an air identification capability. Thus on 1 June, 1965, No.228 OCU began work again, this time based at Leuchars where there was a Javelin F(AW)Mk.9 full flight simulator as well as the four Javelin T.3s belonging to Fighter Command's Instrument Rating Squadron. In addition to these four trainers, a number of Javelin F(AW)Mk.9 aircraft were delivered to the unit, being drawn mainly from Nos.5 and 11 Squadrons in Germany and No.27 MU. In common with a number of second line units, No.228 OCU had an operational rôle in the event of an emergency and during the latter part of its life its aircraft carried the markings of No.11 Squadron. No.228 OCU was finally disbanded in November 1966, having become the last unit regularly to fly the Javelin in the United Kingdom. Among its aircraft was an F(AW)Mk.9, XH898, which was believed to be unique in that it had a non-standard natural metal finish and

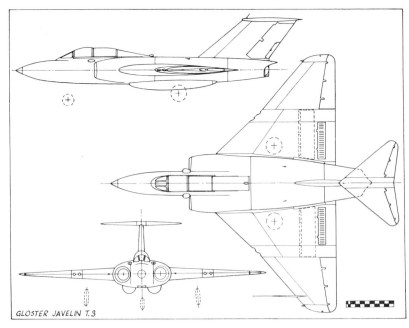

GLOSTER JAVELIN T.3

WT841 as it appeared in the 1956 SBAC Flying Display at Farnborough.

carried the letters GHB on its fin, the initials of the unit's commanding officer, Sqdn Ldr G. H. Beaton.

Apart from WT841 which was used by Glosters for trial installations of equipment, XK577 was used as a trials aircraft by A and AEE until scrapped on 16 October, 1961, and XM336 went to CFE at West Raynham.

Javelin F(AW)Mk.4

Originally projected with a one-piece slab tailplane, all production Javelins up to the 41st aircraft, XA629, had an adjustable tailplane with orthodox power-boosted elevators. At high indicated airspeeds, however, the stick forces were unacceptably high and a fully-powered all-moving tailplane with elevators acting as anti-balance tabs was introduced on XA629, the first production Javelin F(AW)Mk.4. An all-moving tailplane had been tested earlier on XA545, the second production Javelin 1, and, to speed up the flying and acceptance trials, XA629 was brought forward in Glosters' production line sequence from 41st to 11th position. It flew for the first time on 19 September, 1955, piloted by Peter Varley. This aeroplane was later used for trial installation of an audible stall warning and still later was fitted with Kuchemann, or Whitcombe, 'bumps'. Known at Glosters as 'carrots', these were streamlined bodies initially mounted on the trailing edge of the wing just inboard of the ailerons, but also later fitted at the wingtips. They were used to weaken shock waves and reduce airflow separation at high subsonic speeds in order to extend the buffet

XA630, the second production Javelin F(AW)4, prepared for its first flight from Hucclecote in March 1956.

331

Used for operational reliability trials by Glosters, this Javelin F(AW)4, XA631, had an all-metal nose and lacked Q-feel pitot heads.

boundary. The first flight with these 'carrots' was on 28 March, 1956, after extensive model testing, and about 30 hr flight testing was completed by Glosters. Tests were also made with two rows of vortex-generator vanes along the leading edge of the outer wing panels, and with thickened trailing edges on the ailerons; both measures proved useful and, because of their lower weight and cost, were adopted instead of the 'carrots' which had produced similar results. This Javelin variant was given CA release on 7 December, 1956.

Fifty Javelin F(AW)Mk.4s were built, 18 by Gloster Aircraft at Hucclecote and the remainder by Armstrong Whitworth Aircraft at Coventry. They were issued initially on 3 January, 1957, to No.141 Squadron normally based at RAF Coltishall but, at the time of their re-equipment, 'lodging' at RAF Horsham St Faith while runway improvements were made at their own base. This squadron had previously flown Venom NF.3s but converted to the Javelin without difficulty through the assistance

XA630 equipped with 'bosom' ventral fuel tanks for flight trials of the fuel system.

332

A Javelin with Kuchemann 'bumps'. These large streamlined bodies known as 'carrots' were fitted on the trailing edge of XA629's wing to weaken shock waves. (*Courtesy F. G. Swanborough*)

of flight commanders posted in from No.46 Squadron. The potent new Javelin enabled the RAF to undertake the immediate readiness rôle, which had the code name Fabulous, previously the responsibility of the USAF. 'Fabulous' aircraft were positioned on the immediate readiness platform (or 'scramble pan') adjoining the duty runway, with the crews, who were changed every hour, strapped into their seats and the tele-scramble telephone line connected while other aircraft stood by with their crews at readiness.

Another view of the 'carrots' fitted to XA629.

The tail unit of a No.46 Sqdn Javelin F(AW)4. Note the all-flying tailplane, 'pen nib' jet-pipe fairing and the thick-edged ailerons.

Pilot's cockpit of the Javelin F(AW)4. Compare this with those on pages 209 and 266.

The Javelin F(AW)Mk.4 also flew with Nos.3, 11, 23, 41, 72, 87, 96 and 141 Squadrons replacing variously Venom and Meteor night fighters as well as earlier Javelin variants.

Apart from XA629 fitted with 'carrots', other aircraft used for trials included XA630, XA634 and XA644 flown on handling trials by Glosters and A and AEE Boscombe Down; XA720, XA721 and XA723 which went to CEFE, Climatic Detachment, Nameo, Canada, for winterization trials in October 1956; and XA763 and XA764 used for development trials at CFE, West Raynham.

Three Javelin F(AW)5s of No.228 OCU, with a T.3 in the box.
(*Flight International*)

Javelin F(AW)Mk.5

The operating range of earlier Javelin variants had always been considered marginal when flying without external fuel tanks and this feature had been particularly criticized by the various evaluation teams from the USAF and from European air forces who had flown the Javelin at Moreton Valence. The Javelin F(AW)Mk.5, which was similar in all outward appearances to the F(AW)Mk.4, carried an additional 125 gal of fuel in each wing. Provision was also made for carrying four de Havilland Firestreak guided missiles on underwing pylons.

335

A standard Javelin F(AW)5. A crew mounting ladder is attached to the port side of the front fuselage.

The first F(AW)Mk.5, XA641, was first flown on 26 July, 1956, by R. F. Martin, and CA release was received on 4 March, 1957. A total of 64 aircraft was built, 20 by Glosters and the remainder by Armstrong Whitworth Aircraft, and all except six were issued to RAF squadrons. They went first to No.151 Squadron at Leuchars on 2 April, 1957, and later to Nos.5, 11, 23, 41, 72, 87 and 137 Squadrons. No.228 OCU at Leeming had 23 aircraft, and the Central Fighter Establishment at West Raynham operated two Javelin F(AW)Mk.5s.

Javelin F(AW)Mk.6

This mark of Javelin bore the same relationship to the earlier Mk.5 as did the Mk.2 to the Mk.1 in that it carried the US-built AI.22 radar under a slightly modified radome. XA815, the first of 33 examples of this Javelin variant to be built at Hucclecote, made its first flight on 14 December, 1956, piloted by R. F. Martin, and CA release was obtained with XA821

XH692, an Armstrong Whitworth built Javelin F(AW)5 of No.228 OCU, RAF Leeming. Note the special mounting ladder used by the crew to cross the air intake en route to the cockpits. (*Flight International*)

XA836, a Javelin F(AW)6, taking-off from Hucclecote piloted by Geoff Worrall.

on 15 August, 1957. Thirty-one aircraft were issued to RAF squadrons commencing with No.89 (later No.85) early in 1958 and continuing with Nos.29 and 46.

Javelin F(AW)Mk.7

Some fundamental changes were made with the introduction of the Javelin F(AW)Mk.7 which was the first production variant to carry de Havilland Firestreak infra-red homing air-to-air missiles, plus two 30 mm Aden guns, as standard armament. More of this Javelin variant were built than any other, a total of 142 being produced, 85 by Glosters and the remainder by Armstrong Whitworth Aircraft at Coventry.

Powered by the 11,000 lb thrust Sapphire Sa.7, the maximum all-up weight of the Javelin rose to over 40,000 lb when carrying four 100 gal drop tanks under the wings in addition to the two 250 gal ventral tanks. The flying-control system was also extensively modified to include pitch auto-stabilization by a Gloster-developed system, fully-powered hydraulic

A Javelin F(AW)7, powered by Sapphire Sa.7s, with extended rear fuselage, and aileron vortex generators. The light-coloured patch on the fuselage is an unpainted access door.

XH780, an Armstrong Whitworth built Javelin F(AW)7, was used for trials of flight-refuelling probes and systems with a Canberra tanker aircraft.

The lance-type flight-refuelling probe developed for late versions of the Javelin, here seen fitted to the 57th F(AW)7.

The extended rear fuselage and angled jet-pipe nozzles on the Javelin F(AW)7.

XH712 was fitted with a metal nose fairing with a pitot and yaw vane boom for Javelin F(AW)7 handling trials at A and AEE Boscombe Down.

operation of the rudder with a yaw stabilizer and electro-hydraulic three-axes control autopilot with an automatic approach and altitude control. To reduce the base drag which was higher than calculated, the rear fuselage was extended and the top line raised; vortex generators were fitted to the wings, and ailerons having thickened trailing edges were used. The under-wing launching pylons for the Firestreak missiles were extensively flight tested and were of complex shape. Because of high local Mach numbers in the region of the pylons and the need to avoid excessive drag rise which would reduce the aircraft's range, a sophisticated design was ultimately evolved. The pylons were swept back at an angle from the missile to the undersurface of the wing, were waisted in end elevation and had a

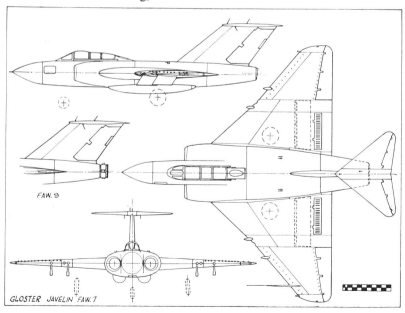

XH758, a Javelin F(AW)7, carrying two Firestreak guided missiles and two Microcell rocket pods on underwing pylons.

thickness/chord ratio of 10 per cent at the top and bottom reducing to a constant 6 per cent over the central portion.

The first Javelin F(AW)Mk.7, XH704, first flew on 9 November, 1956, piloted by Dicky Martin, and CA release was obtained with XH710 on 7 January, 1958. The second Javelin Mk.7, XH705, was a production tryout for the Firestreak installation, and it was not until the 30th aircraft, XH753, which was brought forward in production sequence from its proper position, that this installation was embodied on the assembly line. All earlier aircraft of this mark were equipped retrospectively. Of the total number of Javelin F(AW)Mk.7s built, 24 were initially retained for various trials and the remainder were issued to the RAF squadrons, beginning with first deliveries to the MUs on 30 May, 1958, and to No.33 Squadron in the following August. Subsequently Javelin Mk.7s were issued to Nos.23, 25 and 64 Squadrons. No.25 Squadron promptly applied their squadron markings, consisting of two black bars, to the fins of their Firestreak missiles as well as to their aircraft.

Among the Javelin Mk.7s retained for trials were XH706, (handling and

A close-up view of the starboard Firestreak guided missile and rocket pod on XH758.

340

autostabilizer), XH713 (tropical trials), XH754 (autopilot and vision in rain trials), XH756 and XH757 (missile trials) and XH758 (final conference aircraft).

A total of 76 Javelin F(AW)Mk.7s were subsequently converted to Javelin F(AW)Mk.8 standards and redesignated F(AW)Mk.9.

Javelin F(AW)Mk.8

This was the final production version of the Javelin and was the first to be powered with the 11,000 lb thrust Sapphire Sa.7R which had limited reheat. Operable above 20,000 ft this reheat system provided a 12 per cent increase in thrust to give a total thrust of 12,300 lb. The Javelin Mk.8 was fitted with a Sperry autopilot and had the Gloster-developed pitch auto-stabilizer, the Louis Newmark yaw stabilizer, and fully-powered rudder, with drooped leading edge to the mainplane and two rows of vortex generators. The US-built AI.22 radar was carried, and provision was made for the standard armament of four Firestreak air-to-air missiles on under-wing pylons and two 30 mm Aden guns in the outer positions in the main-planes.

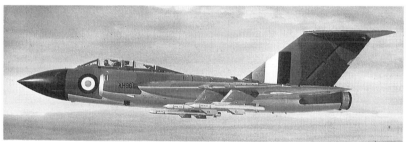

In common with all Javelin F(AW)8s, the first production aircraft, XH966, was powered by reheated Sapphire Sa.7R engines.

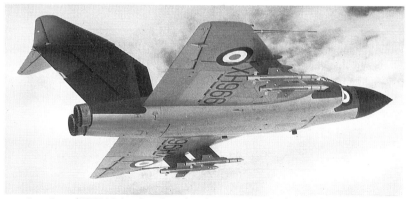

Another view of XH966 showing the twin reheat nozzles, the four underwing Firestreaks and the second pitot head boom on the starboard wingtip.

341

Javelin F(AW)8, XJ125, lining up for take-off at the 1961 SBAC Flying Display at Farnborough. (*Courtesy Rolls-Royce*)

Forty-seven Javelin F(AW)Mk.8s were built by Glosters at Hucclecote, and the first, XH966, flew on 9 May, 1958, piloted by Dicky Martin. The last, XJ165, was assembled at Moreton Valence and left there on 16 August, 1960, on a delivery flight to No.41 Squadron at Wattisham and was, in fact, the last aircraft to be built by Glosters. The 41st production Javelin Mk.8, XJ125, was advanced in the production line sequence from 289th to 233rd position to replace the 4th aircraft, XH969, so that the production tryout of mod.1011, pitch stabilizer, could be completed as early as possible.

The Javelin F(AW)Mk.8 was first delivered to MUs on 1 October, 1959, and reached No.41 Squadron in the spring of 1960. This variant was subsequently delivered to Nos.23, 72 and 85 Squadrons. Four aircraft, XH966, XH968—970 were retained by Glosters for CA release work and various auto-stabilizer trials. A and AEE had five Javelin Mk.8s, XH966–970 for handling, performance and other trials; and Armstrong Siddeley Motors were allocated XJ125 for development flying with their Sapphire Sa.7R engines.

Javelin F(AW)Mk.9

In squadron service the massive all-weather Javelin performed its tasks with great efficiency and surprised many of its critics by outperforming the Hunter, particularly on the climb to 50,000 ft, and its ability to carry infinitely superior armament. At high altitude, however, the Javelin F(AW)Mk.7 lacked the manoeuvrability of its more powerful successor, the F(AW)Mk.8 with its reheated Sapphire engines and aerodynamic

XH768, a Javelin F(AW)9, carrying ventral fuel tanks.

342

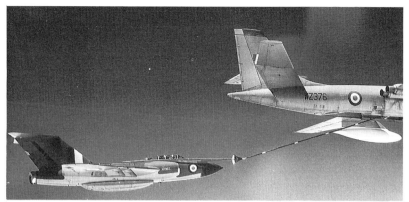

A Valiant tanker aircraft was used for 'wet hook-ups' during flight-refuelling trials of the Javelin F(AW)9.

refinements. In consequence, in 1960, it was decided to modify a large number of Javelin Mk.7s to bring them up to the same standard as the Javelin Mk.8. In this form the aircraft were redesignated Javelin F(AW)Mk.9, and the first to be so converted was XH959 on 15 January, 1960.

The ever present threat, at that time, of the loss of RAF airfields and staging posts around the world, particularly in the Middle and Far East, where the confrontation with Indonesia was brewing up, focused attention on the reinforcing range of all RAF aircraft and especially fighters. Some rather inconclusive flight-refuelling trials of the 'dry hook-up' type had earlier been undertaken with the Javelin Mk.4 XA634, having a wing-

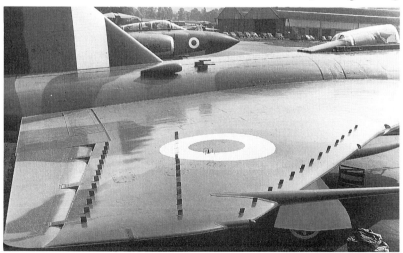

Two tailplane and two rudder Q-feel pitot heads, two cooling air intakes, three rows of vortex generators, stall-warning vane and an additional pitot head boom adorn this Javelin F(AW)9 at Moreton Valence.

M

343

Believed unique among Javelins, this F(AW)9, flown by Sqdn Ldr G. H. Beaton of No.228 OCU at RAF Leeming, was in natural metal finish and bore his initials in black on the fin. (*Courtesy Roger Levy*)

mounted probe, and a Canberra tanker. In later trials with two Javelin Mk.9s, XH780 and XH965, and Valiant and Canberra tankers, a large fixed probe some 20 ft in length was mounted high on the starboard side of the front fuselage. This position was much more successful, and 22 Javelin Mk.9s were ultimately fitted with this type of probe. Other modifications included the drooped leading edge on the outer mainplanes, jet-pipes with variable-area nozzles and the inclusion of an autopilot.

The first of these rejuvenated Javelins entered RAF service with No.25 Squadron in the summer of 1960 and, throughout the remainder of the year and into 1961, deliveries were made to Nos.23, 29, 60 and 64 Squadrons. In October 1960 four Javelin F(AW)Mk.9s of No.23 Squadron flew nonstop from the United Kingdom to Singapore, flight refuelling from Valiant tanker aircraft *en route*.

The last United Kingdom based operational unit with Javelin F(AW)Mk.9s (and with Gloster aeroplanes) was No.25 Squadron based

The reheat nozzles of the Sapphire Sa.7Rs powering No.23 Sqdn's Javelin F(AW)9s. The second aircraft is carrying a black dummy Firestreak missile. (*Rolls-Royce*)

344

A Javelin F(AW)9 of No.5 Sqdn, with empty missile pylons, taxi-ing at Bodø in Arctic Norway during the 1964 NATO exercise Northern Express. (*Courtesy William Green*).

at Leuchars who flew the Javelins until October 1964 when they were replaced by English Electric Lightnings. Overseas, No.11 Squadron at Geilenkirchen in Germany retained Javelins until February 1966, while No.29 Squadron, serving in Cyprus, flew their Javelins until April 1967 when they converted to Lightnings at Wattisham. No.29 Squadron went to Ndola in Zambia during the early days of the Rhodesian UDI crisis in 1966.

In June 1967, at Tengah, No.64 Squadron flew a final flypast to mark their disbandment; this was in conjunction with No.60 Squadron and, with 14 Javelins airborne, this was the last time that so many were seen in the air together.

Three generations of fighters are represented by this formation of a Javelin F(AW)4, a Meteor NF.14 and the Gladiator.

TECHNICAL DATA

Description: Two-seat all-weather fighter (Mks.1, 2, 4, 5, 6, 7, 8 and 9). Two-seat trainer (Mk.3). Metal stressed-skin construction.

Accommodation: Pilot and crew in enclosed cockpits.

Powerplant: Two 8,000 lb (3,628 kg) thrust Armstrong Siddeley Sapphire Sa.6 Mk.10201 (port) and 10301 (starboard) turbojets (Mks.1, 4 and 5).

Two 8,000 lb (3,628 kg) thrust Armstrong Siddeley Sapphire Sa.6 Mk.10701 (port) and 10301 (starboard) turbojets (Mks.2 and 5).

Two 8,000 lb (3,628 kg) thrust Armstrong Siddeley Sapphire Sa.6 Mk.11201 (port) and 11301 (starboard) turbojets (Mk.3).

Two 11,000 lb (4,990 kg) thrust Armstrong Siddeley Sapphire Sa.7 Mk.20301 (port) and 20401 (starboard) turbojets (Mk.7).

Two 11,000 lb (4,990 kg) thrust Armstrong Siddleey Sapphire Sa.7R Mk.20501R (port) and 20601R (starboard) turbojets with 12 per cent limited reheat to provide 12,300 lb. (5,579 kg) thrust above 20,000 ft (6,096 m) altitude (Mk.8).

Two 11,000 lb (4,900 kg) thrust Armstrong Siddeley Sapphire Sa.7R Mk.20901R (port) and 21001R (starboard) turbojets with 12 per cent limited reheat to provide 12,300 lb (5,579 kg) thrust above 20,000 ft (6,096 m) altitude (Mk.9).

Fuel 765 gal (3,475 litres) (Mks.1, 2 and 4); 1,064 gal (4,836 litres) (Mk.3); 995 gal (4,340 litres) (Mks.5 and 6); 915 gal (4,158 litres) (Mk.7); 950 gal (4,318 litres) (Mks. 8 and 9). All variants could carry two 250 gal (1,136 litres) ventral tanks and Mks.7, 8 and 9 had provision for four 100 gal (454 litres) tanks on underwing pylons.

Armament: Four fixed Aden 30 mm cannon mounted in the outer mainplanes. Mks.7, 8 and 9 also had provision for four de Havilland Firestreak air-to-air guided weapons carried on underwing pylons.

Dimensions:	Mk.1	Mk.2	Mk.3	Mk.4	Mk.5
Span	52 ft 0 in	52 ft 0 in	52 ft 0 in	52 ft 0 in	52 ft 0 in
	(15·8 m)	(15·8 m)	(15·8 m)	(15·8 m)	(15·8 m)
Length	56 ft 3 in	56 ft 3 in	59 ft 11 in	56 ft 3 in	56 ft 3 in
	(17·1 m)	(17·1 m)	(18·2 m)	(17·1 m)	(17·1 m)
Height	16 ft 0 in	16 ft 0 in	16 ft 0 in	16 ft 0 in	16 ft 0 in
	(4·8 m)	(4·8 m)	(4·8 m)	(4·8 m)	(4·8 m)
Wing area	927 sq ft	927 sq ft	927 sq ft	927 sq ft	927 sq ft
	(86 sq m)	(86 sq m)	(86 sq m)	(86 sq m)	(86 sq m)

Mainplane and tailplane aerofoil section: RAE 101. Thickness/chord ratio 0·010 (inner wing), 0·0089 (outer wing); track 23 ft 4 in (7·1 m).

Weights:	Mk.1	Mk.2	Mk.3	Mk.4	Mk.5
Take-off	31,580 lb	32,100 lb	38,000 lb	32,800 lb	34,990 lb
(clean aircraft)	(14,324 kg)	(14,500 kg)	(17,237 kg)	(14,877 kg)	(15,871 kg)
Overload (two	36,690 lb	37,200 lb	42,000 lb	37,480 lb	39,370 lh
ventral tanks)	(16,641 kg)	(16,873 kg)	(19,051 kg)	(17,000 kg)	(17,857 kg)
Performance:					
Maximum speed	616 kt	616 kt	555 kt	610 kt	612 kt
at sea level	(0·925 MN)	(0·925 MN)	(0·83MN)	(0·915 MN)	(0·92 MN)
(clean aircraft)	(1,141 km/h)	(1,141 km/h)	(1,028 km/h)	(1,130 km/h)	(1,134 km/h)
Maximum speed	—	—	523 kt	—	—
at 35,000 ft			(0·91 MN)		
(10,669 m)			(969 km/h)		
Maximum speed	540 kt	540 kt	—	550 kt	535 kt
at 40,000 ft	(0·94 MN)	(0·94 MN)		(0·955 MN)	(0·93 MN)
(12,192 m)	(1,000 km/h)	(1,000 km/h)		(1,019 km/h)	(991 km/h)
Climb to 45,000 ft					
(13,716 m)	9·8 min	9·8 min	22 min	8 min	10·3 min
Service ceiling	52,500 ft	52,500 ft	46,000 ft	50,700 ft	50,100 ft
	(16,001 m)	(16,001 m)	(14,020 m)	(15,453 m)	(15,270 m)
Absolute ceiling	55,000 ft	55,000 ft	49,500 ft	52,000 ft	51,600 ft
	(16,764 m)	(16,764 m)	(15,087 m)	(15,849 m)	(15,726 m)

	Mk.6	Mk.7	Mk.8	Mk.9
Dimensions:				
Span	52 ft 0 in	52 ft 0 in	52 ft 0 in	52 ft 0 in
	(15·8 m)	(15·8 m)	(15·8 m)	(15·8 m)
Length	56 ft 3 in	56 ft 3 in	56 ft 3 in	56 ft 9 in
	(17·1 m)	(17·1 m)	(17·1m)	(17·2 m)
Height	16 ft 0 in	16 ft 0 in	16 ft 0 in	16 ft 0 in
	(4·8 m)	(4·8 m)	(4·8 m)	(4·8 m)
Wing area	927 sq ft	927 sq ft	927 sq ft	927 sq ft
	(86 sq m)	(86 sq m)	(86 sq m)	(86 sq m)

Mainplane and tailplane aerofoil section: RAE 101. Thickness/chord ratio 0·010 (inner wing), 0·0089 (outer wing); track 23 ft 4 in (7·1 m).

	Mk.6	Mk.7	Mk.8	Mk.9
Weights:				
Take-off	35,810 lb	35,690 lb	37,410 lb	38,100 lb
(clean aircraft)	(16,243 kg)	(16,188 kg)	(16,968 kg)	(17,272 kg)
Overload (two	40,600 lb	40,270 lb	42,510 lb	43,165 lb
ventral tanks)	(18,416 kg)	18,266 kg)	(19,282 kg)	(19,578 kg)
Performance:				
Maximum speed	612 kt	616 kt	610 kt	610 kt
at sea level	(0·92 MN)	(0·925 MN)	(0·915 MN)	(0·915 MN)
(clean aircraft)	(1,134 km/h)	(1,141 km/h)	(1,130 km/h)	(1,130 km/h)
Maximum speed	—	—	534 kt	534 kt
at 35,000 ft			(0·925 MN)	(0·925MN)
(10,669 m)			(989 km/h)	(989 km/h)
Maximum speed	535 kt	—	—	—
at 40,000 ft	(0·93 MN)			
(12,192 m)	(991 km/h)			
Maximum speed	—	540 kt	—	—
at 45,000 ft		(0·945 MN)		
(13,716 m)		(1,000 km/h)		
Climb to 45,000 ft				
(13,716 m)	10·3 min	6·6 min		
Climb to 50,000 ft				
(15,240 m)	—	—	9·25 min	9·25 min
Service ceiling	50,100 ft	52,800 ft	52,000 ft	52,000 ft
	(15,270 m)	(16,039 m)	(15,849 m)	(15,849 m)
Absolute ceiling	51,600 ft	54,100 ft	54,000 ft	54,000 ft
	(15,726 m)	(16,489 m)	(16,459 m)	(16,459 m)

Production: A total of 302 GA.5s and Javelins produced by Gloster Aircraft Co Ltd, Hucclecote, Glos. during 1949–59 and 133 Javelins produced by Sir W. G. Armstrong Whitworth Aircraft Ltd, Baginton, Coventry, during 1956–59 as follows:

7 prototypes 1949–54.
40 Javelin Mk.1 production aircraft 1952–54.
30 Javelin Mk.2 production aircraft 1955–57.
22 Javelin Mk.3 production aircraft 1955–57.
50 Javelin Mk.4 production aircraft 1955–58.
64 Javelin Mk.5 production aircraft 1955–57.
33 Javelin Mk.6 production aircraft 1954–56.
142 Javelin Mk.7 production aircraft 1954–57.
47 Javelin Mk.8 production aircraft 1957–59.
76 Javelin Mk.9 converted from Mk.7 aircraft 1960–61.

Allocation: See Individual Aircraft Notes pages 369–373.

Individual Aircraft Notes

In this section will be found basic data on production quantities and service of every Gloster type with details, where available, of contract and airframe serial numbers, dates of first flights and deliveries. Because of space restrictions, generally details of only the first location to which an aircraft was delivered are given; where aircraft were assigned to Ministry Establishments or other manufacturers for trials, wherever possible the duty on which the individual aircraft were engaged is also included.

Abbreviations most frequently used in these notes refer to the following:

A and AEE	Aircraft and Armament Experimental Establishment
AEE	Aircraft Experimental Establishment
AFDS	Air Fighting Development Squadron
AFS	Advanced Flying School
AGS	Air Gunnery School
AI	Airborne Interception radar
AIEU	Armament and Instrument Experimental Unit
AM	Air Ministry
ANS	Air Navigation School
APS	Armament Practice Squadron
ASM	Armstrong Siddeley Motors Ltd
AWA	Sir W. G. Armstrong Whitworth Aircraft Ltd
AWFLS	All Weather Fighter Leader School
B	Bomber
CA	Controller of Aircraft (at Ministry of Supply)
CFE	Central Fighter Establishment
CFS	Central Flying School
CGS	Central Gunnery School
Comms	Communications
CSA	Controller of Supplies (Air)
CU	Conversion Units
DFLS	Day Fighter Leader School
DH	de Havilland Aircraft Co Ltd
EAAS	Empire Air Armament School
EFTS	Elementary Flying Training School
ETPS	Empire Test Pilots School
F	Fighter
F(AW)	Fighter (All Weather)
FCCS	Fighter Command Communications Squadron
Flt	Flight
FR	Fighter Reconnaissance
FRS	Flying Refresher School
FTS	Flying Training School
FWS	Fighter Weapons School

G.A.C.	Gloster Aircraft Company Ltd
HAL	Hawker Aircraft Ltd
HVAR	High Velocity Aircraft Rocket
MAP	Ministry of Aircraft Production
MoD	Ministry of Defence
MU	Maintenance Unit
NF	Night Fighter
PR	Photographic Reconnaissance
RAAF	Royal Australian Air Force
RAE	Royal Aircraft Establishment
RAFFC	Royal Air Force Flying College
RCAF	Royal Canadian Air Force
RNethAF	Royal Netherlands Air Force
RNZAF	Royal New Zealand Air Force
SAAF	South African Air Force
S of TT	School of Technical Training
Sqdn	Squadron
STU	Service Trials Unit
T	Trainer
TI	Trial Installation of equipment
TRE	Telecommunications Research Establishment
TT	Target Tug
Wg	Wing

Gloster Mars I. One aircraft, G-EAXZ, built by Gloucestershire Aircraft Company Ltd as a private venture. First flown on 20 June, 1921, by J. H. James. Napier Lion II engine. Named Bamel, it won the Aerial Derby in 1921, 1922 and, renamed Gloster I, again in 1923. Was the only entrant in 1924 and 1925 when the race was abandoned on both occasions. Bought by the Air Ministry in December 1923 for £3,000 and with serial J7234 was mounted on floats to become a trainer for the RAF's 1925 and 1927 Schneider Trophy contest pilots. Scrapped at end of 1927.

Gloster Mars II. Thirty aircraft, JN400, JN402–430, built by Gloucestershire Aircraft Company Ltd in 1921 for the Imperial Japanese Navy as Sparrowhawk I. Bentley B.R.2 rotary engine. Modified Nighthawk airframe.

Gloster Mars III. Ten aircraft, JN401, JN431–439, built by Gloucestershire Aircraft Company Ltd in 1921 for the Imperial Japanese Navy as Sparrowhawk II. Bentley B.R.2 rotary engine. Two-seat version of Sparrowhawk I. One aircraft, G-EAYN, built as private-venture demonstrator. First flown in April 1922. Competed in 1922 Aerial Derby but retired. Was converted to Grouse I in 1923.

Gloster Mars IV. Ten aircraft, JN442–451, built by Gloucestershire Aircraft Company Ltd in 1921 for Imperial Japanese Navy as Sparrowhawk III. Bentley B.R.2 rotary engine. Sparrowhawk I with flotation gear, hydrovanes and arrester gear.

Mars VI Nighthawk. About 29 Nieuport Nighthawk airframes converted to Mars VI by Gloucestershire Aircraft Company during 1922–23 under contract No.3467703/22 dated 13 October, 1922. Powered either by Armstrong Siddeley Jaguar II or Bristol Jupiter III engine. Prototype, H8544, first flown in June 1922.

Representative aircraft in service: No.1 Sqdn H8544; No.8 Sqdn J6925–6; RAE J6927.

Greek Mars VI Nighthawk. Twenty-five of the Nieuport Nighthawk airframes converted to Mars VI standard were ordered by the Greek Government in 1922 and delivered during the same year. Greek serial numbers unknown.

Mars X Nightjar. Twenty-two Nieuport Nighthawk airframes converted to Mars X by Gloucestershire Aircraft Company during 1922–23 under contract No.AM373763/22 dated 8 January, 1923. Powered by Bentley B.R.2 rotary engine.

Representative aircraft in service with No.203 Sqdn, No.401 Flight and a Training Flight at Leuchars were H8535–6, H8538–9, J6928–30, J6932, J6941; RAE H8535; AEE H8539.

Gloster Grouse I. The Mars II/Sparrowhawk I G-EAYN demonstrator modified in 1923 to embody Gloster H.L.B. wing combination. Bentley B.R.2 rotary engine.

Gloster Grouse II. G-EAYN modified as *ab initio* trainer in 1924. Armstrong Siddeley Lynx engine. C of A reissued on 21 April, 1925. Sold to Sweden on 9 December, 1925, modified to embody oleo landing gear.

Gloster Gannet One aircraft, G-EBHU, built by Gloucestershire Aircraft Company. First flown on 23 November, 1923. 750 cc Carden two-stroke engine. Flew in the 1923 *Daily Mail* Light Aeroplane competition at Lympne, was re-engined in 1924 with 698 cc Blackburne Tomtit. Sold for scrap in 1932 to R. V. Coley and Son.

Gloster Grebe. Three prototype aircraft, J6969, J6970, J6971, built by Gloucestershire Aircraft Company during 1923 and ordered under contract No.402023/23 as Nighthawk (thick-winged). Powered by Armstrong Siddeley Jaguar III engine. First flown in May 1923. A fourth aircraft, G-EBHA, which was built as a company demonstrator, first flew on 6 July, 1923, piloted by L. Carter, and a C of A was issued on 11 July, 1923. G-EBHA was scrapped 1930. A and AEE, J6969, J6970; G.A.C., J6971, G-EBHA.

Gloster Grebe Mk.II. A total of 129 aircraft, J7283–J7294, J7357–J7402, J7406–J7417, J7519–J7538, J7568–J7603, and J7784–J7786, built by Gloucestershire Aircraft Company during 1923–27 in five batches. First flight of J7283 in August 1923, piloted by L. Carter. Powered by Armstrong Siddeley Jaguar IV engine. Deliveries began in October 1923 and were completed in 1928.

Representative aircraft in Royal Air Force squadron service: No.19 Sqdn J7407; No.25 Sqdn J7284–J7294, J7363, J7368, J7372, J7392, J7402, J7538; No.29 Sqdn J7520, J7521; No.32 Sqdn J7599; No.56 Sqdn J7406, J7408–J7417, J7583; No.111 Sqdn (one flight only). Other aircraft: J7283 (A and AEE), J7381, J7394 (Sold to New Zealand), J7400 (Trials in conjunction with airship R-33), J7519 (Converted to two-seat trainer).

Gloster II. Two aircraft, J7504 and J7505, were built by Gloucestershire Aircraft Company Ltd in 1924 to an Air Ministry specification for the Schneider Trophy contest. Both aircraft were powered by the Napier Lion engine. J7504 sank during pre-race trials at Felixstowe in September 1924 and was written off. Fitted with a wheeled landing gear, J7505 crash-landed at Cranwell during high-speed trials in 1925.

Gloster Gamecock. Three prototype aircraft, J7497, J7756 and J7757 designed to Air Ministry specification 37/23, built by Gloucestershire Aircraft Company during 1924–25 and ordered as Grebe IIs. First flight of J7497 in February 1925, piloted by H. Saint, with Grebe-type tail unit and powered by Bristol Jupiter IV engine. J7756 had Jupiter IV, and J7757 had a Jupiter VI engine.

A and AEE, J7497 (Handling and performance trials); G.A.C. and Bristol Aeroplane Company, J7756, J7757 (Development and engine trials).

Gloster Gamecock Mk.I. Ninety aircraft, J7891–J7920, J8033–J8047, J8069–J8095 and J8405–J8422, designed to Air Ministry specification 18/25, built by Gloucestershire/Gloster Aircraft Company during 1925–27 in three production batches ordered in September 1925, July 1926 and November 1926. Powered by Bristol Jupiter VI engine. Armament was two Vickers Mk.I ·303 in machine-guns with 600 rounds per gun. Deliveries began in May 1926.

Representative aircraft in RAF Sqdn service: No.3 Sqdn J8407, J8410, J8411; No.17 Sqdn J8405, J8408, J8414; No.23 Sqdn J7894, J7895, J7898, J7903, J7907, J7914, J7915, J8040, J8041, J8082, J8084, J8406, J8409, J8420, J8421; No.32 Sqdn J7907, J7909, J8044, J8420; No.43 Sqdn J7904, J7905, J7908, J7919, J7920, J8037, J8090, J8415, J8418, J8421. Other aircraft: J7910 (G.A.C. and RAE handling trials), J8046, J8047, J8075 (Mercury IIA development trials), J8089 (CFS), J8033, J8034 (AGS), G-EBNT and G-EBOE (G.A.C. demonstrator aircraft civil registrations).

Gloster Gamecock Mk.II. One aircraft, J8804, built by Gloster Aircraft Company in 1927, plus two pattern airframes for Finland delivered in November 1928. Fitted with larger rudder, narrow-chord ailerons, new windscreen, and centre section introduced in upper mainplanes. J8075, Gamecock I, used for flight development of Mercury II engine, and J7910, Gamecock I, used for anti-flutter trials, were brought up to Mk.II standard.

Gloster III. Two aircraft, N194, and N195 subsequently G-EBLJ, were built by Gloucestershire Aircraft Co Ltd to an Air Ministry order in 1925 for the Schneider Trophy contest in Baltimore. Fitted with 700 hp Napier Lion engine. First flight of N194 was on 20 August, 1925, and of N195 a few days later. Redesignated Gloster IIIA after modification. N195 broke float struts during taxi-ing tests and was withdrawn from contest. N194 took second place in the race. With further modifications, designation changed to Gloster IIIB. N194 delivered to Felixstowe in June 1926 and N195 in November 1926, where both aircraft were used as trainers by the High Speed Flight.

Gloster Gorcock. Three aircraft, J7501–3, built by Gloster Aircraft Company during 1926–28 to Air Ministry contract, first two with all-metal fuselage and wooden wings, third Gorcock was company's first all-metal aircraft. First flew in 1925 and delivered RAE Farnborough in 1927. Napier Lion IV and VIII geared and direct-drive engines.

Gloster Guan. Three aircraft ordered from Gloucestershire Aircraft Company by Air Ministry in 1925, but only two, J7722–3, were built during 1926–27. All-metal fuselage and wooden wings. First flew in June 1926 and delivered to RAE Farnborough in August. Subsequent aircraft delivered early 1927. Napier Lion IV and VI geared and direct-drive engines fitted with exhaust driven turbo-supercharger.

Gloster Goral. One aircraft, J8763, built by Gloster Aircraft Company during 1926–27 under Air Ministry contract to specification 26/27. First flown on 8 February, 1927, and delivered to A and AEE Martlesham Heath for type competition. Bristol Jupiter VIA radial engine.

Gloster Goring. One aircraft, J8674, built by Gloucestershire Aircraft Company during 1926 as a private venture to specification 23/25 and 24/25. First flown in March 1927 powered by Bristol Jupiter VI. Converted to seaplane in 1930 fitted with Jupiter VIII. On conversion back to landplane new vertical tail surface fitted and a Jupiter XF engine installed. Taken on charge by the Air Ministry in 1932 and transferred to Filton for flight tests of Mercury VIIA, Pegasus II and Perseus IIL by the Bristol company.

Gloster Goldfinch. One aircraft, J7940, built by Gloster Aircraft Company during 1926–1927 to Air Ministry contract. All-metal construction. First flew in the summer of 1927 and delivered to A and AEE Martlesham for competitive trials but Bristol Bulldog was awarded the contract. Bristol Jupiter VIIF supercharged engine.

Gloster IV. One aircraft, N224, was ordered and built by Gloucestershire Aircraft Company Ltd to Air Ministry specification 5/26 in 1926 for the Schneider Trophy contest. Fitted with a 900 hp Napier Lion VIIA direct-drive engine. Delivered to Calshot for the High Speed Flight in July 1926 for flight trials. Transferred to Felixstowe in November 1926 and used, with various modifications, for flight development and training. In 1930 sold to Amherst Villiers for proposed attempt on world's speed record.

351

Gloster IVA. One aircraft, N222, was ordered and built to Air Ministry specification 5/26 in 1926. Fitted with 900 hp Napier Lion VIIA direct-drive engine. Delivered to Calshot for the High Speed Flight on 29 July, 1926, and shipped to Venice on 16 August. Was reserve aircraft in the Schneider Trophy contest and shipped to Felixstowe on 4 October, 1926. Returned to Sunningend on 21 February, 1928, and after modification and conversion for training rôle was delivered to Felixstowe in July 1928. Returned again to factory in March 1929 for modifications to tail unit and delivered back to Felixstowe in following June. Completed 147 flights during 1929–31 on training and research flying by the High Speed Flight.

Gloster IVB. One aircraft, N223, was ordered and built to Air Ministry specification 5/26 in 1926. Fitted with a geared 885 hp Napier Lion VIIB. Delivered to Calshot for the High Speed Flight in August 1926 and shipped to Venice on 16 August. Flown in Schneider Trophy contest on 20 September, 1927, but retired after five laps and shipped back to Felixstowe on 4 October for flight trials. Returned to Sunningend on 21 February, 1928, and after modification and conversion for training was delivered to Felixstowe in July 1928. Returned again to factory in March 1929 for modifications to tail unit and delivered back to Felixstowe and Calshot for high speed research and training until it crashed while alighting in fog on 19 December, 1930.

Gloster Gambet. One aircraft built by Gloster Aircraft Company as a private venture. First flew 12 December, 1927. Sold as pattern aircraft to Nakajima Hikoki K.K., Japan, who acquired production rights. Bristol Jupiter VI radial engine. Aircraft won type competition in Japan and ordered into production in April 1929 as A1N1 carrierborne fighter for the Imperial Japanese Navy. Fifty aircraft built during 1929–30 with Nakajima Jupiter VI engine. One hundred A1N2s built during 1930–32 with Nakajima Kotobuki 2 radial engines. J-AAMB, a civil registered A1N1, was fitted with a sliding cockpit canopy.

Gloster Gnatsnapper I. Two aircraft, N227 and N254, built by Gloster Aircraft Company during 1927–30 to meet Air Ministry specification N.21/26. Powered by a Bristol Mercury IIA or Bristol Jupiter VII.

Gloster Gnatsnapper II. N227 and N254 modified and powered by an Armstrong Siddeley Jaguar VIII engine.

Gloster Gnatsnapper III. N227 further modified to incorporate two-bay wings. Used by Rolls-Royce as flying test-bed for the Kestrel IIS and Goshawk engines, and until 1934 as a company hack.

Gloster SS.18. One aircraft, J9125, originally designed to specification F.9/26 and progressively developed during the period 1929–1934. Fitted with a Bristol Mercury IIA engine in 1927 to specification F.20/27. Engine replaced by Bristol Jupiter VII and aircraft redesignated SS.18A. Engine replaced by Armstrong Siddeley Panther III and aircraft redesignated SS.18B in 1930. Engine replaced by Bristol Jupiter VIIF, armament increased to four Lewis and two Vickers guns and aircraft redesignated SS.19. Lewis guns removed in 1931, tail unit was modified and aircraft redesignated SS.19A. In 1933 Bristol Mercury VIS and later VIS2 engine was fitted and aircraft redesignated SS.19B, and the production Gauntlet to specification 24/33 was based on this.

Gloster Gauntlet I. Production batch of 24 aircraft, K4081–K4104, built by Gloster Aircraft Company, Hucclecote, to specification 24/33 and ordered under contract No.285263/35. Bristol Mercury VIS2 engine, two-blade wooden fixed-pitch propeller and two Vickers Mk.III machine-guns with 600 rounds per gun. No.6 Sqdn K4085, K4088, K4091, K4093, K4101, K4104; No.19 Sqdn K4082–K4102, K4104, K4087 (crashed 26/1/37); Aircraft Storage Unit, Waddington, 1935: K4101–K4104. Ground Instruction Machines: K4082 (later 867M), K4086 (later 1290M), K4090 (later 2126M),

K4098 (later 1137M), K4102 (later 2127M), K4103 (later 2216M). Other aircraft: K4081 (A and AEE, handling and performance development trials, 1935), K4082 (A and AEE, production performance checks, 1935), K4103 (A and AEE, tests with hydraulic and pneumatic flap operation, July 1936), K4090 (No.9 FTS), K4098 (No.1 Anti-Aircraft School), K4094—Browning gun installation. Aircraft sold to Denmark: K4081.

Gloster Gauntlet II. Second production batch of 104 aircraft, K5264–K5367, built by Gloster Aircraft Company, during 1935–36 and ordered under contract No.396880/35. Bristol Mercury VIS2 engine, two-blade wooden, or three-blade metal, fixed-pitch propeller and two Vickers Mk.V machine-guns with 600 rounds per gun. Hawker-type construction in rear fuselage and wings.

 Operated by RAF Squadrons: Nos. 3, 6, 17, 19, 32, 33, 46, 54, 56, 65, 66, 74, 79, 80, 111, 112, 151, 213, 601, 602, 605, 615, 616.

Aircraft sold to Finland, February 1940: K5267, K5270, K5271, K5288, K5293, K5313, K5324, K5326, K5338, K5341, K5352, K5358, K5364, K5365.

Aircraft sold to Rhodesia, October 1936: K5277, K5347.

Aircraft sold to South Africa, July 1940: K5276, K5330.

Gloster Gauntlet II. Third production batch of 100 aircraft, K7792–K7891, built by Gloster Aircraft Company, during 1936 and ordered under contract No. 442477/36. Hawker-type construction used throughout.

Operated by RAF Squadrons: Nos. 3, 6, 17, 19, 32, 46, 54, 56, 65, 66, 74, 79, 80, 111, 123, 151, 601, 602, 615.

Aircraft sold to Finland, January/February 1940: K7807, K7813, K7826, K7837, K7839, K7857, K7858, K7865, K7867, K7869, K7878.

Aircraft sold to Rhodesia, 1939: K7825.

Aircraft sold to South Africa, July 1940: K7831, K7833.

K7866 transferred to Admiralty charge; to A Flt RNAS Ford.

K7882 three-blade propeller de-icing trials at Rotol Ltd.

Gloster VI. Two aircraft, N249 and N250, were built by Gloster Aircraft Company in 1928–9 to an Air Ministry order. Powered by supercharged Napier Lion VIID engine. N249 was first flown by Sqdn Ldr A. H. Orlebar at Calshot on 25 August and N250 on 31 August, 1929. Withdrawn from 1929 Schneider Trophy contest due to engine trouble. N249 established Absolute Speed Record of 336·3 mph on 10 September, 1929. Both aircraft subsequently used by RAF High Speed Flight at Felixstowe.

Gloster AS.31. Two aircraft, G-AADO and K2603, built by Gloster Aircraft Company in 1929. Developed from the D.H.67 design for the Aircraft Operating Company. Powered by two 525 hp Bristol Jupiter XI engines. G-AADO first flew in June 1929 and was delivered to Aircraft Operating Company at Heston Air Park on 25 January, 1930. Aerial survey of Northern Rhodesia 1930–31. Sold to South African Air Force in May 1935. Serialled 250. K2603 exhibited in skeleton form at Olympia International Aero Exhibition in July 1929. Delivered to RAE Farnborough on 19 November, 1931, for wireless telegraphy experiments and last used there on 17 September, 1936.

Gloster TC.33. One prototype, J9832, was built by Gloster Aircraft Company during 1931 to meet Air Ministry specification C.16/28 and ordered under contract No. 935509/29. Glosters' largest aeroplane. First flew on 23 February, 1932. Powered by two 580 hp Rolls-Royce Kestrel IIIS and two Kestrel IIS engines. To A and AEE Martlesham Heath in October 1932.

Gloster T.S.R.38. One aircraft, S1705, built by Gloster Aircraft Company 1931–32 under Air Ministry contract to meet the S.9/30 specification and bearing the company designation F.S.36. First flown in 1932 with Rolls-Royce Kestrel IIMS engine. Modified during 1933 to meet S.15/33 specification and delivered to A and AEE Martlesham Heath powered by Rolls-Royce Goshawk VIII. Dummy deck-landing trials at Gosport in 1934, before joining HMS *Courageous*. Returned to Gosport.

Gloster SS.37 Gladiator. One prototype, K5200, designed, developed and built as a private venture by Gloster Aircraft Company, Hucclecote, during 1934. Submitted to meet specification F.7/30. Bristol Mercury VIS2 engine (later a Mercury IX), two-blade wooden fixed-pitch propeller. Gloster-type construction throughout with Dowty internally-sprung wheels on fixed cantilever landing gear legs. Two fuselage-mounted Vickers Mk.III machine-guns with 600 rounds per gun and two Lewis machine-guns under the lower wings with 97 rounds per gun. Trials at Martlesham Heath in 1935 and taken on Air Ministry charge on 3 April, 1935. Contract No. 395996/35. Service trials with No.1 Sqdn, April 1935; Glosters, A and AEE and RAE between May 1935 and March 1937; to Bristols, April 1937; Glosters, 20 April, 1937; RAE, 17 April, 1939; 24 (C) Sqdn, 27 April, 1941; Hurn TFU, 27 October, 1941; No.2 AACU, 8 April, 1942. Struck off charge, 12 November, 1942, with 473 flying hours.

Gloster Gladiator I. First production batch of 23 aircraft, K6129–K6151, built by Gloster Aircraft Company during 1936–37 to specification F.14/35 and ordered under contract No.419392/36. Bristol Mercury XI engine with Watts wooden two-blade fixed-pitch propeller. Hawker-type construction throughout. Two fuselage-mounted Vickers Mk.V machine-guns with 600 rounds per gun and either two Lewis guns with 97 rounds per gun or two Vickers machine-guns with 100 rounds per gun under the lower wings. First aircraft was taken on Air Ministry charge on 16 February, 1937, and the last aircraft on 4 March, 1937.

Operated by RAF Squadrons: Nos. 3, 25, 33, 56, 72, 73, 74, 112, 261, 263, 605, 607.

Aircraft transferred to Royal Hellenic Air Force, December 1940: K6135.

Aircraft transferred to Iraqi Air Force, April 1941: K6140, K6141, K6147.

Other aircraft: K6129 (production check trials, A and AEE, 1937; development trials for Sea Gladiator, Jan–Feb 1939; taken on Admiralty charge, February 1939 and issued to No.800 Sqdn Fleet Air Arm), K6130 (squadron trials to compare benefits of 0·50 and 0·572 ratio airscrew reduction gears), K6139 (development trials for Sea Gladiator, December 1938–March 1939).

Gloster Gladiator I. Second production batch of 180 aircraft, K7892–K8055, L7608–L7623, built by Gloster Aircraft Company during 1937 to the amended specification F.14/35 and ordered under contract No. 442476/36. Similar production standard to first batch, but lower wings carried universal armament mounting. Bristol Mercury XI engine. First 37 aircraft fitted with Lewis machine-guns below wings which were later changed to Vickers Mk.III or V and then to Browning machine-guns. Aircraft 38 to 47 had Vickers K gas-operated machine-guns and remaining 133 aircraft were fitted with Colt/Browning machine-guns.

Operated by RAF Squadrons: Nos. 3, 25, 33, 54, 56, 65, 72, 73, 74, 80, 85, 87, 94, 112, 127, 141, 152, 247, 261, 263, 521 (Metcal), 603, 605, 607, 615.

Aircraft transferred to Royal Hellenic Air Force: K7892, K7923, K7932, K7956, K7973, K8013, K8017, K8018, K8031, K8047, K8054, L7609, L7611, L7620, L7621, L7623.

Aircraft transferred to Iraqi Air Force: K7897, K7907, K7928, K7947, K7989, K8005.

Aircraft transferred to South African Air Force for evaluation, January 1939: K7922 (ex-No.72 Sqdn).

Other aircraft: K7919 (Gladiator II instrument panel trial installation), K7922 (performance trials at Filton, Hucclecote and Martlesham Heath with Fairey three-blade metal propeller, 1937), K7929 (first production aircraft with Vickers K gas-operated underwing guns), K7939 (first production aircraft with Browning underwing guns), K8049 (trials at A and AEE, with 0·572 ratio airscrew reduction gear), K7976 (crashed during test: not taken on Air Ministry charge), K8039 (A and AEE, Sea Gladiator development trials), K8040 (trials at Rotol Ltd, 1939, with paints and wood blade coverings on three-blade Rotol internal cylinder propeller).

Gloster Gladiator I. Third production order for 28 aircraft, L8005–L8032, built by Gloster Aircraft Company during 1937. Similar production standard to earlier batches. Browning machine-guns below lower wings during 1938. No.80 Sqdn, L8010, L8011. Transferred to Royal Hellenic Air Force, December 1940: L8011.

Sold to Egypt, April 1939: L8005, L8012–L8028 (these aircraft are believed to have had Egyptian serials K1331–K1348). Some were subsequently taken back on RAFME charge.

Other aircraft: L8005–L8028 (all these aircraft were modified to Gladiator Mk.II standard at No.27 MU in January 1939 and were consigned for transfer to RAF Storage Unit at Aboukir, Egypt, in March 1939. Most were subsequently transferred to the Royal Egyptian Air Force). L8032 delivered to No.27 MU at Shawbury for assembly in October 1938 and was issued to No.2 AACU on 11 October, 1938. Transferred to Glosters 23 February, 1948, and to Air Service Training, Hamble, on 15 November, 1950. Sold to V. Bellamy, Flightways Ltd, in 1952. Fitted with engine and propeller from N5903 and registered G-AMRK. Bought by Glosters on 12 August, 1953, and after restoration was serialled K8032 with No.72 Sqdn markings. Transferred to Shuttleworth Trust on 7 November, 1960.

Gloster Latvian Gladiator I. Production order for 26 aircraft built by Gloster Aircraft Company during 1937. Order received from Latvian Government in May 1937 and aircraft were paid for from proceeds of a State lottery. Delivery by sea August–November 1937. Normal production standard. Four Vickers Mk.VM 7·7 mm machine-guns.

Gloster Lithuanian Gladiator I. Production order for 14 aircraft built by Gloster Aircraft Company during 1937. Order received from the Lithuanian Government in May 1937. Delivery by sea during October–December 1937 for final erection at Vilna and Kaunas. Normal production standard. Four Vickers Mk.VM 7·7 mm machine-guns.

Gloster Norwegian Gladiator I. Production order for six aircraft built by Gloster Aircraft Company during 1937. Order received from Norwegian Government in June 1937. Delivery by air during September–October 1937. Normal production standard but all six aircraft were later brought up to Gladiator Mk.II standard.

Gloster Swedish Gladiator I. Production order for 37 aircraft built by Gloster Aircraft Company in 1937–38. Order received from Swedish Government in June 1937. Normal production standard. Nohab licence-built Bristol Mercury VIS2 engines. Swedish Air Force designation, J8.

Gloster Belgian Gladiator I. Production order for 22 aircraft built by Gloster Aircraft Company during 1937. Order received from Belgian Government in June 1937. Delivery by air 1937–38. Normal production standard. Four Vickers Mk.V machine-guns.

Gloster Chinese Gladiator I. Production order for 36 aircraft built by Gloster Aircraft Company during 1937–38. Order received from Chinese Government in October 1937. Delivery by sea to Hongkong and final erection at various places near Canton. Normal production standard. Four Vickers Mk.V machine-guns.

Gloster Irish Gladiator I. Production order for four aircraft built by Gloster Aircraft Company during 1937–38. Order received from Irish Government in November 1937. Delivery by air in 1938. Normal production standard. Serialled 23–26.

Gloster Greek Gladiator I. In 1938 Zarparkis Homogenos paid Glosters £9,200 for two aircraft for presentation to the Royal Hellenic Air Force. Seventeen other aircraft transferred from the RAF to the Royal Hellenic Air Force during December 1940–March 1941.

Gloster Egyptian Gladiator I. Eighteen aircraft were transferred in March 1939 from the RAF to the Royal Egyptian Air Force after having been brought up to Gladiator II standard.

Gloster Iraqi Gladiator I. During October 1940–December 1942 nine aircraft were transferred from the RAF Middle East to the Iraqi Air Force.

Gloster Gladiator II and Sea Gladiator (Interim). First production batch of 50 aircraft, N2265–N2314 built by Gloster Aircraft Company during 1938. N2265–N2302 were modified and produced to Sea Gladiator (Interim) standard with deck arrester hook and taken on Admiralty charge during December 1938. The remaining 12 aircraft N2303–N2314, produced to full Mk.II standard to meet specification F.36/37. Bristol Mercury VIIIA with auto-mixture control, electric starter, Vokes air cleaner, carburettor intake filters and Browning machine-guns.

Operated by RAF Squadrons: Nos. 94, 247, 521 (Metcal), 605, 615.

Fleet Air Arm Units: N2265–N2277, N2281 (RNAS, Worthy Down, December 1938); N2285–N2290, N2292, N2294, N2296, N2299, N2300 (RNAS, Donibristle).

Aircraft transferred to the South African Air Force, 18 April, 1941: N2278, N2280, N2283, N2285–2290, N2292, N2294.

Gloster Gladiator II and Sea Gladiator. Main production order for 300 aircraft, N5500–N5549, N5565–N5594, N5620–N5649, N5680–N5729, N5750–N5789, N5810–N5859, N5875–N5924, built by Gloster Aircraft Company during 1938–39 to specification F.36/37 and ordered under contract No. 952950/38. Bristol Mercury VIIIA and VIIIAS engines with automatic boost control carburettors. Four Browning machine-guns. First 60 airframes transferred to Admiralty during manufacture and produced to full Sea Gladiator standard with deck arrester hook, ventral dinghy stowage, extended ammunition empty case and link chutes and catapult strong points. The remaining 240 aircraft produced to Mk.II standard. For clarity this order is detailed under individual blocks of serial numbers.

N5500–N5549 (50 aircraft, all Sea Gladiators)

N5565–N5594 (30 aircraft, N5565–N5574 Sea Gladiators; N5575–N5594 Gladiator Mk.IIs)

N5620–N5649 (30 aircraft, all Gladiator Mk.IIs)

N5680–N5729 (50 aircraft, all Gladiator Mk.IIs)

N5750–N5789 (40 aircraft, all Gladiator Mk.IIs)

N5810–N5859 (50 aircraft, all Gladiator Mk.IIs)

N5875–N5924 (50 aircraft, all Gladiator Mk.IIs)

Gladiator Mk.II: Operated by RAF Squadrons: Nos. 6, 33, 80, 94, 141, 152, 247, 263, 521 (Metcal), 605, 615.

Aircraft sold to Finland, December 1939: N5584, N5683, N5685–N5689, N5691, N5692, N5694, N5696, N5700, N5704, N5706–N5713, N5715, N5718, N5721, N5722, N5724, N5726–N5729.

Aircraft transferred to the Egyptian Air Force, 1941: N5755, N5758, N5760, N5762, N5767, N5771, N5875–N5892 (renumbered L9030–L9047).

Aircraft transferred to the Iraqi Air Force, 1 March, 1944; N5780, N5825, N5828, N5830, N5857.

Aircraft sold to Portugal: N5835–N5849.

Aircraft sold to Norway, 1939: N5919–N5924.

Sea Gladiator: Operated by No. 33 Sqdn RAF and by Fleet Air Arm Squadrons Nos. 769 (Training), 801, and 802 HMS *Glorious*.

Gloster Swedish Gladiator II. Production order for 18 aircraft built by Gloster Aircraft Company during 1938. Order received from Swedish Government in 1930. Normal production standard. Nohab licence-produced Bristol Mercury VIIIS.3 engine with Fairey three-blade metal propeller. Swedish Air Force designation, J8A.

Gloster Norwegian Gladiator II. Production order for six new aircraft built by Gloster Aircraft Company (diverted from Air Ministry contract No. 773235/38). Order received from Norwegian Government in 1939. Normal production standard. Four Colt machine-guns.

Gloster Portuguese Gladiator II. Production order for 15 new aircraft built by Gloster Aircraft Company (diverted from Air Ministry contract No. 773235/38). Order received from Portuguese Government in 1939. Normal production standard. G5 was test flown at A and AEE during 19–27 July, 1938.

Gloster Finnish Gladiator II. Thirty aircraft were transferred from the RAF to the Finnish Air Force during December 1939–January 1940.

Gloster Greek Gladiator II. During 1940–41 eight aircraft were transferred from the RAF to the Royal Hellenic Air Force.

Gloster Egyptian Gladiator II. Twenty-seven aircraft were transferred from RAF Middle East to the Royal Egyptian Air Force during 1941.

Gloster South African Gladiator II. Beginning in April 1941 eleven aircraft were transferred from the RAF to the South African Air Force.

Gloster Iraqi Gladiator II. On 1 March, 1944, five aircraft were transferred from RAF Middle East to the Iraqi Air Force.

Gloster F.5/34. Two prototypes, K5604 and K8089, were built by Gloster Aircraft Company during 1936–38 to meet Air Ministry specification F.5/34 and ordered under contract No. 395989/35. Fitted with 840 hp Bristol Mercury engine. Were Glosters' first aircraft with retractable landing gear. K5604 first flew in December 1937 and K8089 in March 1938. Became ground instructional airframes in May 1941 re-serialled 2232M and 2231M respectively.

Gloster F.9/37. Two prototypes, L7999 and L8002, were designed and built by Gloster Aircraft Company to Air Ministry contract No. 697972/37 during 1938–40. L7999 first flew on 3 April, 1939, powered by two 1,050 hp Bristol Taurus TE/1 engines. Rebuilt in July 1939, following a landing accident at Boscombe Down, and re-engined with 900 hp Taurus III engines.

L8002 was fitted with two 885 hp Rolls-Royce Peregrine engines.

Gloster E.28/39. Two aircraft, W4041 and W4046, were designed and built by Gloster Aircraft Company to specification E.28/39 under contract No. SB/3229 dated 3 February, 1940. W4041 fitted with Power Jets W.1X turbojet for taxi-ing only, and first flew on 15 May, 1941, at Cranwell powered by 860 lb thrust W.1 turbojet. Delivered to RAE Farnborough in November 1941. 1,700 lb thrust W.2/500 engine fitted for development programme flying from Barford St John. Fitted with high-speed E-type wing on 5 July, 1943. Delivered engineless to RAE and fitted with auxiliary fins, a jettisonable hood and a new 1,760 lb thrust W.2/500 engine. Ten hours flying completed. W4041 was put on permanent display in Science Museum, London, on 28 April, 1946.

W4046 flew for the first time on 1 March, 1943, at Edgehill, powered by a 1,200 lb thrust Rover W.2B turbojet and on 17 April, 1943, made the first cross-country jet flight in Britain, from Edgehill to Hatfield. Delivered to RAE Farnborough on 3 May, 1943, and fitted with a 1,526 lb thrust W.2B engine. Crashed on 30 July, 1943, following an inverted spin from 37,000 ft.

Gloster F.9/40. Eight prototype aircraft, DG202/G to DG209/G, designed and developed to meet specification F.9/40 and ordered under contract SB 21179/C 23(2) dated 6

357

February, 1941. DG202/G powered by W.2B/23 turbojets and first flown on 24 July, 1943, from Barford St John. Subsequently used for flight trials at Newmarket, Moreton Valence and Rolls-Royce, Hucknall. DG203/G powered by W.2/500 turbojets and first flown on 9 November, 1943, from Moreton Valence. Used for flight trials of W.2/700 engines and finally became instructional airframe 5926M. DG204/G, powered by Metropolitan Vickers F.2 axial-flow turbojets and first flown on 13 November, 1943, from the Royal Aircraft Establishment, Farnborough. Engine trials from RAE before crashing on 1 April, 1944. DG205/G powered by W.2B/23 turbojets, first flown on 12 June, 1943, from Barford St John. Crashed at Moreton Valence on 27 April, 1944, after trials with Gloster and at Hatfield. DG206/G, powered by de Havilland Halford H.1 engines, was first flown by Michael Daunt on 5 March, 1943, from Cranwell, and was the first F.9/40 to fly. Used for flight trials at RAE Farnborough and by Gloster and National Gas Turbine Establishment. DG207/G powered by H.1b engines was first flown on 24 July, 1945, from Moreton Valence. This aircraft was the sole prototype Meteor F.2 and was used by de Havilland Engine Company for trials. DG208/G, powered by W.2B/23 engines, was first flown on 20 January, 1944, was used for various aerodynamic trials by Gloster before going to de Havilland. DG209/G powered by W.2B/37 engines and first flown on 18 April, 1944, from Moreton Valence. Used for engine trials by Rolls-Royce at Hucknall, and scrapped at RAE Farnborough in July 1946.

Gloster Meteor F.Mk.1. First production batch of 20 aircraft, EE210/G to EE229, built by Gloster Aircraft during 1943–44, and ordered under contract No. A/C 1490/41, dated 8 August, 1941. EE210/G first flown in March 1944. W.2B/23 Welland 1 engines fitted in 17 aircraft; EE220 had W.2/700 engines; EE222 and EE229 were fitted with W.2B/23B Welland engines.

No.616 Sqdn, EE213–EE222, EE224–EE229.

Other aircraft: EE210/G (Went to Muroc Air Force Base, USA, in exchange for Bell XP-59 Airacomet, February 1944), EE211/G, EE212/G (RAE Farnborough), EE223 (Rolls-Royce).

Gloster Meteor F.Mk.3. First production batch of 210 aircraft, EE230–EE254, EE269–EE318, EE331–EE369, EE384–EE429, EE444–EE493, built in five sub batches by Gloster Aircraft Co Ltd during 1944–46 and ordered under contract No. 6/ACFT/1490.C.B.7(b). EE230 first flown on 11 September, 1944. First 15 aircraft, EE230–EE244, powered by Welland Series 1 engines and remainder, EE245–EE493, powered by Derwent Series 1 engines. Last 15 aircraft, EE479–EE493, were fitted with long-chord engine nacelles.

Operated by RAF Squadrons: Nos. 1, 56, 63, 66, 74, 92, 124, 222, 245, 257, 263, 266, 500, 504, 616.

Other aircraft: EE230 (Flame damping trials A and AEE); EE249 (A and AEE); EE238, EE283, EE284, EE294 (RAE Farnborough); EE311 (Winterization trials, RCAF, Rockliffe, Canada); EE281 (CFE); EE314 (Central Gunnery School); EE291 (Power Jets); EE317 (Carrier trials); EE337 (Carrier trials, A and AEE); EE361 (Winterization trials, Canada); EE356 (CGS); EE338, EE351, EE367 (RAE Farnborough); EE350 (ETPS); EE359 (CFS); EE360, EE363 (Long-chord nacelle trials, Rolls-Royce); EE395 (became NZ6001, RNZAF); EE396 (A and AEE); EE408 (CFE); EE397, EE398 (ETPS); EE403 (RAE); EE415, EE416 (Ejector seat trials, Martin Baker); EE426 (FCCS); EE427 (Trials in Australia); EE429 (RAE); EE445 (Griffiths wing, boundary layer control trials, Armstrong Whitworth Aircraft); EE444, EE451 (CFE); EE454, EE455 (RAF High Speed Flight for World Speed Record attempt, 7 November, 1945); EE456 (CRD); EE472 (CFE); EE465–EE467, EE477, EE493 (ECFS).

Gloster Meteor F.Mk.4. First production batch of 170 aircraft, EE517–EE554, EE568–EE599, RA365–RA398, RA413–RA457, RA473–RA493, in five sub batches by Gloster

A Meteor F.4 of No.257 Sqdn. (*Courtesy Bruce Robertson*)

Aircraft Cộ Ltd during 1945–47 and ordered under contract No. S.B.1490/C.23(a). EE517 first flown on 12 April, 1945. Derwent 5 engines of various powers were installed in these aircraft. A number of F.4s were built with long-span wings similar to the F.3, but the majority had the short-span wing.

Operated by RAF Squadrons: Nos. 1, 19, 56, 66, 74, 92, 222, 245, 257, 263, 500, 501, 504, 600, 610, 611.

Other aircraft: EE526, EE527, EE532, EE544, EE546, EE547, EE551–EE554, EE569–EE572, EE574–EE577, EE580–EE583, EE585–EE589, RA370, RA384, RA386, RA388–RA391 (Sold to the Argentine Republic in 1947); EE517 (Engine trials, Rolls-Royce); EE518, EE519 (CA Moreton Valence); EE520 (Landing gear drop tests at G.A.C.); EE521, EE545 (G.A.C.); EE531 (Folding wing experiments Heston Aircraft Ltd, 1946); EE527, EE529, EE530, EE548, EE549, EE550 (RAF High Speed Flight for World Speed Record attempt 1946); EE578, EE579 (Increased span for high altitude trials at G.A.C.); EE568, EE599 (RAE Farnborough); EE597 (Rolls-Royce); RA377 (CFE); RA365, RA367 (CGS); RA382 (Long-nose F.4 trials, G.A.C.); RA394 (G.A.C.); RA417, RA420, RA438 (A and AEE, miscellaneous trials); RA429, RA453–RA456 (CFE); RA424 (RAE); RA430, RA435 (Miscellaneous engine trials, Rolls-Royce); RA486 (Cockpit pressurization trials, A and AEE); RA475, RA478 (CFE); RA479 (ETPS); RA490 (Fitted with Metropolitan Vickers F.2/4 Beryl axial-flow engine in 1947; later fitted with Rolls-Royce Nene engines by Westland Aircraft for jet deflection trials in 1954); RA491 (Fitted with Rolls-Royce Avon RA.2 axial-flow engines in 1948. Sold to France in 1951 for flight trials of SNECMA Atar 101.B21 engines).

Gloster Meteor F.Mk.4. Second production batch of 200 aircraft, VT102–VT150, VT168–VT199, VT213–VT247, VT256–VT294, VT303–VT347, built in five sub batches by Gloster Aircraft Co Ltd during 1947–48 and ordered under contract No. 6/ACFT/658 C.B. 7(b) dated 22 November, 1946. Deliveries began on 4 February, 1948. All aircraft powered by Rolls-Royce Derwent 5 engines and fitted with short-span wings.

Operated by RAF Squadrons: Nos. 1, 43, 56, 63, 66, 74, 92, 222, 245, 257, 263, 266, 500, 504, 611, 616.

Other aircraft: VT135 (APS); VT105, VT107, VT117, VT130, VT144 (CFE); VT141 (ECFS); VT150 (Became prototype Meteor F.8, first flew 12 October, 1948); VT176 (CU); VT190 (CFE); VT196 (Flight trials of Canadian reheat installation for Avro Orenda engine at NAE, 1954); VT220, VT224, VT228, VT235, VT236 (CFE); VT223 (CGS); VT241 (G.A.C.); VT215 (RAFFC); VT259 (Armament trials, RAE); VT262 (CFE); VT264, VT271 (CGS); VT306, VT335 (CFE); VT312, VT317 (CGS); VT333 (Sold to Netherlands); VT338 (Vickers-Armstrongs); VT340 (TRE); VT347 (Miscellaneous trials, G.A.C.).

Gloster Meteor F.Mk.4. Third production batch of 119 aircraft, VW255–VW315

VW780–VW791, built in two sub batches by Gloster Aircraft Co Ltd during 1948–49 and ordered under contract No. 6/ACFT/1389 C.B.7(b) dated 2 August, 1947. Remainder built by Armstrong Whitworth. Operated by RAF Squadrons: Nos. 1, 66, 74, 92, 222, 245, 257, 263, 500, 504, 600, 611.

Other aircraft: VW278, VW282, VW296 (CFE); VW308, VW316, VW357 (Diverted to Belgian contract); VW286, VW291 (Sold to Netherlands); VW302, VW303 (RAE Farnborough); VW288, VW305–VW307, VW309, VW310, VW313, VW315 (Sold to Netherlands); VW780 (Cabin pressurization, heating and ventilating trials at A and AEE); VW782 (CFE); VW790 (MoS trials with Vickers rocket missile).

Gloster Meteor F.Mk.4. Fourth production batch of 46 aircraft, VZ386–VZ429, VZ436–VZ437, built by Sir W. G. Armstrong Whitworth Aircraft Ltd, part of the 119 aircraft batch ordered under contract No. 6/ACFT/1389 C.B.7(b) dated 2 August, 1947. First four aircraft, VZ386–VZ389, of two sub batches were ordered under contract No. 6/ACFT/2430 C.B.7(b) dated 4 September, 1948.

Operated by RAF Squadrons: Nos. 1, 56, 63, 66, 92, 245, 500, 504, 600, 615.

Other aircraft: VZ416 (CFE); VZ419, VZ427 (CGS); VZ420, VZ421–VZ426 (Sold to Egypt); VZ386 (RAFFC); VZ389 (Flight refuelling trials, Flight Refuelling Ltd); VZ387, VZ388, VZ391, VZ394–VZ400, VZ402, VZ408, VZ409 (Sold to the Netherlands).

Gloster Meteor T.Mk.7. First production batch of 70 aircraft, VW410–VW459, VW470–VW489, built by Gloster Aircraft Co Ltd in two sub batches during 1948–49, and ordered under contract No. 6/ACFT/1389 C.B.7(b) dated 2 August, 1947. VW410 first flown on 26 October, 1948. Early production Meteor T.Mk.7s powered by Derwent 5 engines, and later aircraft had Derwent engines and large-diameter intakes. Some aircraft had Meteor F.8 type tail units but majority fitted with F.4 tail unit. Two F.4s, EE530 and EE573, were converted to T.7 standard.

Operated by RAF Squadrons: Nos. 1, 6, 43, 54, 74, 245, 257, 604, 702.

Other aircraft: VW411 (Target drone trials RAE Farnborough and radio acceptance trials A and AEE Boscombe Down); VW412 (Automatic air brake trials A and AEE); VW413 (Became aerodynamic prototype for NF.11, Armstrong Whitworth Aircraft); VW414 (BLEU): VW431, VW432, VW434, VW451, VW452, VW454 (CFE); VW433 (Firestreak trials photography, de Havilland Propellers Ltd); VW435, VW437, VW438 (CFS); VW418 (EAAS); VW417 (FCCS); VW410 (G.A.C.); VW441 (RAE); VW470 (Air Pass Weapons systems trials, Ferranti Ltd); VW474, VW477 (EAAS); VW478 (CFE); VW481 (CFS); VW483 (CGS).

Gloster Meteor T.Mk.7. Second production batch of 21 aircraft, VZ629–VZ649, built by Gloster Aircraft Co Ltd during 1949 and ordered under contract No. 6/ACFT/2430 C.B.7(b) dated 4 September, 1948. Deliveries began in July 1949.

Operated by RAF Squadrons: Nos. 63, 66, 72, 92, 222, 247, 500, 614, 616, 702, 759.

Other aircraft: VZ641 (CFE); VZ642 (CFS); VZ646, VZ647 (RNAS).

Gloster Meteor T.Mk.7. Third production batch of 137 aircraft, WA590–WA639, WA649–WA698, WA709–WA743, built by Gloster Aircraft Co Ltd, in three sub batches during 1948–49, and ordered under contract No. 6/ACFT/2982 C.B.7(b) dated 25 November, 1948. Deliveries began in June 1948.

Operated by RAF Squadrons: Nos. 2, 6, 28, 54, 56, 72, 73, 81, 96, 213, 245, 247, 249, 501, 504, 600, 601, 605, 608, 609, 611, 614, 615, 702.

Other aircraft: WA597 (CGS); WA599 (APS); WA602, WA603 (ITS); WA607, WA609 (FTU); WA623, WA626, WA633 (Sold to the Netherlands); WA634 (Zero feet ejector seat trials, G.A.C. and Martin Baker. Fitted with E.1/44 type tail 1952); WA636 (Handling trials RAE); WA638 (Ejector seat trials, Martin Baker 1962); WA649, WA650 (RNAS); WA654 (EAAS); WA659, WA678, WA694 (CFE); WA660, WA668, WA679,

WA698 (CFS); WA662 (FCCS); WA708, WA741 (CFS); WA709 (Miscellaneous trials G.A.C); WA722 (CFE); WA731, WA732 (Sold to Australia).

Gloster Meteor T.Mk.7. Fourth production batch of 89 aircraft, WF766–WF795, WF813–WF862, WF875–WF883, built by Gloster Aircraft Co Ltd in three sub batches during 1950–51 and ordered under contract No. 6/ACFT/5044 C.B.7(b) dated 4 May, 1950. Deliveries began in January 1951.

Operated by RAF Squadrons: Nos. 19, 25, 26, 41, 64, 65, 66, 67, 71, 85, 94, 96, 222, 500, 502, 504, 601, 602, 603, 607, 608, 609, 611, 613, 615.

Other aircraft: WF795 (A.V.Roe and Co); WF769, WF772 (CFS); WF780, WF784 (FTU); WF781 (Missile trials, Fairey Aviation Ltd); WF796 (RAE Farnborough); WF815 (CFE); WF822 (Fitted with radar nose for trials of Meteor NF.11 AI radar, Armstrong Whitworth Aircraft); WF826 (FTU); WF840, WF852 (CFS); WF841 (CFE).

Gloster Meteor T.Mk.7. Fifth production batch of 160 aircraft, WG935–WG950, WG961–WG999, WH112–WH136, WH164–WH209, WH215–WH248, built by Gloster Aircraft Co Ltd in five sub batches during 1950–52 and ordered under contract No. 6/ACFT/5621 C.B.7(b) dated 8 August, 1950. Deliveries began in August 1951.

Operated by RAF Squadrons: Nos. 1, 2, 81, 87, 92, 141, 145, 151, 256, 264, 500, 541, 600, 610, 611, 614.

Other aircraft: WG937, WG940 (CGS); WG942 (JCU); WG981, WG983, WG987 (CFS); WG974, WG977 (Leased to RAAF, Korea, 1951, as conversion trainers, re-serialled A77-380 and A77-577 respectively and later became A77-703 and A77-704 respectively. Latter aircraft crashed on 6 September, 1952); WH118, WH131 (CFS); WH117 (STU); WH177 (CFS); WH189 (RAFFC); WH195 (FTU); WH217–WH219, WH241, WH245, WH247, WH248 (CFS); WH220, WH238 (Sold to Australia).

Gloster Meteor T.Mk.7. Sixth production batch of 139 aircraft, WL332–WL381, WL397–WL436, WL453–WL488, WN309–WN321, built by Gloster Aircraft Co Ltd in four sub batches during 1951–53 and ordered under contract No. 6/ACFT/6066 C.B.7(b) dated 15 January, 1951. Deliveries began in April 1952.

Operated by RAF Squadrons: Nos. 2, 3, 4, 26, 34, 65, 72, 74, 79, 96, 222, 256, 266, 504, 612, 702, 759.

Other aircraft: WL333–WL335, WL352 (RNAS); WL359, WL369, WL373, WL374, WL381 (CFE); WL364 (G.A.C.); WL375 (Fitted with an F.R. nose and E.1/44 type tail assembly, RAE Farnborough); WL377 (ETPS); WL309, WL405 (FTU); WL419, WL436, WL465, WL470, WL473, WL478 (CFE); WL481 (CFS); WL487 (Sold to Netherlands); WL488 (ETPS); WN318 (FTU); WN321 (Sold to Australia).

Gloster Meteor T.Mk.7. Seventh production batch of 15 aircraft, WS103–WS117, built by Gloster Aircraft Co Ltd during 1953, and ordered under contract No. 6/ACFT/6410 C.B.7(b) dated 28 April, 1951. Deliveries began in May 1953, and the whole batch was delivered to two Royal Navy Squadrons.

Gloster Meteor T.Mk.7. Eighth production batch of nine aircraft, WS140–WS141, XF273–XF279, built by Gloster Aircraft Co Ltd in two batches during 1953–54 and ordered under contract No. 6/ACFT/6411 C.B.7(b) dated 28 April, 1951. Deliveries began in November 1953.

Gloster Meteor F.Mk.8. First production batch of 128 aircraft, VZ438–VZ485, VZ493–VZ517, built by Gloster Aircraft Co Ltd in two sub batches during 1949–50, and VZ518–VZ532, VZ540–VZ569 built by Sir W. G. Armstrong Whitworth Aircraft Ltd, Coventry, in two sub batches and ordered under contract No. 6/ACFT/2430 C.B.7(b) dated 4 September, 1949. First flight by prototype Meteor F.8, (VT150) on 12 October, 1949. Powered by Rolls-Royce Derwent 8 engines, early aircraft had small-diameter air intakes, two-piece canopy with metal rear fairing and geared-tab ailerons. Later production aircraft had large-diameter air intakes, one-piece clear-view canopy and spring-tab ailerons. Extra 95 gal fuel tank fitted in 30 in insert in front fuselage and E.1/44 type tail unit used on all aircraft.

Operated by RAF Squadrons: Nos. 1, 43, 56, 63, 65, 66, 72, 74, 92, 222, 245, 247, 257, 263, 500, 609, 611.

Other aircraft: VZ439 (Pressurization trials with metal canopy, G.A.C.); VZ442 (Hood jettison trials at RAE and G.A.C.); VZ443, VZ447 (CFE); VZ445 (RAFFC); VZ450 (Sold to Belgium); VZ457 (G.A.C.); VZ459 (Sold to Belgium); VZ460 (RP and bomb trials, G.A.C.); VZ473 (RP and bomb trials, A and AEE); VZ493, VZ500 (CFE); VZ504 (G.A.C.); VZ506 (Gun firing trials, APS); VZ508 (CFE); VZ517 (Fitted with Armstrong Siddeley Screamer rocket motor); VZ522 (APS); VZ530 (CFE).

Gloster Meteor F.Mk.8. Second production batch of 210 aircraft, WA755–WA794, WA808–WA812, WA965–WA969, WA981—WA999, WB105–WB112, built in five sub batches by Sir W. G. Armstrong Whitworth Aircraft Ltd, Coventry, during 1950–51, and WA813–WA857, WA867–WA909, WA920–WA964, built in three sub batches by Gloster Aircraft Co Ltd during 1950–51, and ordered under contract No. 6/ACFT/2983 C.B.7(b) dated 25 November, 1949.

Meteor F.8s of No.41 Squadron, RAF, were a familiar sight in the skies over southeast England in 1951.

Operated by RAF Squadrons: Nos. 1, 19, 41, 43, 56, 63, 64, 65, 66, 74, 92, 222, 245, 257, 263, 500, 600, 614, 615.

Other aircraft: WA772 (CFE); WA775 (Hunter nose radar fitted for use with de Havilland Firestreak air-to-air missile); WA782, WA783, WA786 (Sold to Australia); WA784, WA790, WA810, WA811 (CFE); WA809 (G.A.C.); WA820 (Fitted with Sapphire engines); WA857 (Trials with US HVAR projectiles and air brake assessment, A and AEE); WA878 (G.A.C.); WA901 (Sold to Australia); WA931, WA932 (CFE); WA934, WA937, WA939, WA941, WA944, WA947, WA950–WA952, WA954, WA956–WA958, WA960, WA961, WA964 (Sold to Australia); WA966, WA968 (CFE).

Gloster Meteor F.Mk.8. Third production batch of 120 aircraft, WE852–WE891, WE895–WE902, built by Sir W. G. Armstrong Whitworth Aircraft Ltd in two sub batches during 1949–51, and WE903–WE939, WE942–WE976, built by Gloster Aircraft Co Ltd in two sub batches during 1950–51, and ordered under contract No. 6/ACFT/4040 C.B.7(b) dated 29 September, 1949. Deliveries began in March 1951.

Operated by RAF Squadrons: Nos. 1, 19, 41, 43, 56, 63, 64, 65, 66, 92, 245, 247, 263, 609, 610, 611, 614, 616.

Other aircraft: WE879, WE882, WE887 (CGS); WE874, WE877, WE880, WE886, WE890, WE895, WE898 (Sold to Australia); WE917, WE931, WE932, WE936 (CGS); WE919 (RATOG trials, de Havilland Aircraft, later to RAE Farnborough); WE930 (CSE); WE903, WE905, WE906, WE908, WE918, WE928 (Sold to Australia); WE944, WE945, WE953, WE960 (CFE); WE966 (M.L. Aviation); WE971 (Sold to Australia).

Gloster Meteor F.Mk.8. Fourth production batch of 89 aircraft, WF639–WF662, WF677–WF688 built by Sir W. G. Armstrong Whitworth Aircraft Ltd in two sub batches during 1951, and WF689–WF716, WF736–WF760 built by Gloster Aircraft Co Ltd in two batches during 1951, and ordered under contract No. 6/ACFT/5043 C.B.7(b) dated 4 May, 1950. Deliveries began in June 1951.

Operated by RAF Squadrons: Nos. 1, 19, 34, 41, 56, 63, 64, 65, 66, 72, 74, 92, 245, 257, 263, 500, 504, 600, 609, 611, 615.

Other aircraft: WF653 (Sold to Australia); WF683 (FCCS); WF690 (CGS); WF696–WF699, WF701 (Sold to the Netherlands); WF739 (CFE); WF745, WF748 (CGS); WF752 (Guided missile trials, de Havilland); WF746, WF750 (Sold to Australia).

Gloster Meteor F.Mk.8. Fifth production batch of 200 aircraft, WH249–WH263, WH272–WH320, WH342–WH386, WH395–WH426, WH442–WH444, WH445–WH484, WH498–WH513, built by Sir W. G. Armstrong Whitworth Aircraft Ltd, Coventry, in seven batches during 1951–52, and ordered under contract No. 6/ACFT/5621 C.B.7(b), dated 8 August, 1950. Deliveries began in August 1951.

Operated by RAF Squadrons: Nos. 1, 12, 19, 41, 54, 56, 63, 64, 65, 66, 72, 74, 92, 222, 245, 247, 257, 263, 500, 504, 600, 601, 604, 605, 610, 611, 615, 616.

Other aircraft: WH249 (CFE); WH251, WH252, WH254, WH259 (Sold to Australia); WH260 (Sold to Syria); WH279 (APS); WH272 (CFE); WH274 (CFS); WH284 (TRE, later a U.Mk.16); WH312 (ETPS); WH363 (APS); WH347, WH353 (CGS); WH355, WH356, WH358, WH371 (Fitted with windscreen wipers and braking parachute for RAE Farnborough trials); WH379, WH380 (CFE); WH385 (CGS); WH411, WH412, WH413, WH419 (CGS); WH409, WH414, WH417 (Sold to Australia); WH457, WH458, WH481 (CGS); WH482 (CFE); WH479 (RAFFC); WH483 (Spring-tab aileron trials); WH498 (ETPS); WH508, WH509, WH511, WH512 (CFE).

Gloster Meteor F.Mk.8. Sixth production batch of 343 aircraft, WK647–WK696, WK783–WK827, WK849–WK893, WK935–WK955, WK966–WK994, WL104–WL143, WL158–WL191, built by Gloster Aircraft Co Ltd in seven sub batches during 1951–54, and WK707–WK756, WK906–WK934 built by Sir W. G. Armstrong Whitworth Aircraft Ltd in two sub batches during 1951–53 and ordered under contract No. 6/ACFT/6066 C.B.7(b) dated 15 January, 1951. Deliveries began in March 1953; they ended with the last Meteor, WL191, flown from Hucclecote on 9 April, 1954, by Jim Cooksey, which was delivered in May 1954 and subsequently sold to Egypt in 1955.

Operated by RAF Squadrons: Nos. 1, 19, 34, 41, 43, 54, 56, 63, 64, 65, 66, 72, 74, 92, 111, 222, 245, 247, 257, 263, 500, 600, 601, 604, 609, 615, 616.

Other aircraft: WK649, WK652, WK661, WK694 (APS); WK650 (Sold to Australia); WK655, WK665 (CFE); WK660 (30 mm cannon trials); WK675, WK678, WK690, WK695 (CGS); WK650, WK670, WK674, WK682, WK686 (Sold to Australia); WK720 (CFE); WK723, WK729, WK731, WK732, WK746 (CGS); WK755 (FCCS); WK730 (Sold to Australia); WK786, WK788, WK793, WK794 (APS); WK797 (G.A.C.); WK806, WK815, WK824 (Windscreen wiper and braking parachute trials, CFE); WK878 (Sold to Australia); WK876 (RAFFC); WK909, WK913 (Sold to Australia); WK915 (CGS); WK926 (TRE); WK930 (CGS); WK935 (Prone pilot Meteor); WK937 (Sold to Australia); WK942 (CFE); WK967 (CGS); WK973 (Sold to Australia); WK981 (FCCS); WK988 (CGS); WL166 (RAFFC); WL183, WL185–WL188, WL191 (Sold to Egypt).

Gloster Meteor FR.Mk.9. First production batch of 12 aircraft, VW360–VW371, built by Gloster Aircraft Co Ltd during 1949–50 and ordered under contract No. 6/ACFT/1389 C.B.7(b) dated 2 August, 1947. First flight of prototype Meteor FR.9 VW360 on 22 March, 1950, piloted by J. Zurakowski. Early production aircraft had metal rear fairings on the cockpit canopy; later aircraft had clear-view canopy. Two Derwent 8 engines. Deliveries began in July 1950 and were completed in December 1950. No.2 Sqdn. VW361, VW364, VW371; No.208 Sqdn. VW363, VW367, VW368–VW370.

Other aircraft: VW360 (HVAR projectile trials, G.A.C.); VW362 (Gun and camera heating trials. Later fitted with wingtip-mounted spotlights by Ferranti); VW366 (CFE).

Gloster Meteor FR.Mk.9. Second production batch of 35 aircraft, VZ577–VZ611, built by Gloster Aircraft Co Ltd during 1949–51 and ordered under contract No. 6/ACFT/2430 C.B.7(b) dated 4 September, 1948. Deliveries began in December 1950 and were completed in April 1951.

Operated by RAF Squadrons: Nos. 2, 79, 208.

Other aircraft: VZ597 (Sold to Ecuador); VZ608 (Derwent 8 and RB.108 engine trials, Rolls-Royce).

Gloster Meteor FR.Mk.9. Third production batch of 23 aircraft, WB114–WB125, WB133–WB143, built by Gloster Aircraft Co Ltd in two sub batches during 1950–51 and ordered under contract No. 6/ACFT/2983 C.B.7(b) dated 25 November, 1948. Deliveries began in April 1951 and were completed in September 1951.

Operated by RAF Squadrons: Nos. 2, 79, 208.

Other aircraft: WB123 (Sold to Israel); WB134 (Miscellaneous T Is, G.A.C.); WB136 (Sold to Ecuador); WB140 (Sold to Israel).

Gloster Meteor FR.Mk.9. Fourth production batch of 25 aircraft, WH533–WH557, built by Gloster Aircraft Co Ltd during 1951–52 and ordered under contract No. 6/ACFT/5621 C.B.7(b) dated 8 August, 1950. Deliveries began in January 1952 and were completed in June 1952.

Operated by RAF Squadrons: Nos. 2, 79.

Other aircraft: WH540, WH543, WH547, WH549, WH550, WH553–WH555 (Sold to Ecuador).

Gloster Meteor FR.Mk.9. Fifth production batch of 11 aircraft, WL255–WL265, built by Gloster Aircraft Co Ltd during 1951–52 and ordered under contract No. 6/ACFT/6066 C.B.7(b) dated 15 January, 1951. Deliveries began in April 1952 and were completed in July 1952.

Operated by RAF Squadrons: Nos. 2, 79.

Other aircraft: WL259 (Sold to Israel).

Gloster Meteor FR.Mk.9 Sixth production batch of 20 aircraft, WX962–WX981, built by Gloster Aircraft Co Ltd during 1951–52 and ordered under contract No. 6/ACFT/7252 C.B.7(b) dated 17 August, 1951. Deliveries began in June 1952 and were completed in August 1952.

Operated by RAF Squadrons: Nos. 2, 79.

Other aircraft: WX963 (Sold to Israel); WX964 (CFE); WX967, WX975, WX980 (Sold to Israel); WX979 (RAE).

Gloster Meteor PR.Mk.10. First production batch of 20 aircraft, VS968–VS987, built by Gloster Aircraft Co Ltd during 1950–51 and ordered under contract No. 6/ACFT/658 C.B.7(b) dated 22 November, 1946. First prototype Meteor PR.10 VS968 first flown on 29 March, 1960, by Capt F. Vyzelaar (RNethAF). Early production aircraft had cockpit canopy with metal rear fairing but later aircraft had a clear-view canopy. Two Derwent 8 engines. Deliveries began in February 1951 and were completed in April 1951. One Meteor PR.10, VZ620, was built under contract No. 6/ACFT/2430 C.B.7(b) which covered Meteor T.7. It was delivered to RAF Merryfield and was later taken on charge by G.A.C.

Operated by RAF Squadrons: Nos. 25, 81, 541.

Other aircraft: VS969 (Miscellaneous trials CA to G.A.C.).

Gloster Meteor PR.Mk.10. Second production batch of four aircraft, VW376–VW379, built by Gloster Aircraft Co Ltd during 1950–51 and ordered under contract No. 6/ACFT/1389 C.B.7(b) dated 2 August, 1948. Deliveries began in January 1951 and were completed in April 1951.

Operated by RAF Squadrons: Nos. 81, 541.

Gloster Meteor PR.Mk.10. Third production batch of 29 aircraft, WB153–WB181, built by Gloster Aircraft Co Ltd during 1950–51 and ordered under contract No. 6/ACFT/2983 C.B.7(b) dated 25 November, 1948. Deliveries began in May 1951 and were completed in September 1951.

Operated by RAF Squadrons: Nos. 2, 13, 81, 541.

Gloster Meteor PR.Mk.10. Fourth production batch of five aircraft, WH569–WH573, built by Gloster Aircraft Co Ltd during 1951 and ordered under contract No. 6/ACFT/5621 C.B.7(b) dated 8 August, 1950. Deliveries began in February 1952 and were completed in April 1952.

Operated by RAF Squadrons: Nos. 13, 541.

Gloster Meteor NF.Mk.11. Three prototype aircraft, WA546, WA547, WB543, built by Sir W. G. Armstrong Whitworth Aircraft Ltd and ordered under contract No. 6/ACFT/3433 C.B.5(b). The first prototype built to specification F.24/48, WA546, was first flown on 31 May, 1950, by Eric Franklin. Four British Hispano 20 mm cannon mounted in the outer mainplanes. Two Derwent 8 engines.

WA546, WA547 (A and AEE Boscombe Down); WB543 (TRE and RAE).

Gloster Meteor NF.Mk.11. First production batch of 200 aircraft, WD585–WD634, WD640–WD689, WD696–WD745, WD751–WD800, built by Sir W. G. Armstrong Whitworth Aircraft Ltd, during 1950–52 in four sub batches and built under contract No. 6/ACFT/3433 C.B.5(b). Deliveries began in October 1950.

Operated by RAF Squadrons: Nos. 29, 68, 85, 87, 96, 141, 151, 256, 264.

Other aircraft: WD585 (CFE); WD586 (Di-electric nose trials TRE); WD587 (TRE); WD588, WD589 (RAE); WD591 (CFE); WD593 (Pressure cabin trials, A.W.A.); WD594 (Tropical trials); WD595 (CFE); WD596 (DV panel trials CFE); WD597 (Rolls-Royce); WD604 (Wingtip tank installation and trials); WD646 (CSE); WD648 (CFE); WD686 (TRE); WD687 (A and AEE); WD727–WD730 (Sold to Belgium); WD743–WD745 (Fireflash missile trials, Fairey Aviation); WD765, WD769 (ETPS); WD775 (Sold to Belgium); WD785, WD791 (Modified to NF.12 standard for trials at Ferranti Ltd); WD797 (A and AEE).

Gloster Meteor NF.Mk.11. Second production batch of 111 aircraft, WM143–WM192, WM221–WM270, WM292–WM302, built by Sir W. G. Armstrong Whitworth Aircraft Ltd in three sub batches and ordered under contract No. 6/ACFT/6141 C.B.5(b). Deliveries began in July 1951.

Operated by RAF Squadrons: Nos. 29, 68, 85, 87, 96, 141, 151, 256, 264.

Other aircraft: WM180 (TRE); WM184 (CSE); WM191 (CFE); WM232 (Firestreak missile trials, de Havilland Propellers); WM252 (S.C.1 trials chase aircraft and cabin pressurization trials); WM261 (NF.14 development TIs and ultimately the NF.14 prototype); WM262, WM295 (Vickers Blue Boar missile trials); WM296–WM302 (Sold to France).

WM372–WM375 were built as missile test aircraft for use by Fairey Aviation Ltd for Fireflash air-to-air missile trials.

Twenty NF.11s sold to Denmark in 1952 were on Armstrong Whitworth production lines as WM384–WM403. These aircraft were diverted to the Danish contract and re-serialled. Deliveries began in February 1952 and were completed in February 1953.

Gloster Meteor NF.Mk.12. First production batch of 100 aircraft, WS590–WS639, WS658–WS700, WS715–WS721, built by Sir W. G. Armstrong Whitworth Aircraft Ltd in three sub batches and ordered under contract No. 6/ACFT/6412 C.B.5(b).

Operated by RAF Squadrons: Nos. 25, 46, 64, 72, 85, 152, 153.

Gloster Meteor NF.Mk.13. First production batch of 40 aircraft, WM308–WM341, WM362–WM367, built by Sir W. G. Armstrong Whitworth Aircraft Ltd in two sub batches and ordered under contract No. 6/ACFT/6141 C.B.5(b). First prototype, WM308, first flown on 23 December, 1952, by J. O. Lancaster. Tropicalized version of Meteor NF.11. Two Derwent 9 engines.

Operated by RAF Squadrons: Nos. 39, 213, 219.

Meteor NF.12s and NF.14s of No.46 Sqdn, RAF, photographed in 1955, with each mark having a different camouflage scheme.

Gloster Meteor NF.Mk.14. First production batch of 100 aircraft, WS722–WS760, WS774–WS812, WS827–WS848, built by Sir W. G. Armstrong Whitworth Aircraft Ltd in three sub batches and ordered under contract No. 6/ACFT/6412 C.B.5(b). First prototype, WM261, first flown on 23 October, 1953, by W. H. Else. Two-piece canopy, spring-tab ailerons, auto-stabilizer fitted. Two Derwent 8 engines.

Operated by RAF Squadrons: Nos. 25, 33, 46, 64, 85, 96, 152, 153, 213, 264.

Gloster Meteor U.Mk.15. A total of 92 Meteor F.Mk.4 aircraft were converted to U.Mk.15 standards by Flight Refuelling Ltd, Tarrant Rushton, during 1955–69. Camera pods, command aerials, infra-red homing flares and automatic control equipment fitted. The majority powered by Derwent 5 engines with small-diameter air intakes. First Meteor F.4 airframe converted to a target drone, RA421, made first fully-automatic take-off controlled from the ground on 11 March, 1955.

Royal Aircraft Establishment, Llanbedr: RA373, RA375 (second production U.Mk.15, destroyed 6 May, 1960), RA397, RA415, RA420 (Development trials, Flight Refuelling), RA432, RA439, RA442, RA457 (Later to Royal Navy, Malta), VT104, VT110, VT135, VT168, VT196, VT268, VT291 (Camera installation trials, RAE), VT332, VT338, VW258, VW280 (Development trials), VW285, VW293, VW299, VW415.

Weapons Research Establishment, Woomera, Australia: EE524, RA367, RA371,

RA398, RA417, RA421 (First U.Mk.15 produced in joint RAE/Flight Refuelling programme), RA430, RA433, RA438, RA441, RA454, RA473, VT105, VT106, VT112, VT113, VT118, VT130, VT139, VT142, VT175, VT177, VT179, VT184, VT187, VT191, VT192, VT197, VT219, VT220, VT222, VT226, VT230, VT256, VT259, VT262, VT270, VT286, VT289, VT294, VT310, VT316, VT319, VT329, VT330, VT334, VW266 (First U.Mk.15 delivered to Australia, 23 July, 1957), VW273, VW275, VW303, VW308, VW781, VW791, VZ386, VZ389, VZ401, VZ403, VZ407, VZ414.

No.728 Sqdn: RA387, RA479, VT107 (Development trials, Flight Refuelling), VT243, VT282, VW276, VZ417.

Gloster Meteor U.Mk.16. A total of about 108 Meteor F.Mk.8 aircraft were converted to U.Mk.16 standards by Flight Refuelling Ltd, Tarrant Rushton, during 1956–69. An automatic pilot, radio link and camera equipment, command aerials and a lengthened nose embodied in F.Mk.8 airframe. First flight by U.Mk.16, WA775, on 22 October, 1956.

Royal Aircraft Establishment, Llanbedr: including VZ445, VZ485, VZ506, VZ514, VZ551, WA756, WA775 (Auto-pilot development trials), WA842, WA982, WE867, WE915, WF707, WF741, WF751, WF756, WH258, WH284 (First U.Mk.15 to be delivered to RAE Llanbedr), WH320 (Development trials, RAE), WH344, WH349, WH359, WH365, WH372, WH499, WH500, WH505, WH506, WK717, WK729. WK812, WK852, WK867, WK870, WK925, WK926 (First production U.Mk.16), WK942, WK980, WK993, WK994, WL124, WL127, WL160, WL162.

Weapons Research Establishment, Woomera, Australia: including VZ455, VZ503, WE902, WE960 (Converted to U.Mk.21), WF659, WH460, WK710, WK797 (Converted to U.Mk.21), WK879, WL136.

Other aircraft: including VZ439, VZ448, VZ458, VZ462, VZ513, VZ520, VZ530, VZ554, WA781, WA850, WA984, WA991, WE881, WE919, WE925, WE946, WF646, WF685, WH281 (all U.16 spares); WH369 (Development drone trials, Flight Refuelling); WH381 (Abandoned long-range project, Flight Refuelling); WH420 (Fitted with towed target flares for Jindivik 102 B and rearward-facing cameras); WK660 (Provided wings for WA982); WK738 (U.16 spares).

Gloster Meteor TT.Mk.20. A total of 20 Meteor NF.11 aircraft were converted for

A Meteor TT.20 showing the wind-driven winch, target-towing cable and tail-mounted deflector. (*Courtesy William Green*)

367

Royal Navy use to TT.Mk.20 standards. M.L.Aviation Type G fully-feathering wind-driven winch carried in streamlined pylon on starboard centre section with 6,100 ft of cable. Four high speed radar responsive, or non-responsive, targets stowed in rear fuselage. Winch operator's controls in the rear cockpit.

Meteor NF.11 aircraft so converted were WD592, WD606, WD626, WD630, WD645, WD646, WD647, WD649, WD652, WD657, WD678, WD679, WD702, WD767, WD780, WM148, WM223, WM224, WM270 and WM293. Four NF.11s of the Royal Danish Air Force, 508, 512, 517, and 519, were similarly converted to TT.Mk.20 standards and subsequently registered SE-DCH, SE-DCF, SE-DCG and SE-DCI respectively. SE-DCF and SE-DCH were sold to Kjeld Mortensen in Denmark in March 1969 after all four aircraft had been operated by Swedair Ltd for target-towing duties in Denmark. These two TT.Mk.20s were later sold to West Germany, but in February 1970 were being advertized for sale again by Mortensen.

Meteor Export Production

Argentinian Meteor F.4. Production order for 50 aircraft, serialled I-051 to I-100, built by Gloster Aircraft Company during 1947–48. Normal production standard. All delivered by sea between May 1947 and January 1949 to be assembled and test flown at El Palomar Air Base near Buenos Aires.

Belgian Meteor F.4. Production order for 48 aircraft, serialled EF-1 to EF-48, built by Gloster Aircraft Company in 1949. Normal production standard. Delivery flights were completed in September 1949 and the aircraft were operated by Nos.349 and 350 Squadrons, Belgian Air Force.

Danish Meteor F.4. Production order for 20 aircraft, serialled 461 to 480, built by Gloster Aircraft Company in 1949–50. Order received from Danish Government in May 1949. Normal production standard. Delivery flights were completed by March 1950.

Egyptian Meteor F.4. Production orders for 12 aircraft, serialled 1401 to 1412, built by Gloster Aircraft Company in 1948–50. Orders received from Egyptian Government for three batches of two, three and seven aircraft in August 1948, January 1949 and November 1949 respectively. Normal production standard plus tropical equipment. Delivery flights were interrupted by British Government embargoes but were completed in May 1950.

Dutch Meteor F.4. Production orders for 38 aircraft, serialled I-21 to I-58, built by Gloster Aircraft Company in 1947–50. Orders received from Netherlands Government for four batches of five, five, 24 and four aircraft in June 1947, August 1948, April 1949 and March 1950. Normal production standard. Delivery flights began in June 1948 and were completed in September 1950.

Belgian Meteor T.7. Production order for three aircraft, serialled ED-1 to ED-3, built by Gloster Aircraft Company in 1948. Order received from Belgian Government in May 1948. Normal production standard. Delivery flights were undertaken in September and December 1948.

Danish Meteor T.7. Production order for nine aircraft, serialled 261 to 269, built by Gloster Aircraft Company in 1949–50. Normal production standard. Delivery by air. These aircraft served initially with 3rd Air Flotilla of the Naval Air Service which became No.723 Squadron, Danish Air Force, in January 1951.

Egyptian Meteor T.7. Production orders for three aircraft, serialled 1400, 1413 and 1414, built by Gloster Aircraft Company in 1949. Normal production standard. Orders received from Egyptian Government for one aircraft in August 1948 and for two aircraft in October 1948. Delivery flights were delayed by British Government embargo until

July 1949, February and May 1950.

Dutch Meteor T.7. Production order for 43 aircraft, built by Gloster Aircraft Company in 1949–50. Order received from the Netherlands Government in November 1948. First aircraft delivered was I-1 which was originally Glosters' PV Meteor T.7 G-AKPK. Normal production standard. Delivery flights were completed in 1956.

French Meteor T.7. Production order for two aircraft, serialled F1 and F2, built by Gloster Aircraft Company in 1950. Order received from French Government in September 1950. Normal production standard. Delivery was made in February 1951. Aircraft were operated by CEV at Bretigny.

Syrian Meteor T.7. Production order for two aircraft, serialled 91 and 92, built by Gloster Aircraft Company in 1950. Order received from Syrian Government in January 1950. Aircraft were accepted by a Syrian Government representative at Glosters' Moreton Valence factory but British Government embargo prevented their delivery flight to Syria. These aircraft were diverted to the French Air Force in February 1951.

Israeli Meteor T.7. Production order for four aircraft, serialled 2162 to 2165, built by Gloster Aircraft Company in 1953. Order received from the Israeli Government in February 1963. Normal production standard with target-towing equipment.

Brazilian Meteor T.7. Production order for ten aircraft, serialled 4300 to 4309 built by Gloster Aircraft Company in 1953. Order received from Brazilian Government in October 1952. Part of deal for 70 Meteors exchanged for 15,000 tons of raw cotton. First two aircraft were ex-RAF.

Brazilian Meteor F.8. Production order for 60 aircraft, serialled 4400 to 4459, built by Gloster Aircraft Company in 1953–54. Order received from Brazilian Government in October 1952. These aircraft were exchanged for 15,000 tons of raw cotton. Delivery by sea was completed in 1954.

Danish Meteor F.8. Production order for 20 aircraft, serialled 481 to 500, built by Gloster Aircraft Company in 1950–51. Order received from Danish Government in April 1950. Normal production standard. Delivery flights were completed during 1951. These aircraft served primarily with No.742 Squadron, Danish Air Force.

Israeli Meteor F.8. Production order for 11 aircraft, serialled 2166 to 2169 and 2172 to 2178, built by Gloster Aircraft Company in 1953. Order received from Israeli Government in February 1953. Normal production standard except that provision was made for carriage of US-built HVAR projectiles under the wings, and Israeli Government supplied the four-cannon armament. Delivery flights were made between August 1953 and January 1954.

Danish Meteor NF.11. Production order for 20 aircraft, serialled 501 to 520, built by Sir W. G. Armstrong Whitworth Aircraft in 1952–53. Order received from Danish Government in 1952. Normal production standard. Delivery flights between November 1952 and March 1953. These aircraft served with No.723 Squadron, Danish Air Force.

Gloster E.1/44. Six prototypes, SM801, SM805, SM809, TX145, TX148 and TX150, built or partially built by Gloster Aircraft Company during 1944–49. The first two airframes, on which construction was abandoned, bore the Gloster GA.1 designation; the next three were designated GA.2 and the sixth, which was also abandoned before completion, was GA.3. GA.4 was allocated to the proposed production of GA.2 to specification 24/46 P. Pre-production prototype, TX145, first flown at A and AEE Boscombe Down on 9 March, 1948, by W. A. Waterton. Powered by Rolls-Royce Nene 2 turbojet.

Gloster GA.5. Five prototypes, WD804, WD808, WT827, WT830 and WT836, built by Gloster Aircraft Company during 1949–54 to meet specification F.4/48. WD804 powered by Armstrong Siddeley Sapphire Sa.3 engines of 7,500 lb thrust and first flown on 26 November, 1951, from Moreton Valence. Written off in a heavy landing after loss of elevators on 29 June, 1952, at Boscombe Down. WD808 first flown on 21 August, 1952, from Moreton Valence. Crashed on 11 June, 1953, at Flax Bourton after experiencing super stall conditions. WT827 first flown on 7 March, 1953, from Moreton Valence. First prototype to carry armament, radar and radome. WT830 first flown on 14 January, 1954, the first GA.5 to fly from Hucclecote. WT836 first flown on 20 July, 1954, from Hucclecote.

Gloster Javelin F(AW)Mk.1. First production batch of 40 aircraft, XA544–XA572, XA618–XA628, built by Gloster Aircraft Co Ltd during 1952–54 and ordered under contract No.6/Aircraft/8336 dated 14 July, 1952. Armstrong Siddeley Sapphire Sa.6 engines. AI.17 radar. Electrically-operated variable-incidence tailplane. First flight by XA544 on 22 July, 1954.

Operated by RAF Squadrons: Nos. 46, 87.

G.A.C. trials aircraft: XA544 (Radar and gunnery), XA545 (Flying controls), XA546 (Crashed 21 October, 1954), XA547 (Missiles), XA548 (Spinning), XA549 (Radar, later 7717M), XA551, XA552 (Later de Havilland Gyron Junior engines installed), XA553 (Electrical, later 7470M), XA554, XA555, XA556 (Flew at Paris Air Show 1955), XA558 (Intensive flying, crashed RAF Brüggen 5 June, 1958), XA559 (Miscellaneous TIs), XA560 (Engine trials, Sapphire Sa.7 reheat); A and AEE: XA563 (Handling, later 7627M); Armstrong Siddeley Motors Ltd: XA557 (Engine and instruments); Rolls-Royce Ltd: XA562 (Avon RA.24 installation); Boulton Paul Aircraft: XA561 (Spinning trials, crashed 8 December, 1955), XA567 (Radar trials); Bristol Aeroplane Co Ltd: XA564 (later 7464M); RAE: XA550.

Gloster Javelin F(AW)Mk.2. First production batch of 30 aircraft, XA768–XA781, XA799–XA814, built by Gloster Aircraft Co Ltd during 1955–57 and ordered under contract No. 6/Aircraft/8336 dated 14 July, 1952. Armstrong Siddeley Sapphire Sa.6 engines. AI.22 radar. All-flying tail. First flight by XA768 on 25 April, 1956. One prototype, XD158, also built and first flew 31 October, 1955.

Operated by RAF Squadrons: Nos. 46, 85, 89.

G.A.C. trials aircraft: XA769 (Radar and generators), XA770 (Armament controls), XA771 (Missiles), XA778 (Later pacer aircraft at A and AEE, March 1961); A and AEE: XD158 (Radar trials).

Gloster Javelin T.Mk.3. Production batch of 22 aircraft, XH390–XH397, XH432–XH438, XH443–XH447, XK577, XM336, built by Gloster Aircraft Co Ltd during 1955–57 and ordered under contract No. 6/Aircraft/11262 dated 27 September, 1954. Armstrong Siddeley Sapphire Sa.6 engines. All-flying tail. One prototype WT841, also built. First flight by WT841 on 26 August, 1956.

Operated by RAF Squadrons: Nos. 5, 11, 23, 25, 29, 33, 41, 46, 60, 64, 72, 85, 96, 151.

Gloster Javelin F(AW)Mk.4. Production batch of 50 aircraft, XA629–XA640, XA644, XA763–XA767 built by Gloster Aircraft Co Ltd and XA720–XA737, XA749–XA762 built by Sir W. G. Armstrong Whitworth Aircraft Ltd during 1955–58 and ordered under contract No. 6/Aircraft/8336 dated 14 July, 1952. Armstrong Siddeley Sapphire Sa.6 engines. AI.17 radar. All-flying tail. First flight by XA629 on 19 September, 1955.

Operated by RAF Squadrons: Nos. 3, 11, 23, 41, 72, 87, 96, 141.

G.A.C. trials aircraft: XA629 (Kuchemann 'carrots' fitted), XA630 (Handling), XA631 (Operational reliability), XA632, XA634 (Later 7641M), XA644 (Handling), XA720, XA721, XA723 (Later to CEFE, Climatic Detachment, Nameo, Canada, for winterization trials, 3 October, 1956), XA765; CFE: XA763–4.

Gloster Javelin F(AW)Mk.5. First production batch of 58 aircraft, XA641–XA643, XA645–XA661 built by Gloster Aircraft Co Ltd, and XA662–XA667, XA688–XA719 built by Sir W. G. Armstrong Whitworth Aircraft Ltd during 1955–57 and ordered under contract No. 6/Aircraft/8336 dated 14 July, 1952. Armstrong Siddeley Sapphire Sa.6 Mks.10201 and 10301 engines. AI.17 radar. All-flying tail. First flight by XA641 on 26 July, 1956.

Operated by RAF Squadrons: Nos. 5, 11, 23, 41, 72, 87, 151.

G.A.C. trials aircraft: XA641, XA709 (Also A and AEE armament trials); CFE: XA642 (Lost at sea 6 December, 1957), XA648 (Crashed 20 September, 1958), XA665, XA688, XA696–7, XA704; A and AEE: XA649 (Handling squadron); RAE: XA692 (Institute of Aviation Medicine); Armstrong Siddeley Motors Ltd: XA711 (Later A and AEE gun firing).

Note: Components of XA643, XA645, XA646, XA654–XA658 manufactured by Gloster Aircraft Co Ltd and assembled by Sir W. G. Armstrong Whitworth Aircraft Ltd. First AWA-built Javelin 5 to be delivered was XA699 which went to No.19 MU at St Athan on 17 April, 1957. The last Gloster-built Javelin 5 was XA660 which also went to St Athan, on 16 September, 1957.

Gloster Javelin F(AW)Mk.5. Second production batch of six aircraft, XH687–XH692, built by Sir W. G. Armstrong Whitworth Aircraft Ltd and ordered under contract No. 6/Aircraft/11329 dated 19 October, 1954.

Operated by RAF Squadrons: Nos. 5, 11, 151.

Gloster Javelin F(AW)Mk.6. First production batch of 22 aircraft, XA815–XA836, built by Gloster Aircraft Co Ltd during 1956–57 and ordered under contract No. 6/Aircraft/8336 dated 14 July, 1952. Armstrong Siddeley Sapphire Sa.6 Mks.10701 and 10801 engines. AI.22 radar. All-flying tail. First flight by XA815 on 14 December, 1956. Operated by RAF Squadrons: Nos. 29, 46, 85, 89.

G.A.C. trials aircraft XA821; A and AEE: XA821 (CA release), XA834 (Handling and fuel consumption checks); RAE: XA831.

Gloster Javelin F(AW)Mk.6. Second production batch of 11 aircraft, XH693–XH703, built by Gloster Aircraft Co Ltd and ordered under contract No. 6/Aircraft/11329 dated 19 October, 1954.

Operated by RAF Squadrons: Nos. 29, 46, 85, 89.

Gloster Javelin F(AW)Mk.7. Production batch of 142 aircraft, XH704–XH725, XH746–XH784, XH900–XH912, XH955–XH965, built by Gloster Aircraft Co Ltd, and XH785–XH795, XH833–XH849, XH871–XH899 built by Sir W. G. Armstrong Whitworth Aircraft Ltd and ordered under contract No. 6/Aircraft/11329 C.B.7(b) dated 19 October, 1954. Armstrong Siddeley Sapphire Sa.7 Mks.20301 and 20401 engines. AI.17 radar. All-flying tail. First flight by XH704 on 9 November, 1956. (Note: Seventy-six aircraft were subsequently converted to Javelin F(AW)Mk.8 standard and redesignated Javelin F(AW)Mk.9. Where the serial number alone is given the aircraft remained a Mk.7; where the serial number has an asterisk the aircraft was converted after delivery but before being taken on charge by the unit indicated; the date of the conversion is given in parentheses after those aircraft converted at Moreton Valence to Mk.8 standard; where the serial number is in parentheses the aircraft was issued to its first unit as a Mk.9; where an asterisk and the date are given the aircraft returned to the same unit after conversion.)

No.23 Sqdn: (XH763), XH774 (2 Feb. 1961), XH775 (Crashed after mid-air collision with XH781, 1 Sept. 1959), XH777 (2 Feb. 1961), XH778 (19 Dec. 1960), XH779 (8 Mar. 1961), XH781 (Crashed after mid-air collision with XH775), (XH793), (XH845), (XH848), (XH849), (XH885–XH895), XH904 (19 Dec. 1960), XH958 (16 Jan. 1961), XH960 (13 Jan. 1961), XH962 (26 Jan. 1961), XH963 (26 April, 1961), XH964 (21 Dec. 1960). No.25 Sqdn: (XH760, later 7892M), (XH767, later 7955M), (XH769–XH772),

Firestreak-armed Javelin F(AW)9s of No.25 Sqdn. Note that missiles are carried only on the outboard pylons.

XH776*, (XH880), (XH881–XH884), XH897 (9 Nov. 1960), XH898* (24 Oct. 1960), XH899 (5 Oct. 1961), XH905 (21 Oct. 1960), XH906* (28 Oct. 1960), XH907 (28 Nov. 1960), XH908 (6 Dec. 1961), XH909* (24 Oct. 1960), XH910 (31 May, 1961), XH911 (4 Nov. 1960), XH912 (29 Nov. 1960), XH955 (26 July, 1961), XH956 (5 Jan. 1961), XH957 (8 Nov. 1960), XH959 (15 Jan. 1960), XH961 (21 Sept. 1961). No.29 Sqdn: XH725*, XH749*, XH752*, XH777*, XH778*, XH779*, XH792*, XH834*, XH910*, XH956*, XH958*, XH960*, XH962*, XH963*. No.33 Sqdn: XH713*, XH715 (10 Jan. 1962), XH716 (30 Oct. 1961), XH718 (10 Jan. 1961), XH719 (29 June, 1961), XH720 (Scrapped after crash landing, Nicosia, 14 Oct. 1959), XH721 (28 July, 1961), XH750 (Crashed 10 July, 1959), XH751 (8 Sept. 1961), XH755*, XH756*, XH758*, XH773*, XH780*, XH786 (16 Jan. 1961), XH794 (31 May, 1961. Crashed, Wildenrath, 12 June, 1962), XH795 (20 Jan. 1961), XH833 (27 Sept. 1961), XH835 (21 June, 1961), XH836 (25 July, 1961), XH837 (20 Jan. 1961), XH838 (Scrapped 23 Oct. 1960), XH839 (28 Aug. 1961), XH897*, XH903* (Later 7938M), XH904*, XH905*, XH907*, XH911*, XH912*, XH957*. No.60 Sqdn: XH721*, XH722*, XH724*, XH747*, XH751*, XH785*, XH787*, XH788*, XH791* (Crashed, Dacca, 5 Aug. 1961), XH835*, XH836*, XH839*, XH840–XH842*, XH846*. No.64 Sqdn: XH708*, (XH709), XH717 (18 April, 1961), XH719*, XH723, XH724 (28 June, 1961), XH725 (21 April, 1961), (XH762), (XH764), (XH765), (XH766), (XH768), XH785 (26 May, 1961), XH787 (31 May, 1961), XH788 (27 June, 1961), XH789, XH791 (29 June, 1961), XH794 (31 May, 1961), XH834 (14 Mar. 1961), XH840 (25 May, 1961), XH841 (25 May, 1961), XH842 (27 Mar. 1961), XH844*, XH846 (26 May, 1961), (XH871–XH874), (XH875. Destroyed by fire, Nicosia, 26 May, 1961), (XH876), (XH877), (XH878. Crashed Waterbeach, 26 Nov. 1961), (XH879), (XH887), (XH896).

G.A.C. trials aircraft: XH704 (Performance. Converted 3 Mar. 1960), XH705, XH706 (Handling and autostabilizer. Converted 10 May, 1960), XH780 (2 Dec. 1960). A and AEE: XH704, XH705 (Missile trials. Scrapped 12 Oct. 1961), XH706 (Pitch stabilizer. Converted 10 May, 1960), XH708 (Engineering. Converted 22 Aug. 1960), XH710 (CA release), XH712 (Handling. Converted 28 Oct. 1960), XH713 (Tropical trials, Bahrein, August 1957. Converted 9 Jan. 1961), XH753 (16 Oct. 1961), XH754 (Autopilot and vision in rain trials), XH757 (Tropical trials, Kano, September 1957), XH759 (Handling), XH964*, XH965. Airwork Ltd: XH711 (10 Jan. 1962); GWTS: XH782–XH784; AWDS: XH790, XH792 (1 Mar. 1961), XH900 (Later 7811M), XH901–2; CFE: XH747 (26 April, 1961), XH748 (13 Jan. 1961), XH749 (14 Mar. 1961), XH752 (27 Feb. 1961), XH755 (30 Nov. 1960), XH756 (2 Dec. 1960), XH758 (18 Jan. 1961); No.19 MU: XH844 (18 Sept. 1959), XH959*; No.23 MU: XH707*, XH711*, XH712*,

(XH761), XH773 (30 Sept. 1960), XH776 (4 Oct. 1960), XH843 (31 Aug. 1960), XH847 (15 Sept. 1960); Armstrong Siddeley Motors Ltd: XH707* (Engine development), XH746.

Gloster Javelin F(AW)Mk.8. Production batch of 47 aircraft, XH966–XH993, XJ113–XJ130, XJ165, built by Gloster Aircraft Co Ltd during 1957–60 and ordered under contract No. 6/Aircraft/11329 dated 19 October, 1954. Armstrong Siddeley Sapphire Sa.7 Mks.20501R and 20601R engines with limited reheat. AI.22 radar. All-flying tail. First flight by XH966 on 9 May, 1958, and last flight by a Gloster-built aeroplane from Hucclecote was by XJ128 on 8 April, 1960, piloted by R. F. Martin. (Note: XJ166–XJ178 were allocated but cancelled).

Operated by RAF Squadrons: Nos. 23, 41, 72, 85.

G.A.C. trials aircraft: XH966, XH968, XH969, XH970; A and AEE: XH966–XH970; AFDS: XH972, XH975–6; AWDS: XH975–6; Armstrong Siddeley Motors Ltd: XJ125.

Gloster Projects

The following unbuilt projects fall into three broad chronological groups: (a) the period from just after World War I until the end of World War II, (b) a second period up to the time of the 1957 White Paper on Defence, and (c) the final three years of Glosters' life.

Period (a) 1922–1945

These 23 years saw the development of the piston-engined biplane not only reach its peak but also its demise, prior to World War II, coupled with the growing supremacy of the monoplane and the turbine engine. Glosters' projects of this period therefore range from single-engined fighters and transport biplanes to four-jet bomber monoplanes. The drawings and descriptive material relative to these projects reveal the very practical approach to many of the specifications.

Period (b) 1946–1957

This was the era when, for a short period, the British aircraft industry, spurred on by the political and military scene in Europe and the Far East, achieved a measure of supremacy in fighter development but lost the initiative through delaying the introduction of sweptwing aircraft. Then the 1957 Defence White Paper halted work on this class of manned military aircraft. During these years Glosters' projects reflect the pace of technological development and include many types of subsonic and transonic fighter and research aircraft which would have carried the company into the supersonic era just getting under way in the United Kingdom. Possibly due to military security of this period, but more likely due to disinterested 'arsonists', little more than three-view drawings have survived but many original Gloster drawings are used to illustrate these years of endeavour.

Period (c) 1958–1961

For Glosters time was running out and this was a period of desperate efforts being made to apply 43 years' experience in the production of military aircraft to the needs of civil aviation in many of its forms. Thus the projects of this era run the gamut of turbine- and piston-engine powered transports, from small executive aeroplanes to transonic airliners, some with V/STOL capabilities, and an unmanned crop-spraying helicopter. Three-view drawings exist for all Gloster projects from P.392 to P.534 and 16 of the more interesting have been chosen to illustrate these, possibly, most productive three years of Glosters' project office.

From 1917 until 1942 a number of systems were used by Gloucestershire and Gloster Aircraft Company to designate their projects. In some cases a name and mark number were employed, in others the duty and type of engine or the Air Ministry specification to which they were designed were used. In 1942 a system was adopted in which projects were given a 'P number' designation, although many drawings showing fuselage lines, wing geometry, engine and armament installation were also given this designation and account for most of the gaps in the following list. Unfortunately it is believed that no complete record of company projects survives; those given below therefore comprise the fullest available.

Designation		Date	
Mars V reconnaissance aircraft		1922	Schemed
Mars VII single-seat fighter		1922	Design study
Mars VIII single-engine nine-seat transport		1922	Schemed
Mars IX single-engine seven-seat transport		1922	Schemed
Goodwood single-engine freight aircraft		1925	Construction begun
Twin-engine bomber to B.9/32		1932	Design study
Single-engine day bomber to P.27/32		1933	Design study
Twin-engine turret-armed fighter to F.5/33		1933	Design study
SS.34 monoplane fighter		1934	Design study
Twin-engine turret-armed fighter to F.34/35		1935	Tendered
Twin-engine turret-armed fighter to F.11/37		1937	Tendered
Single-engine twin-boom fighter to F.18/37		1938	Mock-up begun
Four-engine bomber to B.1/39		1939	Tendered
Single-engine turret-armed fighter to N.9/39		1939	Tendered
Twin-engine day/night interceptor to F.18/40		1940	Mock-up begun
Twin-engine night fighter to F.29/40		1940	Tendered
Four-jet bomber		1941	Schemed
Single-engine fighter to E.5/42		1942	Tendered
P.199	E.1/44 with AJ.65 engine	1945	Schemed
P.203	High-altitude Meteor	1946	Schemed
P.209	Twin-jet fighter with AJ.65 engines	1946	Schemed
P.228	Night fighter to F.44/46	1946	Design study
P.231	Twin-jet fighter to N.40/46	1946	Design study
P.234	Single-seat interceptor with AJ.65 engines to F.43/46	1947	Schemed
P.238	Day and night interceptor	1947	Schemed
P.240	Day and night interceptor with F.9 engines	1947	Schemed
P.241	Delta-wing development of P.240	1947	Schemed
P.248	Design to F.43/46 with 4½ in recoilless gun	1947	Schemed
P.250	Design to F.43/46 with two 30 mm guns	1947	Schemed
P.258	Two-seat fighter with six rocket tubes	1947	Schemed
P.259	Two-seat fighter with Sapphire or Avon engines	1947	Schemed
P.262	Meteor with delta wing	1947	Schemed
P.263	Development of P.262	1947	Design study
P.272	Two-seat night fighter with four 4½ in recoilless guns	1948	Design study
P.275	Single-seat day fighter to F.3/48	1948	Design proposal
P.276	Two-seat night fighter to F.4/48	1948	Tendered, became Javelin
P.279	Two-seat night fighter with Sapphire engines to F.4/48	1948	Design study
P.280	Two-seat day/night fighter to F.4/48	1949	Design study

P.203. High-altitude version of the Meteor 4 schemed in January 1946.

376

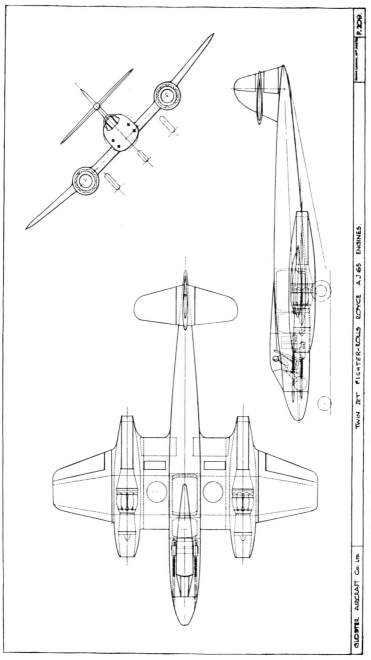

GLOSTER AIRCRAFT Co. LTD.   TWIN JET FIGHTER-ROLLS ROYCE AJ 65 ENGINES.   P.209.

P.209. Development of the Meteor 4 with Rolls-Royce AJ.65 axial-flow engines, June 1946.

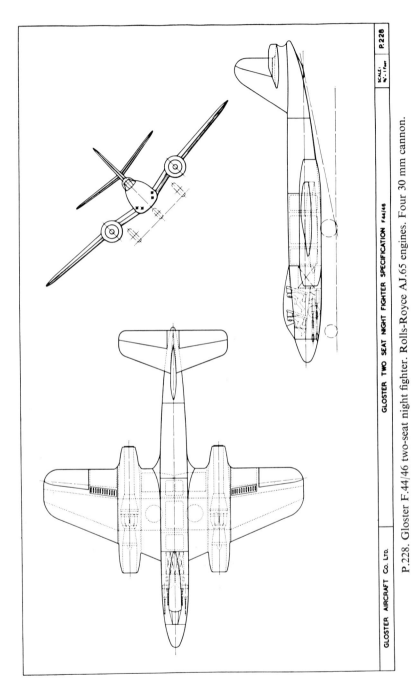

GLOSTER TWO SEAT NIGHT FIGHTER SPECIFICATION F.44/46

SCALE:
N°: 1 foot

P.228

P.228. Gloster F.44/46 two-seat night fighter. Rolls-Royce AJ.65 engines. Four 30 mm cannon.

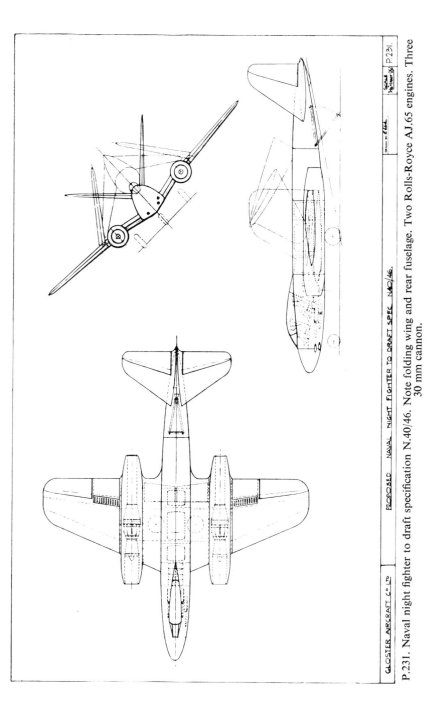

GLOSTER AIRCRAFT Cº LTD   PROPOSED NAVAL NIGHT FIGHTER TO DRAFT SPEC N40/46.   P.231.

P.231. Naval night fighter to draft specification N.40/46. Note folding wing and rear fuselage. Two Rolls-Royce AJ.65 engines. Three 30 mm cannon.

379

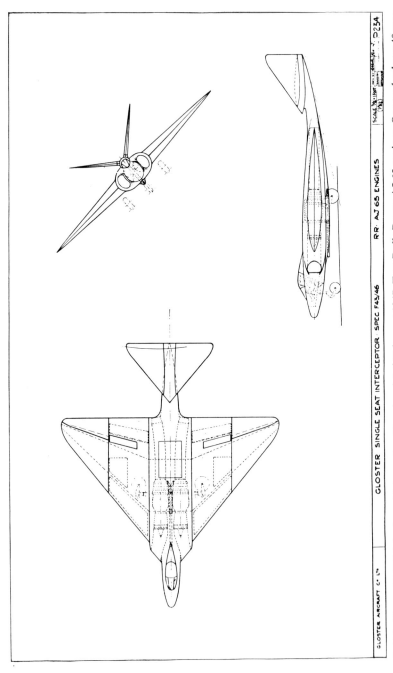

GLOSTER AIRCRAFT Cº Lº   GLOSTER SINGLE SEAT INTERCEPTOR. SPEC F.43/46   RR. AJ 65 ENGINES   SCALE... P.234

P.234. Gloster F.43/46 single-seat interceptor. Drawing dated February 1947. Two Rolls-Royce AJ.65 engines. One underslung 40 mm gun.

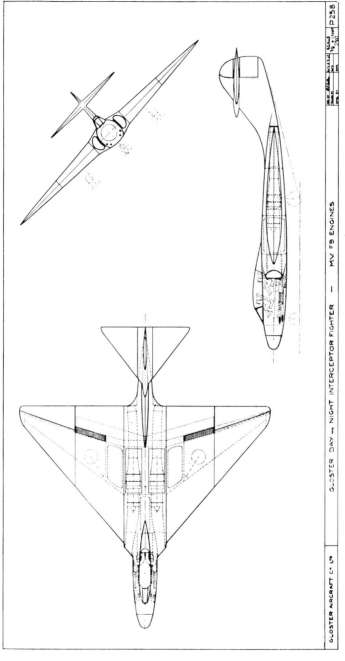

P.238. Gloster day and night interceptor with Metropolitan Vickers F.9 engines and slab tailplane. Drawing dated March 1947. Four 30 mm guns.

381

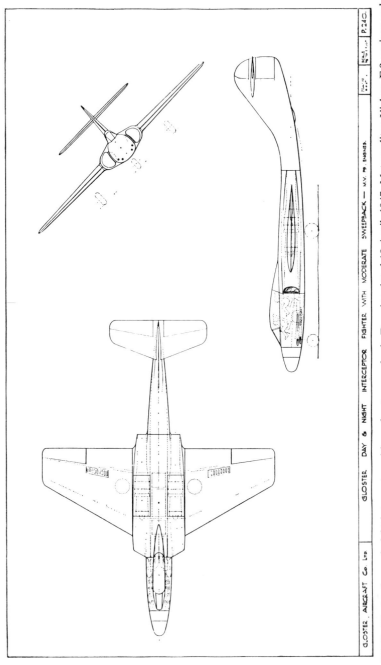

P.240. Gloster day and night interceptor with moderate sweepback. Drawing dated 18 April, 1947. Metropolitan Vickers F.9 engines and four 30 mm guns.

382

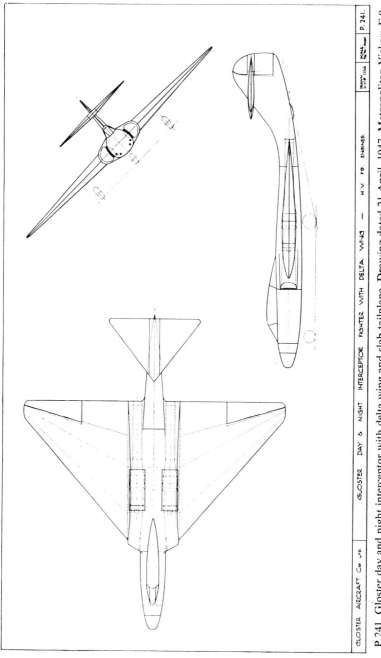

P.241. Gloster day and night interceptor with delta wing and slab tailplane. Drawing dated 21 April, 1947. Metropolitan Vickers F.9 engines. Four 30 mm guns.

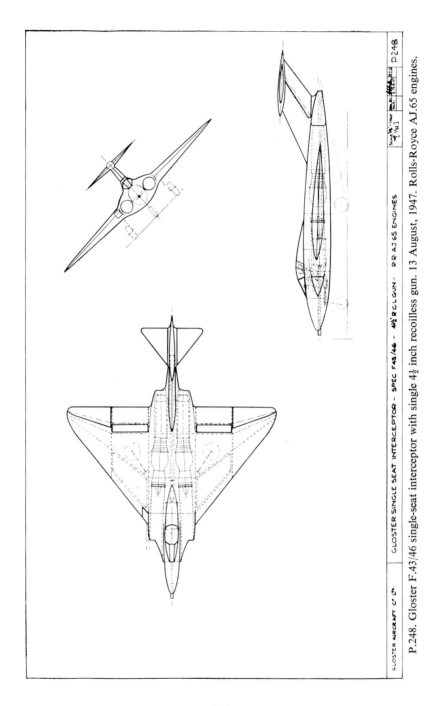

GLOSTER AIRCRAFT C° L°   GLOSTER SINGLE SEAT INTERCEPTOR - SPEC F43/46 - 4½" R.CL GUN - R.R A.J 65 ENGINES   P.248

P.248. Gloster F.43/46 single-seat interceptor with single 4½ inch recoilless gun. 13 August, 1947. Rolls-Royce AJ.65 engines.

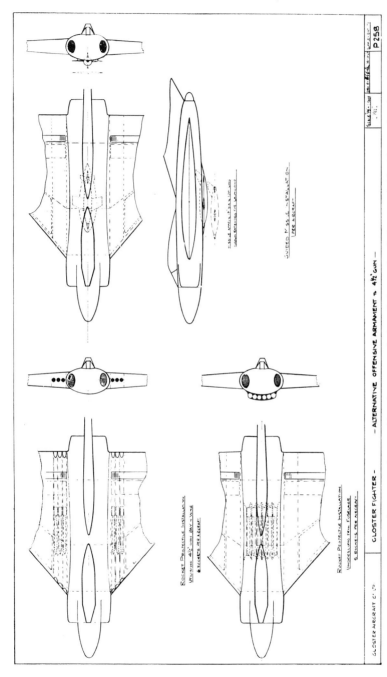

P.258. Heavy armament was always a major consideration in the design of all-weather fighters and this Gloster drawing, dated October 1947, shows a six rocket projectile battery carried internally and externally and the use of a semi-retractable guided missile.

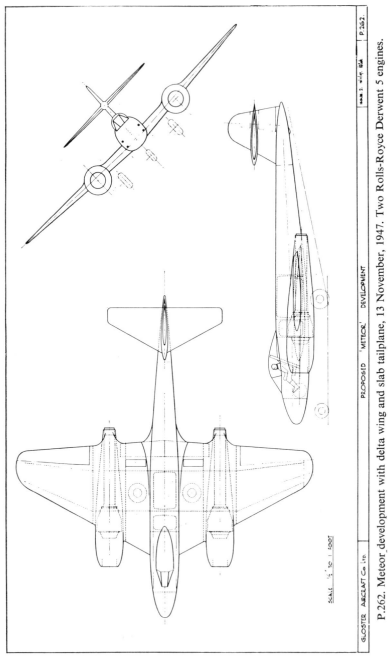

GLOSTER AIRCRAFT Co. LTD.   PROPOSED 'METEOR' DEVELOPMENT   P.262.

SCALE ½" TO 1 FOOT

P.262. Meteor development with delta wing and slab tailplane, 13 November, 1947. Two Rolls-Royce Derwent 5 engines.

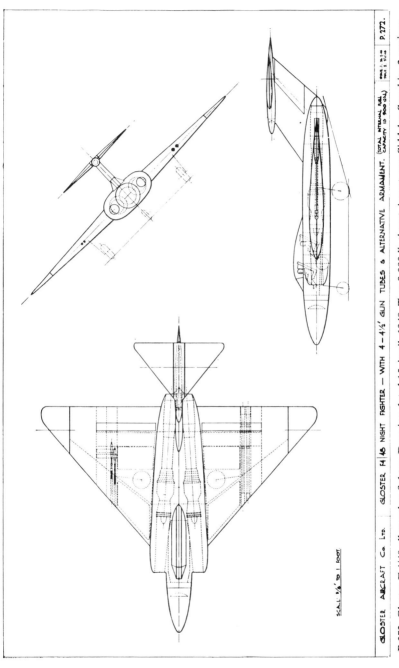

SCALE 1/6 TO 1 FOOT

GLOSTER AIRCRAFT Co. LTD. GLOSTER F4/48 NIGHT FIGHTER — WITH 4 - 4½" GUN TUBES & ALTERNATIVE ARMAMENT. (TOTAL INTERNAL FUEL CAPACITY 10 900 GAL) P.272.

P.272. Gloster F.4/48 all-weather fighter. Drawing dated 15 April, 1948. Two 9,000 lb thrust Armstrong Siddeley Sapphire 2 engines. Four 30 mm guns or four 4½ inch guns. Rotating wingtip controls and slab tailplane.

387

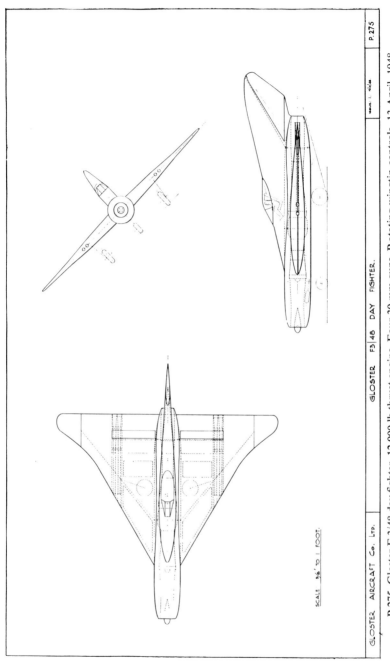

GLOSTER AIRCRAFT Co. LTD.　　　GLOSTER F3/48 DAY FIGHTER.　　　P.275

SCALE ⅟₁₆' to I FOOT.

P.275. Gloster F.3/48 day fighter. 12,000 lb thrust engine. Four 30 mm guns. Rotating wingtip controls. 13 April, 1948.

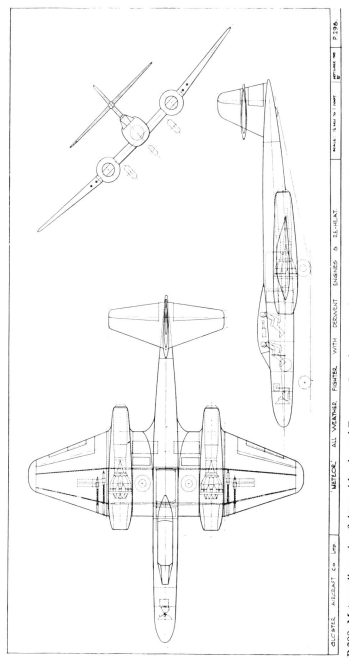

GLOSTER AIRCRAFT Co LTD | 'METEOR' ALL WEATHER FIGHTER WITH DERWENT ENGINES & RE-HEAT. | SCALE 12 INCH TO 1 FOOT | SEPTEMBER 1949 BY | P.298.

P.298. Meteor all-weather fighter with reheated Derwent 5 engines. Drawing dated September 1949. Note wing-mounted armament and constant-chord centre section.

389

Designation		Date	
P.281	Meteor development	1948	Schemed
P.284	Transonic research aircraft—prone pilot position	1948	Design study
P.285	Transonic research aircraft—conventional pilot position	1948	Design study
P.292	Meteor development with Avon engines	1949	RA491
P.298	Meteor all-weather fighter with reheat Derwent engines	1949	Design study
P.300	Development of P.298 with swept wing	1949	Schemed
P.303	Meteor ground-attack fighter with bombs	1950	Meteor G-7-1
P.304	Meteor ground-attack fighter with rocket projectiles	1950	Meteor G-7-1
P.305	Meteor ground-attack fighter with long-range tanks	1950	Meteor G-7-1
P.306	Meteor ground-attack fighter with long-span wings	1950	Meteor G-7-1
P.307	Meteor armed trainer	1950	Design study
P.308	Development of P.307 with long-range tanks	1950	Schemed
P.315	Two-seat long-range fighter	1950	Design study
P.316	Single-seat long-range fighter	1950	Design study
P.317	Long-range fighter-bomber	1950	Schemed
P.318	Two-seat long-range rocket armed fighter	1950	Schemed
P.319	Dual control version of F.4/48	1950	Schemed
P.322	Interceptor development of F.4/48 with AS.Sa.50 engines	1950	Design study
P.323	Long-range fighter development of P.322	1950	Design study
P.324	Fighter-bomber and rocket-armed development of P.322	1950	Design study
P.325	High-altitude escort fighter	1951	Schemed
P.346	PR development of F.4/48—Scheme 1	1952	Design study
P.347	PR development of F.4/48—Scheme 2	1952	Design study
P.348	P.347 with wing cameras	1952	Design study
P.350	PR development of F.4/48 to PR.118D and P	1952	Tendered
P.356	Thin-wing development of Javelin	1953	Tendered
P.370	Thin-wing development of Javelin with Olympus to F.153D	1953	Detail construction begun
P.371	P.370 armed with two Red Dean	1953	Design proposal
P.372	P.370 armed with four Firestreak	1953	Design proposal
P.376	Development of F.153D as supersonic fighter	1956	Design proposal
P.382	Javelin 7 with two Scorpion rocket motors	1957	Design study
P.392	30-seat transport with two or four paired Orpheus engines	1958	Schemed
P.393	30-seat transport with three rear-mounted Orpheus engines	1958	Schemed
P.394	30-seat transport with four Orpheus engines	1958	Schemed
P.404	38/56-seat 'double bubble' fuselage transport	1958	Design investigation
P.405	38/56-seat transport with area-ruled fuselage	1958	Schemed
P.409	52-seat transport with conventional fuselage	1958	Schemed
P.411	14-seat VTOL transport with two BE.53/2 engines	1958	Schemed
P.414	80-seat transport with area-ruled fuselage 1958	1958	Schemed
P.418	160-seat transport with area-ruled fuselage	1958	Schemed
P.426	Twin-boom VTOL aircraft with three BE.53/2s	1958	Schemed

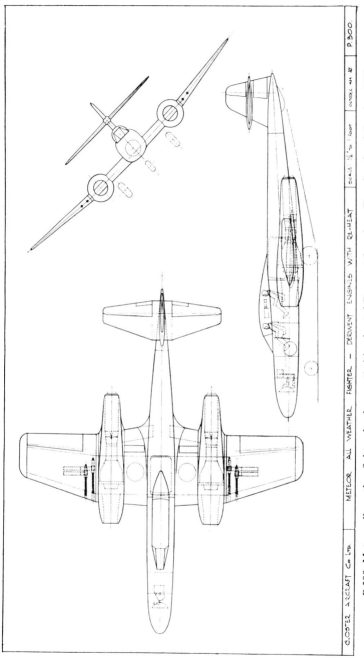

GLOSTER AIRCRAFT Co LTD | METEOR ALL WEATHER FIGHTER — DERWENT ENGINES WITH RE-HEAT | SCALE ⅛″ to 1 FOOT | GLOSA. № 16 | P.300

P.300. Meteor all-weather fighter development with reheated Derwent 5 engines. Drawing dated October 1949.

Designation		Date	
P.428	VTOL aircraft with four BE.53/2 engines	1958	Schemed
P.429	VTOL aircraft with four pylon-mounted engines	1958	Schemed
P.443	Unmanned crop-spraying helicopter	1960	Detail design
P.454	Development of P.418	1958	Schemed
P.458	P.418 with landing gear in trailing edge of wing	1958	Schemed
P.459	36-seat transport with two BE.61 engines	1958	Schemed
P.460	36-seat transport with two derated BE.61 engines	1958	Schemed
P.461	Four-jet 150,000 lb AUW strategic transport	1958	Schemed
P.462	STOL version of P.458	1958	Schemed
P.463	Development of P.458 with elliptical wing	1958	Schemed
P.464	STOL development of P.458	1958	Schemed
P.465	54-seat transport with elliptical wing	1958	Schemed
P.467	Alternative STOL version of P.458	1958	Schemed
P.471	80-seat transport version of P.465	1959	Schemed
P.473	54-seat transport version of P.458	1959	Schemed
P.474	54-seat transport with four-abreast seats	1959	Schemed
P.475	54-seat transport with three-abreast seats	1959	Schemed
P.476	Development of P.475	1959	Schemed
P.479	67-high-density-seat transport	1959	Schemed
P.480	Two-deck 141-seat transport	1959	Schemed
P.486	Two-deck 144-seat transport	1959	Schemed
P.492	Transonic transport with six Olympus 591 engines	1959	Schemed
P.493	P.492 with alternative engine layout	1959	Schemed
P.494	Twin-jet 18-seat light transport	1960	Schemed
P.496	Twin-engined 6-seat light transport	1960	Schemed
P.497	VTOL Meteor 8 with twelve RB.108 engines	1960	Schemed

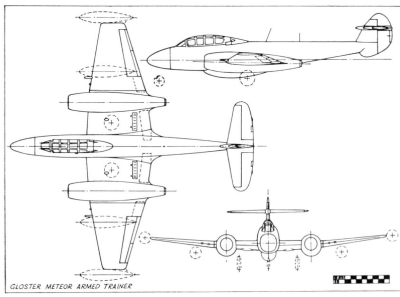

GLOSTER METEOR ARMED TRAINER

Project P.307 of 1950 was a Meteor T.7 fuselage with NF.11 armed wings.

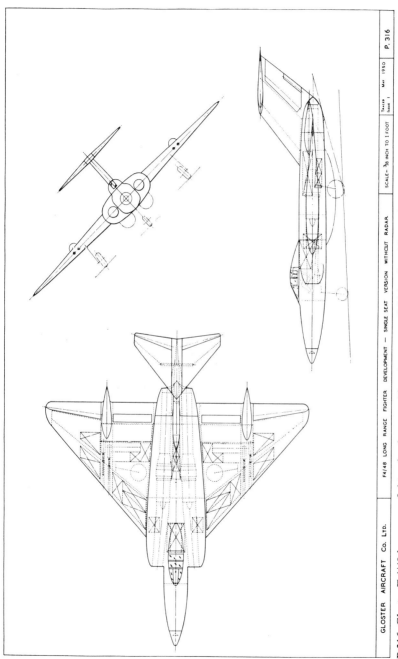

GLOSTER AIRCRAFT CO. LTD.   F4/48 LONG RANGE FIGHTER DEVELOPMENT — SINGLE SEAT VERSION WITHOUT RADAR   SCALE - 3⁄8 INCH TO 1 FOOT   TRACED MAY 1950 ISSUE 1   P. 316

P.316. Gloster F.4/48 long-range fighter development. Two Armstrong Siddeley Sapphire engines. Single-seat version without AI radar. Note 'carrots' on wings.

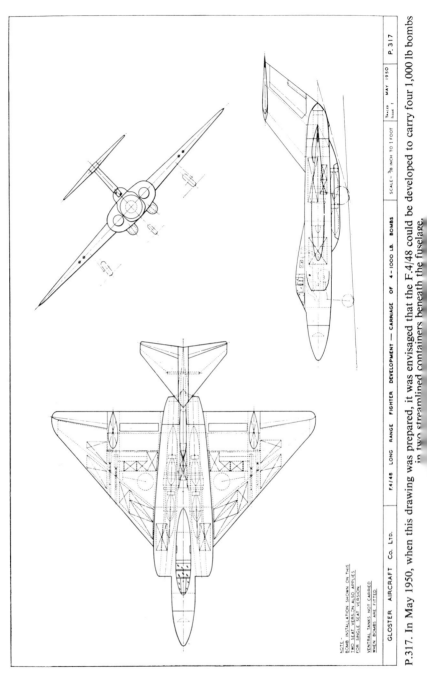

GLOSTER AIRCRAFT CO. LTD. | F.4/48 LONG RANGE FIGHTER DEVELOPMENT — CARRIAGE OF 4 - 1000 LB. BOMBS | SCALE - ³⁄₈ INCH TO 1 FOOT | TRACED MAY 1950 | P. 317 ISSUE 1

P.317. In May 1950, when this drawing was prepared, it was envisaged that the F.4/48 could be developed to carry four 1,000 lb bombs in two streamlined containers beneath the fuselage.

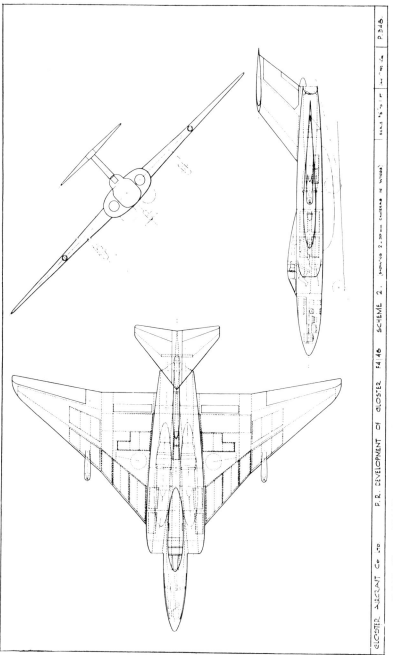

P.348. Gloster F.4/48 unarmed PR development. Nose camera pack. Rearward-looking radar. 11 January, 1952.

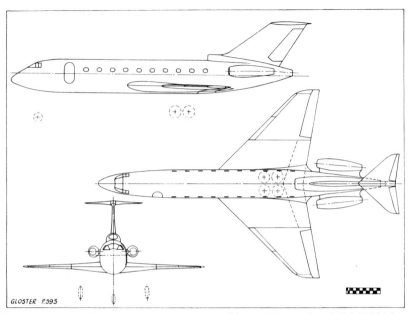

An early civil project was a 30-seat transport with two, three or four Bristol Siddeley Orpheus engines. All-up weight was 40,000 lb. Drawing dated 7 March, 1958.

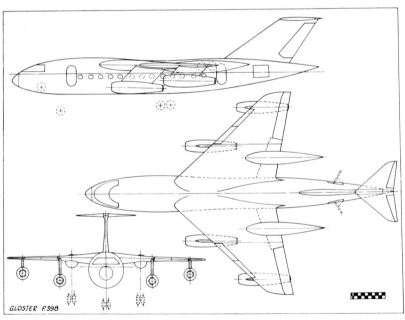

High-wing 39-seat civil transport with an area-ruled fuselage. Drawing dated 11 April, 1958. Four podded Orpheus engines. All-up weight about 40,000 lb.

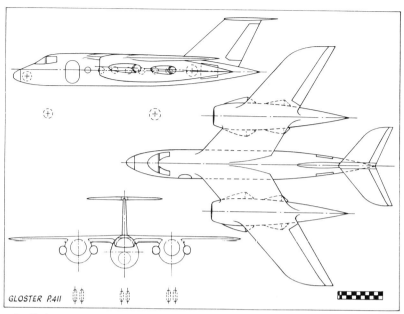

Preliminary scheme for a 14-seat VTOL transport. Two Bristol Siddeley BE.53/2 lift/thrust engines. Drawing dated 19 June, 1958.

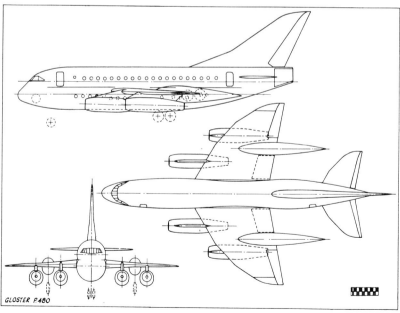

Double-decked 141-seat transport with area-ruled fuselage and elliptical wing. Four Bristol Siddeley BE.50 engines. Drawing dated 6 March, 1959.

397

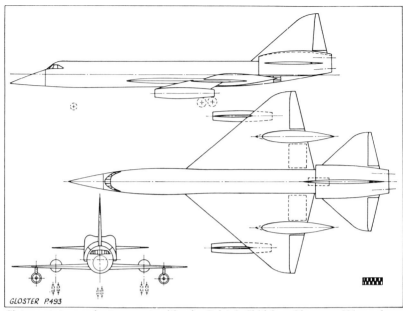

Sixty-seat transonic transport with six Bristol Siddeley Olympus 591 engines. Alternative scheme with four underwing and two rear-mounted engines. Drawing dated 13 January, 1960.

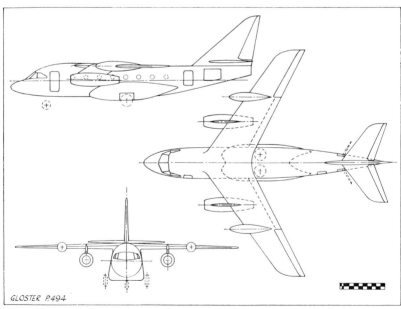

Proposal for an 18-seat light transport with 17,000 lb all-up weight. Two Orpheus engines. Drawing dated 5 April, 1960.

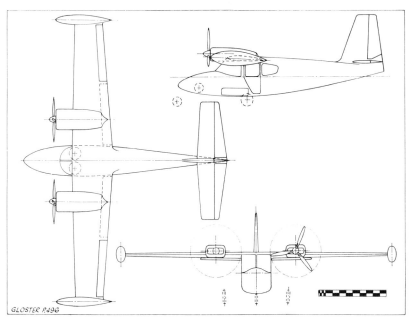

Six-seat executive light aircraft. Two 250 hp Continental engines. Drawn on 3 June, 1960.

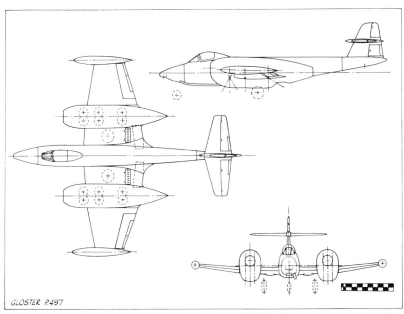

A V/STOL version of the Meteor F.8 with twelve RB.108 lift engines in two nacelles. Strengthened landing gear and centre section structure. Dated 8 June, 1960.

Designation		Date	
P.499	Twin-engined 6-seat light transport	1960	Schemed
P.500	Twin-engined 6/7-seat light aircraft	1960	Schemed
P.501	Twin-engined 4/5-seat light transport	1960	Schemed
P.503	VTOL Meteor 7 with twelve RB.108 engines	1960	Schemed
P.504	VTOL Meteor 7 with eighteen RB.108 engines	1960	Schemed
P.505	STOL tactical strike reconnaissance aircraft to GOR.2	1960	Schemed
P.507	VTOL strike reconnaissance aircraft	1960	Schemed
P.511	VTOL 40-seat transport	1960	Schemed
P.512	VTOL aircraft with ten BE.59 and four Orpheus engines	1960	Schemed
P.514	60-seat VTOL transport	1960	Schemed
P.515	Development of P.514 with hinged rear fuselage	1960	Schemed
P.516	80-seat VTOL transport	1960	Schemed
P.517	V/STOL tactical transport	1960	Schemed
P.519	80-seat VTOL military transport	1960	Schemed
P.520	82-seat VTOL transport	1960	Schemed
P.524	VTOL military transport	1961	Schemed
P.526	VTOL military transport with rear loading doors	1961	Schemed
P.527	VTOL military transport	1961	Schemed
P.529	STOL medium transport	1961	Schemed
P.532	V/STOL twin-boom military transport	1961	Schemed
P.533	Development of P.529	1961	Schemed

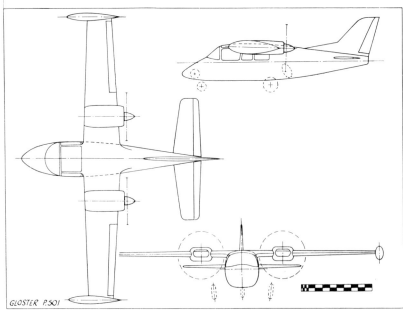

GLOSTER P.501

Proposed 4/5-seat 5,000 lb twin-engined executive or sporting aircraft. Two 250 hp Continental engines. Drawing dated 30 June, 1960.

400

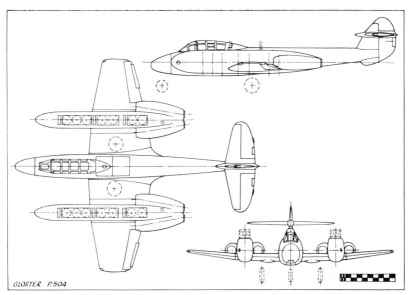

Proposed conversion of a Meteor T.7 for VTOL research. The original drawing, dated 9 August, 1960, details a loaded weight of 18,680 lb, with 26,320 lb lift from fourteen of the aircraft's eighteen Rolls-Royce RB.108 engines.

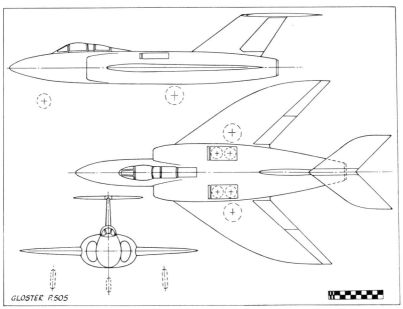

Tactical strike reconnaissance STOL aircraft to a SHAPE requirement. One Rolls-Royce Conway R.Co.11 main propulsion unit and four RB.162 lift engines. All-up weight 30,000 lb. Drawn on 26 August, 1960.

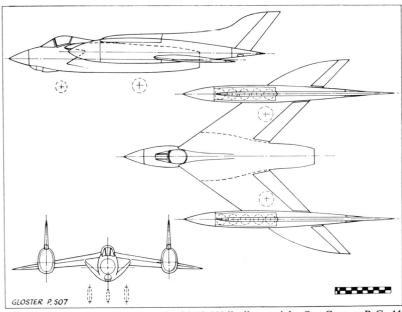

GLOSTER P.507

VTOL strike reconnaissance aircraft with 32,400 lb all-up weight. One Conway R.Co.11 main propulsion engine and ten RB.162 lift engines. Drawn on 7 October, 1960.

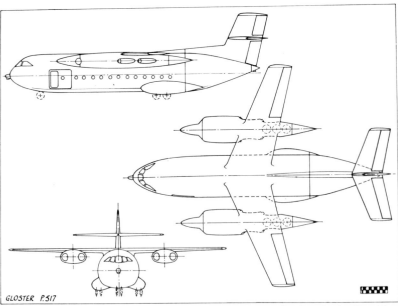

GLOSTER P.517

Large capacity tactical V/STOL transport with hinged rear fuselage for loading. Two Bristol Siddeley BE.53/5 vectored-thrust engines and ten BE.59/7 lift engines. Drawing dated 1 December, 1960.

402

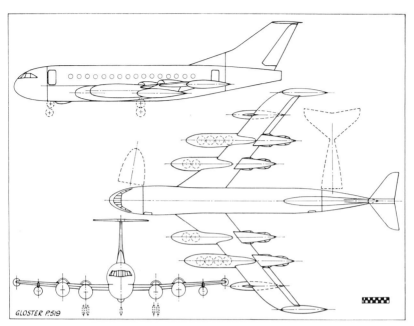

An 80-seat military VTOL transport with hinged nose and rear fuselage for loading. Drawn on 12 December, 1960. Four Bristol Siddeley BS.94 vectored-thrust engines and twelve BS.59/7 lift engines.

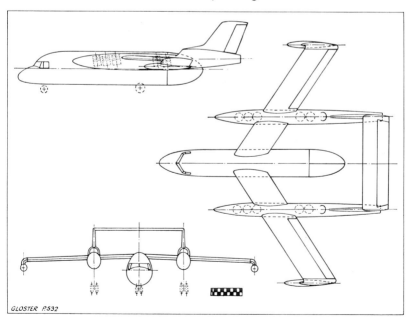

Tactical V/STOL military transport with clamshell rear loading doors. Two Bristol Siddeley BS.75 main propulsion engines and ten BS.59/7 lift engines. Drawing dated 5 February, 1961.

403

Designation	Date
P.534 STOL twin-boom transport	1961 Schemed

Other projects:

PL.16 Two-seat night fighter version of Meteor	1948 Design study
PL.562 Meteor ground-attack fighter with RATOG	1950 T.I. completed

Of the 129 unbuilt projects listed above the following supplementary data for 20 of them are all that have survived.

Mars V. The Mars V was a projected two-seat reconnaissance aircraft for which a layout was prepared in 1922. Construction was steel tube primary structure and wood secondary structure with fabric covering. It would have been powered by a 340 hp Armstrong Siddeley Jaguar III fourteen-cylinder air-cooled radial engine. Many advanced features were to have been incorporated in this aeroplane including a control system employing push rods, bell cranks and levers in place of cables and pulleys, and a tail unit specially devised to give the gunner an unrestricted field of fire. For this reason the fin area and 70 per cent of the rudder were below the fuselage. Estimated maximum speed was 130 mph at sea level and 112 mph at 15,000 ft; landing speed was 53 mph. The climb was 19 min to 15,000 ft and the service ceiling 19,000 ft. Military load was 985 lb. Span 35 ft, length 24 ft 6 in, height 9 ft 11 in, wing area 340 sq ft. Total weight 3,620 lb. Fuel 80 gal, oil 8 gal.

Mars VII. This was a design study in 1922 of a single-seat fighter development of the Mars VI Nighthawk powered either by a 385 hp Bristol Jupiter III nine-cylinder air-cooled radial or a 450 hp Napier Lion II broad-arrow water-cooled engine.

Mars VIII. This was a single-engined, nine-seat transport project schemed in 1922, intended to combine a low landing speed with a good climb performance. The Gloster

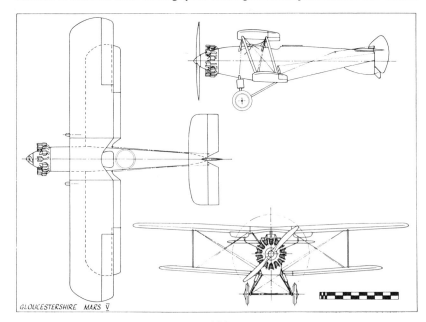

GLOUCESTERSHIRE MARS V

H.L.B. wing combination was specified together with an oleo-type landing gear, push rod and bell crank control system, variable-incidence tailplane and gravity-feed fuel system. Passenger facilities included a luggage compartment and lavatory. The most unusual and interesting feature was the hinged rear fuselage which could be swung to port to open up the whole fuselage cross-section for loading purposes. A partition would have folded down out of the forward fuselage to provide a cargo ramp, and screw jacks under the rear part of the cabin would have supported the aircraft during loading and unloading. The pilot had an outstanding view from a cockpit on top of the fuselage in front of the upper mainplane. To have been powered by a 450 hp Napier Lion twelve-cylinder liquid-cooled broad-arrow engine, the estimated top speed was 108 mph at 5,000 ft and landing speed was 47 mph. The cabin volume was 385 cu ft and the useful load would have been 1,927 lb.

Span 51 ft 6 in, length 39 ft 7 in, height 12 ft 7 in, wing area 534 sq ft. Total weight 6,820 lb. Endurance 4 hr. Fuel 103 gal, oil 11 gal.

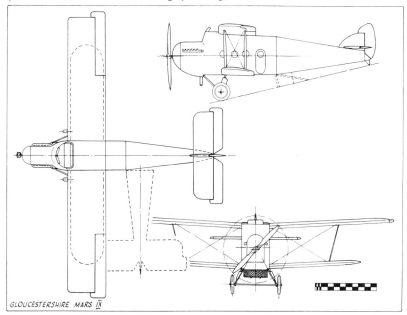

GLOUCESTERSHIRE MARS IX

Mars IX. The Mars IX was a projected single-engined seven-seat version of the Mars VIII project for which a layout was prepared in 1922. It also featured the Gloster H.L.B. wing combination and all the other design characteristics of the Mars VIII including the hinged rear fuselage. Powered by a 360 hp Rolls-Royce Eagle IX twelve-cylinder vee water-cooled geared engine, the estimated maximum speed was 104 mph. The cabin volume was 270 cu ft and a 1,600 lb payload would have been carried.

Span 45 ft, length 34 ft 8 in, height 11 ft 10 in, wing area 415 sq ft. Total weight 5,615 lb. Endurance 4¾ hr. Fuel 86 gal, oil 7 gal.

Goodwood. This was the name allocated to a single-engined freighter aircraft project, produced in 1925, which embodied many features of the Mars VIII and IX projects of 1922. These included the hinged rear fuselage to enable bulky cargo to be easily loaded. Design work and construction of a mock-up were well advanced when the whole project was abandoned. To have been powered by an unspecified 460 hp engine, the estimated top speed was 75 mph and the ceiling 9,500 ft. The total weight would have been about 10,000 lb with a 3,450 lb payload.

Gloster V. In November 1927 design work began on the new Gloster V which was a development of the Gloster IVB and was therefore a biplane. It was to have been built for the 1929 Schneider Trophy contest and in the preliminary wind-tunnel tests the models proved highly satisfactory, but the problems were encountered at a later stage when it was found that the supercharger on the new 1,300 hp Napier Lion VIID twelve-cylinder liquid-cooled engine largely contributed to the weight increase of nearly 300 lb over early Lions. When the design was altered to bring the wings further forward to compensate for the shift in the c.g. it was discovered that the front spar of the biplane's upper wing would come over the Lion's centre cylinder block. Thus it was impossible to reposition the upper wing in this manner and to give an adequate forward view. For this reason the biplane layout was abandoned and a monoplane configuration was adopted for the last of the Gloster racing seaplanes—the Gloster VI.

B.9/32. This was a twin-engined bomber design study of 1932 which had an all-up weight of 12,800 lb, a wing span of 70 ft and would have been powered by two 820 hp Bristol Perseus VI air-cooled radial engines.

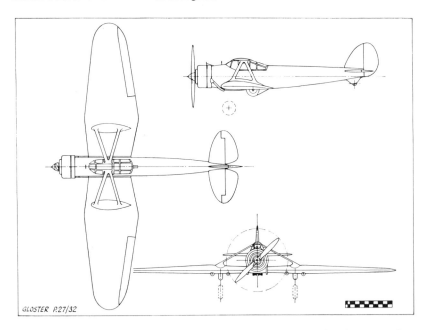

GLOSTER P.27/32

P.27/32. The Gloster P.27/32 was a two-seat single-engine day bomber monoplane project for which a layout was produced in 1933. The pilot had an enclosed cockpit and the gunner's Lewis ·303 in machine-gun was mounted either on a special revolving gun mounting or on a type of Scarff ring. Over the gunner was a sliding roof with side windows which divided into two halves and could be lowered for gun firing. A retractable landing gear was to have been incorporated and four fixed forward firing Vickers ·303 in guns were mounted under the mainplanes. Distinctive inverted V struts passed from the top of the cockpit to the mainplane on each side. Powered by an 810 hp Armstrong Siddeley Tiger VI air-cooled engine, the estimated top speed was 168 mph.

406

Span 57 ft 6 in, length 40 ft, height 10 ft 6 in, wing area 480 sq ft. All-up weight 7,600 lb.

F.5/33. A design study made in 1933 for a twin-engine two-seat fighter with turret armament. Two Bristol Aquila air-cooled radial engines were to have been used.

SS.34. A projected 'monoplane Gladiator' with a retractable landing gear for which design studies were undertaken late in 1934.

F.34/35. A twin-engined, two-seat, turret fighter project of 1935 to which was allocated the RAF serial number K8625. An earlier specification, F.9/35, called for a single-engined aircraft with similar armament but this Gloster project was abandoned when the Boulton Paul Defiant, designed to F.9/35, promised to meet both specifications. The Gloster F.34/35 shared a number of design features with an earlier project, the Bristol Aquila powered F.5/33.

F.11/37. This was an unusual project of 1937 intended to meet the specification F.11/37, issued on 26 May, 1937, for a two-seat day and night fighter for Home Defence or to operate with a Field Force. A heavy armament of four Hispano 20 mm cannon in a power-operated turret was called for and many other exacting requirements to make this aeroplane suitable for operations against fast hostile bombers. The aircraft had to carry internally a 250 lb bomb load 'for use in breaking up enemy formations'.

Glosters produced designs for two variants: one a fighter to be powered either by two 1,760 hp Rolls-Royce Vulture II 24-cylinder liquid-cooled X engines, Armstrong Siddeley Deerhound 21-cylinder triple-banked engines or two 1,600 hp Bristol Hercules 14-cylinder air-cooled radials; the other an associated bomber with two 1,650 hp Bristol Hercules VI engines. The fighter followed the basic design of the F.9/37, the main difference being the use of more powerful engines, the provision of the turret (which could accommodate two Madsen 23 mm guns as an alternative to the Hispano cannon) and a number of detail modifications. The main landing gear retracted into the engine nacelles and the pilot was seated forward of the mainplane with the gunner's turret positioned immediately aft of the rear spar. The turret was fully retractable and was flush with the fuselage top line when in the 'down' position. A fixed tailplane was to have been used with twin fins and rudders. Estimated maximum speed with Vulture engines was 378 mph at 15,000 ft and the estimated climb was 8·7 min to 25,000 ft.

Span 63 ft, length 45 ft 6 in, height 13 ft 6 in, wing area 565 sq ft, all-up weight 17,100 lb; fuel 280 gal.

The bomber version utilized virtually the same outer mainplanes and centre section and much of the rest of the airframe of the fighter; a specially designed fuselage was to have been used to accommodate nine 250 lb or six 500 lb bombs or one 2,000 lb torpedo. The estimated maximum speed with Hercules engines was 353 mph at 15,000 ft.

Span 60 ft, length 45 ft 6 in, height 13 ft 10 in, wing area 525 sq ft, all-up weight 20,530 lb, range 2,000 miles.

F.18/37. Glosters departed markedly from conventional design in 1938 with this projected single-seat twin-boom fighter to meet specification F.18/37. It was claimed that it would offer great advantages over existing types in that all of its 12 Browning ·303 in machine-guns were concentrated in a battery in the fuselage nose with the 2,100 hp Napier Sabre I 24-cylinder liquid-cooled horizontally-opposed engine driving a pusher propeller aft of the pilot's cabin. Radiators were mounted in the leading edge of the wing and the airflow through them exhausted below the tail booms. A retractable tricycle-type landing gear was to have been used. Maximum speed was estimated at 418 mph at 17,500 ft and ejector exhausts were expected to add a further 5 mph to this figure. The climb was 4·1 min to 15,000 ft and the service ceiling 38,000 ft. This project was abandoned mainly due to the uncertain performance of the Sabre engine.

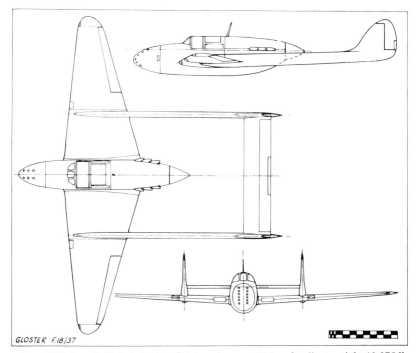

GLOSTER F.18/37

Span 46 ft, length 39 ft, height 12 ft 9 in, wing area 290 sq ft, all-up weight 10,375 lb, fuel 57 gal, oil 5 gal.

B.1/39. One of the few four-engined projects by Glosters, this aircraft was to meet specification B.1/39 calling for a bomber for worldwide use to replace all medium and heavy bomber types then in service. A deep wing housed most of the main 9,400 lb bomb load, (only two 500 lb bombs were to be carried externally below the outer main-planes), the four 1,550 hp Bristol Hercules VI, 14-cylinder air cooled radials, the main units of the tricycle-type landing gear, and the fuel. For improved altitude performance it was proposed to use turbo-supercharged Hercules or to replace the two inboard Hercules VIs with Bristol Centaurus engines. Dorsal and ventral gun turrets carried two Hispano 20 mm guns each. Provision for a bomb aimer's position in the extreme nose and an observer's position in the tail. Removable seating in the fuselage would have accommodated 36 troops. This aircraft would have had a seven-man crew. Estimated maximum speed was 265 mph at 16,000 ft with full load.

Span 115 ft, length 91 ft 6 in, height 23 ft 6 in, wing area 1,840 sq ft, track 27 ft, all-up weight 72,000 lb.

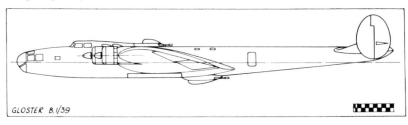

GLOSTER B.1/39

408

N.9/39. This was a projected two-seat, single-engined, turret fighter to specification N.9/39, issued to produce a fleet fighter for operation from aircraft carriers, which was to have been powered either by a 1,550 hp Bristol Hercules VI or a Napier Sabre I. The Blackburn wing-folding technique was adopted and would have reduced the span to only 11 ft. An hydraulic Nash and Thompson turret, mounted above the rear spar, housed four Browning ·303 in guns. Estimated maximum speed was 321 mph at 17,000 ft with a 2·2 min climb to 5,000 ft and 11·1 min to 20,000 ft. Endurance was to have been 6 hr at 138 mph at 15,000 ft.

Span 50 ft, length 39 ft 1 in, height 16 ft 2 in (tail up), wing area 396 sq ft, track 10 ft, all-up weight 10,000 lb.

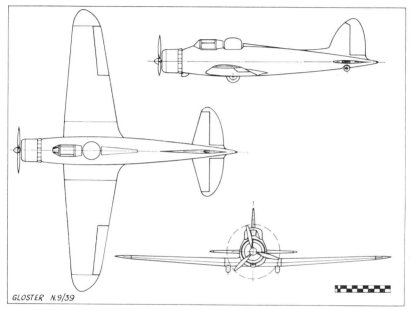

GLOSTER N.9/39

F.18/40. Specification F.18/40 called for a two-seat twin-engine fighter, powered by Rolls-Royce Merlins, and having a fixed gun armament for day and night interceptor duties. A mock-up was prepared and tests were undertaken with L8002, a correctly ballasted F.9/37, but following preliminary trials the project was abandoned.

Gloster Jet Bomber. Within three months of the first flight of the E.28/39 in May 1941, George Carter turned his attention to a four-jet bomber project which was intended to operate at very high speed and at high altitude. Carter described it as being 'somewhat idealistic in conception in as much as no provision has been made for defensive armament.'

Powered by four Whittle W.2.B turbojets expected to deliver 2,000 lb thrust each, this aircraft would have had a maximum speed of 454 mph at 36,000 ft. The flight plan for a typical operation envisaged an outward leg at 440 mph at 40,000 ft and a return leg at 445 mph at 45,000 ft. As a rational development of the F.9/40 the jet bomber incorporated the main features of the fighter and the same basic layout.

Span 84 ft, length 62 ft 6 in, height 19 ft 6 in, wing area 900 sq ft, track 19 ft, all-up weight 31,500 lb. Fuel 1,225 gal, oil 18 gal. Bomb load 4,000 lb or 8,000 lb (overload). Range 1,500 miles plus 20 min cruise over target area. Ceiling 55,300 ft.

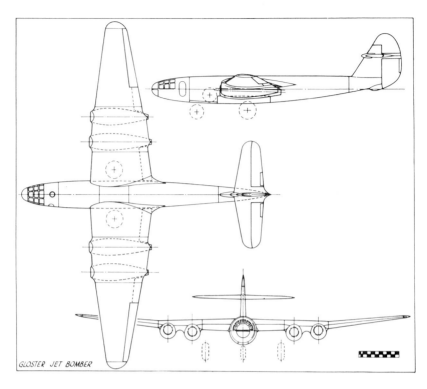

GLOSTER JET BOMBER

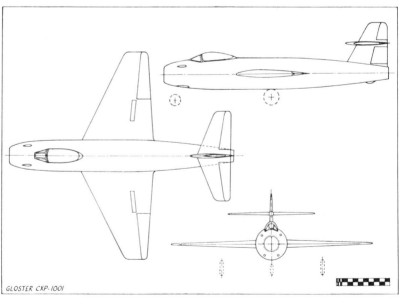

GLOSTER CXP-1001

410

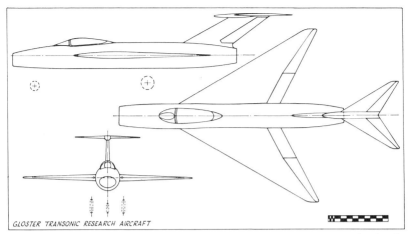

GLOSTER TRANSONIC RESEARCH AIRCRAFT

CXP-1001. In 1946 the Chinese Nationalist Government was eager to modernize the Chinese Air Force and sent technical missions to the United Kingdom and the United States. Their tasks were to investigate the design and construction of prototype jet fighter and bomber aircraft and suitable powerplants for them.

Glosters agreed to collaborate with a small team of Chinese design engineers in the creation of a single-seat jet fighter to be powered initially either by a Rolls-Royce Nene or a de Havilland Ghost turbojet. The original design, designated CXP-102, was developed to produce a fighter closely resembling the Gloster E.1/44 in configuration and armed with four fixed 20 mm cannon in the nose.

A number of components were produced but due to the political situation in China the project was abandoned and the mission returned home after about a year's work.

Span 38 ft, length 41 ft 10 in, height 14 ft 10 in, wing area 360 sq ft, thickness/chord ratio 0·011, incidence 1 deg, sweepback 20 deg, weight 8,960 lb (empty) and 13,900 lb (loaded). Fuel 470 gal (internal) with provision for two 200 gal underwing drop tanks.

Transonic Research Aircraft. A design study undertaken in 1948 to the specification issued in that year for a single-engined transonic fighter. Two basic variants were pro-

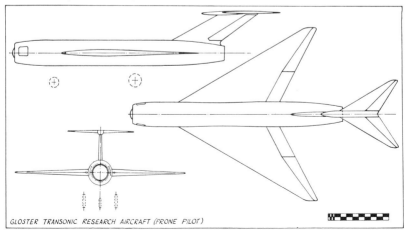

GLOSTER TRANSONIC RESEARCH AIRCRAFT (PRONE PILOT)

411

jected; one with the pilot seated normally, and the other having provision for a prone pilot in the intake centre body. A 7,500 lb thrust (or 9,450 lb with reheat) Armstrong Siddeley Sapphire Sa.2 turbojet was calculated to give a maximum speed of Mach 1·2 (700 kt) at 45,000 ft with the conventional cockpit and Mach 1·25 (725 kt) at 45,000 ft with the prone cockpit. The maximum rate of climb would have been 35,000 ft/min at sea level and the absolute ceiling 63,000 ft. The wing had 61 deg sweepback and the all-up wing loading was 45 lb sq ft. No provision was made for radar, armour protection, engine fire protection or inert gas system for the fuel tanks. Two 30 mm guns with ammunition for eight seconds fire were specified. These economies were to reduce the size and weight as much as possible to achieve high performance with relatively low thrust.

Span 28 ft, length 46 ft 6 in, height 11 ft 9 in, wing area 290 sq ft. Wing thickness/chord ratio, root 6 per cent and tip 10 per cent. All-up weight 13,000 lb. Fuel 280 gal.

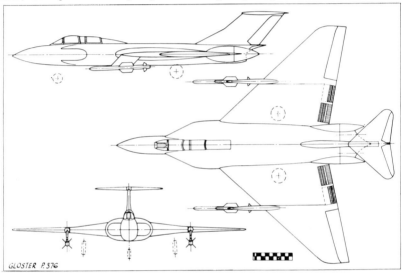

F.153D. The initial conception of the F.153D was as a subsonic/transonic aircraft with a pursuit or collision course weapon system and 30 mm Aden guns as secondary armament. By May 1956, with the prospect of further increases in hostile target speeds, it was believed that this concept would fall short of future requirements. For this reason Richard Walker gave consideration to the further development of the F.153D into a supersonic fighter by extending the fuselage fore and aft to improve the area-rule distribution and fit thin wings of five per cent mean thickness/chord ratio. This second measure was abandoned as it would have reduced the internal fuel capacity. Powered by two 20,000 lb thrust Bristol Ol.21R turbojets with reheat, this big fighter, which had a maximum design take-off weight of 60,300 lb, had a calculated maximum speed of Mach 1·82 at 36,000 ft and a sea level rate of climb of 57,000 ft/min. Typical projected interception plans envisaged the destruction of hostile targets 200 nautical miles from base and at 50,000 ft only 23 min after take-off. Preliminary estimates of design and manufacturing effort indicated that a prototype could be ready for flight trials by December 1958, and component and sub-assembly manufacture began. However, this project was cancelled in July 1956 following a change of Government defence policy. The F.153D bore the project number P.376.

412

Span 60 ft 8 in, length 72 ft, height (over canopy) 12 ft, wing area, 1,235 sq ft, sweep-back 41·4 deg. Attack weight 50,500 lb. Armament two Red Dean air-to-air guided weapons. Fuel 2,200 gal, oil 11 gal.

Lightweight Crop Sprayer. In 1960 Glosters undertook a highly detailed design study of a lightweight unmanned crop sprayer of unusual configuration. Basically a four-rotor helicopter, it consisted of a central box structure with four folding booms radiating from it, to form an X configuration in plan view, which carried the two-bladed rotors.

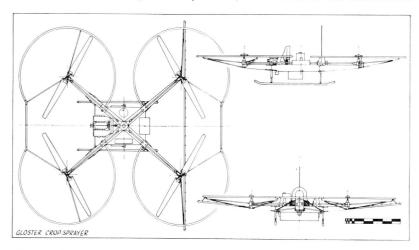

GLOSTER CROP-SPRAYER

This central box provided a platform for the 20 gal plastic spray tank, the 105 hp Potez 4E flat four-cylinder air-cooled engine, the central gear-box, command radio equipment, hydraulic and other systems. Guard rings were provided around the four rotor discs and the 22 ft spray-bar was carried below the two rearmost rotor booms. It was planned to carry the folded crop sprayer between farms on a special transporter towed by a Land Rover type vehicle. Two controllers were required, each taking over control of the machine as it approached across the field being sprayed and turning it back toward the other operator. In this way the machine could not overshoot the field—and possibly spray weedkiller on other crops—since it would have been always homing onto a controller rather than flying away on an outgoing course.

The advantages of this unmanned helicopter were that a simplified design, free from the stringent requirements of the Air Registration Board, was possible; most of the weight normally allowed for a pilot provided more payload; the machine could be operated direct from the spraying site with no lost time in flying to and from an airstrip; more precise spraying could be undertaken within the bounds of small fields and, of course, the risks of a fatal accident were minimal. Glosters estimated that about £40,000 would need to be spent in producing a prototype and that such a machine could be sold for £3,800 in the United Kingdom where the market was assessed at being around 150.

Unfortunately, although the company made out a sound case for the production of such a machine, it did not find favour with the Hawker Siddeley Board and the project was abandoned.

Rotor diameter 10 ft, total geometric disc area 314 sq ft, length 22 ft 10 in, width 20 ft 7 in, height (excluding aerial) 3 ft.

413

Wartime Expansion

Expansion of the 750,000 sq ft of factory floor area at Hucclecote began on 19 August, 1938, when the first turf was cut on the 43-acre site for a new shadow factory. When finally completed in 1940 it provided 24 acres of buildings for production work and associated services. This No.2 Factory was used during World War II for the manufacture, and/or assembly and flight testing of Hawker Hurricanes and Typhoons, Armstrong Whitworth Albemarles, Short Stirlings and Stinson Sentinels.

By the end of 1940 no fewer than 34 other premises in the Gloucester-Cheltenham area had been taken over and converted for use as workshops, design offices and stores; moreover, six new dispersal factories had been built by the end of March 1941. Thus within 18 months of the outbreak of war, Glosters had nearly 1¾ million sq ft of floor area devoted to aircraft production and a labour force of some 14,000 employees.

In the spring of 1943 the company began negotiations to use part of a 360-acre RAF airfield at Moreton Valence, about eight miles south of Hucclecote. By June, MAP and Air Ministry approval was obtained for the main runway to be lengthened to 2,100 yd and for a new hangar to be erected for Glosters' use. The Flight Development department moved to Moreton Valence in October 1943. During the ensuing 18 years the floor area was gradually built up to a total of 282,000 sq ft with 53 acres of runways and perimeter tracks and nearly eight acres of aprons, hard standings and roadways.

Premises taken over for use as dispersal factories.

No.4	Bentley Piano Works	Woodchester, Stroud	Assembly
No.5	H. H. Martyn Ltd	Cheltenham	Machine shop
No.6	Albion Cabinet Works	Cheltenham	Assembly
No.7	Belle Vue Hotel Garage	Cheltenham	Stores
No.8	Cheltenham Original Brewery	Cheltenham	Assembly
No.9	Victory Motor Co	Cheltenham	Stores
No.10	Edwards & Marshalls	Cheltenham	Heat treatment
No.11	Bristol Tramway Depot	Gloucester	Assembly
No.12	Hough and Whitmore Garage	Gloucester	Assembly
No.13	Hatherley Step Works	Gloucester	Assembly
No.14	Norman Sawyer Co	Cheltenham	Tool room
No.15	Wycliffe Motors Ltd	Cheltenham	Press shop
No.16	North Street Motors	Cheltenham	Assembly
No.17	Post Office Garage	Cheltenham	Assembly
No.18	Standard Match Co	Gloucester	Sheet metal
No.19	St Aldate Garage	Gloucester	Assembly
No.20	The Ford Garage	Gloucester	Spray shop
No.21	T. Bond Worth & Sons	Thrupp, Stroud	Machine shop
No.22	The Car Mart	Cheltenham	Stores
No.23	Chinn's Motors	Cheltenham	Stores
No.24	Crabtree's Garage	Cheltenham	Experimental dept
No.25	Regent Motors	Cheltenham	Stores
No.26	Gloucester Incubator Co	Woodchester, Stroud	Stores

No.27	Cordwell's Central Garage	Ebley, Stroud	Rolling mills
No.28	Montpellier Pavillion	Cheltenham	General stores
No.29	Thirlstaine House	Cheltenham	Offices
No.30	Bridges Garage	Cirencester	Stores
No.31	Glevum Billiard Hall	Gloucester	Canteen
No.32	Army Mechanisation Depot	Ledbury	Wing assembly
No.33	Barnes Garage	Gloucester .	Stores
No.34	Cleeve House and Manor House	Bishop's Cleeve	Drawing office
No.35	Savoy Billiard Hall	Cheltenham	Drawing office
No.36	St James Mission Hall	Gloucester	Canteen
No.37	Chas Dickens' Garage	Cheltenham	Stores

New Dispersal Factories

No.38		Ledbury	Wing assembly
No.39		Stoke Orchard	Assembly
No.40		Stoke Orchard	Flight shed
No.41		Uckington, Glos	Tool room, fitting shop and presses
No.42		Bentham, Glos	Experimental design office and factory
No.43		Newent, Glos	Sheet metal

APPENDIX C

Aircraft Production Data

Gloucestershire Aircraft Company Ltd, 1917–1926
Gloster Aircraft Company Ltd, 1926–1961

The year by year production figures listed below refer to aircraft manufactured at Sunningend, Cheltenham, at Hucclecote, and Bentham, Glos: airframes and components manufactured at Sunningend by H. H. Martyn and Co between 1915 and 1917 under direct sub-contract to the Aircraft Manufacturing Company are also shown. In these data are included 1,067 Meteor and 133 Javelin variants built by Sir W. G. Armstrong Whitworth Aircraft Ltd at Baginton, Coventry. The licensed production of 15 Game-cocks by the Finnish State Aircraft Factory in Helsinki; 150 Gambets (A1N1 and A1N2) by Nakajima Hikoki K.K. in Japan; 17 Gauntlet IIs by Flyvertroppernes Vaerksteder in Copenhagen, Denmark; and 330 Meteor Mk.8s (plus 30 sets of components for assembly by Avions Fairey in Belgium) by N. V. Koninklijke Nederlandse Vliegtuigen-fabriek Fokker at Amsterdam in the Netherlands must be added to these data. This latter company sub-contracted some of this work to Aviolanda N.V. Maatschappij Voor Vliegtuigbouw at Woensdrecht.

Aircraft names in italics indicate original design by other companies with only manufacture and/or modification design undertaken by Gloster Aircraft Company Ltd. Production figures in parentheses indicate that the aircraft is a conversion from an earlier prototype or production airframe listed earlier.

Column groupings (left to right): **H. H. Martyn** (1915–1917) · **Gloucestershire Aircraft Co Ltd** (1917–1926) · **Gloster Aircraft Co Ltd** (1926–1937)

Aircraft	1915	1916	1917	1918	1919	1920	1921	1922	1923	1924	1925	1926	1927	1928	1929	1930	1931	1932	1933	1934	1935	1936	1937	Totals
Longhorn components	×																							×
Shorthorn components		×																						×
BE.2c components	×	×	×																					× × × ×
DH.4 (Airco)			×	×																				
DH.5 (Airco)			×	×																				
DH.6/DH.9 (Airco)			150																					150
F.2.B (Bristol Fighter)				156	165	140																		461
Nighthawk					12	18																		30
Mars I							1																	1
Mars II/Sparrowhawk I							30																	30
Mars III/Sparrowhawk II							11																	11
Mars IV/Sparrowhawk III							10																	10
Mars VI								38	16															54
Mars X Nightjar								7	15															22
Gloster I									(1)															(1)
Grouse									(1)															(1)
Gannet									1															1
Grebe									4	60	47	22												133
Panther (Parnall)										18														18
Gloster II										1	1													2
Gamecock											2	30	62	2										96
Gloster III											2													2
Gorcock												2	1											3
Guan												1	1											2
Goral												1												1
Goring												1												1
Goldfinch													1											1
Gloster IV												1	2											3
Siskin (Armstrong Whitworth)													3	10	51	10								74
Gambet													1											1
Gnatsnapper													1		1									2
SS.18														1										1
Gloster VI															2									2

Aircraft	1950	1951	1955	1956	1957	1958	Totals
AS.31	1	1					2
Monospar							1
TC.33			1				1
FS.36			1				1
SS.19			(1)				(1)
TRS.38			(1)				(1)
Hardy (Hawker)				9	27	10	47

× Indicates quantities not known. (1) Indicates use of an earlier airframe.

Gloster Aircraft Co Ltd

Aircraft	1934	1935	1936	1937	1938	1939	1940	1941	1942	1943	1944	1945	1946	1947	1948	1949	1950	1951	1952	1953	1954	1955	1956	1957	1958	1959	1960	Totals
Audax (Hawker)		25																										25
Hart (Hawker)	1	65	6																									72
Gauntlet		24	192	12																								228
Hartbees (Hawker)			2																									
Gladiator				252	158	320	16																					747
F.5/34				1	1																							2
Henley (Hawker)					10	171	19																					200
Hurricane (Hawker)						32	1,211	1,359	148																			2,750
F.9/37						1	1																					2
E.28/39								1	1																			2
Typhoon (Hawker)								28	677	1,131	1,165	299																3,300
F.9/40									2	5	1																	8
Meteor (F & NF)*											30	169	98	114	187	306	406	530	466	233	110							2,649
Meteor (T)															6	135	129	176	136	104	16	10						712
Meteor (FR)																	24	46	56									126
Meteor (PR)																	14	40	4									58
E.1/44													1	1	1	2	1											6
GA.5																		1	2	1	1							5
Javelin (F(AW))**																				2	23	84	128	119	31	17	3	407
Javelin (T)																							1	10	6	4	2	23
F.153D***																							1					1

* Includes 1,067 aircraft built by Armstrong Whitworth. ** Includes 133 aircraft built by Armstrong Whitworth. *** Major sub-assemblies completed.

Aircraft supplied to the Royal Air Force and Fleet Air Arm

	Mars VI	Mars X	Grebe II	Gamecock II	Gauntlet I	Gauntlet II	Gladiator I	Gladiator II	Sea Gladiator (Interim)	Sea Gladiator II	Meteor (F and NF)	Meteor (FR)	Meteor (PR)	Meteor (T)	Javelin (FAW)	Javelin (T)	Totals
Royal Air Force	4	22	129	82	24	204	231	252	38	60	2,354	126	58	602	407	23	4,496
Fleet Air Arm											3			38			161

Aircraft supplied to Overseas Customers

Numbers in parentheses are for ex-RAF aircraft

Countries	Mars II	Mars III	Mars IV	Mars VI	Grouse	Grebe	Gamecock	Gambet	Gauntlet	Gladiator	Meteor 3	Meteor 4	Meteor 7	Meteor 8	Meteor 9	Meteor 11	Meteor 13	Meteor 14	Totals New	Ex-RAF
Argentina												50(50)							50	50
Australia											(1)		(2)	(89)						92
Belgium *										22		48	3	(23)		(24)			73	47
Brazil													8(2)	60					68	2
Canada											(1)									1

Country																		Total
China														36			36	
Denmark **												20	20	(12)			12	69
Ecuador																		
Egypt									12	3 (3)	(8)	(6)	(13)		15			85
Eire									4					4				
Finland ***				(25)	2	(55)	(30)						(32)	2				55
France				25				1 (1)	2 (12)	3 (3)			(2)	3		(1)		48
Greece							2 (6)		43		(5)			27				6
Holland †									38 (27)					81				32
Iraq							(14)					(7)						14
Israel	30									4	11		(6)	15				13
Japan ††		10						1						51				
Latvia						26								26				
Lithuania						14								14				
New Zealand					3	(1)								3				1
Norway							6 (6)							6				6
Portugal						(15)												15
South Africa †††			1			(11)	(1)		(4)									16
Sweden							55			(3)				56				3
Syria				2				1		(2)	(2)		(6)	12				17
Total new aircraft	30	10	25	25	1	10	165	169	76	107	132	21	62	611	20	27		
Total ex-RAF aircraft	30	10		2	3		29	4	137	78	18	21	62		20	1		515

419

* Fokker produced 145 Meteor F.8s for the Belgian Air Force and 30 as sub-assemblies for completion by Avions Fairey.
** Flyvertroppernes Vaerksteder produced 17 Gauntlets for the Danish Army Air Service.
*** Finnish National Aircraft Factory produced 15 Gamecocks for the Finnish Air Force.
† Fokker produced 155 Meteor F.8s for the Royal Netherlands Air Force.
†† Nakajima Hikoki produced 150 Gambets for the Imperial Japanese Naval Air Service.
††† South African Air Force purchased AS.31 G-AADO from the Aircraft Operating Company.

Records Established and Races Won by Gloster Aeroplanes 1921–1951

Between 1921 and 1951 Gloster aeroplanes established one British and three world air speed records, five capital-to-capital records, two closed-circuit records and a 'time to height record', won six air races and took second place in a Schneider Trophy contest.

Aircraft	Date	Pilot	Achievement
Mars I/Bamel G-EAXZ	17 July, 1921	J. H. James	Winner of Aerial Derby at 163·3 mph. Winner of Aerial Derby Handicap Cup
Mars I/Bamel G-EAXZ	12 December, 1921	J. H. James	British Air Speed Record of 196·4 mph
Mars I/Bamel G-EAXZ	7 August, 1922	J. H. James	Winner of Aerial Derby at 177·85 mph
Gloster I G-EAXZ	6 August, 1923	L. L. Carter	Winner of Aerial Derby at 192·4 mph
Grebe G-EBHA	1923	L. L. Carter	Fastest circuit in King's Cup race
Grebe G-EBHA	1923	Flt Lieut Bird	Rotterdam-Gothenburg Swedish Government prize
Gloster IIIA N194	26 October, 1925	H. Broad	Second place in Schneider Trophy contest at 199·16 mph
Gamecock I	1927	Flg Off Montgomery Flt Lieut Collier Flg Off Macdonald	First (J8073), second and third places in RAF inter-squadron handicap race for the Sassoon Cup
Gloster VI N249	10 September, 1929	Flt Lieut G. H. Stainforth	World Speed Record of 336·3 mph
Gauntlet I	September 1935	No.19 Squadron	Brooke-Popham Air Firing Challenge Trophy
Gauntlet I	1936	No.19 Squadron	Brooke-Popham Air Firing Challenge Trophy
Gauntlet II	November 1938	No.74 Squadron	Sassoon Flight Attack Challenge Trophy
Meteor IV EE454	7 November, 1945	Grp Capt H. J. Wilson	World Speed Record of 606·26 mph
Meteor IV EE549	7 September, 1946	Grp Capt E. M. Donaldson	World Speed Record of 616·16 mph
Meteor 4 EE549	16 January, 1947	W. A. Waterton	Paris–London at 618·4 mph.

Aircraft	Date	Pilot	Achievement
Meteor 4 G-AIDC	21 April, 1947	D. Cotes-Preedy	Brussels-Copenhagen at 630 mph
Meteor 4 VT103	6 February, 1948	W. A. Waterton	100 km Closed-Circuit Record of 542·9 mph
Meteor 8 VZ468	4 April, 1950	Jan Zurakowski	London–Copenhagen at 541 mph
Meteor 8 VZ468	4 April, 1950	Jan Zurakowski	Copenhagen–London at 500·37 mph
Meteor 8 VZ468	4 April, 1950	Jan Zurakowski	London–Copenhagen– London at 480·29 mph
Meteor 8 VZ496	11 May, 1950	J. R. Cooksey	1,000 km Closed–Circuit Record of 510 mph
Meteor 8 WA820	31 August, 1951	R. B. Prickett	Time to height from standing start records 3,000 m (9,843 ft) in 1 min 16 sec, 6,000 m (19,686 ft) in 1 min 50 sec, 9,000 m (29,529 ft) in 2 min 25 sec, 12,000 m (39,372 ft) in 3 min 7 sec

APPENDIX F

Test Pilots of Gloucestershire Aircraft Company 1919–1926 and Gloster Aircraft Company Limited 1926–1961

John James	1919–23	Bamel, Gloster I, Sparrowhawks, Nighthawks, Nightjars. Also flew in Aerial Derby and King's Cup events.
Larry Carter	1923–26	Gloster I, Grouse, Gannet, Grebes, Gloster II.
Rex Stocken	1927–30	Grebes, Gamecocks, Goral, Goring.
Howard Saint	1927–35	Chief test pilot. Grebes, Gamecocks, Gorcocks, Gloster IIIs, Guan, Goral, Goring, Goldfinch, Gambet, Gnatsnappers, SS.18s, SS.19s, Gauntlets, Gladiators.
Maurice Piercey	1926–27	Grebes, Gamecocks.
Maurice Summers	1935–40	Production pilot. Gauntlets, Gladiators.
P. E. G. Sayer	1934–42	Chief test pilot. Gauntlets, Gladiators, F.5/34, F.9/37s, Henleys, Hurricanes, Typhoons. Made Great Britain's first jet flight in E.28/39, 1941. Killed in a Typhoon.
Michael Daunt	1937–44	Production (later chief) test pilot. Gladiators, F.5/34, F.9/37, Henleys, Hurricanes, Typhoons, F.9/40, Meteors.

John James (*left*), Glosters' first test pilot, flew the Bamel and the Gloster I to a number of notable victories in the Aerial Derbies during 1921–23. Hubert Broad (*right*), who was a highly experienced test pilot, joined the Gloster team for the 1925 Schneider Trophy contest in Baltimore.

Arthur Berkeley	1938–41	Production test pilot. Henleys, Hurricanes.
Jack Hathorn	1939–40	Production test pilot. Henleys, Hurricanes. Killed in a Hurricane.
John Grierson	1941–45	Production and experimental test pilot. Hurricanes, Typhoons, E.28/39, F.9/40s, Meteors.
Max Williams	1941–44	Production test pilot. Hurricanes, Typhoons.
John Crosby-Warren	1940–44	Production and experimental test pilot. Henleys, Hurricanes, Typhoons, E.28/39, F.9/40, Meteors. Killed in a Meteor.
Llewellyn Moss	1943–46	Production test pilot. Typhoons, Meteors. Killed in a Meteor.
Digby Cotes-Preedy	1946–49	Production and development test pilot. Meteors.
Peter Cadbury	1943–46	Production test pilot. Typhoons, Meteors.
Eric Greenwood	1944–47	Chief test pilot. Meteors. Made first flight in Trent-Meteor, 1945.

Howard Saint (*left*) probably flew more Gloster types than any pilot during his eight years with the company. P. E. G. Sayer (*right*) made history with his first flight of the E.28/39, only to die in a piston-engined aircraft.

Jack Hathorn (*left*) an experienced pilot who lost his life when a production Hurricane crashed into Robinswood Hill near Gloucester. His successor at Glosters was Michael Daunt (*right*), an ex-RAF pilot, whose colourful career encompassed the first flight of the F.9/40, forced landings in a Typhoon and a parachute descent from a Folland flying test bed. (*Courtesy N. Daunt*)

Roland Beamont	1946	Development test pilot. Meteors.
Philip Stanbury	1943–47	Production test pilot. Typhoons, Meteors.
W. A. Waterton	1946–54	Development (later chief) test pilot. Meteors, E.1/44, GA.5s and Javelins.
J. Bridges	1946–47	Production test pilot. Meteors. Killed in a Meteor.
James Cooksey	1947–54	Chief production test pilot. Meteors, Javelins.
Rodney Dryland	1946–49	Production and development test pilot. Meteors. Killed in a Meteor.
Jan Zurakowski	1947–52	Chief development test pilot. Meteors, E.1/44, GA.5s and Javelins.

John Grierson (*left*) brought a wealth of aviation experience to his four years' test flying with Glosters. Over 6 ft 8 in tall, John Crosby-Warren (*right*) shared the early burden of jet aircraft development before his untimely death in a Meteor. (*Courtesy John Grierson*)

423

Digby Cotes-Preedy (*left*) who went to the Argentine to check-fly Meteors after assembly there, and Philip Stanbury (*right*), seconded to Glosters from the RAF, who nearly lost his life in a Meteor windscreen failure incident.

Michael Kilburn	1949–53	Production and development test pilot. Meteors, GA.5s and Javelins.
Brian Smith	1950–56	Production and development test pilot. Meteors, Javelins. Killed in a Javelin.
Geoffrey Worrall	1950–61	Production (later chief) test pilot. Meteors, Javelins.
Peter Lawrence	1952–53	Development test pilot. Meteors and Javelins. Killed in a Javelin.
R. F. Martin	1953–60	Chief test pilot. Javelins.
Peter Varley	1955–60	Assistant chief test pilot. Javelins.
Michael Morss	1955–57	Production test pilot. Javelins.
John Towle	1957–60	Production test pilot. Javelins.
O. J. Hawkins	1957–60	Production test pilot. Javelins.

Eric Greenwood (*left*), who claimed to be the first pilot to exceed 400, 500 and 600 mph indicated airspeed, with Grp Capt H. J. Wilson, RAF (*right*), with whom he successfully established a world speed record in 1945.

Peter Cadbury (*left*) flew for Glosters as a production test pilot in Typhoons and Meteors. Much decorated Roland Beamont (*right*), renowned war-time Typhoon pilot, was with Glosters for a short period for development of the Meteor. (*British Aircraft Corporation*)

W. A. Waterton (*left*) flew the first Gloster GA.5 and Avro Canada's CF-100 prototypes. Jim Cooksey (*right*) set a new 1,000 km closed-circuit record in a Meteor F.8.

Rodney Dryland (*left*) who contributed much to Meteor development before crashing in the FR.5 prototype. Polish born Jan Zurakowski (*right*) was a rare combination of skilled engineer, painstaking test pilot and unparalleled display pilot.

425

Both Michael Kilburn (*left*), who flew Meteors and Javelins during his four years with Glosters, and Brian Smith (*right*), who, while flying a Javelin, was tragically killed in collision with an RAF Hunter, developed the techniques of test flying jet aircraft.

Geoffrey Worrall (*left*), joined Glosters' pilots in September 1950. Peter Lawrence (*right*), who came to Glosters from English Electric, was the first pilot to lose his life after experiencing a deep stall in a sweptwing aircraft.

R. F. 'Dickie' Martin (*left*), ETPS instructor, RAF and RAE pilot, who carried much of the burden of Javelin development flying and its introduction into RAF service. Peter Varley (*right*) joined Glosters in 1955 to become assistant chief test pilot.

Michael Morss (*left*), production pilot on Javelins, who also ferried Meteors to overseas air forces, and John Towle (*right*), who undertook similar duties.

New Zealander O. J. 'Ossie' Hawkins (*left*), flew Javelins at Glosters for three years. Capt Fitz Vyzelaar (*right*) of the RNethAF was seconded to Glosters to check-fly Meteors being exported to the Netherlands.

Sqdn Ldr P. Scott (*left*) was the RAF liaison pilot concerned with Javelin production and development. Flt Lieut A. Morgan (*right*), an RAF radar operator/navigator, was attached to Glosters during 1955–1959.

427

In 1956 Sqdn Ldr D. W. H. Smith (*left*) succeeded Sqdn Ldr Scott as Fighter Command liaison pilot with Glosters. When he was posted to RAF Staff College in 1957 his successor was Sqdn Ldr L. C. Gregory (*right*) who successfully landed a Javelin having experienced flying control hydraulics failure.

Flt Lt R. Jeffries (*left*), an RAF radar operator/navigator, survived after ejection from the Javelin in which Brian Smith lost his life. Don Lucey (*right*) was seconded to Glosters from Hawker Aircraft to help test-fly the last batch of Javelins prior to closure of the factory.

From time to time RAF, civilian and foreign pilots were attached to or flew for the company for various flying duties. They include H. Broad, B. Hinkler, R. C. Graveley, Flt Lieuts A. Dredge and R. Stark (RAF), Capt F. Vyzelaar (RNethAF), R. A. Sutherland, D. J. Cockshead, A. McDowell, Flt Lieut R. Ross, Sqdn Ldrs P. Scott, D. W. H. Smith and L. C. Gregory (RAF), D. Lucey (HAL). In addition, R. Percival (G.A.C.), Flt Lieuts R. Jeffries and A. J. Morgan (RAF) served as navigator/observers during the period 1954–61.

Gloster Aeroplanes Extant

Less than three per cent of the 5,900-plus Gloster aircraft still exist. Operational losses, obsolescence, moths and rust have accounted for most of the remainder, but the wrecker's axe and cutting torch have destroyed many others which should have been accorded an honoured place in some collection of unique historical aircraft. Of those which remain some stand guard at the gates of Royal Air Force and other Ministry Establishments while a few are in, or destined for, museums, while a handful more are still engaged on flying duties.

The oldest of these is the Shuttleworth Trust's Gladiator I (now K8032) which was originally delivered as an airframe to No.27 MU, Shawbury, on 4 October, 1938, for assembly and installation of a Bristol Mercury VIIIA engine. It was delivered to No.2 AACU, as L8032, on 11 October. In February 1939 it moved to No.8 MU and, as far as can be established, remained there until October 1943 when it was delivered to No.61 OTU. It was returned to No.8 MU in September 1944 and soon after went back to Hucclecote, with Gladiator N5903, to be modified for use on meteorological duties. Both aircraft remained at Glosters' factory, un-modified, until November 1950 when L8032 went by road to Air Service Training's school at Hamble and N5903 to the Ansty school where they were used as ground instructional airframes. In 1952 they were acquired by Flightways Ltd, Southampton, who cannibalized N5903 to get L8032 into an airworthy condition. When complete it was registered G-AMRK and flew in a number of displays piloted by V. Bellamy. In August 1953 G-AMRK was bought by Glosters and was gradually restored to operational condition with armament, gun sight, control column and TR.9 wireless set. Permission was given by the Air Ministry for this aircraft to carry No.72 Sqdn markings and the spurious serial K8032 as the first batch of Gladiators in this squadron carried K serials. On 7 November, 1960, it flew from Hucclecote to Old Warden in Bedfordshire on being handed over to the Shuttleworth Trust. It now carries its original serial L8032.

The following list shows Gloster aeroplanes reported to be still extant at August 1970.

Type	Serial No	Location	Remarks
Gladiator I	L8032	Old Warden, Bedfordshire	Shuttleworth Trust.
Gladiator I	K8042	RAF Henlow, Bedfordshire	RAF Museum collection.
Sea Gladiator	N5520	National War Museum, Valletta, Malta	Restored fuselage with engine and propeller.
Gladiator II	N5641	Dovre, Norway	Ex-No.263 Sqdn RAF.
Gladiator II	N5903	RNAS Yeovilton, Fleet Air Arm Museum	Serialled N2276.
E.28/39	W4041/G	Science Museum, London	First British jet aircraft to fly.

429

Type	Serial No	Location	Remarks
F.9/40	DG202/G	RAF Cosford, Staffs	First Meteor prototype.
Meteor F.3	EE416	Science Museum, London	Partial display shows installation used for first live ejection.
Meteor F.3	EE419	RAF Coltishall, Norfolk	Reserialled 7247M.
Meteor F.4	Forty-four aircraft serviceable or under repair in the Argentine.		
Meteor F.4	EE531	Lasham airfield, Hampshire	
Meteor F.4	EE549	RAF St Athan, Glamorgan	For RAF Museum.
Meteor F.4	VT229	RAF Colerne, Wiltshire	Reserialled 7151M.
Meteor F.4	VT260	Winterbourne Gunner, Dorset	Was with Civil Defence.
Meteor F.4	I-025	Moron Air Base, Argentina	Ex-RAF EE532.
Meteor F.4	461	Copenhagen, Denmark	
Meteor F.4	469	RDAF Skrydstrup, Denmark	
Meteor F.4	I-69	Soesterberg Air Base, Netherlands	
Meteor T.7	A small number of aircraft serviceable in Brazil.		
Meteor T.7	WA591	RAF Kemble, Glos	Reserialled 7917M.
Meteor T.7	WA662	RAE Llanbedr, Merionethshire	
Meteor T.7	WF784	RAF Quedgeley, Glos	Reserialled 7895M.
Meteor T.7	WF825	RAF Lyneham, Wiltshire	
Meteor T.7	WH132	Chelmsford, Essex	Reserialled 7906M. With No.276 Sqdn ATC.
Meteor T.7	WH226	Seletar, Singapore	Reserialled 7818M.
Meteor T.7	WL332	RAF Manston, Kent	
Meteor T.7	WL360	RAF Locking, Somerset	At gate.
Meteor T.7	WL375	RAE Farnborough, Hampshire	Flying duties.
Meteor T.7	WL405	RAE Farnborough	Flying duties.
Meteor T.7	VW417	Beek Airport, Netherlands	
Meteor T.7	XF274	RAE Farnborough	Flying duties.
Meteor T.7	I-19	Woensdrecht Airfield, Netherlands	
Meteor T.7	A77-707	Moorabbin Airport, Victoria, Australia	Australian Air Restoration Group collection.
Meteor T.7	SE-CAS	Visby Airport, Sweden	Operated by Swedair Ltd.
Meteor T.7	SE-DCC	Visby Airport, Sweden	Was G-ANSO.
Meteor F.8	More than 40 aircraft serviceable in Brazil.		
Meteor F.8	VZ438	RAE West Freugh, Wigtownshire	
Meteor F.8	VZ477	Bristol	
Meteor F.8	WA833	Chadderton, Manchester	
Meteor F.8	WA952	Canberra, Australia	RAAF serial A77-368.
Meteor F.8	WF756	Chadderton, Manchester	
Meteor F.8	WH301	RAF Henlow, Bedfordshire	RAF Museum collection.
Meteor F.8	WH443	Hucknall, Nottinghamshire	

Type	Serial No	Location	Remarks
Meteor F.8	WK674	Technical College, Sydney, Australia	RAAF serial A77-868.
Meteor F.8	WK791	School of Technical Training, Wagga Wagga, Australia	At gate. RAAF serial A77-874.
Meteor F.8	WK910	RAAF Williamtown, Australia	RAAF serial A77-880.
Meteor F.8	WK935	RAF Colerne, Wiltshire	Prone pilot research aircraft.
Meteor F.8	WK968	RAF Odiham, Wiltshire	At gate.
Meteor F.8	WK991	Imperial War Museum, London	
Meteor F.8	WL168	RAF Finningley, Yorkshire	Carries serial WH456.
Meteor F.8	490	Aalborg Airfield, Denmark	Used in playground.
Meteor F.8	491	Karup Air Base, Denmark	
Meteor F.8	I-200	Voorst Airfield, Netherlands	
Meteor F.8	7-E5	Soesterberg Air Base, Netherlands	
Meteor F.8	9Y-25	Lensderheide Airfield, Netherlands	
Meteor F.8	EG18	Chièvres Air Base, Belgium	
Meteor F.8	EG79	Brustem Air Base, Belgium	
Meteor F.8	EG224	Brussels, Belgium	Musée de l'Armée et d'Histoire Militaire.
Meteor F.8	A77-702	RAAF Laverton, Victoria, Australia	Was A77-305.
Meteor FR.9		Eight aircraft reported in service in Ecuador in November 1969.	
Meteor FR.9	VZ608	Newark, Nottinghamshire	Air Museum.
Meteor NF.11	WD724	RAF Patrington, Yorkshire	At gate.
Meteor NF.11	WD790	RRE, Pershore, Worcestershire	Flying duties.
Meteor NF.11	501	Aalborg Airfield, Denmark	First RDAF NF.11.
Meteor NF.12	WS692	RAF College, Cranwell, Lincolnshire	
Meteor NF.13	WM367	A and AEE, Boscombe Down, Wiltshire	Flying duties.
Meteor NF.14	WM261	Turnhouse Airport, Edinburgh	With Ferranti Ltd, re-registered G-ARCX.
Meteor NF.14	WS726	Royton, Lancs	With No.1855 Sqdn ATC.
Meteor NF.14	WS739	RAF Church Fenton, Yorkshire	At gate.
Meteor NF.14	WS744	RAF Leeming, Yorkshire	
Meteor NF.14	WS747	Bretigny, France	Flying duties with Centre d'Éssais en Vol serialled NF14-747.
Meteor NF.14	WS766	RAF North Luffenham	At gate.
Meteor NF.14	WS777	RAF Buchan, Scotland	At gate.
Meteor NF.14	WS787	Tengah, Singapore	

Type	Serial No	Location	Remarks
Meteor NF.14	WS792	RAF Cosford, Staffordshire	With museum.
Meteor NF.14	WS804	RAE Bedford, Bedfordshire	Flying duties.
Meteor NF.14	WS807	RAF Watton, Norfolk	At gate of Eastern Radar Headquarters.
Meteor NF.14	WS838	A and AEE, Boscombe Down, Wiltshire	Flying duties.
Meteor NF.14	WS840	RAF Bishopscourt, N. Ireland	Reserialled 7969M.
Meteor NF.14	WS843	RAF St Athan, Glamorgan	For RAF Museum.
Meteor TT.20	WD630	Exeter Airport, Devonshire	Operated by No.3 CAACU.
Meteor TT.20	WD646	Exeter Airport, Devonshire	Operated by No.3 CAACU.
Meteor TT.20	WD647	Exeter Airport, Devonshire	Operated by No.3 CAACU.
Meteor TT.20	WD679	Exeter Airport, Devonshire	Operated by No.3 CAACU.
Meteor TT.20	WD702	Exeter Airport, Devonshire	Operated by No.3 CAACU.
Meteor TT.20	WD767	A and AEE, Boscombe Down, Wiltshire	
Meteor TT.20	WD780	Hurn Airfield, Hampshire	
Meteor TT.20	WM148	Exeter Airport, Devonshire	Operated by No.3 CAACU.
Meteor TT.20	WM223	Exeter Airport, Devonshire	Operated by No.3 CAACU.
Meteor TT.20	WM224	Exeter Airport, Devonshire	Operated by No.3 CAACU.
Meteor TT.20	WM270	Exeter Airport, Devonshire	Operated by No.3 CAACU.
Meteor TT.20	WM292	RNAS Yeovilton, Somerset	
Meteor TT.20	WM293	Exeter Airport, Devonshire	Operated by No.3 CAACU.
Meteor TT.20	SE-DCF	Cologne, West Germany	Was operated by Swedair.
Meteor TT.20	SE-DCH	Cologne, West Germany	Was operated by Swedair.
Javelin F(AW)1	XA549	RAF Swanton Morley, Norfolk	
Javelin F(AW)1	XA553	RAF Stanmore Park, Middlesex	At gate, reserialled 7470M.
Javelin F(AW)1	XA564	RAF Cosford, Staffordshire	Reserialled 7464M.
Javelin F(AW)2	XA801	RAF Stafford, Staffordshire	
Javelin F(AW)4	XA634	RAF Colerne, Wiltshire	Reserialled 7641M.
Javelin F(AW)5	XA699	RAF Cosford, Staffordshire	Reserialled 7809M.
Javelin F(AW)6	XA821	RAF Hartlebury, Staffs	At gate.
Javelin F(AW)6	XA829	RAF Manston, Kent	
Javelin F(AW)8	XH882	RAF Cosford, Staffordshire	
Javelin F(AW)8	XH967	Worcester, Worcestershire	With ATC, reserialled 7955M.
Javelin F(AW)8	XH980	RAF Stafford, Staffordshire	
Javelin F(AW)8	XH986	RAF Swanton Morley, Norfolk	
Javelin F(AW)8	XH991	RAF College, Cranwell, Lincolnshire	
Javelin F(AW)9	XH764	RAF Manston, Kent	
Javelin F(AW)9	XH892	RAF Shawbury, Shropshire	
Javelin F(AW)9	XH897	A and AEE, Boscombe Down, Wiltshire	Flying duties.
Javelin F(AW)9	XH903	RAF Innsworth, Glos	At gate, reserialled 7938M.

APPENDIX H

The Gladiators of Lesjaskog

On 2 August, 1968, a little over 28 years after the ill-fated but gallant attempt to operate Gladiators of No.263 Squadron RAF from the frozen, but melting, Lake Lesjaskog in Norway in support of a British Expeditionary Force landing north of Trondheim, a second 'expeditionary force', in the form of the Royal Air Force College's Sub-Aqua Club, landed at Trondheim in an Argosy of RAF Air Support Command. With the object of developing character, leadership, hardihood and resource, the Royal Air Force permits expeditions of a rigorous and testing nature, with some hazards to be overcome, to be organized. The self-imposed task of the Sub-Aqua Club was to seek and salvage parts of those Gladiators which, having been attacked by the Luftwaffe as they stood on the ice of Lake Lesjaskog, had sunk to the bottom where they could occasionally be seen from the surface.

The Club's Diving Officer and in charge of the expedition was Flt Lieut Alex Thomas who had spent many months in its planning and making extensive enquiries through HM Air Attaché in Oslo and the Lillehammer Sub-Aqua Club about diplomatic clearance for the team, the requirements for the subsequent 'export' back to the United Kingdom of any Gladiator remains salvaged, the temperature of the water in the lake and the availability of other diving facilities. To each of these queries Flt Lieut Thomas received the most encouraging response and so, after a long period of preparation, the

Some of the first pieces of Gladiator recovered were lying in 6 ft of water. One underwing gun fairing and the top portion of the rudder of N5632 are identifiable in this photograph. (*Courtesy Flt Lieut Thomas*)

433

Flt Cadets Rees and Proctor with the tail section of N5628 soon after it had been raised to the surface of Lake Lesjaskog. (*Courtesy Flt Lieut Thomas*)

team of eleven officers and cadets assembled at Trondheim for the road journey to Lesjaskog where they were to stay with a farmer having three—but not the hoped for eleven—charming daughters.

At their first attempt to find the Gladiators, using snorkel equipment only, the team were disappointed to find that although the water was surprisingly warm, despite the presence of snow on the mountain slopes, the vertical visibility was limited to about 10 ft. Thus they were forced to dive to this depth and swim horizontally and look further down into the depths of the lake until they had to surface for more breath. This initial disappointment was eased however when a local resident rowing on the lake offered to show them a complete aircraft preserved in a shed near to the point where they were diving. There, surrounded by logs, stood a Gladiator airframe minus its fabric covering, with the wings stowed above it and complete with engine and propeller which could still be turned over by hand. Seven machine-guns in excellent condition were fastened to the walls. This survivor of the 18 Gladiators which had landed on the lake on 24

Flg Off P. Gates, SAC A. Gray and Flt Cadet A. Proctor with N5628's tail section at the lake's edge. (*Courtesy Flt Lieut Thomas*)

April, 1940, having been brought to within 150 miles of the Norwegian coast by the aircraft carrier HMS *Glorious*, had been purchased from a scrap merchant in 1946 for the equivalent of £10. When a panel was removed from the airframe the serial number was found to be N5641, one of the main production batch of Gladiator IIs built during 1937–38. Their guide also told them that another aircraft had been pulled from the lake with a tractor, the undamaged portions retained and the rest thrown back into the water.

When diving began and two Gladiators in various stages of destruction had been discovered, lost, and then found again, it was decided to make an attempt to raise the more complete airframe even though the longerons were badly corroded where fire had attacked the protective treatment of the metal. Three inflatable rubber dinghies were secured to the airframe; one under each wing adjacent to the landing gear legs and the third below the fuselage just aft of the cockpit. The plan was to inflate the dinghies under water and so lift the Gladiator to the surface. Unfortunately, with representatives of the local press seated in boats above waiting for N5628 to rise from the waters like Aphrodite, the dinghies failed to inflate correctly. The one under the fuselage worked perfectly but the port one inflated unevenly and inverted itself and the one under the starboard wing blew out of its securing ropes. In addition the fuselage finally broke in two parts at the point where the longerons were corroded and, sinking back to the lake bottom, nearly hit Flt Lieut Thomas who was swimming near to it. Only a colleague's assistance in drawing him clear averted what could have been an accident.

Undaunted by this apparent failure one of the team made a restraining net for the one remaining serviceable dinghy and this was attached to the lifting eye of the Gladiator's Mercury engine. As Flt Lieut Thomas inflated this dinghy he reports that 'Suddenly I got the impression that I was descending because the aircraft was closer to my feet but—and what a wonderful feeling—Gloster Gladiator N5628 was moving again for the first time in 28 years'. Ropes were then attached to the landing gear legs and passed to a boat on the surface which towed the airframe into shallower water. With little time remaining before the teams returned home they decided to remove as much as possible from the airframe and ultimately stripped off the port upper wing and bracing wires, flare ejector boxes, instruments, and collected many rounds of ·303 in ammunition. All this evidence of their discovery was crated for the return journey by Argosy to the United Kingdom and the Royal Air Force Museum.

The team arrived back having achieved its objectives in terms of character and leadership development and had undertaken a task of a rigorous, testing and at times, hazardous nature; they had all experienced the unusual sensation of encountering aircraft in an unnatural element and gained experience of working under water—yet they felt that they had left a job only half done. .

At least they know where there is half a Gladiator in a lake in Norway, they know there are others there too and perhaps these will provide a challenge to enterprising young airmen in future years.

APPENDIX I

Air Attacks on Hucclecote Factories

Although three direct attacks were made in daylight by the Luftwaffe and several more were made during the night, only a few high explosive bombs, of the several score which were dropped in the vicinity, fell within the factory perimeter.

During one daylight attack in October 1940 an oil bomb struck the roof of No.7 Machine Shop and Toolroom causing considerable damage and injury to the occupants, while the remaining high explosive bombs of that particular stick fell on open ground nearby. On 4 April, 1942—Easter Saturday—another attack was made in the late afternoon as the dayshift workers were leaving the factory. One bomb, of a stick of five which straddled the airfield, factory and adjoining houses, fell into the car and bus park killing 13 people and injuring many times that number. On a third occasion, when the factory alarm sent employees streaming out to the air raid shelters on the edge of the airfield, a Junkers 88 broke cloud at about 3,000 ft over the factory itself. A solitary Home Guard gunner hopefully fired a number of rounds from a Lewis gun but the enemy aircraft slipped back into the cloud and dropped bombs on Gloucester a few minutes later.

APPENDIX J

Glosters' Royal Visitors

Glosters' factory was visited by several members of the Royal Family during the war years. On 10 February, 1940, HM King George VI accompanied by HM The Queen toured the Hucclecote works and in October of the same year HRH the Duke of Kent visited the company. HM Queen Mary, who for a long period of the war resided at Badminton House, the home of the Duke of Beaufort, was a visitor to Glosters on two occasions.

Index

ABC Dragonfly engine, 7, 68
Admiralty, 214, 215, 216, 356
Aerial Derby, 9, 11, 69, 70, 72, 73, 78, 83, 107, 349
Aichi Tokei Denki K.K., 157, 159
Air Board, 5, 9, 18, 84
Aircraft Manufacturing Company, 1, 2, 3, 4, 5
Aircraft Operating Co Ltd, 21, 189, 190, 193, 353
Aircraft Technical Services, 25
Air Ministry, 12, 15, 21, 23, 25, 28, 31, 36, 40, 42, 43, 48, 55, 68, 75, 76, 81, 97, 98, 99, 107, 110, 113, 119, 124, 129, 130, 133, 136, 145, 157, 159, 171, 172, 185, 193, 199, 205, 206, 207, 210, 214, 215, 218, 223, 230, 237, 245, 285, 349, 350, 351, 352, 353, 354, 355, 357, 374, 414, 429
Air Mission to Japan 1921, 8, 75
Air Service Training, 62, 217, 329, 355
Airship Development Programme, 12, 103
Airship R-33, 12, 103, 104, 350
Antoni, Signor Ugo, 22, 23
Argentine Air Force, 262, 288, 359, 368
Argentine Purchasing Mission 1931, 139
Argus, HMS, 268
Armée de l'Air, 271, 295
Armstrong Siddeley Motors Ltd, 43, 44, 62, 342, 370, 371, 373
Armstrong Siddeley engines:
  Deerhound, 407
  Jaguar, 10, 17, 80, 81, 85, 91, 92, 97, 98, 100, 103, 104, 106, 110, 163, 165, 192, 349, 350, 352, 404
  Lynx, 90, 92, 350
  Panther, 171, 352
  Sapphire, 60, 277, 279, 311, 315, 321, 329, 337, 342, 344, 369, 373, 375, 387, 393, 412
  Screamer rocket motor, 277, 278, 279, 362
Armstrong Siddeley Snarler rocket motor Tiger, 34, 406
Armstrong Whitworth Aircraft Ltd, Sir W. G., 25, 51, 62, 64, 66, 259, 268, 277, 279, 280, 295, 297, 302, 332, 335, 336, 338, 358, 360, 361, 363, 365, 366, 369
Armstrong Whitworth Albemarle production, 40, 41
Armstrong Whitworth Argosy, 66, 431
Armstrong Whitworth AW.34, 231

Armstrong Whitworth AW.XVI, 169
Armstrong Whitworth Siskin, 20, 97, 104, 167
Atcherley, Flt Lieut R. D. R., 101
Atkinson, R. V., 53, 62, 64
Austin Motor Co, 42
Aviation Traders Accountant, 65, 66
Avions Fairey, 270, 280, 281
Avro Blue Steel stand-off bomb, 66
Avro CF-100, 425
Avro Vulcan, 66
Avro 504, 92
Avro 707, 314
Avro 748, 66
Avro Whitworth Division of Hawker Siddeley Aviation, 66

Baginton factory, 51
Balbo, General, 199
Balloon Factory, Farnborough, 2
Barford St John airfield, 244
Beacham, T. E., 16
Beamont, Roland, 423, 425
Beaton, Sqdn Ldr G. H., 331
Belgian Air Force, 35, 49, 222, 262, 263, 270, 280, 281, 282, 368
Belgium, 47, 48, 49, 222, 270, 280, 293, 296, 356, 360, 361, 365
Bell Airacomet, 247, 358
Bellamy, V. H., 217, 355
Bentham factory, 48, 247, 248, 307
Bentley BR.2 rotary engine, 10, 12, 69, 76, 79, 85, 88, 89, 93, 349, 350
Beuger, Col G. de, 323
BE.2c, 4
Biaird, Capt H. C., 127
Bjarkov, Maj H. L. V., 182
Blackburn Aircraft Ltd, 426
Blackburne Tomtit engine, 95, 96, 350
Bloodhound missile, 300
Blue Jay missile, 300
Blue Sky missile, 300
Boeing 218, 160
Boscombe Down (A and AEE), 38, 234, 235, 247, 252, 257, 274, 275, 296, 286, 287, 291, 294, 295, 309, 310, 321, 322, 328, 335, 339, 342, 357, 358, 359, 360, 365, 370, 371, 373
Boothman, Flt Lieut J., 152
Boulton and Paul Aircraft Ltd, 25, 370
Boulton Paul Aircraft Ltd, 174, 314
Boulton Paul Defiant, 231
Boulton Paul Partridge, 169

437

439

Nakajima A1N1 and A1N2, 159, 160, 161, 352, 415
Nakajima Hikoki K. K., 19, 157, 159, 252, 415
Nakajima Kotobuki engine, 159, 352
D. Napier and Son Ltd, 25
Napier Lion engine, 12, 14, 15, 25, 30, 31, 68, 69, 70, 75, 107, 110, 124, 128, 129, 130, 132, 133, 134, 136, 150, 151, 152. 154, 155, 156, 186, 187, 188, 349, 350, 351, 352, 404, 405, 406
Napier Lioness engine, 134
Napier Rapier engine, 23, 24
Napier Sabre engine, 42, 409
Napier Scorpion rocket motor, 390
Napier take-over bid for Glosters, 25
National Research Council of Canada, 260
Netherlands, 49, 262, 263, 359, 360, 361, 363, 368, 369
Newark Air Museum, 288
New Zealand Permanent Air Force, 104, 105, 106
Nieuport and General Aircraft Co, 7, 84
Nieuport BN.1, 8
Nieuport Goshawk, 69
Nieuport London, 8
Nighthawk, 4, 5, 7, 8, 9, 11, 68, 69, 80, 83, 84, 85, 349, 421
North American F-86 Sabre 49
North American F-100 Super Sabre, 324
North Atlantic Treaty Organisation, 345
North, J. D., 1, 25
Norway, 35, 212, 213, 355, 356, 357, 419, 433–435
Norwegian Air Force, 36, 220
Norwegian air operations, 36, 212, 213, 220, 433–435

Oddfellows Inn, Shurdington, 18
O'Gorman and Cozens-Hardy company, 2
O'Gorman, Mervyn, 2
Okura company, 17
Olympia International Aero Shows, 17, 96, 193, 353
Operational Requirements:
    OR227, 311
    OR228, 311
    OR234, 80
    OR278, 59, 328
    OR309, 59
Orlebar, Sqdn Ldr A. H., 187, 188, 353

Palestine air operations, 33, 182
Paris Air Show 1955, 323, 325, 370
Parnall Panther, 12
Pattle, Flt Lieut M. T. St. J., 212
Peck, G., 1, 3, 4
Pittman fish fryers, 27
Portugal, 223, 356, 357, 419
Potez 4E engine, 413
Power Jets Ltd, 43, 238, 242, 243, 252, 358
Power Jets W.1A engine, 243

Power Jets W.1X engine, 357
Power Jets W.2/500 engine, 244, 245, 304, 357
Pratt & Whitney Hornet engine, 192
Preston, H. E., 9, 149, 186
Pye, Dr., 43

Red Dean missile, 60, 61, 62, 63, 268, 300
Red Duster (Bloodhound) missile, 300
Red Hawk missile, 313
Red Shoes (Thunderbird) missile, 300
Redrup axial lever engine, 24
Regent Motors Ltd, 239, 240, 414
Regia Aeronautica, 212, 216
Reynolds, Sqdn Ldr J. McC., 42, 43
Rhodesia, 182, 353
Roe and Co Ltd, A.V., 66, 99, 314, 361
Rolls-Royce Ltd, 18, 45, 48, 51, 166, 249, 252, 254, 257, 288, 292, 299, 322, 326, 358, 359, 364, 365
Rolls-Royce engines:
    AJ.65 Avon, 56, 261, 311, 313, 359, 375, 377, 378, 379, 380, 384, 390
    B.41 Nene, 54, 257, 260, 307, 309, 310, 314, 359, 369 411
    Continental engines 399, 400
    Conway, 401, 402
    Dart, 66
    Derwent, 253, 254, 257, 259, 260, 265, 267, 270, 271, 276, 305, 358, 361, 364, 366, 385, 389
    Eagle, 10, 405
    F.XI Felix, 17
    Goshawk, 34, 164, 203, 204, 205, 206, 352
    Kestrel, 167, 196, 197, 200, 201, 203, 205, 352, 353
    Peregrin, 234, 235, 236, 357
    RA.24R, 322, 326
    Soar, 278
    Trent, 251, 252
    RB.108, 66, 288, 364, 392, 399, 400, 401
    RB.162, 402
    Vulture, 407
    W.2/700, 358
    W.2B/23C Welland, 47, 247, 249, 250, 253, 304, 305, 358
Roman, Col C., 323
Ross, Flt Lieut R. J., 323, 428
Rotol Airscrews Ltd, 353
Rotol propellers, 234, 236, 251, 252, 355
Rover Motors Ltd, 7, 46, 247, 306
Rover W.2/500 engine, 46, 304
Rover W.2B engine, 46, 244, 245, 247, 249, 252, 304, 357
Royal Aero Club, 72
Royal Aircraft Establishment (RAE) Farnborough, 18, 24, 26, 33, 43, 81, 87, 103, 110, 115, 118, 132, 133, 164, 176, 179, 193, 211, 230, 244, 247, 249, 251, 268, 274, 280, 300, 308, 309, 314, 323, 324, 351, 353, 357–367, 370, 371, 426, 432

442